Routes to Success

Routes to Success

Case Studies of 40 UK Small Business Ventures

Colin Barrow

Kogan Page

Copyright © Colin Barrow and contributors 1986

All rights reserved

First published in Great Britain in 1986
by Kogan Page Ltd, 120 Pentonville Road, London N1 9JN

British Library Cataloguing in Publication Data

Routes to success: case studies of 40 UK small business ventures.
   1.   Small business—Great Britain—Case studies
   I.   Barrow, Colin
   338.6'42'0722   HD2346.G7

ISBN 0-85038-955-0

Typeset by Mathematical Composition Setters Ltd, Salisbury, Wiltshire

Printed and bound by Billing & Sons Ltd, Worcester

Contents

Preface

Starting a new business is no longer just a spectator sport. There are now 2.5 million self-employed people who represent about one in ten of the labour force. In the first quarter of 1985 26,800 new ventures registered with the Companies Registration Office, some 11 per cent more than in the first quarter of the preceding year.

There is also strong evidence beginning to emerge, which suggests that those entrepreneurs who take the time and trouble to prepare, and to plan their strategies carefully have a significantly greater chance of success than those who do not.

This book is aimed at those who are seriously interested in starting their own business, or in expanding an existing one. It is also intended for use on a more formal programme of business studies, for students who are examining business policy or entre-preneurial issues. It is not written in the style of a text book, with the possible exception of the introduction. Rather a privileged insight into the minds of the entrepreneurs has been presented, at the time they were formulating their business plans and strategies. It deals with the problems and opportunities faced by entrepreneurs as they tackle decisions about the future of their firms. Because there is no general theory of the firm that provides a standard form of reference for resolving all the issues of small business management, the book is in the form of a series of case studies.

By observing the experiences of others one can learn about the judgements that a successful entrepreneur must make and so develop analytical skills that can be applied to other enterprises, including your own.

The cases reflect the commercial and organisational issues of the 1980s. With the exception of two firms based in Ireland, they all describe British businesses. The cases have been carefully chosen so that together they provide the basis for a complete introductory course in small business management or in business policy, for students at many levels.

The cases have also been selected to be representative of the types of small enterprise currently being started and operated in the UK; and of the types of people who are running those businesses.

For example, the 24 per cent rise since 1981 in women working for themselves has not gone unnoticed. Nor has the growing number of young graduates at one end of the spectrum, and those taking early retirement or voluntary redundancy at the other.

The cases cover manufacturing firms, the service sector, retailing, high and low technology, and management buy-outs.

In terms of legal structure, companies, partnerships and sole traders are well represented, and two cases covering the increasingly important field of franchising have also been included.

You can just plough through the cases from beginning to end as they are intended to be a good read. An adventure in enterprise. Alternatively, you could select a case that covers an industry or a topic of particular interest from the brief description provided on the contents pages.

The cases are listed in three groups: Dreams of Success (before start-up); the Dawn of Reality (one to three years); and Growing Concerns (three years and over). The reasoning behind this is that the nature of the risks ahead of the proposed venture are very different at these critical points in its life.

Before a business can get started it usually runs considerable development risks. Can they actually produce the product they plan to make, or find the right location for their retail outlet? The gulf between the business idea and the market-place is vast. In the start-up cases you have only the personality of the entrepreneur and the market evidence as portrayed in the business plan to guide you.

Once the business has started up, the results show whether the risks were worth taking. Then attention swings to the management's ability to respond to the business environment. The business begins to compete directly with established companies, and to become successful it has to concentrate on introducing economies of scale and improving internal reporting and financial controls.

For example, in the West Cornwall Woodwork case, they dreamt of working in pine, launched the business with originals in ash, but made their money out of producing reproduction furniture to Liberty designs.

By the third year it should be becoming clear whether or not the venture has real growth potential. Having started up on a shoe string the management is now in a position to go out to sources of finance with a 'track-record'. This is also the time at which the organisational structure of the business should take shape. The original partnerships may be under strain and new management may be being taken on board. During this stage of the business's life the owner/manager has to make the difficult decision to delegate day-to-day responsibility for key areas, which may hitherto have been their own pet projects. Relinquishing responsibility is a necessity: it allows the company to grow.

When tackling the cases on your own you can read the cases with your own criteria in mind, or you can use the questions posed at the end of each case as a means of extracting the useful information.

To help with the latter approach we describe below a dozen issues that are of importance to most types of small enterprise during the formative years.

I would like to thank all those who have contributed case material, without which there could have been no book. The diligent research of all these 'practitioners' in the field is, I believe, a heartening confirmation that entrepreneurship is staging a decisive come-back.

Thanks are particularly due to Lucius Cary of *Venture Capital Report* for his considerable help in assembling material; to my colleague Godfrey Golzen for permission to use his material in the franchise case studies; and to:

Dr Michael Scott of Durham University Business School
Stephen Pettit of the National Institute for Higher Education, Limerick
Graham Beaver of Trent Polytechnic
Dr Everett Jacobs of Sheffield University
Maureen and Graham Davey of West Cornwall Woodwork
Dr David Kirby of the University of Wales
Jill and Bob Crowther of the Shaftesbury Hotel
Roger McMullan of Bolton Business Ventures
Dr John Murray and Nora O'Donnell of the Enterprise Centre at Dublin University
Richard Thorpe of Blackburn College
John Thompson of Huddersfield Polytechnic
Michael Beaumont of Oldham College of Technology
John Howdle and Peter Chadwick of Bristol Polytechnic
Nigel Campbell, Paul Washbourne and Stuart Craimer of Manchester Business School

Finally I would like to thank my colleagues at Cranfield for their help with questions at the end of some of the case studies. Any mistakes, errors or omissions are, of course, all mine.

Colin Barrow
October 1985

Some Key Issues in Small Business Management

1. The skills for success

To launch a venture successfully, you need at least three aces in your hand. You have to be the right sort of person to start a business; your business idea must be right for the market; and your timing must be spot on. The world of business failures is full of products that were 'ahead of their time'.

The entrepreneur is frequently seen as someone who is always bursting with new ideas, is highly enthusiastic, hyperactive and insatiably curious. But the more you try to create a picture of the typical entrepreneur, the more elusive he becomes.

Peter Drucker, the international business guru, captured the problem clearly with this description:

> 'Some are eccentrics, others painfully correct conformists; some are fat and some are lean; some are worriers, some relaxed; some drink quite heavily, others are total abstainers; some are men of great charm and warmth, some have no more personality than a frozen mackerel.'

Having said that, there are certain characteristics which successful newcomers to business do have in common.

- *Self-confident all-rounders*. Entrepreneurs are rarely geniuses. There are nearly always people in their business who have more competence, in one field, than they could ever aspire to. But they have a wide range of ability, and a willingness to turn their hands to anything that has to be done to make the venture succeed. They can usually make the product, market it and count the money, but above all they have self-confidence that lets them move comfortably through uncharted waters.
- *The ability to bounce back*. Henry Ford was a two-time loser before he became a winner. His first businesses, created in 1899 and 1901, folded. It was not until 1903, when he was 40, that he borrowed $28,000 to launch the Ford Motor Company. Sir Clive Sinclair suffered a disaster with his digital black watch

in 1976, but has since become a multi-millionaire. Business set-backs are not always of these proportions, but they always exist. Entrepreneurs must be resilient if they are to make it past the winning post (and it certainly helps if they are healthy too).

- *Innovative skills.* Almost by definition, entrepreneurs are innovators who either tackle the unknown, or do old things in new ways. It is this inventive streak that allows them to carve out a new niche, often invisible to others. In 'For a few pence more' John Holnbrook brings management innovation to bear on his new venture, while in the Windancer case, Tim Langley re-invents the wheel!

- *Results-orientated.* Successful people set themselves goals and get pleasure out of trying to achieve them. Once a goal has been reached, they have to get the next target in view as quickly as possible. This restlessness is very characteristic. Tom Porter, in the River Inn case, is one such example.

- *Professional risk-taker.* The high failure rate shows that small businesses are faced with many dangers. An essential characteristic of someone starting a business is a willingness to make decisions and to take risks. This does not mean gambling on hunches. It means carefully calculating the odds and deciding which risks to take and when to take them.

- *Having total commitment.* You will need complete faith in your area. How else will you convince anyone else it is a worthwhile venture? You will also need single-mindedness, energy and a lot of hard work to get things started; working 18-hour days is not uncommon. This can put a strain on other relationships, particularly within your family – so they too have to become involved and committed, if you are going to succeed.

All too often budding entrepreneurs believe themselves to be the right sort of person to set up a business. Unfortunately the capacity for self-deception is enormous. When a random sample of male adults were asked recently to rank themselves on leadership ability, 70 per cent rated themselves in the top 25 per cent, only 2 per cent felt they were below average as leaders. In an area in which self-deception ought to be difficult, 60 per cent said they were well above average in athletic ability, only 6 per cent said they were below.

A common mistake made in assessing entrepreneurial talent is to assume that success in big business management will automatically guarantee success in a small business.

Lore Harp, who took her company Vector Graphics from a

$6,000 investment to a $25 million company in five years, when asked if a grooming at IBM would have helped her on her way, replied:

> 'We were one of the pioneers of the microcomputer explosion. The buying, as well as the selling, process in this industry is different from what it had been before for computers. Buyers were much less sophisticated; they really didn't know what they wanted. So I think the principles that I may have learned at IBM, DEC, or any other computer company would probably not have served me well at all. We are dealing with a totally new element.'

When you are looking at the way in which strategy was developed at Medsoft, it may be useful to consider the appropriateness of a big company management style to a small company structure.

2. Choosing and using professional advice

A Dun and Bradstreet study concluded that 'inexperience and incompetence' accounted for most small business failures. This should not be taken to mean that there are fewer competent people in small companies than in large. But it does suggest that the margin for error is much narrower and managerial resources are spread thinner. Owner managers face a daily onslaught of business problems. Many problems are ones they have never faced before, and some they may not meet again for months or even years. For example: drawing up contracts of employment; hiring and firing; raising capital; starting exporting; instituting a stock control system; or changing a pricing policy.

The ability to recognise when to use outside advisers and where to find them is essential to small business owners.

In the case studies you will see many and various approaches. Chantal Coady, for example, attempts to anticipate problems by talking to lawyers, accountants, bank managers and surveyors before she sets up Rococo. At Medsoft the problems have become almost intractable before consultants are called in. In the Shaftesbury Hotel case, the importance of spending time in choosing professional advisers before using them is made clear.

3. Market research

The Duke of Wellington called reconnaissance 'the art of knowing what is on the other side of the hill'. Market research is the business equivalent of that activity.

Market research is the name given to the process of collecting, recording, classifying and analysing data on customers, competitors and any other factors influencing the buying chain. It is the breadth of the gulf between a new business and its customers that makes this information gathering so vital.

Entrepreneurs are often deterred by the rigours of market research, or simply do not know how to carry it out cheaply. They rely instead on their own subjective judgement; they develop the iceberg syndrome, believing that the small number of customers they see are a sure indication of the mass of other customers. It is a fundamental mistake to believe that people are simply waiting to be sold to and that competitors are blind or lazy. New businesses need a clear and detailed picture of their market well before they launch.

The range of possible research topics is wide, and what is appropriate to one business could be irrelevant to another. However, there are certain questions which need to be answered by more or less all potential businesses.

Where is my market?

The starting point in any market appreciation has to be a definition of the scope of the market you are aiming for. A small general shop may only service the needs of a few dozen streets. A specialist restaurant will have to call on a much larger catchment area.

You may eventually decide to sell to different markets. For example, a retail business can serve a local area through the shop and a national area by mail order. A small manufacturing business could branch out into exporting.

People all too often flounder in initial market research by describing their markets too broadly. For example, saying that they are in the motor industry when they really mean secondhand car sales in Perth.

While it is helpful to know about trends in the wider market, this must not obscure the need to focus on the precise area that you have to serve.

How big is that market?

You need some idea of the market size in order to work out how much you can realistically expect to sell. If you were in the home improvements market your calculations might run as follows. On average, people in the UK spend £11 per year on home improvement products; so if the catchment population for a retail outlet is 25,000 people, the total market potential for that area is £11 × 25,000 = £275,000. Using the same data for previous years, you can work out how fast the market is expanding or contracting.

Who are my competitors and what are their strengths and weaknesses?

Most businesses have competitors. To some extent this is reassuring because you know in advance that customers need what you have to offer. But you have to identify who they are and how they can affect your business. You have to know everything about them; their product range, prices, discount structure, delivery arrangements, specifications, minimum order quantities and terms of trade.

How can I differentiate my business from the competition?

There has to be something unique about either you or your product that makes you stand out from your competitors. It could be something as obvious as being open later or longer. Or it may be a policy, such as the John Lewis Partnership's 'never knowingly undersold' message. Whatever your unique selling proposition is, communicate it effectively.

What should I charge?

The greatest danger in setting a price for the first time is to pitch it too low. Raising a price is always more difficult than lowering one. There are great temptations to undercut the competition at the outset.

Every product or service has its own demand curve, relating sales volume to selling price, showing that the lower the price the greater the quantity sold. This can help you to think out how a change in price will affect your sales volume.

The sensitivity of demand to price changes is called 'price elasticity'. If demand increases more than proportionally when a product price is reduced, then the demand is elastic. If it does not, it is inelastic. Sales of Rolls Royces are not likely to be improved significantly by lowering prices. In fact, the snob appeal may be diminished, so this is an inelastic demand curve. You have quickly to get a feel for how your sales volume is affected by price changes.

What is my message and where is the medium?

Lord Leverhulme is reported to have said that half the money he spent on advertising was wasted, but no one could tell him which half. A key element in your marketing strategy has to be what to tell whom and how to tell them.

If you start off by deciding how many people you want to influence, and what you want them to do as a result of seeing your advertisement, then you are off to a good start. In some media, response ratios are well established. For example, planning for more than 2 per cent response from a direct mail shot would be unrealistic.

4. Developing a product market strategy

People starting a new business almost always define their product in physical terms. Customers, on the other hand, want their needs satisfied. Compare a Bic and a Parker. In basic physical terms they are very similar. They both write well; their caps protect your pocket from ink stains; both have clips that hold them in place; and they are comfortable to grip. But one costs around 10p and the other from about £3.00. Customers pay the extra £2.90 for largely intangible benefits such as status, or the pleasure the pen will bring as a gift. Bic and Parker are both successful products, but the needs they satisfy are poles apart.Customers' needs must be defined before the business can begin to assemble a product to satisfy them.

Name names

Without customers no business can get off the ground, let alone survive. Some people believe that customers arrive after the firm 'opens its doors'. This is clearly nonsense. A business needs customers before it can even think of launching. The customers themselves are a vital part of a successful business strategy, and are not simply the passive recipients of new products or services. Even those ventures that start off with a handful of clients, perhaps poached from a previous employer, need the certainty of a wider customer base if they are to survive and prosper. Over-dependence on a few important customers is an all too common problem for the new business.

Naming names of customers, both actual and potential, is a start, but then these customers must be looked at in terms of the group or category into which they fall. For example, train users divide into commuters and off-peak travellers: those who have to get to a certain destination by a certain time, and those who do not. The relative intensity of need allows a premium price to be charged for the former and a price incentive is offered to the latter to induce them away from using their cars.

Satisfy needs

When asked what his business did, the founder of a successful cosmetics firm replied: 'In the factories we make perfume and in the shops we sell dreams'. This same philosophy is true of every product or service.

Maslow, the eminent American psychologist, suggested that 'all consumers are goal seekers who gratify their needs by purchase and consumption'. He classified consumer needs in a five-stage pyramid known as the 'hierarchy of needs'. The first and largest need was physiological (hunger and thirst), followed by safety, social, self-esteem and, at the top of the pyramid, self-realisation. Every product or service is bought to satisfy one or more of these needs. So, for example, as people's hunger and thirst needs are satisfied, they move up the hierarchy, to satisfy other needs.

Defining the product/market strategy

Everyone needs a purpose to their lives to make it worthwhile and rewarding. A business also needs a purpose to keep it headed in the right direction, amid the welter of distractions that threaten to divert even the most dedicated entrepreneur from his other chosen goal. That purpose should be defined as simply as possible in terms of what the business does and for whom it does it.

For example, Blooming Marvellous, a competitor to Mothercare, defines its activities as follows. 'We design, make and market clothes for the fashion conscious mother-to-be.' This statement is proof that the business has defined its product/market strategy and knows exactly where it is going. With the same skills they could make clothes for children, or for women who were not pregnant, but pursuing these markets would dilute their scarce resources leaving them vulnerable and open to attack on too many fronts.

Some further product issues

- *Is one product enough?* One-product businesses are the natural output of the inventor, but they are extremely vulnerable to competition, changes in fashion and to technological obsolescence. Having only one product can also limit the growth potential of the enterprise. Several of the case studies focus on the aspirations of businesses in this situation: a question mark must inevitably hang over them until they can broaden out their product base.
- *Single-sale products.* In the Medsoft case study the business is

21

focused on selling a microcomputer and a tailor-made software package to a hospital doctor. Unfortunately the management had no idea of the cost and effort required to sell each unit. Worse still, there were no repeat sales. It was not that customers did not like the product: they did; but each user needed only one product. This meant that all the money and time spent on building up a 'loyal' customer was largely wasted. In another type of venture, for example selling company cars, you could reasonably expect a satisfied customer to come back every two or three years. In the restaurant business the repeat purchase cycle might be every two to three months.

• *Non-essential products.* Entrepreneurs tend to be attracted to fad, fashion and luxury items because of the short response time associated with their promotion and sale. Companies producing for these markets frequently run into financial difficulties arising out of sudden market shifts. Market security is more readily gained by having products that are viewed as 'essential'.

• *Too simple a product.* Simplicity, usually a desirable feature, can be a drawback. If a business idea is so basic that little management or marketing expertise is required for success, this is likely to make the cost of entry low and the value added minimal. This makes it easy for every Tom, Dick or Harry to duplicate the product idea, and impossible for the original company to defend its market, except by lowering the price.

The video rental business was a classic example of the 'too simple product' phenomenon. Too many people jumped on the bandwagon as virtually anyone with a couple of thousand pounds could set themselves up. Rental prices fell from pounds to pence in a year or so, and hundreds of businesses folded.

5. Winning the cash flow war

Most business starters think their problems are over once customers start to roll in. Unfortunately, they may have only just begun. One of the characteristics that most new or small businesses have in common is a tendency to change their size and shape quickly. In the early weeks and months customers are few, and each new customer (or a particularly big order) can mean a large percentage increase in sales.

A large increase in sales in turn means an increase in raw materials and perhaps more wages and other expenses. Generally, these expenses have to be met before your customer pays up. But until the money comes in, the business has to find cash to meet its bills. If it cannot find the cash to meet these day-to-day bills it very often goes bankrupt.

Bankers have a name for it. They call it overtrading. It means taking on more business than you have the cash to finance. Consider this example.

High Note is a new music shop selling sheet music, instruments, classical records and cassettes. Customers include schools and colleges who expect trade credit, and members of the public who pay cash. The owner put in £10,000 and borrowed a further £10,000 from his bank. When he started up these seemed enough funds to meet the £12,500 bill for shop fixtures and fittings, and the opening stock of £5,500.

As people heard about him and his reputation grew, he expected sales to build up to a satisfactory level. In any case, he felt that he could rely on his cash customers to meet his day-to-day expenses and any increases in stock. But he had reckoned without calculating the effect on cash flow of paying on the nail for supplies, and having to give trade credit, while his sales were growing rapidly.

He opened in April. By the middle of June he had run out of cash, and by August he needed an overdraft equivalent to 30 per cent of the entire capital of the business. What was particularly galling was that the growth in sales exceeded his wildest dreams.

The cash picture over the first few months is set out in the table. The top of this cash picture shows the sales as they were achieved and the percentage rate of sales growth. Below that is the cash that comes in from the customers. (In the first month the start-up capital is also coming in.)

From May, when credit sales began, the gap between sales achieved and cash coming in grew rapidly. This was because purchases of stock had to stay in line with the growth in sales achieved, and not with the cash coming in. So, for example, in July High Note actually paid out more for stock than it received in cash. And the overheads had still to be paid.

What High Note's worried owner did not know in August was that his negative cash flow had peaked. As average monthly sales growth slowed down from a meteoric 70 per cent between April and August to a more modest 27 per cent between August and September, his rate of cash consumption would drop too. Eventually, as the business began to stabilise, a cash surplus would appear – and not before time.

High Notes's cash problem is by no means an uncommon one.

The cash picture

	April	May	June	July	Aug	Sept
			ACTUAL RESULTS			FORECAST
	£	£	£	£	£	£
Sales Achieved	4,000	6,000	7,000	9,000	15,000	19,000
Sales Growth			70% per month			27%
Sales Receipts	4,000	5,000	6,000	7,000	12,000	15,000
Owner's Capital	10,000					
Loan Capital	10,000					
Total Cash in	24,000	5,000	5,000	7,000	12,000	15,000
Cash Payments out						
Purchases	5,500	2,950	4,220	7,416	9,332	9,690
Rent/Rates etc	2,300	2,300	2,300	2,300	2,300	2,300
Wages	1,000	1,000	1,000	1,000	1,000	1,000
Advertising	250	250	250	250	250	250
Fixtures and Fittings	12,500	–	–	–	–	–
Total Cash out	21,550	6,500	7,770	10,966	12,882	13,240
Cash Balances						
Monthly Cash Balance	2,450	(1,500)	(2,770)	(3,966)	(882)	1,760
Balance brought forward	–	2,450	950	(1,820)	(5,786)	(6,668)
Balance to carry forward or Net Cash Flow	2,450	950	(1,820)	(5,786)	(6,668)	(4,908)

And there is a cure. Once a business is successfully launched, its sales pattern passes through four distinct stages (see graph).

The 'introduction' stage occurs while contacts, customers and a reputation are being built up. Typically, sales and the rate of sales growth are modest and start-up cash resources are adequate.

The next 'early growth' stage is when the problems begin. Rapid sales growth is as natural to a successful new business as physical growth is to a baby. And just as a baby runs out of new clothes, new businesses run out of cash – usually about halfway up the curve.

It is not until the rate of growth has slowed down during the third 'growth' phase that a positive cash flow begins to appear, and much later still before the cumulative net cash flow is in the black.

The fourth stage, 'maturity', is only reached by those who survive the earlier cash flow crisis. This phase is typified by positive cash flow, and a stable sales platform from which to build a strong business.

The key to survival lies in having a good cash flow forecast, prepared in advance and modified in the light of changing events. This should be used to negotiate an adequate overdraft facility in advance. But as well as getting help from the bank, small firms

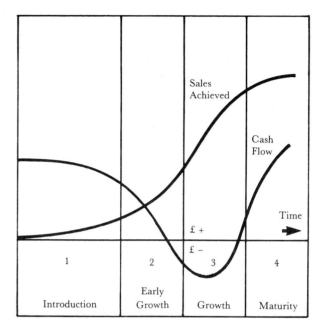

Sales and cash cycle for a new business

can help themselves. The following measures will help you to minimise the need for extra cash to finance sales growth.

- *Send bills out promptly.* Someone new to an area asked his neighbour to recommend a good local builder. His reply was that there was little to choose in workmanship between Brown and Smith, two local firms, but he always used Smith as they settled up once a year! Get a system right at the start to get bills, statements and reminders out promptly. Have a hit list of debtors: those who owe money must be chased up for payment. It is a good idea to list debtors by age of debt as this shows who owes how much and for how long. Take a no-nonsense approach with them and stop supplies to people who take too long to pay or threaten to sue.
- *Check credit ratings.* Before taking on a new or big customer have them checked out. If they are 'blue-chip' you may be able to factor the debt and get up to 80 per cent of the cash owed immediately. Alternatively, offer discount for cash and charge interest on overdue accounts.
- *Keep stock levels down.* The chances are that the opening stock

will be out of line with customer demand. After all, before the start companies have to guess what will sell. Once a pattern begins to emerge order accordingly. Too many new ventures spend all their cash on opening stock, only to find they are left with products that won't sell and have no cash to buy those that will.

- *Take credit.* As a rule of thumb successful businessmen try to take as much credit as they are giving. So if their customers take a month to pay, they aim to take a month's credit from their suppliers.

6. Breaking even

While some businesses have difficulty raising start-up capital, paradoxically one of the main reasons small businesses fail in the early stages is that too much start-up capital is used to buy fixed assets. Some equipment is obviously essential at the start, other purchases could be postponed. This may mean that 'desirable' and labour saving devices have to be borrowed or hired for a specific period.

This is not as nice as having them to hand all the time but if, for example, photocopiers, electronic typewriters, word processors, micros and even delivery vans, are brought into the business, they become part of the fixed costs.

The market place dictates the selling price

The higher the fixed cost plateau, the longer it usually takes to reach break-even and then profitability. And time is not usually on the side of the small, new business. It has to become profitable relatively quickly, or it will simply run out of money and die.

Difficulties usually begin when people become confused by the different characteristics of costs. Some costs, for instance, do not change, however much you sell. If you are running a shop, the rent and the rates are constant figures, quite independent of the volume of sales. On the other hand, the cost of the products sold from the shop is completely dependent on volume. The more you sell, the more it 'costs' to buy stock. The first type of cost is called 'fixed' and the second 'variable' and you cannot add them together to arrive at total costs, until you have made some assumptions about sales.

Let's take an elementary example: a business plans to sell only one product and has only one fixed cost, the rent.

In the chart opposite, the vertical axis shows the value of sales

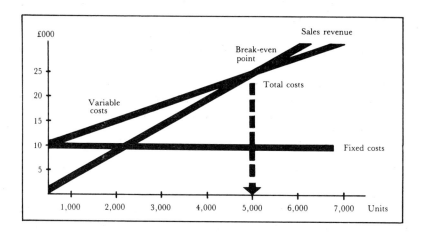

and costs and the horizontal shows the number of units sold. The second horizontal line represents the fixed costs, those that do not change as volume increases. In this case it is the rent of £10,000. The angled line running from the top of the fixed costs line is the variable costs. In this example we plan to buy in at £3 per unit, so every unit we sell adds that much to our variable costs.

Only one element is needed to complete the picture, the sales line. That is the line moving up at an angle from the bottom left-hand corner of the chart. We plan to sell at £5 per unit, so this line is calculated by multiplying the units sold by that price. The break-even point is the stage when a business starts to make a profit. That is when the sales revenue begins to exceed both the fixed and variable costs. In our example the break-even point is 5,000 units.

A formula, deduced from the chart, will make your calculations easier.

$$\text{Break-even point} = \frac{\text{Fixed Costs}}{\text{Unit Selling Price} - \text{Variable Costs per Unit}}$$

Thus; in our example: $\frac{10,000}{5-3} = 5,000$ units

Look at two new small businesses, Company A and Company B. They are making and selling identical products at the same price, £10. They plan to sell 10,000 units each in the first year.

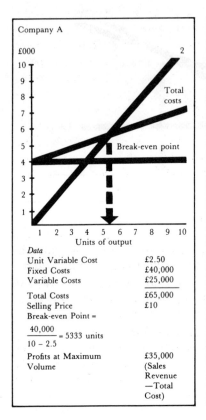

Company A

£000

Total costs

Break-even point

Units of output

Data
Unit Variable Cost	£2.50
Fixed Costs	£40,000
Variable Costs	£25,000
Total Costs	£65,000
Selling Price	£10

Break-even Point =

$$\frac{40,000}{10-2.5} = 5333 \text{ units}$$

Profits at Maximum Volume	£35,000 (Sales Revenue —Total Cost)

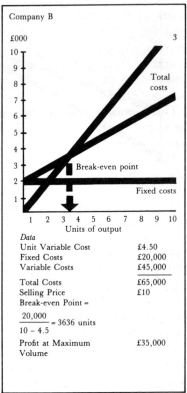

Company B

£000

Total costs

Break-even point

Fixed costs

Units of output

Data
Unit Variable Cost	£4.50
Fixed Costs	£20,000
Variable Costs	£45,000
Total Costs	£65,000
Selling Price	£10

Break-even Point =

$$\frac{20,000}{10-4.5} = 3636 \text{ units}$$

Profit at Maximum Volume	£35,000

The owner of Company A plans to get fully equipped at the start. His fixed costs will be £40,000, double those of Company B. This is largely because, as well as his own car, he has bought such things as a delivery van, new equipment and a photocopier. Much of this will not be fully used for some time, but will save some money now. This extra expenditure will result in a lower unit variable cost than Company B can achieve, a typical capital intensive result.

Company B's owner, on the other hand, proposes to start up on a shoestring. Only £20,000 will go into fixed costs but, of course, his unit variable cost will be higher, at £4.50. The variable cost is higher because, for example, he has to pay an outside carrier to deliver, while A uses his own van and pays only for petrol.

The break-even position for each business is shown in the charts opposite. You can see that total costs for 10,000 units are the same for each company, so total possible profits, if 10,000 units are sold, are also the same. The key difference is that Company B starts making profits after 3,636 units have been sold. Company A has to wait until 5,333 units have been sold, and it may not be able to wait that long.

This is a hypothetical case. But the real world is littered with the corpses of businesses that spent too much too soon. The market-place dictates the selling price and your costs have to fall in line with that, if you are to have any hope of survival. Ask these questions before committing to capital expenditure.

Are fixed cost estimates realistic?

A West Country self-employed builder became bored with paying out fancy prices for paint, wallpaper and other materials. He decided to open a decorating shop and get his wife to look after it. He bought one with a flat above, in a pretty run-down condition. That did not bother him as he knew he could do most of the renovation work himself. What he did not know was that the fire regulations required a fire resistant wall and ceiling between the shop and the living accommodation. This additional work put nearly £6,000 on his start-up costs and pushed his break-even point out to the second year. That was beyond his cash resources and the shop is now up for sale.

Is everything on the shopping list essential?

One of the problems with becoming a company director is the great danger of behaving like the chairman of a successful multinational at the outset. Sure, a Range Rover could double as a delivery van, but so could a Cavalier estate at half the price.

Can it be begged, borrowed or stolen?

A piece of equipment may be essential to get started, but it doesn't have to be owned. Perhaps begging or stealing are unacceptable options, but leasing certainly is not. Despite the changes in taxation on capital allowances, leasing is still a favourite way for small businesses to have the use of an asset and keep start-up costs low. In the West Cornwall Woodwork case, for example, Maureen and Graham Davey have the use of a new diesel van and a purpose-built factory for an initial outlay of under £1,000. Had they set out to buy these assets they would have used up every penny of their capital before they had made their first sale.

7. Understanding the nature of profit

A significant number of new small ventures operate largely on a cash basis. That is, most of their transactions and income come in either as cheques or in folding notes. While it is certainly very pleasant to be able to conduct your business affairs in this way, cash can often give rise to misleading financial signals.

It is very tempting for the owner manager to believe that the cash he has in hand is pretty much the same as the profit he will end up with. And either through feeling flush, or sheer personal necessity, he may end up spending more than he can really afford.

The whole problem arises from the difference between the accounting definition of profit, and the 'commonsense' definition of cash. Cash and profits are not the same thing, even in a cash business, and a business needs both cash and profits to survive.

To make matters even more confusing, there are at least three sorts of profit to keep track of! This case history will give you some idea of the problems that can arise.

Henry Nicholson had worked for a packaging company for five years before it went into liquidation. He had been the area representative for the south-east of London, and had very good contacts with a number of important buyers. His old firm had imported its most profitable lines from Sweden, and when he decided to go into business for himself it was on these that he chose to concentrate.

He took a small warehouse near Southwark Bridge, with an office and telephone. He hired a telephone-sales girl, who chased up orders and 'looked after' things while he was on the road.

The first month's results were quite spectacular, and with nearly £3,000 in his hand he felt his future was assured. He had received some £10,000 in sales, and although he still had some of that to deliver, the customers had paid up. They were keen to maintain a source of supply, and wanted to do everything they could to help him to get started.

He still owed his Swedish suppliers a small amount for one shipment, and he expected some other bills would come in late in the year. Certainly not every month would be as good as this one and, of course, the taxman would eventually have to be paid. But nothing could alter the fact that he had cash in hand.

Nicholson's profit and loss account 1 May – 1 April 1984	
	£
Sales receipts	10,000
Less payments for	
Materials	5,000
Wages etc	1,000
Rent	500
Advertising	500
Profit for the month	3,000

Nicholson was a little surprised that neither his bank manager, nor his financial adviser were quite as enthusiastic about his trading results as he was. After an hour of probing questions

Profit and loss account – 1 May – 1 April 1984		
	£	£
Sales income		9,000
Less cost of sales		
Opening stock	0	
Purchases in month	6,000	
	6,000	
Less closing stock	500	
Cost of goods sold		5,000
Gross profit		3,500
Less operating expenses		
Materials		
Wages etc	1,000	
Rent	500	
Advertising	500	
Rates	100	
Telephone	80	
Electricity and gas	80	
Total expenses		2,600
Operating (or trading) profit		1,240
Non-operating expenses		
Loan interest		70
Provision for a personal pension		70
Profit before income tax		1,100
Tax		330
Class II – NI stamps		22
To reserves for future needs		448
Profit available for drawings (net profit)		300

a new profit and loss account was constructed by his financial adviser, with explanations given for the difference between the statements.

The fundamental differences between cash and profits can best be explained under the following headings.

1. The realisation concept

A particularly prudent sales manager once said that an order was not an order until the customer's cheque had cleared, he had consumed the product, had not died as a result and, finally, had shown every indication of wanting to buy again. Most of us know quite different salesmen who can 'anticipate' the most unlikely volume of sales. In accounting, income is usually recognised as having been earned when the goods (or services) are despatched and the invoice sent out – not when an order is received, or on the assumption of a firm order, or the expectation of prompt payment.

It is possible that some of the products despatched may be returned at some later date. This means that income, and consequently profit, can be achieved in one period, and have to be removed later on. Obviously, if returns can be estimated accurately, then an adjustment can be made to income at the time.

Nicholson has received a 'pre-payment' for £1,000-worth of goods not yet despatched. This cannot be included in his figure for sales income which has to appear as only £9,000 and not the £10,000 he has received in cash.

2. The cost of sales

Obviously, goods which have not yet been despatched must still be held in stock. A vital calculation is that of exactly how much stock has been used up over the period. This is calculated by adding the opening stock to any purchases you have made, and taking away the stock that is left. To get this right, you will have to take a physical stock check periodically, but if the volumes involved are large, you may have to rely on your paperwork in the meantime.

The 'materials' used in a business are usually a major element of expense and as such are separated off from the rest of the expenses. For a manufacturing company materials are easy to define. For a service business the sum is less obvious, but still necessary. So, for example, a travel agency's account might look like this:

Sunbeam Travel

	£
Sales	200,000
Payment to carriers	130,000
Net commission income	
(Gross profit)	70,000
Expenses etc	
(as for any other business)	

The money that is left after Sunbeam Travel has paid the companies that carry their customers is the gross profit.

3. Matching expenses

Expenses is the general name given to the costs incurred in selling, marketing, administering, distributing and advertising a company's products or services. Some of these expenses may be for items not yet paid for. The profit and loss account sets out to 'match' income and expenditure to the time period they were incurred. In the example above, Nicholson does not have a bill for the telephone, electricity or gas, but he cannot enter a nil expense. An estimate of what has been spent is entered. Accountants call this accruing.

A number of other expenses are not allowed for in Nicholson's naive estimate of his profits and once these have been deducted, he is left with £300 to draw as his salary: a far cry from the £3,000 he originally thinks he has.

8. Management accounts

Liquidators say almost all the businesses they are called in to wind up have no reliable management accounts. 'If only I'd known the financial situation earlier' is the cry of many a failed entrepreneur. New businessmen often see accounting as a bureaucratic nuisance carried out for the Inland Revenue's benefit alone. Those same people would never drive a car without a fuel gauge, speedometer and oil pressure indicator. Yet they set off at breakneck speed, running their business with only the annual accounts to guide them – and break their necks. For them, the end of the first year is often the end of the business.

So it is essential at the outset for the owner manager to be able to demonstrate how the enterprise is to be controlled. This entails knowing what information is needed for decision making, who will collect it, and how it will be processed and presented. Outside professional advice will almost certainly be needed, but the entrepreneur must anticipate the need, understand the data and be able to make timely decisions working from the management accounts.

9. Teamwork

The company misfit, who may have many of the characteristics of the ideal entrepreneur, is usually short on the skills that are needed to manage a growing business.

The new enterprise has rapidly to develop a management team and an organisational structure that can handle the business in a competitive environment.

Apple Computers is a classic example of this principle, taking its two founder entrepreneurs and two professional managers into Forbes 1984 listing of the Richest Four Hundred People in America on the way. In March 1976 Jobs and Wozniak formed a partnership and by June they were selling printed-circuit boards. By selling Jobs' Volkswagen bus and Wozniak's Hewlett Packard calculator they raised the money to design their personal computer, the Apple II. By the end of 1976 sales were $200,000, and by the beginning of 1977 neither man wanted to continue to have responsibility for the day-to-day operation. They brought in AC Markula, marketing manager of Intel, a leading semi-conductor manufacturer, as Chairman; and later added Michael Scott, president of National Semi-Conductors, as President. By the end of 1977 the key management team was in place and $3 million capital had been raised. On 12 December 1980, Apple made a $96.8 million public share offer which was rapidly taken up, making all four multi-millionaires overnight.

A word of caution must be added on the subject of partnerships. As both success and failure put great strains on relationships it is important to choose business partners carefully and to take advice at the outset in formalising that relationship, its rewards and obligations.

10. Funding

Reading through the cases, you will notice one theme which they all have in common. There is a constant search for funds to finance start-up capital, the cash flow for sales growth, or a major new project.

A motorist having bought a new car, does not suddenly

discover that he has to buy petrol before it will go anywhere, and that the further he wants it to go the more petrol he will have to buy. Similarly, it should come as no surprise to the budding entrepreneur that a large proportion of his time must be spent looking for new money.

There are three main types of finance that a small business can pursue.

Venture capital

First there is the money introduced by the proprietor(s), or, if the business is a limited company, by the shareholders. This is risk capital in the sense that, unless profits are made, the shareholders get no reward. Typically, the reward for venture capital, as this risk money is often called, would be dividends and growth in the value of the shares.

Start-up and early-stage entrepreneurs looking for venture capital often believe that retaining a minimum of 51 per cent of the shares is essential to be able to control the company. This view assumes that control depends on legal percentage of ownership rather than on management's behaviour. A glance at the share register of any successful mature company will show that this is a misconception, but it is one which leads some entrepreneurs to starve themselves of essential capital and not only stifle growth, but threaten the very survival of their venture. In short, 51 per cent of nothing is nothing.

Sound investment partners do not want to run the company – they invest in the entrepreneur and his team. In fact a substantial investment by a venture capital firm is a vote of confidence in that team. Research carried out on companies in the USA started with the aid of venture capital suggests that 65 to 80 per cent survive and succeed. This compares very favourably with the success rate of the 'go it alone', business starter.

Loan capital

After exploring their own resources and those of other potential investors, small businessmen usually turn to the clearing banks and to other sources of loan capital, such as mortgages and hire-purchase. The common feature of all such loans is that the business has to pay interest on the money, and eventually repay the capital, whether or not it is successful. On the other hand if the business is a spectacular success these lenders, unlike shareholders, will not share in the profits.

Organisations providing either share capital or loan capital to a new or small business look very carefully at their relative levels of involvement. So, for example, a bank advancing a loan would normally expect the owner and his fellow shareholders to match that loan £1 for £1. This relationship is known as the debt/equity ratio.

Similarly, once a business has started trading and is looking for new share capital, a too high proportion of debt could be a deterrent. After all, interest has to be paid on that debt before any profits are available to shareholders, and with loan interest running at 15 to 25 per cent (credit cards are 26 per cent +) that profit can be a long time coming.

Owner managers are thus not only always raising money, but they are managing their debt/equity ratio. Sensitive to this problem, financial institutions are becoming innovative in providing 'off balance sheet' financing, such as leasing, which can be treated in the accounts as an expense and not as a source of funds.

Share options

One major clearing bank is believed to be producing a scheme which involves the bank taking a share option. Loans ranging from £25,000 to £200,000 will be unsecured for up to ten years. Repayment arrangements will be flexible.

The key innovation is that the loan will be subordinated to other creditors, with the bank repaid before shareholders but after all the other creditors if the company fails. In return for this risk, the bank is likely to want an option on up to 25 per cent of the company's capital.

Finally, once the business has got started and is making profits, it can plough some of those profits back into finance growth, and consequently reduce the debt/equity ratio! (These undistributed profits retained in the business belong to the shareholders so are treated in the accounts as an increase in share capital or equity.)

11. The business plan

The accepted way in which proposals for funds are put forward is through a business plan. The business plan brings together the marketing and operational aspects of the business or proposed business, and is presented in terms that a financial institution will understand, complete with financial statements and projections.

The development of such a business plan is neither quick nor easy. It can take anything from 200 to 400 hours. If these hours have to be found during evenings and weekends, the process will take between six months and a year.

It is often felt that a more effective approach would be to commission outside professionals to prepare the business plan, while the entrepreneur concentrates on getting things going quickly. However, this is unlikely to prove a short-cut in the end, as the careful preparation of a business plan represents an excellent opportunity to think through all facets of a new venture. You can examine the consequences of different strategies and tactics and determine the human and financial requirements for launching and building the venture, all at no risk or cost.

In both the Windancer and Medsoft case studies the consequences of the founders not preparing a comprehensive business plan are clearly visible. In other cases, particularly those where a specific proposal for funds is involved, you might like to put yourself in the shoes of a potential investor.

This is not to suggest that outside advice and help are not essential. Quite the contrary. But the plan itself must be prepared by the people who are going to have to implement it.

Presenting business plans to financiers

Owners/managers sometimes think that having to present their plans to outside people such as their bank manager is a nuisance to be avoided. It is possible to have some sympathy with this point of view, but if your business needs cash then there is no alternative. On the positive side, having to present a plan does make sure it is prepared in the first place, and prepared to a certain standard. If you need outside money then a 'banker' will need to look carefully at both the proposal and the proposer.

The proposer's experience, ability, drive, integrity and resilience in times of trouble, will all be areas subject to examination. So you, the proposer, must be prepared to make your presentation with sufficient information and style to let these qualities be seen.

The proposal itself, even if made in person, should be supported with comprehensive back-up documentation. This should be sent in advance, after an appointment to 'present' has been made. This will give the 'banker' a chance to prepare himself and so be ready to give a quick decision. The information need not contain as much detail as your own business plans. You want, instead, to produce a summary, but one that demonstrates that a thorough approach has been taken.

The presentation should include as much of the following

information as possible:

1. A description of the business, its history and past achievements. Include details of all products/services and perhaps literature. (Obviously a start-up proposal will not have any trading history, so more emphasis must be placed on showing the management's competence and the business idea's viability.)
2. Details of the experience, education and background of the directors and key managers. This should include other directorships and business interests.
3. If applicable, the management structure, with details of the responsibilities of each director/manager.
4. A list and details of other shareholders. If they are prestigious or with good business experience, emphasise any other help they may be able to give you.
5. Audited accounts as far back as possible, and current management accounts.
6. For a start-up proposal, details of the type of financial controls to be used, and who will provide them.
7. An appraisal of the present and future markets for your products, with details of major competitors.
8. A detailed statement on the current order book, showing number and type of customers. Compare this with the past year or so.
9. The finance now required. How it is to be used. By what means it will be repaid.
10. Projections for the years ahead. This is a summary of your current budget and three-year plan, containing a profit and loss account for each year; a cash flow forecast month-by-month for the first year and then quarterly for three years; opening and closing balance sheets for each year.

Keep the documentation as brief and simple as possible, but do not miss out anything important. Read it through asking yourself four questions as you do so. Is it clear, concise, complete and correct? Also explain technical terms, and, if possible, bring along the end product or at least a picture of it.

Timing is crucial

Anything as complex as starting up a business or launching a new product calls for careful time management. First, break the whole task into its component parts, setting targets and deadlines for each. Initially the plan should be made in big bold chunks of time, only filling in the detail later.

For a new business the first of these component parts could be described as pre-launch activities, that is all the work to be done before you can open for business. It starts as soon as you decide to commit time, money, or both, to a business idea. Finding suppliers, premises, marketing channels and key staff are all included.

The second component could be launch activities: what is to happen a few days before and after opening day. For Chantal Coady's Rococo this meant organising a stream of launch parties for the press and important customers. This was supported by local advertising and other public relations work. It also meant recruiting temporary staff to help out in the first few weeks until things settled down. The crucial thing here is to open on the right day. Every business has a seasonal peak, and opening just after it is asking for trouble.

The third component could be post-launch activities. A small new business is so demanding that entrepreneurs have to be very selective about how they spend their time, or important development tasks will be neglected.

Two entrepreneurs found that a week after they launched their mail order business, they had been transformed from managing director and chairman into a couple of 'mail boys'. After a day spent collecting, packing and running down to the post office they had no time or energy left. And yet they both knew they had to build on their initial success and extend their product and customer base. So they farmed out their business to a mail order house, which took over everything from processing customers' cheques to despatching the goods. Their computer produced weekly sales figures, customer lists and even told them how effective each advertisement or editorial had been. Fortunately, the two entrepreneurs had planned to do this if the situation called for it.

Contingency plans are needed for each of these planning stages. It is no good waiting until things go wrong before thinking about what to do. Some things will not go as planned and when that happens you must be prepared. Obviously you cannot cater for every eventuality but, in critical areas, planning is essential.

Prepare a chart timetable bringing all these key events together. The length of the 'bar' for each activity is the time between the earliest start date and the latest completion date. In the example below the search for premises starts in November,

Priority	Activity	Nov	Dec	Jan	Feb	Mar	Apr
1	Find premises	███	███				
2	Refit premises			███	███	███	
3	Buy in stock					███	
4	Open shop for Easter						███

and must be completed by January. Everything hinges around this, as the premises cannot be fitted out until they have been found, and the stock cannot be bought in until fitting out is well under way.

Allow some slack in the timetable, between the opening day and the last activity. This will prevent a disaster if the preceding events take longer than at first expected. This 'planning slack' should be a realistic amount of time. Less than 30 per cent is unlikely to be enough.

Review progress regularly by recording results on the chart as you go along. In this way the impact of any delay in completing a task can easily be seen and allowed for. If you are running behind with fitting out the premises, for example, delay ordering stock, or taking on staff. Otherwise you will run out of cash as well as time.

The very process of planning how to spend your time over this crucial business start-up period can be an education in itself.

Talk your plan through with someone who has done something similar before. They will quickly tell you if your timing is realistic.

12. The effects of inflation

Inflation in the UK and elsewhere has persisted at high enough rates for a long enough period of time to make many of its debilitating effects well known.

Beyond rising prices and an inducement to speculate which affect all businesses, inflation causes a particular problem for the small firm, as it distorts the financial yardsticks by which outsiders and managers make decisions. This problem is further exacerbated because small company managers often try to minimise or exaggerate their financial accomplishments depending on whether they are preparing tax forms or seeking loans. With such important interests in mind, managers are likely to ignore the effects of inflation on financial results. This example will serve to illustrate the point.

A company was reviewing its sales performance over a two-year period. At first sight the figures set out in Table A show a substantial growth in sales in each of the past two years.

Table A

Year	Sales	Sales Growth	Percentage Growth year on year
	£	£	
1	100,000	–	
2	130,000	30,000	30
3	145,000	15,000	11.5

However, the purchasing power of a pound in year 1 is not the same as in year 3. To compare these figures properly we need an 'index' such as that for consumer prices. Such indices usually take 100 as their base at some time in the past, for example 1975. Then an index value for each subsequent year is produced showing the relative movement in the item being indexed.

If this company's management used a consumer price index for the appropriate time period to adjust these sales figures, the years could be properly compared. Let us assume that the indices for years 1, 2 and 3 were 104, 120 and 135 respectively. Year 3 is the most recent set of figures, and therefore the one we want to use as the base for comparison.

So to convert pounds from years 1 and 2 to 'current pounds', we use this sum:

$$\text{Current Pounds} = \frac{\text{Index for Current year}}{\text{Index for Historic year}} = \text{Historic Pounds}$$

For year 1 sales now become 135/104 × £100,000 = £129,808
For year 2 sales now become 135/120 × £130,000 = £146,250
For year 3 sales now become 135/135 × £145,000 = £145,000

We can now show in Table B, the real sales growth over the past three years.

Table B

Year	Adjusted Sales	Adjusted Sales Growth	Percentage Growth
1	129,808	–	–
2	146,250	16,442	12.7
3	145,000	– 1,250	– 0.9

The real situation is nothing like as rosy as we first thought. Far from growing, the company's sales are actually in decline. The effects of inflation have fundamentally concealed the company's true trading position.

Part 1: Dreams of Success
(Before start-up)

Case 1

Rococo

Colin Barrow

Christmas 1981 marked a watershed in 22-year-old Chantal Coady's life. After two years in Harrods' confectionery department where she had both designed packaging and sold chocolates, she felt the time had come to branch out on her own (see Appendix 1, Résumé).

With her art college education she decided to apply fashion to some field which had never been fashionable – and sweet shops hadn't changed since Edwardian days. The customers she was aiming for were the young, the eccentric, people greedy for new ideas, all visually orientated. The description covered the range from dowagers to designers buying to match their decor. (Two years on Jasper Conran was to ask Chantal to provide boxes of sugared almonds to match his spring collection.)

After several months' thinking around the idea she put pen to paper and described her proposed venture in these terms.

'I will be in the business of selling chocolates, aiming at the top end of the market. The products will range from Belgian fresh cream chocolates and truffles to the more unusual 'Rococo' chocolates. These will include chocolate cherubs and sugar crystal tiaras, to appeal to the younger *avant-garde* chocolate buyers.

The kernel of the idea is that chocolates equal pornography and when two friends meet in my shop they say, "God! What are you doing here?" as if they had met in a sex shop.

Location is crucial to the success or failure of my business, therefore I have chosen the World's End section of the King's Road, Chelsea, at the junction of Beaufort Street. This is conveniently located for the Chelsea/Knightsbridge clientele. There a good passing trade, and a generally creative ambience on this road, and no other specialist chocolate shop in the vicinity.

The Rococo personality will be a major theme for the decor of the shop; it will be based on an Adam interior and filled with cupids, chandeliers, candelabra, *trompe l'oeil* and stucco plaster work. This will also be reflected in the packaging, which has been designed to form an essential part of the service which I am offering ie gifts. There will also be a range of greeting cards.

The reclining cupid (or slouching cherub) is to be the trade mark or "signature" of the project.'

World's End was not chosen simply on a whim, it was the subject of a most careful study. While Chantal was confident that her 'Rococo' concept was unique, she was enough of a realist to recognise that at one level it could be seen as just another up-market chocolate shop. As such her shop needed its own distinctive catchment area. She drew up a list of chocolate shops situated in Central London (Appendix 2), which verified her closest competitors to be in Knightsbridge – in Central London terms, another world.

A further subject of concern was the nature of the passing trade in the vicinity of the proposed World's End shop. The local residents could be polled by direct leafleting, but she decided to find out more about the passing trade by means of a questionnaire (Appendix 3). About half the people questioned responded favourably to the 'Rococo' concept. Slightly more worrying, nearly 70 per cent of the passing trade were in socio-economic groups that were unlikely to be major customers.

By the summer of 1982 Chantal had attended a 10-week small business course at Thames Polytechnic, sponsored by the Manpower Services Commission, and her plans were well developed. She had also taken professional advice from a score of experts (Appendix 4). A summary of the plan she took to her bank manager is set out below. She also included details from her market research activity.

Statement of objectives

The population of Kensington and Chelsea is 241,000, so from this figure I have reached a target audience of the same number, comprising one-third local trade and two-thirds passing trade. The market size would be approximately £480,000. I would be aiming to take a 25 per cent share of this, ie £120,000, by my third full year of trading.

Financial strategy

The project is to be financed by:

Share capital	£5,000
Loan under government Loan Guarantee Scheme	£20,000
	£25,000

The loan will be repaid over seven years.
Future growth will be funded by profits.
I do not intend to open another shop in the near future.

The three-year profit and loss accounts, one-year cash flow, and opening and first-year end balance sheets are shown in Appendix 5.

Launch strategy

High prices and quality
Medium promotion
High product awareness
Little competition

The launching of the business, like the location, is of key importance, therefore there will be a launch party. The press, ie *Vogue*, *Harpers & Queen*, *The Face*, *Ritz*, the Sunday papers, local press and other magazines such as *Interiors* will be invited, along with a mystery guest to cut the ribbon (wouldn't you love to know who?).

Premises

Shops in the area that Chantal required were relatively expensive and came on the market infrequently. One shop, 315 King's Road, SW3, seemed almost ideal. It was prominently situated on the south side of the King's Road, just to the east of Beaufort Street. The frontage was 15 ft and in all the ground floor and basement provided some 800 sq ft. The rent was £7,850 per annum, and the premium sought offers in excess of £15,000. Chantal planned for relatively simple fixtures and fittings and her schedule of costs is set out below:

Costs of fixtures and fittings

	£
2 or 3 gilt mirrors	300
1 chaise longue	300
1 long cabinet with rococo trim	400
2 tables	400
8 chairs	400
2 chandeliers and candelabra	600
Casts from the British Museum	500
Coffee machine	200
Cups etc	100
	3,200
Plus: Plaster mouldings, paint and sundry expenses	1,800
	5,000

Suppliers

Harringtons of Royal Tunbridge Wells
Bendicks of Mayfair
Della (Belgian fresh cream chocolate importer)
Costa's
Lindt
Bassetts
Droste
Just Because (sugar crystal)
Japanese company for novelty chocs – to be verified
Bakers recommended by Harringtons
Loseley ice cream

Printing and packaging

Ribbon:	Caldecotts
	Swan Porth Textiles
Paper:	Cartwright Bryce
	Spicer Cowan
	Mentmore Graphic Arts
	Mary Totman
Boxes:	M Fish & Son
	SE Milbourne Ltd
Moulds:	Ray White
Gold embossed labels:	Walsall Litho Co.

Terms of trade. All cash up front until creditworthiness is established.

Products

In chocolate, such as cupids, shoes, oysters, cameras, walkmans, tape-recorders, records, handcuffs, calculators.

In sugar crystal, such as tiaras, engagement rings, chandeliers, earrings, cocktail glasses, glass slippers, champagne buckets.

Other lines (standard and traditional): yoghurt raisins, honey-dipped fruit, toffee, gobstoppers, jelly beans, nuts, old-fashioned humbugs, lollipops, sugared almonds.

Contingency plans

Leave in £3,000 from a reduction in leasehold premium for any unforeseen emergencies.

The provision of selling cakes and ice cream to help with any downturn in summer chocolate sales.

In case of personal accident or injury, there are executives available to handle emergency administrative problems. The full-time member of staff would not be expected to take on any additional responsibilities.

The Retail Staff Agency could be called upon to supply extra staff and there is a possibility that the Saturday girls would be willing to stand in in such an emergency.

I will carry a line of relatively non-perishable chocolates (boxed) to cope with unexpectedly large orders. In addition to this, I have suppliers who can produce fresh chocolates at very short notice (one day).

The future possibility of exploiting the mail order gift market.

Appendix 1

Résumé

Name	Chantal Coady
Address	111 London Rd, London, SE23 3XW
Telephone	01-699 0840
Date of Birth	17 April 1959
Marital Status	Single
Education	1969–75 St Leonard's-Mayfield.
	1975–77 Mary Datchelor Girls School
	1975 GCE O levels: art, biology, chemistry, physics, maths, English literature, English language, French, Italian.

	1977 GCE A levels: art (printed textiles), French. 1977–78 Foundation course at St Martin's School of Art, London. 1978–81 BA Hons in fashion/textiles at Camberwell School of Art and Crafts.
Summary of Working Experience	General filing, accounting, invoicing, basic typing, operating PABX switchboard, checking computer printouts. Designed range of special boxes and packaging for Harrods' confectionery dept. Special commissions: special birthday cake in the shape of car for rock star. Hand-made truffles for Ray Batchelor's store. 10-week course at Thames Polytechnic, covering all aspects of running a small business, such as bookkeeping.
Details of Working Experience	July 1976: three weeks in France as an au pair. July/Aug 1977: worked as painter/decorator. July/Aug 1978: worked as receptionist/telephonist for Godden & Holme solicitors. July/Aug 1979: Worked for Davy International. Helped prepare accounts for audit and checked computer printouts after accounting system had been updated. Touch-typing course at Dynamic Typing. Aug 1979: with Sogex, preparing personnel data for computer input. 1979–81: Harrods' confectionery dept designing, packaging and selling chocolates.

Appendix 2

Other chocolate shops in London

Charbonnel and Walker, Bond Street
Prestats, South Molton Street
Thorntons, Covent Garden
Elena, Hampstead, Edgware and St John's Wood
Harrods and Selfridges
Clare's, Regent's Park
Ackermans, Smithfield and NW6
Bendicks, Sloane Street and Mayfair

Richoux, Knightsbridge
Newmans, City and Shaftesbury Avenue

None of these shops offers the kind of service I am proposing.

Appendix 3

Market Research Questionnaire

Date: Location: Time:

I am interested in people who buy chocolate – can you tell me how often you buy the following:

	Every day	Every week	Once a month	Special occasions
Bars				
Boxes				
Loose chocs				

Where do you buy these chocs?
Supermarket
Sweet shop
Woolworths
Specialist shop
Other

When was the last time you were given chocs as a present? Some people enjoy receiving chocs as a gift; where would you put yourself on this scale?

Overjoyed	Very pleased	Mod pleased	Indifferent	Ungrateful

Do you ever buy chocs as a present for anyone?

The last time you bought chocs for someone, who was it for?

Where did you buy it from?

How much did you spend? Up to £1 ☐ Up to £5 ☐ Over £5 ☐

Was it wrapped in the shop (as a gift)?

Do you have a favourite chocolate bar or box?

Any preferences for: Dark ☐ Milk ☐ White ☐?

Do you have a favourite from any particular country?

English	French	German	Belgian	Swiss	Other

Some people say that the existing chocolates on the market are rather boring; would you agree?

If there were a shop which sold a unique range of gifts in chocolate, and high quality loose and boxed chocs, how interested would you be in buying them?

Extremely	Very	Moderately	Indifferent	Not interested

Age Group
Up to 20
21 – 25
26 – 30
31 – 40
41 – 50
Over 50

Profession:

Income bracket
Up to £5,000
Up to 10,000
Up to 15,000
Up to 20,000
Over 20,000

Any other comments:

Objectives of questionnaire

1. Purpose:
   a) To quantify positive response: as a percentage.
   b) To establish the 'character' of the positive respondent in terms of socio-economic grading, ie profession/income bracket; their buying habits and their unfulfilled requirements.
   c) To clarify problem gift areas.

2. The character of the target market can be split into main parts:

   The passing trade – of which the weekday and Saturday influx constitutes different subdivisions.

   The genuine residents, many of whom have lived in the area for generations.

I have decided to poll the residents in their own right by direct leafleting. There will be an incentive to reply (such as a reduction in the price of a box of chocolates). At the same time I shall be sampling the passing trade by means of the questionnaire. Thus

I expect to obtain information about these different market sectors.

The sample
The figures below represent the first 100 questionnaires. Early results bear out expectations that the Saturday afternoon shoppers on the King's Road are made up of a large number of under 20-years-olds, D&E (up to £5,000 per annum).

Total sample to date: 100 (50 male : 50 female)

Age		Socio-economic grading	
			%
30 aged up to 20	which	E under £5,000	
20 aged 21–26	converts	D under £5,000	42
20 aged 26–30	to:	C_2 up to £10,000	28
10 aged 31–40		C_1 up to £15,000	11
10 aged 41–50		B up to £20,000	8
10 aged over 50		A over £20,000	11
100			100

General information drawn from the sample
90 per cent of this sample buys chocolate bars more than once a week.

60 per cent bought boxes of chocolates for special occasions, such as birthdays, Christmas, Easter, Mother's Day, or for a thank-you present.

Only 10 per cent said that they never bought boxed chocolates.

When asked if they had ever bought chocolate as a gift for a particular person, 86 per cent responded positively, and the categories of people for whom the gift was bought are as follows:

	%
Friends	44
Mothers	26
Relations	15
Grandparents	8
Wives	4
Lovers	3
	100

When asked how much they had spent on the last box of chocolates bought as a gift:

15 per cent spent under £1
75 per cent spent up to £5
10 per cent spent over £5

96 per cent responded positively when asked if they had ever been given chocolate as a gift. Their reactions to receiving chocolate as a gift were:

45 per cent were very pleased or overjoyed.

Only 3 per cent were ungrateful: one suffered from migraine, one preferred Scotch, one was on a diet.

20 per cent of the sample bought chocs from specialist shops, the rest were bought in sweet-shops, garages, or supermarkets.

Chocolate preferred (by nationality type):

	%
Swiss	37
English	25
Belgian	16
French	7
German	3
American	1
Italian	1

Trades and professions in the sample were widely varied:

Student
Secretary
Civil servant
Teacher
Financier
Hotelier
Roof tiler
Jelly baby maker and others

The diversity of favourites showed no clear pattern, and ranged through specialist Belgian fresh cream chocs such as Godiva and Leonidas, standard boxes, such as Lindt and Bendicks, to Mars bars and Double Deckers.

When asked if they thought the existing chocolates on the market were boring (and this was evidently a question that they had not considered):

43 per cent said that they found them boring.
57 per cent were negative.

An attempt was made to test the response to the 'Rococo' concept of fanciful product lines, without leading the respondent:

18 per cent were extremely interested
16 per cent were very interested
21 per cent were moderately interested
20 per cent were indifferent
25 per cent were not interested

100 per cent

These figures show that 55 per cent responded to 'Rococo' positively.

When examined in terms of age groups and income brackets a pattern quickly became evident, that the A/Bs showed a high degree of awareness, and an established buying pattern of high quality chocolates. They were also interested in a shop which offered a service superior to that otherwise available.

Examination of the lower income brackets showed less awareness of available products and less readiness to spend money on them.

In the age groupings, the over 50s showed little desire to buy novelty chocolates, though the As, Bs and Cs aged 26–50 seemed to have a definite appetite for high class, well-presented chocolates.

Of the positive respondents only 12 per cent had been offered a gift wrapping service in the shop where they had bought the chocolate.

Summary of findings so far
The overall habits of the chocolate buying public (which is the majority of the population) are supported by the early findings: that is that the average Briton eats 8oz of chocolate per head per week; and so I will carry a wide range of chocolate bars for every-day consumption.

It also appears that at some time in the year, most people will buy chocolate as a gift. When chocolate is purchased in the normal way, it would not come with a gift presentation.

The awareness of certain 'Rococo' product lines will have to be heightened by advertising in the appropriate media; for example: chocolate cameras in the *British Journal of Photography*.

Appendix 4

Professional advice

Paul Curtin:	Harrods confectionery buyer
Solicitor:	Michael Rapinet
	Kidd, Rapinet & Badge
Accountant:	Robert Churchhouse
	Price Waterhouse
Bank managers:	Mr C F Thorpe
	Barclays Bank, Forest Hill
	Mario Aresti
	Lloyds Head Office, Fish St
	John Phillips
	National Westminster, Croydon
Other financial advice:	John Stafford Howarth
	Howard Ashforth Associates
Estate agents:	Jones Lang Wooton
	John Buckingham
	Philip Wragg
Insurance:	Mr Rogers
	Prudential Insurance

Other advice

Printing and packaging:	Mary Totman
Chocolates:	Mike Clibbens
	Harringtons
Cakes and ice cream:	John Turley
	Harringtons
Thames Polytechnic Small Business Course:	Colin Barrow, Geoffrey Randall, Jackie Severn, Peter Saunders, Ian Keenan, Paul Vaughan, Margaret Gabarak

Appendix 5

Profit and Loss Account, Year 1

	£
Sales	78,000
Cost of sales	46,800
Gross profit	31,200

Other expenditure	£	
Wages	7,500	
Heat, light and power	700	
Water	700	
Telephone	570	
Rent	7,850	
Rates	2,050	
Stationery	200	
Advertising	1,200	
Packaging	1,000	
Legal	1,000	
Weighing scales and cash register	244	
Accountant	300	
Shrinkage	2,510	
Bank interest	3,720	
Insurance	300	
Depreciation	250	
Amortisation	850	
	30,244	30,244

Net profit	956
Less drawings	(2,880)
Net loss	(1,924)

Profit and Loss Account, Year 2

	£	£
Sales		99,360
Cost of sales		59,000
Gross profit		40,360
Other expenditure		
Wages	8,100	
Heat, light and water	1,018	
Telephone	570	
Rent	7,850	
Rates	2,225	
Stationery	216	
Advertising	1,296	
Packaging	1,080	
Cash registers etc	264	
Accountant	432	
Interest on loan	3,720	
Depreciation	250	
Amortisation	850	
Shrinkage	2,980	
	31,176	31,176
Net profit		9,184
Less drawings		(5,000)
		4,184

Profit and Loss Account, Year 3

	£
Sales	124,900
Cost of sales	74,940
Gross profit	50,040

	£	
Other expenditure		
Wages	8,748	
Heat, light and power	1,099	
Telephone	610	
Rent	7,850	
Rates	2,403	
Stationery	233	
Advertising	1,400	
Packaging	1,167	
Cash register etc	286	
Shrinkage	3,750	
Insurance	350	
Depreciation	250	
Amortisation	850	
	32,716	32,716
Net profit		17,324
Less drawings		(7,000)
		10,324

Balance Sheet

Opening balance	£
Lease	15,000
Fixtures and fittings	5,000
	20,000

Deferred revenue	
Expenditure	1,300
	21,300
Cash	3,700
	25,000

Financed by capital	5,000
Bank loan	20,000
	25,000

Closing balance

	Cost	Depreciation	£
Fixed assets			
Lease	15,000	850	14,150
Fixtures and fittings	5,000	250	4,750
	20,000	1,000	18,900
Current assets			
Stock	1,200		
Cash	2,976		
	4,176		4,176
			23,076
Financed by			
Capital account	5,000		
Add profit '	956		
	5,956		
Less drawings	2,880		
			3,076
Bank loan			20,000
			23,076

Cash flow

		Feb	Mar	Apr	May	June	July	Aug	Sept	Oct	Nov	Dec	Jan	
Cash sales	1	8,000	8,000	15,000	3,000	3,000	4,000	4,000	5,000	6,000	7,000	12,000	3,000	78,000
VAT on sales	2	1,200	1,200	2,250	450	450	600	600	750	900	1,050	1,800	450	11,700
Share capital	3	5,000												5,000
Bank loan	4	20,000												20,000
	5													
Total income	A	34,200	9,200	17,250	3,450	3,450	4,600	4,600	5,750	6,900	8,050	13,800	3,450	114,700
Expenditure	6	6,000	4,800	9,000	1,800	1,800	2,400	2,400	3,000	3,600	4,200	7,200	1,800	48,000
VAT on stock	7	900	720	1,350	270	270	360	360	450	540	630	1,080	270	7,200
Wages and drawings	8	865	865	865	865	865	865	865	865	865	865	865	865	10,380
Capital items*	9	21,300												21,300
Rent/rates	10	2,475			2,475			2,475			2,475			9,900
Heat, light and power	11	300			150			100			150			700
Advertising	12	500	250								200	250		1,200
Transport and packaging	13	500					500							1,000
Bank interest	14	310	310	310	310	310	310	310	310	310	310	310	310	3,720
Accountant	15	100											200	300
Cash register and scales	16	49	6	6	49	6	6	49	6	6	49	6	6	244
VAT outstanding	17			1680			600			900			1,320	4,500
Wastage	18	250	240	450	90	90	120	120	150	180	210	360	250	2,510
Stationery	19	200			200									200
Telephone	20	70						150			150			570
	21													
Total	B	33,819	7,191	13,661	6,209	3,341	5,161	6,829	4,781	6,401	9,239	10,071	5,021	111,724
	A-B	381	2,009	3,589	(2,759)	109	(561)	(2,229)	969	499	(1,189)	3,729	(1,571)	2,976
Balance brought forward	C		381	2,390	5,979	3,220	3,329	2,768	539	1,508	2,007	818	4,547	
Balance carried forward	D	381	2,390	5,979	3,220	3,329	2,768	539	1,508	2,007	818	4,547	2,976	2,976

*Capital items: Lease: £15,000; Fixtures and fitings: £5,000; Legal: £1,000; Insurance: £300 = £21,300.

61

Questions

1. How useful do you think the survey questionnaire was in providing endorsement for the Rococo concept and premises location?
2. Do you think the market share objective of 25 per cent is a realistic aim?
3. Is Chantal's financial strategy soundly based?
4. Do you think the product range will support the business that Chantal aims to achieve?
5. What important pre-launch activities do not appear to have been addressed?

Bob and Carol and Ted and Alice
Michael Scott

Bob

Bob was recently made redundant by British Steel, having worked for 17 years in the weighing section of the local steel works. He began his working life as an apprentice, and worked his way up through the system, until eventually he was manager of the weighing operations. This involved all aspects of weighing, from vehicles through to small and large quantities of chemicals and other raw materials of steel manufacture. He has a good working knowledge of the mechanics of weighing machines and also of the new electronic devices which have slowly been introduced in the last ten years. In particular he has a good knowledge of the calibration process for a variety of weighing systems.

He has £8,000 of his own money to invest, and his house in Hartlepool is also free of any mortgage. He thinks he would like to set up his own business, building on the experience gained at British Steel. He is currently seeking information on what grants are available, and whether any premises could be provided at a reduced rate in the local area. Initially he will be self-employed with some assistance from his wife to look after clerical tasks and answer the telephone. He may also take on a young person to train in the near future. He needs premises to garage a van and also to hold, in security, his calibration equipment. The work will involve travelling around local firms which have weighing equipment and he will carry out calibration tests on site where possible; in other cases he will bring parts of the weighing equipment back to his workshop for calibration. He does not know of any similar services in the local area, and his old contacts suggest that many firms have to rely on visits from their suppliers who are based in other parts of the UK. This is an area with a lot of engineering firms and he is confident that a market exists. He has not yet started trading and, apart from talking to some friends, the only action he has so far taken has been to make an appointment with a counsellor from the Department of Trade and Industry in a week's time.

Bob is married with no children. His wife is presently not working but she has had experience as a personal secretary to the managing director of a small clothing firm.

Carol

Carol is in the process of setting up a business in York to provide historical tours for tourists. She graduated with a good degree in archaeology about eight months ago and cannot find employment in her own profession. During the summer she began to take small groups of tourists for walks around the city in the evenings and at weekends and she found that she could often find a party of 20 to accompany her. She charged 50p per person per tour, and because she had minimal overheads (a small amount of local newspaper and poster advertising) she was able to make a summer income.

She is about to visit her local Enterprise Agency, and specifically wants advice on whether she is charging enough for her services and also whether there are any grants or subsidies from any source which would help her during the winter months. She has approached the English Tourist Board local office who have agreed to provide her with some free advertising space and possibly a publicity article. Otherwise she has had no help from anyone at all.

She has not discovered any direct competitors although there have been rumours that the City Council may hire summer guides to provide a similar service. She knows that the number of tourists, especially foreign, has increased substantially in the past year and that there is a national campaign to 'sell' English cities, other than London, to distribute tourist income more evenly.

Although concentrating at present on City walks, in the longer term she would like to organise guided coach tours to archaeological sites in the vicinity, but does not really know how to go about organising these, nor what help is available. She believes that a link with local hotels might be one way forward.

Carol is single, aged 24 and lives locally with her parents. She is small, quietly spoken, but with a pleasant personality. She gives the impression of knowing her subject extremely well and is very enthusiastic about local history and archaeology. She is currently unemployed, and has about £600 in personal savings.

Ted

Ted is a young man of 19 who wants to set up a butterfly farm. This will involve breeding rare foreign butterflies and selling them mainly through mail order. They will be sold as cocoons to enthusiasts who will hatch them and keep the mature butterflies in glass cases, in the same way as tropical fish are kept. Because butterflies have a short life span, repeat or frequent orders are expected. He knows of several successful butterfly farms in the south of England, has visited one of them and has done a lot of reading around the subject. He needs about £250 for some basic equipment and stock (including special packaging for the cocoons). He can operate from home in Leeds.

Ted has been unemployed for six months since leaving school. He has an A level in biology and seems extremely enthusiastic and knowledgeable about Lepidoptera which have been a hobby for seven years.

He has not yet started trading, but knows where to obtain some equipment and his first supplies of butterflies. He seems to know the hobby journals but has had no experience in running a mail order business. He has about £100 of his own savings which he is prepared to use for the business and he thinks his father could lend him perhaps £500 or £600 for working capital. He has a current account at a local bank but has not been to see the bank manager yet.

Alice

Alice is in the process of starting a business to rent and sell foliage plants for interior decoration. She has recently moved to the Nottingham area having previously worked in a company in London which was in the same business: leasing natural and artificial plants to offices, banks and restaurants to enhance their decor. This business provided a regular weekly service by trained assistants who went round the locations attending to the plants to make sure they were kept in good condition, and replacing them when necessary.

Alice knows that in her area there is nobody providing such a service, yet there are many large organisations which she feels sure could benefit from some greenery. Her main problem is finding potential customers: she knows about Yellow Pages but is unsure about the sources of information which might help her to find clients. She is thinking of approaching her local Citizens'

Advice Bureau to find out whether any organisation exists to give help on how to sell, or whether there are courses available.

Alice is married, with two young children aged four and six. She expects to work from home, and the house has a large Victorian conservatory. Her husband is a senior executive of a multi-national chemical company, who moves around the world at about three-yearly intervals. Alice has a degree in botany. She has good contacts with suppliers of plants, since she was involved in the ordering process when she worked in the same business in London. She is extrovert, very well dressed and articulate.

Questions

Do any or all of these individuals have the requisite ingredients for a successful start-up? In what respects do you feel they are deficient, and what action would you recommend they take next?

In thinking about start-up 'ingredients' you may find this simple model useful.

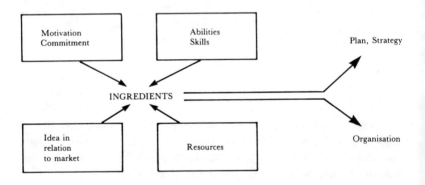

Case 3

Celebration Cakes

Stephen Pettit

Self-employment may offer many attractions to the unemployed, but Jane Dukes and Alice Stewart were already questioning their decision to start their own business as they contemplated the realities of launching Celebration Cakes. Although many people consider themselves good cooks only a few like Jane and Alice want to go further and turn their skills into a business venture. Realising that their lack of business experience could impair overall development they decided to undertake a self-employment course supported by the Manpower Services Commission at the local polytechnic. An integral part of this course is the discussion with appropriate members of staff on the viability and likely effectiveness of the start-up business plan. It was from such a meeting with Stephen James, a lecturer in marketing, that the daunting nature of the task facing them became apparent. Their specific query concerned the suitability of an advertising opportunity in a local magazine, but this developed into a much broader discussion of the total marketing plan. The meeting ended with an agreement to meet again the following week by which time both parties should have had sufficient opportunity to reflect upon the tasks facing Celebration Cakes. Stephen James once again decided to review the various points discussed at their first meeting.

Several years ago Alice attended the local technical college to improve her skills in cake baking and decoration. Although the evening classes lasted only two terms she soon found that her skills were well above average, an opinion supported by staff, fellow students and friends alike. Since that time she often received requests to produce a special birthday, or wedding cake, largely through a network of personal contacts. Despite this continued activity Alice did not describe it as a business, more as a pastime or hobby. At certain times of year she was often receiving two or three orders per month even though no advertising was undertaken.

The idea of Celebration Cakes was born when Alice met Jane one year ago at a Women's Institute meeting in Redcar. Having just moved to Cleveland Jane was keen to supplement her husband's income and she too had expertise in home baking. They decided to form a business partnership to supply a range of decorated cakes for special occasions. Neither of the would-be entrepreneurs expected or even desired to make a fortune from the business. They would be happy to remain small with an income comparable to shop management rates in the Cleveland area; to them the satisfaction of independence and self-fulfilment was compensation in itself. Both were in their early 30s with children aged between 10 and 14 years old.

At an early stage of the self-employment programme, Jane and Alice were required to produce a business plan containing both financial and market projections. The profit and loss account projection is shown in Appendix 1. Although they had decided to work from home in the early years, thus keeping overheads and investment to a minimum, it soon became apparent that there was a major difference between baking for a pastime and baking for a business. In particular they were surprised at the increase in order inflow required to achieve even their modest projections. A breakdown of the sales revenue forecast into different product groups was also developed as a course requirement, but both Jane and Alice readily admitted that their forecasts were based more on aspirations than marketing information (Appendix 2). However, despite the obvious challenge ahead they were both convinced that there was an opportunity for a high quality, designer-made celebration cake service in the Cleveland/North Yorkshire area.

From the meeting with Stephen James a number of issues emerged concerning how the business objectives could be achieved through marketing activities. However, Alice and Jane were unsure as to how to proceed and indeed whether they had the skills and expertise to be both businesswomen and 'master cake bakers'.

Celebration Cakes, although only trading for three months, had already received orders from two main customer groups: the general public and organisations. Sales to the public had mainly come from personal recommendations and were normally for special occasions where quality and style were valued. Initial enquiries from customers were often made over the telephone and Alice would then attempt to arrange a meeting where specific requirements could be discussed and orders taken. She would normally expect to receive two or three enquiries a week, of which conversion to orders would be in the range of 50 to 60 per cent. They both recognised that there would need to be a significant increase in enquiry levels.

It was a large order from an insurance company in Manchester holding its annual sales conference that first alerted Alice and Jane to the organisational market. The order, for 30 iced cakes priced at £25 per cake, came from the recommendation of a friend in the Cleveland area and although the size of the order did place a considerable strain on their production they were both hopeful that this type of business could be developed in the future. The order was supplied to the customer's entire satisfaction and subsequently further orders have been obtained from local charities organising fund-raising dinners. Alice believed that it was far easier and more cost-effective to handle a few large orders rather than many smaller ones from the general public. They were convinced that there must be other organisations placing similar orders on a regular basis and that the problem was in locating them at times when they were likely to buy.

Alice and Jane recognised that they were lacking in market information but considered they had neither the skills nor resources to undertake field research. As the amounts of money at risk in the business were small they planned to make decisions as they went along in response to new opportunities and information. However, they were still unsure which market to concentrate upon and were not sure how to approach either one.

Jane Dukes thought there were only two main competitors in the Cleveland area, Hills and Shipmans, but both of these had large retail chains supplying a wide range of bakery products. She was unsure of their relative share of the market or indeed the size of the market within Cleveland but considered that as Celebration Cakes' planned production was small, market share was not that important. A special feature of the Celebration Cakes concept was that rather than offering a limited range of standard designs, like Hills and Shipmans, they would offer a much wider choice of designs and would be prepared to adapt to individual customer requirements. A breakdown of the product cost levels can be seen in Appendix 3. They considered it counter-productive to provide detailed product cost breakdowns for each item due to the relatively low percentage of material costs to total costs and the need to design in special features, displays etc. It was normal practice to buy ingredients in bulk and then to use them as required until reordering needed to take place. As overheads were minimal no apportioning of cost was undertaken, thus avoiding the need to establish the differences between domestic use of electricity and business use, notional rent and telephone charges etc.

Both Alice and Jane expressed some concern over finding the best price level for their cakes. They had already experienced customer resistance to their quotations when price was mentioned, even though they were comparable with Hills' rates. However, they were around 10 per cent higher than Shipmans' prices, a difference that Alice considered in no way reflected the additional quality and design benefits offered by Celebration Cakes.

Because of the nature of the product, each cake having to be made to order sometimes to a non-standard design, Jane felt that there was little point in trying to sell through retailers. From their own experience they thought it unlikely that the smaller bakery shop would have the expertise or interest in offering the pre- and post-sales services that Celebration Cakes would require. In addition a number of small bakeries would probably have their own facilities and contacts to respond to customer requests even though they would not recognise 'specials' as a priority area within their own business. They were also concerned that the margins would not be available to cover both retailer and Celebration Cakes' expectations, especially when customer price sensitivity was taken into account.

A further problem identified during the self-employment course was that special transport would need to be provided to deliver the finished products. Whereas they had been using their own vehicles to deliver, food regulations require a business to transport edible items in an area separate from the driver. This meant an investment in a second-hand van thus adding to initial start-up costs. It did, however, enable a more flexible, professional delivery service; they had already experienced problems in delivering intact 30 iced cakes to Manchester!

It was in the area of advertising and selling that Alice and Jane expressed the greatest concern, partly due to a lack of knowledge and expertise and partly due to the large costs involved. Although they had budgeted to spend £480 on advertising in the first year this already looked unrealistic when compared to the size of the order inflow required. They had previously advertised in the classified 'superstore' section of the Teesside evening paper which included a range of private, second-hand and business advertisers in a number of categories (carpets, DIY, computers, sporting goods, animals etc). The category chosen by Celebration Cakes was 'Wedding Dept' which included photographic, car hire and other caterers. Although the cost per insertion was small, Jane could not recall any direct enquiries resulting from six insertions. In addition to the *Evening Gazette* a number of insertions were placed in the *Teesside Times*, a classified display advertising paper that was distributed free to over 170,000 readers in the Cleveland area. Again charges were reasonable and the section chosen was 'Catering' where on average 15 to 20 other advertisers offered a complete catering service for weddings and special occasions. Jane was again unsure of the response directly attributable to this paper.

As a result of their experience with newspaper advertising Alice and Jane were questioning whether they should continue with classified insertions. They were concerned that advertising could not really portray to the customer the quality and design offered, particularly if no photographs or drawings were included. Any move towards display advertising was thought a sure way to use up quickly their limited budget. They have been approached by Spec Displays who produce a north-east guide for all hotels and conference organisers. The proposition entailed an expenditure of £250 for a half-page display advertisement guaranteeing them sole rights within their product area. This annual publication contained a wide variety of services from stand erection to catering and video production to cleaning.

Another proposal requiring a decision was whether to exhibit at a 'Bride and Groom' show that was to be held at a local country club the following January. The purpose of the show was to allow those planning their wedding to view under one roof a complete range of wedding services. Alice had produced some mock iced cakes, comprising a wooden box that had been carefully iced and decorated so that exhibiting would be feasible, but again was it worth the £150–£300 quoted for a display stand?

Neither Alice nor Jane had any previous sales experience prior to Celebration Cakes and they were both hesitant about approaching business customers. They had viewed with considerable interest a series of videotapes on professional selling, covering a wide range of selling topics. However, although they knew that they would have to develop their interpersonal skills, there was a certain amount of trepidation about entering into negotiations and even approaching busy hotel managers and conference organisers. Although they were both presentable and articulate it was the need for specific selling skills that concerned them. What skills should they try to develop for the task ahead?

It was with this collection of ideas that Stephen James contemplated the next meeting with Alice and Jane. How should he advise them? He recognised that the obvious limitations in skills and resources were a major factor that must be considered in any proposals. He also recognised that a plea for more information would be inappropriate unless fairly specific directions and guidelines were given. For a moment he wondered whether there was any feasible solution to the marketing tasks facing Alice and Jane during the early years of the business.

Appendix 1

Profit and Loss Account 1984–85

	£	£
Sales		8,200
Labour	—	
Materials	1,852	
Cost of sales		1,852
Gross margin		6,348
Fixed expenses	360	
Selling, administration and interest expenses	1,268	
Partners' remuneration	4,500	
Total expenses		6,098
Net profit before tax		250

Appendix 2

Celebration Cakes: forecast product group sales 1984-85

	Price range £	Expected average price £	Forecast sales	Sales revenue £
Tiffany Range (Single-tier Christmas, birthday cakes etc) – 7 variants in standard range	20–40	25	100	2,500
Linda Range (Single-tier wedding cakes) – 6 variants or special design	40–80	60	30	1,800
Diane Range (Double-tier wedding cakes) – 4 variants or special design	80–120	100	12	1,200
Laura Range (Three-tier wedding cakes) – 4 variants or special design	120–180	150	6	900
Special Orders (Conference, hotels etc)	15 upwards	25	72	1,800
				8,250

Appendix 3

Estimated product costings

Materials cost: normally 20%–30% of selling price

Labour	One-tier Tiffany Range 'woman' hours	Three-tier Laura Range 'woman' hours
Material purchasing	1	2
Baking	6	12
Packing and storage	1	2
Marzipan	1½	5
Coating	2	6
Decorating	3	12
Delivery	2	2
Miscellaneous	1½	5
	18	46

Electricity charges: estimated £240 per annum

Questions

In Stephen James's position, sketch out your advice to Alice and Jane, with particular reference to the following:
1. What skills should they develop and how should they go about it?
2. Why did their classified advertising campaign fail and what steps should they take to get value for money from advertising in the future?
3. How should they set the level of their advertising budget?
4. How should they have prepared so as to make a success of their exhibit at the 'Bride and Groom' show?
5. What is the adequacy or otherwise of their financial controls?
6. What legal structure should they adopt (ie partnership, sole trader and employee, limited company)?

Case 4

A Man of Property

Colin Barrow

As Guy Browning drove home from his dinner with Sam Shield, a successful north country businessman, he tried to put the evening's discussion into some kind of order.

The meeting had been arranged by a mutual Rotary Club acquaintance, after Guy had expressed an interest in setting up a property development business. He and his wife had bought and renovated a farmhouse and two workers' cottages, turning a £50,000 investment into £150,000 in two years. Now he wanted to turn this experience into a full-time business and quit his computer marketing job.

Shield had a property development company to sell, hence the meeting. Plumpton Developments, the company in question, was barely five years old and its main assets were half a million pounds' worth of office sites. Its only working director was Tim Holdsworth, a 35-year-old chartered surveyor who, according to Shield, was a wizard at obtaining planning permissions and getting things done on time and to budget. He had held shares in the company but last year these had been converted into shares in Shield's master company. There was also a team of builders on the pay roll.

Until two years ago the business had made a modest but acceptable profit. It had been cash hungry, but what property company wasn't?

In 1983 things had started to go seriously wrong, and no further profits had been made. Shield attributed the losses to the antics of a former Plumpton director, a one-time estate agent, whose role was to search out and buy suitable development sites. He also handled the cosmetic end of the business, making sure that premises for sale were attractively fitted out. This gave him considerable freedom of action with the company cheque book.

Apparently he had taken his 'cosmetic' role to heart, buying a new Porsche on the company account, and installing his mistress in a flat designated for a caretaker in one of the company's properties. He also led a fairly extravagant life style, wining and dining all and sundry. By the time Shield at the parent company in Lancashire, had noticed what was happening, over £100,000 had been siphoned away.

Stopping only to pick up the company solicitor, Shield had driven south to confront the director and, in the absence of any satisfactory explanation, fired him. Six months later the whole sorry saga was reopened when the company solicitor was himself struck off for misappropriating clients' money – other clients in this case. Armed with this new evidence, the former director sued for wrongful dismissal, claiming that the solicitor had taken Plumpton money too. He lost the case, but Shield had decided that enough was enough – he wanted to be rid of the company. 'Make me an offer' were his parting words.

Shield was doubly anxious to sell, as he planned a full Stock Exchange quotation next year for his master company, and Plumpton would be something of an embarrassment on the balance sheet.

Guy saw that this was an opportunity to get into the property business quickly and at a discount, if he used his negotiating skills. But it was equally obvious that the company could still be a can of worms. He needed to know a lot more before he could even consider an offer – and in any case he didn't have anything like half a million to invest.

Questions

1. Prepare a list of questions you would want answered before you could decide whether to make an offer for Plumpton Properties.
2. What sort of deal should Guy aim for if he decides to bid for the company?
3. What are the advantages and disadvantages of buying this company as opposed to starting up his own company?
4. Do you think Guy's past property success equips him for this new venture?

Case 5

Balloon Bromley

Colin Barrow,
from material collected by *Godfrey Golzen*

Eva Loffsted and Diane Gallacher are the enthusiastic but not uncritical franchisees of Balloon's Bromley (Kent) shop, selling fashionable maternity wear and baby clothes. Eva qualified as a dentist and still practises one day a week and her husband was already in the fashion business. He played a key role in researching the market and finding the site. He knew that Bromley was an ideal place with consumer spending 40 per cent above the national average – but for that reason finding a shop wasn't easy. The site they settled for, a stone's throw from Bromley station, commanded a premium of £30,000 for a £15,000 a year lease.

Diane's husband, a songwriter, managed to get an impressive number of personalities to attend the venture's celebrity launch.

Given Eva and Diane's obvious commitment, intelligence and family support, the question that clearly had to be asked is why they chose to take up a franchise rather than starting up on their own. 'Originally that was what we intended to do,' Eva admits. 'We had an idea for a speciality shop for teenage fashions, but then one of the multiples came along with something very similar and we realised how vulnerable we would be in a small business on our own.' At that particular point she heard of franchising, and of its success rate in getting new businesses off the ground. She read everything she could on it and eventually she and Diane came to the conclusion that it was worth sacrificing a certain amount of independence for the know-how that would otherwise have to be picked up along the hard and expensive route of trial and error. The franchise they eventually plumped for was Balloon, a relative newcomer to the UK franchising scene.

The Balloon concept

Until Véronique Delachaux came on the scene in 1971 most fashion designers felt that glamour stopped when pregnancy began to show. After that women were expected to go into full dress purdah behind garments of indeterminate shape and vaguely floral pattern. That they were longing for something more flatter-ing was demonstrated by the instant success of Madame Delachaux's first Balloon shop in Paris. Her own designs for expectant mothers made pregnancy chic with a whole range of dresses, shirts, skirts, trousers, underwear and even swimwear. Her secret lies not only in clever merchandising and the superb cut that gives Paris fashion its own unmistakable quality, but in the fact that her designs keep their fashionable line throughout the whole period of pregnancy. This contrasts favourably with other maternity wear which tends to look like an outsized version of something bought in slimmer times.

Balloon itself is part of a huge French group, La Redoute, whose turnover is said to be as large as Marks and Spencer's. They opened in the UK in 1981 in Walton Street, a quietly ex-pensive Chelsea backwater where Sloane Rangers do their shop-ping. By 1983 they were satisfied enough to plan a programme of rapid expansion in the UK – spurred, probably, by the fact that others had seen the potential of an annual market of 450,000 women, all willing to spend money on one of the most important phases of their lives. Mothercare, now owned by Conran, had announced a new range of maternity clothes designed by Jasper Conran. In franchising, Edward Young, who runs the highly suc-cessful bridal-wear network, Pronuptia, also moved into the field with his new La Mama franchise. Balloon, however, feel that, 'When it comes to design there is no substitute for French fashions.'

In January 1984 Balloon began to franchise in the UK. Site location is clearly the key to success in retailing and they laid down the following broad guidelines: shops should have a customer base of 200,000 people, an area of 1,000–1,200 sq ft including storage space, and a minimum frontage of 13 ft.

They expected their potential franchise to be able to commit £37,500 to the venture made up as follows:

Initial investment

	£
Licence fee	5,000
Inventory	14,000
Fixtures and fittings	8,000
Legal costs	1,000
Launch	2,000
Training costs	500
Working capital	7,000
	37,500

Balloon proposed to help with selecting the opening stock and to provide fairly generous credit terms: 50 per cent of the first shipment due in three months and the balance after six months.

The licence fee is not due until the contract is signed, which effectively means when a site has been found. The fee includes the service of an architect to prepare plans for layout and interior design. It also includes staff training.

In 1984, at the time of writing, a 2 per cent royalty is under consideration. Balloon did not propose charging their franchisee a royalty on sales, the almost universally recognised formula by which franchisors are rewarded for marketing and maintaining a successful franchise chain. Their main income was to come from the mark-up on goods, as indeed would their franchisees'. Balloon's projected operating statement for an average shop is set out below:

Balloon projected operating statement

Income	£
Sales	90,000
Cost of sales	48,000
Gross margin	42,000
Expenditure	
Rent and rates	12,000
Insurance	800
Services	1,200
Repairs	800
National Advertising	3,600
Local Advertising	600
General and Travelling	1,500
Professional charges	900
Bank charges	700
	22,600
Operating profit	19,400

The expectation on this basis is that the initial investment will be recovered in about 18 months. Balloon justify ignoring in their equation any premium that may have to be paid for the shop, arguing that the income from a prime site will be correspondingly greater.

A note on the franchising industry

'Franchising' is a general title given to a wide range of different business activities. At one end of the scale is product and trade name franchising, typical of which are soft drink manufacturers such as Coca-Cola, and petrol service stations. This is primarily a distribution arrangement in which the franchisee (the person granted the licence) is to some degree identified with the manufacturer's supplies. This type of franchise arrangement dominates the market, accounting for about three-quarters of all sales.

At the other end of the scale is business format franchising, which is characterised by a business relationship between franchisor (the person granting a licence) and franchisee that includes not only the product, service and trade mark, but the entire business format itself – a marketing strategy and plan, operating manuals and standards, quality control, and a continuing day-to-day business involvement. Business format franchising covers a wide and rapidly growing number of business sectors including: restaurants; non-food retailing; personal and business services and property services. This is the fastest growing sector of franchising.

The United States of America

This is the world's largest business format franchise market. In 1983 sales by the 1,700 franchisors were $111 billion compared with $99 billion in 1982 and $89 billion in 1981. Nearly 300,000 establishments existed in 1983 compared with 261,000 in 1981.

Large franchisors, those with 1,000 or more units each, dominate business format franchising, with 57 companies accounting for 53 per cent of all sales and 55 per cent of establishments.

Although this type of franchising is viewed as being a 'safe' way into business, a total of 59 franchisors operating 1,905 outlets failed in 1982. The sales represented by these failed firms amounted to $244 million, which was only a fraction of a per cent of all business format sales. Over the same period 61 franchisors operating 4,124 outlets with sales of $384 million decided to discontinue franchising as a method of doing business.

There is also evidence that franchisees are generally satisfied with their investment. Of 11,515 franchise arrangements that came up for renewal 89 per cent were renewed and 1,237 were not. Of the latter, 245 were not renewed because of objections by the franchisor, 737 because the franchisee did not wish to renew, and 255 by mutual agreement.

The main growth in business format franchising is expected to come from the following activities: financial counselling services; home repair; insurance; legal service centres; accounting service centres; medical services; dental clinics and business brokers. Also high on the list are: weight reduction centres; figure control centres; smoking control centres; exercise studios; computers (hardware, software and counselling) and safe deposit locations.

With maturing home markets American franchisors are looking for international market opportunities in increasing numbers. At present some 300 franchising companies are operating around 22,000 outlets abroad. The table below shows the main geographic split of that activity.

Country or region	Number of franchisors	Number of units
Canada	209	7,068
Japan	63	3,999
Continental Europe	75	3,393
United Kingdom	52	2,113

Last year a further 121 American franchisors indicated that they were looking for opportunities to set up overseas. The interest was expressed mostly by small and medium-sized franchisors, and 'business aids' was the largest market sector to be pioneered.

The United Kingdom

This country is not so well endowed with statistics on the business format franchising sector although, thanks to the British Franchise Association and others, this deficit is rapidly being made good.

In 1984 some 220 franchisors were operating in the UK. Of these, 56 were members of the British Franchise Association, and they operated over 8,000 outlets employing 70,000 people and generated sales in excess of £1 billion per annum.

Franchised outlets have quadrupled since 1979 and the BFA believe that this sector of the economy has a clear prospect of achieving sales of £5 billion per annum in 1989.

The range of franchised businesses in the UK includes: fast food; fast print; health and beauty; motor services and accessories; retailing; personal and professional services; computer services and fashion products.

American involvement is clearly the most significant single factor in this sector and France is next to the USA in the rate of penetration of the UK market by overseas franchisors.

Note: The statistics quoted are drawn from published papers from the US Department of Commerce, the British Franchise Association and *Taking up a Franchise*, 2nd edition (Kogan Page) among others.

Questions

1. Should Eva and Diane have taken up a franchise or would they have been better advised to go their own way?
2. Does the Balloon concept have the ingredients to make a successful UK franchise chain?
3. Do their figures seem realistically based – both for the initial investment and the operating profit?
4. What help and support do you think Eva and Diane should expect from Balloon? (a) Now (b) In the future when a 2 per cent royalty charge is made?

Case 6
Holland & Barrett, Fulham
Colin Barrow,
from material collected by Godfrey Golzen

Getting in on the ground floor of a successful business idea can be very rewarding in every sense, as Paul Geoghegan has discovered. Still in his early 30s, he had five years running his own business, a sauna and workout area in a hotel near Heathrow, when he read that Holland & Barrett were planning to franchise some of their shops. His wife Susan has a degree in nutrition and so of course knew all about Holland & Barrett's products. The fact that the shop on offer was in Fulham, an important west London shopping area, made the proposition doubly attractive.

The company and the concept

Holland & Barrett are a major force in the UK health food market with over 20 per cent of all retail sales. Back in 1967 the company already had 64 outlets but with their acquisition by Booker-McConnell, the £1,000 million a year giant, their involvement in this market grew rapidly. By 1984 they had 150 company-owned outlets all over the country from Newcastle upon Tyne to Plymouth.

Their prominently sited shops sell a comprehensive range of health foods, including wholefoods, vitamin and mineral supplements, natural herbal remedies and natural cosmetics. Today, however, the competition is hotting up. Apart from other specialist shops, even supermarkets now carry shelves of health foods. This does not worry Holland & Barrett boss Ken Mullarkey. 'I think it merely makes people aware of the product. Shops like the Body Shop are complementary to Holland & Barrett since they carry mainly cosmetics and no food lines.' Mullarkey also believes they have another great strategic advantage. 'It's not only that our subsidiary, Associated Health Foods, is a major supplier – we also own Brewhurst, the principal national wholesaler of health foods, with 60 per cent of the market. We even have a subsidiary, Newman Turner Ltd, which is the leading publisher of books and journals on natural living.'

Holland & Barrett believe that the UK can support at least 2,000 health food shops and they aim to have between 400 and 600 of those by 1990. More immediately they plan to have 200 shops by the end of 1985 and will be relying on franchising to generate most of their growth.

'There are some clear reasons why our form of retailing lends itself more to franchising than some others,' Mullarkey believes. 'There's a strong element of personal service – it isn't a supermarket operation. People come in asking for advice on what products they should buy to achieve a particular aim – like healthy ways of losing weight for instance.'

Beginning with a modest two franchises in 1982, they had 17 by 1984 and a further 25 scheduled to open in 1985. The package on offer to potential franchisees is as follows:

The package

One of the attractions of the Holland & Barrett franchise is that although the concept is an unusually well tested one – they have after all been around for a relatively long time – the initial costs are not particularly high. The average investment is said to be around £55,000, of which £5,000 is the franchise fee. The royalty is 10 per cent of turnover paid weekly, although during the first two years of the agreement it is reduced to $7\frac{1}{2}$ per cent. Naturally this is a proposition which the banks find attractive from a lending point of view, so that up to 70 per cent of the start-up costs can be funded by bank borrowing. The typical deal is that 55 per cent of the money is made available as a term loan and the rest is provided in the form of overdraft facilities to even out cash flow variations.

The agreement runs for five years and is automatically renewable thereafter. 'It's a fairly standard franchise contract,' says Mullarkey. 'We charge a small percentage of the price when a franchisee sells the business and, of course, we reserve the right to vet the purchaser, but they don't have to pay a fresh premium for the franchise.'

Site selection

So far, though, no franchise has changed hands in this way and there is usually a wait of three to four months between the time the agreement is signed and the franchisee takes over his or her new outlet. Some of the interval is taken up with shopfitting based on a tried format which encourages customers to browse and then to buy.

The main reason for the wait is the very great importance Holland & Barrett attach to site selection. Mullarkey explains the process: 'We have our own property department which is in constant touch with estate agents who keep a look-out for sites for us. When one comes up it goes through an intensive assessment of its suitability to house a Holland & Barrett shop because not all locations have the kind of socio-economic mix we are looking for.' An evaluation of that factor is accompanied by a systematic pedestrian traffic count, a check on parking and transport facilities and, of course, the viability and exposure of the site. All these elements are then fed into a computer to see if they combine to give the kind of sales volume projection over the period of the agreement which is necessary to reach profit projections.

Finally the site is also visited by a team consisting of Mullarkey himself, key personnel from the property department, and someone who has first-hand knowledge of operational aspects ensures that nothing is left out of the reckoning.

The actual lease is acquired by Holland & Barrett and then sublet to the franchisee. This is where franchising, when it operates under a nationally recognised name, is so advantageous. 'Landlords are reluctant to let property to business newcomers and if they do they are apt to demand a high rental from them,' says Mullarkey. 'On the other hand, having an established name like ours on the tenant roll is a magnet to others and hence a plus point in initial and rent review negotiations.'

As far as the franchisee is concerned, at least part of this time is taken up with training. The core programme is a sandwich of theory and practice designed to develop product knowledge as well as operating methods: two weeks in the classroom, followed by a week in a shop, after which there is a further two weeks' spell of instruction. The timing of the training is geared to the opening date as far as possible but if there are delays franchisees can undertake further periods of practical work at the franchisor's expense.

They are also given a good deal of literature about the products, together with the usual operating manual. The actual shop-opening procedures reflect this careful preparation. There is in fact a 'shop-opener' who takes the franchisee through the initial period and who is an experienced Holland & Barrett executive. 'The average shop stocks about 1,100 lines and the "shop-opener" will help the franchisee make the initial selection, as well as helping to choose and train staff,' Mullarkey explains.

Advertising and promotion

Equally important, though, is the launch of the shop itself. All advertising costs in the first year are devoted to the promotion of the individual outlet and this is indeed unusual in franchising. 'It's an intensive process of making potential customers aware of the outlet, not only through local press advertising but also through leafleting households and distributing our free newspaper, *Health Express*. Even after the first year, 20 per cent of the royalty is still devoted to advertising and promotion, much of it to arouse local interest.'

In the end, however, it is setting up and monitoring financial controls that ensures that the strength of the franchise is also reflected on the bottom line. The shop-opener gradually recedes from the scene – though help is always available on the telephone – but before this happens the shop will have been seen through the first few weeks of the financial reporting that Mullarkey requires.

'I look for key ratios to make sure things are on track,' he says, giving as examples wage costs, drawings and general expenses to sales. These are measured against Holland & Barrett's profit and loss and cash flow predictions for each outlet. The model of the first two years of an investment of £50,000 appears in the table on page 87.

Although Holland & Barrett stress that these figures – which show a pre-tax profit of over £38,000 at the end of the fifth year and a positive cash flow of very nearly that amount – are only for guidance and are not a binding forecast, Mullarkey says that existing franchisees are exceeding this handsomely. 'One thing that means is that we have selected the right franchisees,' he says 'but we can also claim justifiably that they've chosen the right franchise.'

Questions

1. Would you recommend Geoghegan to take out the Fulham Road franchise?
2. Do you think taking over an existing outlet has any special advantages or disadvantages compared with opening up a new franchised outlet?

Model forecast for the first two years of a Holland & Barrett franchise (on an average investment of £50,000)

Profit and Loss Account	Year 1 £	Year 2 £
Sales	182,000	227,500
Opening stock	—	18,460
Purchases	147,679	166,140
Closing stock	18,460	23,075
Gross profit	52,781	65,975
Discounts	14,768	16,614
Gross income	67,549	82,589
Expenses		
Royalty	13,651	17,063
Salaries and NI	11,340	12,012
Rent, rates, utilities	19,424	19,944
Repairs and maintenance	600	750
Insurance	400	500
Telephone, stationery and postage	869	933
Miscellaneous	2,665	1,706
Legal and audit	1,500	500
Depreciation	5,500	5,500
Total	55,949	58,908
Operating profit	11,600	23,681
Loan interest repaid	-4,147	-3,863
Overdraft interest	-927	-912
Pre-tax profit	6,526	18,906

Cash flow projection	Year 1 £	Year 2 £
Outflow		
Franchise fee	5,000	—
Initial investment	50,000	—
Stock movement	18,460	4,615
Creditors' investment	-7,591	-1,898
Loan capital repayments	2,171	2,465
Drawings	7,800	*
VAT payment/receipts	-259	-128
Total outflow	75,581	5,054
Inflow		
Bank loan	34,000	—
Own money	23,201	—
Pre-tax profit	6,526	18,906
Depreciation	5,500	5,500
Total inflow	69,227	24,406
Net in (out) flow	-6,355	19,352

*It is left to the franchisee's discretion how much of the Year 2 surplus of £12,997 he or she wishes to draw out

Balance Sheet	Year 1 £	Year 2 £
Investment	55,000	49,500
Depreciation	-5,500	-5,500
Net investment	49,500	44,000
Stock	18,460	23,075
Creditors	7,591	9,489
Current trading assets	10,869	13,586
VAT net	-259	-387
Net operating	60,110	57,199
Financed by		
Accumulated profits	6,526	17,632
Fixed loan	31,829	29,364
Overdraft	6,355	—
Own capital	23,201	23,201
Drawings	7,000	*
Surplus	—	12,997
Total finance	60,110	57,199

3. What do you think of Holland & Barrett's growth strategy? Specifically, do you believe the UK market can support 2,000 health food shops? (By contrast there are around 12,000 chemists shops.)
4. Do you think that a company can run its own outlets and a franchise chain side by side successfully?
5. Given sufficient resources and a fair degree of personal indifference, would you choose a Balloon or a Holland & Barrett franchise?

Case 7
The Technical Seminar Company

This case study has been prepared by *Colin Barrow* from material originally published in *Venture Capital Report*

During the early months of 1984 Dr Mitra, reader in operational research at Brunel University, was describing the concept that underpinned his plans for a new business: 'The greatest bottleneck in information technology today is information dissemination and one of the best ways through this bottleneck is the technical seminar, at which various products are demonstrated and explained by their authors and architects.'

As the rate of expansion of the information technology industry continues to grow, so the greatest problem of manufacturers and users alike becomes that of keeping abreast of developments. How does a hardware manufacturer or software house with a new product communicate its existence to a market already saturated with literature and advertisements, and how does a potential user in the field inform himself of the relative merits of competing products? The glossiest advertisement may not be for the best product.

This problem is difficult enough when the products concerned are for relatively well-defined functions such as word processing, accounts or stock control, but it becomes even greater as the subject matter becomes more abstruse. For example, it is extremely difficult for a statistician in a large company to compare the merits of the latest computer-assisted decision-making programs from the numerous universities and software houses around the world. It requires a considerable effort even to understand the mathematics and methodology of the systems, and since their inventors are often not primarily interested in selling them they will not come with explanatory manuals.

There are of course literally hundreds of seminars about information processing in the UK each year, but very few are technical, with mathematicians talking about maths and aimed at an academic/scientific audience. Dr Mitra believes that there is a need for such seminars and intends to form a company to mount them.

Test seminar

To test this concept, Dr Mitra arranged a three-day seminar on computer-assisted decision-making at the Tara Hotel to be held from 2 to 4 April 1984. The speakers at this seminar were either academics, scientific computer users or systems designers, and ten particular computer programs were demonstrated.

A simple brochure served to market the seminar and these were distributed as follows:

Members of Operational Research Society	3,500
Mailing list from National Computing Centre	2,400
Mailing list from Brunel University	1,100
Own list of interested academics	1,000
	8,000

In addition to this promotion, advertisements for the seminar appeared in the *Computer Weekly Supplement* (circulation 64,000), the *Computer Bulletin* (circulation 29,000), and the *Computing Training Supplement* (circulation 27,000). The total spent on marketing the seminar including printing the brochure, was less than £5,000, a very small amount by industry norms.

The price structure for the seminar ranged from £100 for a group booking of five students to £200 for academics, £375 for members of the Operational Research Society (£16 per year – 3,500 members), and for members of the British Computing Society (£25 per year – 28,000 members), and £475 for full delegates. By 22 March 1984 some 75 delegates had registered, paying an average of £300 each (£22,500 total), and the test market was considered to have been a success.

Publishing

The second strand to Dr Mitra's strategy is academic publishing. Each speaker at the seminar was required to deliver a written text of his talk for publication and presentation to the delegates. Most speakers were paid only travelling expenses, and were happy to give their talk and present their paper for the honour of participating, and for the benefits that might result from the platform thus afforded to them.

For the test seminar, Dr Mitra made an arrangement with academic publishers North Holland who were to pay royalties of 10 per cent with an advance of £1,000 and who would then print and publish the book, probably at a price of £28 for marketing throughout the world via their specialist catalogues and contacts with academia. This is a no-risk strategy and, if the book sells well, can be quite profitable.

However, in future he plans to do the typesetting and printing himself, having pre-sold 1,000 copies of the book to the publisher for 25 per cent of the market price. Had he done this deal for the test seminar the implications would have been:

Costs	£
Typesetting	3,500
Printing and binding	3,500
	7,000
Advance income	
1,000 × 25% × £28	7,000

The net profit from the first 1,000 books would thus be nothing, but Dr Mitra would receive £7 per book on all sales over 1,000. The prices for such specialist books range from £25 to £100, and had the price been £50 his initial profit would have been £5,500, and he estimates that this will be typical. From time to time, such books become classics of their kind when they mark the first presentation of a theory or program which later becomes widely adopted, and in this case there can be regular sales for years.

The man

Dr Gautam Mitra is 43, married with two young children, and is a fellow of the British Computer Society, a member of the Operational Research Society, and chairman of the Mathematical Programming Study Group of the BCS and has many other interests. He is well known in his field of operational research, having presented papers at many international conferences, had numerous articles published in academic and specialist journals, and is the author of *Theory and Application and Mathematical Programming* (Academic Press, 1976).

Born and brought up in Bengal, he obtained a first class honours degree in electrical engineering at Jadavpur University (Calcutta) in 1962 before coming to the UK, where he obtained an MSc in high voltage techniques at the University of London in 1964. During this time he discovered the delights of computing and having worked as a programmer for one year with Atlas Computing Service at London University, he returned to study and gained his PhD in linear and non-linear optimisation techniques. He then worked as a mathematical consultant with SCICON, and from 1969 to 1971 worked in the same capacity for SIA Ltd, becoming group leader of a joint Anglo-French project. When the entire English group of ten were fired following internal political disagreement between the English and French, he formed Unicom Consultants Ltd with two professors and five other academics from London University.

In 1972 he became the sole owner of Unicom Consultants Ltd, and has been its managing director ever since. Also in 1971 he became a lecturer in operational research at Brunel University and has continued to teach there ever since. Now a reader, he has three research students and a fairly full teaching programme and would like to become a full professor in due course.

Over the years his work at Brunel has occupied between one-half and three-quarters of his time, and Unicom the rest. Unicom has remained small and now has one full-time employee (Mrs Valentine). Another director, Mr Lewis, is fully occupied with an outside assignment, but works for Unicom occasionally, and specialists have been recruited for particular tasks. As an example of a typical assignment, Unicom were asked to design a bus crew scheduling system for Dublin City Services. The total price for this was £50,000 spread over three years. The average sales for Unicom during the last five years have been about £35–£45,000.

Dr Mitra intends to keep on his readership, since this gives him useful contacts in academia as well as giving him ideas for seminars.

There will be three other part-time members of the team of the new seminar/publishing venture. Erik Pordes is 34 and has made a career in academic publishing and book production. In 1980 he formed IMAGO Publishing Ltd whose main business is a print broker, whose turnover now exceeds £1 million, and which has a subsidiary in Singapore. Robert Lewis is 53 and a practising mathematician, lecturing widely on his experience of applying maths and computing to practical problems in many industries. Robert Parslow is 58 and has just retired from being a senior lecturer in computer science at Brunel University where he taught for 20 years. In 1970 he founded Online Conferences which has become one of the largest conference/publishing houses in the UK with sales of about £2.5 million. He sold his shares in this business in 1984. Mr Parslow is on the council of the British Computer Society and is also the European agent for its US counterpart, the

ACM, and in this capacity travels to the USA several times each year. He is thus ideally placed as a link man.

Financial data

The economics of a typical seminar in simple terms are as follows:

	£	£
80 delegates at £300		24,000
Advance sales of book		
1,000 at £12.50		12,500
		36,500
Cost		
Book production costs	7,000	
Brochure and marketing	10,000	
Cost of food and drink for		
delegates and speakers × £45	4,500	
Administration costs	5,000	
		26,500
Profit		10,000

If the book sells well, further royalties of £7,500 per 1,000 sold are generated. If the conference is unpopular and must be cancelled, £10,000 of marketing expenditure may be lost though £5,500 of this may be recovered if the book is produced despite the fact that the conference was cancelled.

Dr Mitra and his three colleagues will be investing £40,000 in a new company to be formed to undertake this business, and he hopes that they will put on eight conferences per year. If one in four of these were to fail, the financial outcome would be:

	£	£
Sales for six conferences	144,000	
Books for eight conferences	100,000	
Total revenue		244,000
Costs for eight conferences at £22,000	176,000	
Food etc for six conferences at £4,500	27,000	
		203,000
Net profit before interest and tax		41,000

It is not expected that more than one in ten conferences will fail; also every so often a book will earn substantial sums, so this profit projection is considered conservative. A further source of income will be from selling the lists of names that the company builds up, which will be of great value to companies selling computer equipment.

While it would be possible to start this company using £40,000, it would mean that the first few conferences would have to be marketed on a small scale and would all have to work in order for sufficient reserves to be built up to withstand a failure. Dr Mitra would rather raise a total of £70,000, which will enable the purchase of some suitable office machinery (£10,000), and take a full six months' planning before launching the conferences at about two-month intervals.

Financial structure

The following structure is proposed for the new company:

Name	Contribution	%
	£	
Dr Mitra	30,000	30
Mr Pordes	3,333	10
Mr Parslow	3,333	10
Mr Lewis	3,333	10
Investor	30,000	40
say	70,000	100

Questions

1. How valid a market test do you believe the Tara Hotel seminar to be?
2. Do you think that a one in four failure rate is a prudent figure on which to base the new company's financial projection?
3. What are the key skills required to set up and run the new company? To what extent do you think Dr Mitra and his team have those skills?
4. In your opinion, are the arguments put forward for the extra £30,000 investment to launch the venture sound ones?

Case 8

Food for Friends

This case study has been prepared by *Colin Barrow* from material originally published in *Venture Capital Report*

Simon Adamson-Hope is 29 and married with one child. After leaving school in 1973 he went to Oxford Polytechnic and graduated in 1976 with an HND in Hotel and Catering Management.

He then joined Trust House Forte as a trainee assistant manager, but decided that his short-term prospects were limited and left in 1977. He began washing up for a vegetarian restaurant in Covent Garden, Food For Thought. The restaurant was very popular but lacked good management, and since it soon became obvious to the owners that Mr Hope was very capable, within six months he became manager and was left to run the business. He ran the restaurant for three and a half years, during which time the turnover increased five-fold. He received seven unsolicited offers from prospective financial backers to help him start his own restaurant, and accepted one from an uncle. They opened a vegetarian restaurant called Food For Friends in Prince Albert Street, Brighton, with a seating capacity of 60. Within three months the restaurant was full every day, with customers queueing in the street during busy times.

The Brighton restaurant

Mr Hope's aim is to provide varied and imaginative vegetarian food and a range of drinks which include house wine, bottled wine and cider. To attract the interest of people of all ages and backgrounds, a comprehensive menu is offered with three starters, three savouries, various salads and dressings, at least four desserts, home-made bread and cakes and soft drinks, together with coffee and a range of different teas. The meals are prepared on the premises daily, using top quality ingredients. The menu is changed twice daily. Fifty per cent of the customers are regulars and Mr Hope believes that 90 per cent of his customers are not vegetarians but use the restaurant because the food is high quality and good value.

The restaurant maintains low prices both for food and drink. Four people can eat out with a litre of wine for £15. The restaurant has high fixed costs, and success is therefore dependent on a fast turnover of customers – there is an average of eight sittings per day.

It became apparent that additional food could be cooked over and above the needs of the restaurant and therefore a take-away service was started, and later some outside catering. The Brighton restaurant has been included in the 1984 and 1985 *Good Food Guides* and also in Egon Ronay's *Just a Bite*. The readers of *Here's Health* magazine voted it one of the top five vegetarian restaurants in Britain. The restaurant is now run by a manager and Mr Hope has plans to open a new one.

The new premises in Covent Garden

Mr Hope is acquiring the lease of a pub/club on the corner of Mercer Street and Shelton Street, an area of Covent Garden which is being redeveloped and is scheduled for completion within 12 months. There will be shops and offices in the surrounding streets. It is within 400 yards of Covent Garden underground station, close to the Royal Opera House and St Martin's School of Art. The area is lively, with many office workers and visitors.

The building has four floors. The basement will house the main seating area, the ground floor, the service counter, the take-away counter and some seating. The first floor will house the kitchens, the second floor, offices, and the top-floor flat has a sitting tenant. The restaurant will have seating capacity of 120.

Mr Hope has negotiated the final price on the lease and has completed talks with the local authority and the fire officer, who have approved his plans. No new planning permission is required, the premises already having the necessary approvals. Mr Hope believes it is council policy not to grant permission for more restaurants in the Covent Garden area.

A cook/manageress who is well known to Mr Hope is keen to join the project. He considers her to be a first class cook and manageress.

The plan is for this restaurant to open between the hours of 8.00 am and 10.00 pm seven days a week, and to have sales of approximately £2,225 per day.

Financial data

The Brighton restaurant with 60 seats has sales of c. £350,000 per annum, a gross profit of 64 per cent and net profits of £50,000 before directors' emoluments. The sales figures and some of the costs for Covent Garden are based on the Brighton results.

The profit and loss forecasts for the first two years of trading in Covent Garden are shown in Table A.

Table A. Profit and Loss forecasts for 1985 and 1986

	1985			1986	
	£	£		£	£
Sales		622,000			684,200
Less cost of sales					
Fresh food	64,000			70,400	
Dry food	100,000			110,000	
Wines	23,000			25,300	
		187,000			205,700
Gross profit		435,000	(70%)		478,500
Wages and NI		165,000			181,500
		270,000			279,000
Less overheads					
Rent and rates	18,200			18,820	
Light and heat	4,200			4,620	
Salaries	1,600			1,760	
Insurance	2,000			2,200	
Stationery	4,000			4,400	
Advertising	2,000			2,200	
Travel	4,000			4,400	
Repairs	4,000			4,400	
Laundry	2,000			2,200	
Sundry	4,000			4,400	
Interest charges	14,900			13,150	
Audit	1,000			1,100	
Directors' salaries	36,779			40,456	
Depreciation	8,125			6,094	
		106,804			110,200
Net profit		163,196			186,800

Notes:
1. Sales—average price of meal is £2.75

		£
Lunch		
120 covers turned over 2.5 times = 300 × £2.75		825
Evening		
120 covers turned over 2 times = 240 × £2.75		660
		1,485
Take-away approximately 33.3% of turnover		742
Daily total		2,227
2227 × 6-day week × 51-week year =		681,462
Less VAT		59,258
Total excluding VAT		622,204

In Brighton each cover is used eight times a day and although there is a gross profit percentage of 64 per cent in Brighton, Mr Hope believes it will be possible to charge higher prices in Covent Garden and thus raise the percentage to 70 per cent.

Also these projections assume a six-day week, whereas the restaurant will probably open seven days a week if there is demand.
2. The restaurant will employ approximately 50 people including part-timers.
3. Loan interest is to allow for servicing the capital.

The funds will be used as shown in Table B.

Table B. Use of funds

	£
Premium for lease	70,000
Professional fees	3,000
Redecoration	7,500
Kitchen extension	4,000
Repairs and renovation	4,000
Chairs	2,000
Serving counter	7,000
Pots, pans, crockery etc	2,000
	99,500
Six months' rent	6,000
Rates	1,000
Wages (2 weeks)	6,000
Food	3,000
	115,500
First month's trading	4,500
	120,000

A cash flow forecast has been prepared and a summary of the first six months is shown below:

Cash flow summary

% of capacity	50%	60%	70%	80%	90%	90%
Month	1	2	3	4	5	6
	£	£	£	£	£	£
Sales	25,917	31,100	36,283	41,467	46,650	46,650
Cost of sales	7,792	9,350	10,908	12,467	14,025	14,025
Wages	13,750	13,750	13,750	13,750	13,750	13,750
Rent and rates	4,550	—	—	6,100	—	—
Heat and lighting	—	—	—	1,400	—	—
Insurance	—	2,000	—	—	—	—
Directors	2,750	3,065	3,065	3,065	3,065	3,065
Other	1,800	1,800	5,525	1,800	1,800	6,025
Total costs	30,642	29,965	33,248	38,582	32,640	36,865
Net flow	(4,725)	1,135	3,035	2,885	14,010	9,785
Opening balances	4,500	(225)	910	3,945	6,830	20,840
Cumulative balance	(225)	910	3,945	6,830	20,840	30,625

Questions

1. How useful do you think Simon Hope's Brighton experiences will be in his proposed Covent Garden restaurant?
2. Are the sales and subsequent profit and loss projections soundly based?
3. Do you think that he has allowed enough money in his use of funds calculations to open a 120-seat restaurant?
4. If you were offered for £70,000 a 30 per cent share of the company set up to run the new restaurant, would you invest (or recommend it to a friend with more money than yourself)?

Case 9

The River Inn, Bishopstoke

This case study has been prepared by *Colin Barrow* from material originally published in *Venture Capital Report* and from additional material provided by *Thomas Porter*

One cold morning in January 1984 the managing director of Northcote Venture Capital was reviewing a proposition for funds passed to him by a colleague. Pinned to the proposal was a recommendation that they meet Porter and an article from that morning's *Times*.

The man

Thomas Chinnal Mansel Porter is 57 and the owner of the Bakers Arms outside Poole, which he converted and opened in 1980, and which was voted 'Babycham Pub of the Year' for the whole of the UK in 1983.

Mr Porter was educated at Cothill Preparatory School, joining the navy and entering Dartmouth Royal Naval College at 13, where he obtained a first class final certificate and the prizes in maths and engineering on leaving to go to sea as a midshipman.

He then served in the Royal Navy from 1944 to 1955, before retiring at his own request with the rank of lieutenant to join the Linoleum Manufacturing Co Ltd where he worked for six years, rising to become export manager.

In 1961 he joined Tintawn (Carpet) Ltd as UK general manager and succeeded in raising sales from £100,000 to £500,000 per annum, but was asked to leave when his commission-related salary became double that of the group chairman.

From 1964 to 1968 he was the sales director of two companies which were owned by a private investor: Colorcel Ltd, a colour photographic processor, and DCHE Ltd, a DIY central heating company. He left when DCHE Ltd was sold, in 1968, and joined Brickwoods Brewery, which was taken over by Whitbread in 1971, for whom he continued to work until he branched out on his own in 1980.

His first post for Brickwoods was as area manager, and he was responsible for seven pubs and for running one depot with three reps. When Whitbread took over both Brickwoods and Strongs in

1971, he became responsible for a large depot in the Isle of Wight with 90 employees serving 130 pubs.

Following a reorganisation in 1973, he then became marketing manager, Wessex, with direct responsibility for all of Whitbread's 1,100 pubs in this region. He remained happily in this job until 1980, but found that it did not provide him with sufficient challenge and he became mildly bored.

In 1980 he finally left with a golden handshake, and purchased a 65-year lease on a derelict thatched pub outside Poole, with a view to opening it again after six years of vandalism. His initial projections forecast annual sales of £200,000.

The lease cost £25,000 and he spent £180,000 on refurbishing, with £45,000 coming from Whitbread, £16,000 from his savings and the balance from a friendly bank manager.

The pub opened as the Bakers Arms in December 1980 and has been an outstanding success; sales have been as follows:

		£
Year to December	1981	440,000
	1982	540,000
	1983	640,000

He has had to acquire a nearby field to convert to an overflow car park.

Mr Porter is an extrovert and enjoys working in his pub, which he does mostly at weekends. However, he has two managers who can run the pub entirely without him, and he says that he has a knack of getting on with his staff and getting the best out of them. This leaves him time for other activities.

His next venture was the purchase of the Happy Cheese, an up-market but somewhat faded restaurant which he converted into a down-market but vigorous pub of the same name. The freehold cost £170,000 and £120,000 was spent on refurbishment. This was to have been funded with a loan from the bank for £190,000 and a loan from a major brewery for £100,000. In the event and at the last minute, the brewery declined to lend more than £75,000, and this created considerable embarrassment. Mr Porter decided to sell out quickly to another brewery which he did at a price of £380,000 making a clear profit of £30,000 after all expenses, including initial trading losses. Nevertheless, the experience left a bad taste, and for this reason he does not wish to become too heavily dependent on any one source of capital for his present venture.

Mr Porter also has various other business interests, all related to pubs:

1. He is very interested in computers and has developed a complete set of programs for pubs, which he uses himself so that he has up-to-the-minute figures on all aspects of his business. He intends to sell this program to other publicans.

2. As the Bakers Arms has become steadily busier, so the tannoy system calling out the numbers of customers' meals as they are ready has become overworked, to the detriment of the pub. In response to this, he has therefore developed a system of TV monitors which are run by a microcomputer, and which can then display messages to customers silently, including time until closing, meals ready, meals not collected and getting cold, quizzes and also messages to individual customers, eg telephone messages received, car lights on etc. He has already sold this system to one nearby pub and intends to market it nationwide in due course.

3. Quiz leagues. Mr Porter has formed a partnership with his old secretary to sell quiz leagues to pubs throughout England. So far about 1,500 pubs have signed up and the business is growing steadily. This activity does not take much of his time. He has provided the funds to launch this and will share 50 per cent of the profits.

Mr Porter also has interests in at least two other large sites for pubs/motels that will be ready to be developed in the next two years, and in which an investor may also be interested.

Happily married for 34 years with three grown-up children, he has also written a book on *How To Do Your Own Divorce*. He also enjoys sailing, shooting and collecting memorabilia, and plans another book.

The new pub

It was in the summer, while driving, that Mr Porter first observed a 'For Sale' board on St Agnes House, a large Victorian three-storey family house that had been used by a local doctor for many years before the present owners acquired it. The house is in Bishopstoke, just outside Southampton, and about 35 miles from the Bakers Arms. The house stands in about 2.5 acres of land and the river Itchin flows at the bottom of the garden on two of the four sides.

'A pub with a pleasant river frontage and large car park is a winner in anybody's language,' was Mr Porter's immediate thought, and he began making enquiries.

Since then the following progress has been made and the following facts are relevant:

1. He has signed contracts to purchase the house for 140,000 and completion was set for February 1984.

2. He has agreed to purchase the cottage and garden in the grounds for £55,000, subject to licensing approval for the pub.

3. He has paid an option for one year, giving him the right to purchase half an acre of adjoining land, which will be necessary for constructing a new access road.

4. He has had architect's outline plans drawn up to build on to St Agnes house to create 5,000 sq ft of selling space which is very large for a pub, but which he believes is warranted by the beauty of the site and the lack of competition. There are approximately one million people of the C/D market for which he is aiming in the catchment area.

5. The basic design for the pub will be a large central bar which will be raised 18 in above three octagonal 'pavilions', where food will be served and where children will be allowed. He has discussed the question of children with the police and planning authorities, and both are keen to encourage a place of entertainment where the whole family can go together, but which will also include a 'pub'. The purpose of raising the bar area 18 in is to designate clearly the area where children will not be allowed.

6. He has received enthusiastic support for this project from the local Labour-controlled council, who are keen to have more places of entertainment in the area, and who would like to see a walk along the river opened up to the public, which is part of the proposal.

7. Planning permission for the project has been granted by the full council, with only two opposing votes.

8. However, the licensing magistrates turned down the licensing application in early December, but Mr Porter is very confident that the application will be granted on appeal, which will be heard by a non-local court in Winchester. The size of the support from the planning council should, Mr Porter feels, carry considerable weight at the licensing appeal hearing.

9. Mr Porter was confident that by mid-February 1984 he would be in possession of all the packages of land required and that all necessary permissions would have been granted for the project to proceed.

Financial data

The total budget for this project is as follows, in round figures:

	£
Site purchase, including all fees etc	250,000
Building and alterations	270,000
Furniture and equipment	80,000
Interest for one year and contingencies(1)	60,000
Total	660,000

(1) Working capital will be provided from cash flow as is normal for pubs/restaurants.

It is suggested that this be provided as follows:

	£	Security
Bank loan (base + 3%)	260,000	First mortgage
Brewery (5%)	140,000	Second mortgage
Hire purchase	60,000	Third mortgage
Mr Porter equity	82,500	55% of equity
Investor	67,500	45% of equity
Loan from investor (0%)	50,000	
Total	660,000	

So far the bank has agreed to provide £260,000 and Bass have agreed to provide £140,000, based on the anticipated barrelage. It is probable that the brewery would be prepared to lend more, but mindful of the problems he experienced with the Happy Cheese, Mr Porter would rather not become too dependent on any one source of funds.

The budget for the first three years of operation is shown in Appendix 2. The actual results for the Bakers Arms in 1982 is set out below:

Profit and loss for the Bakers Arms

(Exc VAT) Income	Bakers Arms 2nd year
	£
Bar sales	238,818
Drink cost	130,383
Bar gross profit	108,435
	(45.5%)
Food sales	251,758
Food cost	113,601
Food gross profit	138,157
	(54.8%)
Fruit m/c profit	5,507
Total sales	495,583
Total gross profit	252,099

105

Expenditure	
Wages – bar	35,531
	(14.8%)
Wages – food	56,379
	(22.3%)
Wages – administration	7,189
Advertising and printing	3,709
Cleaning and garden	10,049
Transport	5,956
Heat and light	9,745
Insurance	665
Bank interest and charges	21,507
HP interest	2,774
Repairs	10,719
Equipment rent	3,555
Rates	3,627
Telephone	1,542
Depreciation	11,660
Sundries	6,117
Total expenditure	190,724
Operating profit	61,375
Cash surplus	73,035

The timetable for this project is as follows:

Feb 1984	Complete purchase of land etc
Feb–May 1984	Finalise building plans
May–Dec 1984	Build
Dec 1984	Open, with huge publicity for Christmas

Mr Porter concedes that this is an extremely tight programme, but thinks that it might just be possible to achieve. It should certainly be possible to open by August 1985 without any undue hurry.

Financial structure

Mr Porter offers 45 per cent of the equity to an investor who will provide £67,500 as equity capital and an interest free loan of £50,000 which will be repaid out of first profits. Mr Porter will invest £82,500 himself for 55 per cent of the equity.

Appendix 1
The number of public houses fell by 6,511, more than a fifth from 1977 to 1981, according to an Hotel and Catering Industry

Training Board report.* In the north, the worst affected region, almost a third of public houses trading in 1977 closed.

Of the 60,800 surviving, almost a third were in the south-east, but the regions with the largest number of pubs per head are in the north-west and Yorkshire and Humberside.

The lowest closure rates were in Scotland (15 per cent) and the south-west (less than one-eighth).

The report says that closures were concentrated among smaller establishments, although they still dominate the industry. Larger establishments increased in number.

There were smaller declines in the number of hotels and guest houses (down by 10 per cent); restaurants, cafes and snack bars (which declined by 12 per cent).

Number of pubs in 1981		% Decline since 1977	Pubs per 10,000 people
Scotland	5,500	− 15	10.7
Wales	2,200	− 24	7.9
North	3,300	− 32	10.6
North-west	8,700	− 27	13.6
Yorks and Humberside	6,000	− 21	12.3
East Midlands	3,800	− 26	10
West Midlands	5,100	− 27	9.9
East Anglia	1,800	− 18	9.6
South-east	19,400	− 15	11.6
South-west	5,000	− 12	11.5
	60,800	− 21	11.2

*Hotel and Catering Establishments in Great Britain: A Regional Analysis. Part 1, (HCITB Publications. PO Box 18, Wembley HA9 7AP).

Appendix 2

```
                 RIVER INN,Bishopstoke  - FINANCIAL INFORMATION
                                         Date of Opening 1st August 1985

                                      Unit of
        QUESTIONS FOR ANSWERING       Answer ANSWERS      NOTES OR REASONS FOR ANSWERING QUESTIONS

                   Day of month opening    No.    1      2(Closed part of 1st month has to be taken into account)
                       Month of opening    No.    8.00   3(Seasonal effect taken into account but not holiday area)

       Est.Inflation rate 2nd year on 1st year    %    5.00   5(Used to add to 1st Year estimated costs - not turnovers.)
       Est.Inflation rate 3rd year on 2nd year    %    5.00   6(Used to add to 2nd Year estimated costs - not turnovers.)

 Total 3rd Year T/O (exc VAT) for Bar + Food   £  750000.00  8(Should be between £110 - £200 per sq ft of sales area.)
 2nd Yr T/O as % of 3rd Yr T/O for Bar + Food   %    85.00   9(Usually about 85% of 3rd Year Turn over)
 1st Yr T/O as % of 3rd Yr T/O for Bar + Food   %    70.00   10(Usually about 70% of 3rd Year Turn over)
 3rd Yr T/O for Fruit & Video M/cs (exc VAT)   £  18000.00   11(1st & 2nd Years are based on Total T/O percentages)
                                                             12

              Bar % of T/O for Bar + Food    %    55.00   13(Important estimation - check on a similar house in area.)
                     Bar Gross Profit %      %    46.00   14(Between 46 - 50% in south, less in north & midlands)
                    Food Gross Profit %      %    53.00   15(Between 50 - 55% in south, less in north, more in London)
                                                          16

           Bar Wages as % of Bar Turnover    %    11.50   17(About 15% of Bar T/O exc. owner or manager's pay)
          Food Wages as % of Food Turnover   %    23.50   18(About 23% of Food T/O exc. owner or manager's pay)
 Management & Admin waages as % of 1st Yr T/O %    3.70    19(Include costs of manager,bookkeeper,accountant,stocktaker
                                                          20(etc,which is likely to be about 3.5% of 1st Yr T/O)

 Print/Advert costs as % 3rd Yr T/O or £ cost  £ or %   0.70   21(Usually about 0.7% of Total T/O.)
 Print/Advert start-up extra costs in 1st Qtr   £    5000.00   22(Usually need £1000+ for 1st qtr for menus, adverts etc.)
 Average weekly entertainment cost in 1st year  £    15.00    23(Weekly cost is easiest way to reckon this)
                                                              24

 Clean/Garden costs as % 1st Yr T/O or £ costs £ or %   1.50   25(About 1.5% of !st Yr T/O if gardener employed)
 Insurance costs as % 1st Yr T/O or £ costs   £ or %   0.40   26(Usually about 0.4% of 1st Yr T/O)
 Bank charges as % 1st Yr T/O or £ cost       % or £  3000.00  27(Bank charges are usually about 0.5% of 1st Yr T/O)
             Owing to Main Lender at opening   £  444000.00   28(Put in the max. allowed to borrow for safety)
 Main Lender's rate of interest at opening     %    19.00   29(Usually Bank Rate + 3%)
                          Period of loan      Yrs  10.00   30(Usually 10 years but can be less)
 Period allowed from start for interest roll-up Yrs  1.00   31(Lender may allow 1 or 2 yrs interest accrual)
 Capital repayments start in ? year, yr        Yr    3.00   32(May allow repayment in last 8 or 9 yrs out of 10)
                                                           33
                                                           34

              Owing to 2nd lender at start-up   £  125000.00  35(Put in max. allowed to borrow for safety)
               2nd lender's rate of interest    %    5.00   36(If a brewery lending to Free Trade a/c then usually 5%)
               Period of loan in years         Yrs  10.00   37(If a brewery - 10 years or less due to EEC regulations)
 Period allowed for interest roll-over         Yrs   1.00   38(1 or 2 yrs interest allowed to accrue to borrowings.)
 Capital repayments start in ? year            Yr    3.00   39(May allow repayment in last 8 or 9 yrs out of 10)
                                                           40
                                                           41

             H.P. Borrowing at Start-up        £  60000.00   42(Usually carpets,furns,kitch.equip etc are so bought)
 Actual rate of interest on borrowing (APR%)   %    18.00   43(APR = actual interest on still owed debt)
                    Period of H.P. Loan        Yrs   3.00   44(Usually never more than 3 years)
                                                           45
                                                           46

 Repairs & Renewals as % 1st Yr T/O          %    1.50   47(Ought to allow 1.5-2.0% of 1st Yr T/O)
 Equipment rent as % 1st Yr T/O or £ cost  % or £  800.00   48(Prudent to allow about 0.2% of 1st Yr T/O)
 Transport costs as % 1st Yr T/O or £ cost % or £  2000.00  49(Car running is min. £1200 p.a. usually more)
 Heat & Light costs as % 1st Yr T/O or £ cost % or £  1.80   50(Allow about 1.7% of 1st Yr T/O)
 Telephone costs as % 1st Yr T/O or £ cost % or £  700.00   51(Allow at least 0.2% of 1st Yr T/O for this)
 Water & Rates as % 1st Yr T/O or £ cost % or £  1.70   52(Allow 1.7% of Total Turnover for this)
                                                        53

 Depreciation as % 1st Yr T/O or £ cost % or £  9000.00  54(Should be 20 - 25% of cost of fixtures and fittings)
 Sundries as % 1st Yr T/O or £ cost   % or £  1.00   55(Allow about 1.0% of 1st T/O for this)
```

- 1 -

THE RIVER INN, BISHOPSTOKE

1st AUGUST 1985 - 31st JULY 1986.

	AUG	SEP	OCT	NOV	DEC	JAN	FEB	MAR	APR	MAY	JUN	JUL	TOTAL
Wks in Month	4	5	4	4	5	4	4	5	4	4	5	4	
YEAR	1												

INCOME (in £'s)

	AUG	SEP	OCT	NOV	DEC	JAN	FEB	MAR	APR	MAY	JUN	JUL	TOTAL
Bar Sales	26796	29741	21079	20501	27720	19635	19924	25988	21656	21945	28298	24544	287826
Drink Cost	13934	15465	10961	10661	14414	10210	10360	13514	11261	11411	14715	12763	149670
Drink G.P.	12862	14276	10118	9841	13306	9425	9563	12474	10395	10534	13583	11781	138156
Food Sales	21924	24334	17246	16774	22680	16065	16301	21263	17719	17955	23153	20081	235494
Food Cost	9866	10950	7761	7548	10206	7229	7336	9568	7973	8080	10419	9037	105972
Food G.P.	12058	13384	9485	9226	12474	8836	8966	11694	9745	9875	12734	11045	129522
Machine take	1169	1298	920	895	1210	857	869	1134	945	958	1235	1071	12560
TOTAL SALES	49889	55373	39245	38170	51610	36557	37094	48384	40320	40858	52685	45696	535880
TOTAL G.P.	26090	28957	20523	19961	26989	19117	19398	25302	21085	21366	27551	23897	280238

EXPENSES (in £'s)

	AUG	SEP	OCT	NOV	DEC	JAN	FEB	MAR	APR	MAY	JUN	JUL	TOTAL
Bar Wages	3832	4253	3014	2932	3964	2808	2849	3716	3097	3138	4047	3510	41159
Food Wages	3069	3407	2414	2348	3175	2249	2282	2977	2481	2514	3241	2811	32969
Admin/Manage	1702	1702	1702	1702	1702	1702	1702	1702	1702	1702	1702	1702	20429
Print/Advert	1891	1891	1891	224	224	224	224	224	224	224	224	224	7688
Entertainment	60	75	60	60	75	60	60	75	60	60	75	60	780
Clean/Garden	774	831	589	573	774	548	556	726	605	613	790	685	8064
Insurance	179	179	179	179	179	179	179	179	179	179	179	179	2150
Bank Charges	0	750	0	0	750	0	0	750	0	0	750	0	3000
Interest-1st	0	10545	0	0	10545	0	0	10545	0	0	10545	0	42180
" 2nd	0	0	0	0	0	0	0	0	0	0	0	0	0
" HP	900	881	861	842	822	801	781	760	738	717	695	673	9470
Reprs/Renews	1344	1344	1344	1344	1344	1344	1344	1344	1344	1344	1344	1344	16128
Equip.Rent	67	67	67	67	67	67	67	67	67	67	67	67	800
Transport	125	125	125	125	125	125	125	125	125	125	125	125	1500
Heat & Light	0	0	1613	0	0	3226	0	0	3226	0	0	1613	9677
Telephone	225	225	225	225	225	225	225	225	225	225	225	225	2700
Rates/Water	627	627	627	627	627	627	627	627	627	627	627	627	7526
Depreciation	667	667	667	667	667	667	667	667	667	667	667	667	8000
Sundries	448	448	448	448	448	448	448	448	448	448	448	448	5376
TOTAL COSTS	15910	28016	15826	12362	25713	15300	12136	25157	15814	12650	25751	14960	219597

PROFITS (in £'s)

	AUG	SEP	OCT	NOV	DEC	JAN	FEB	MAR	APR	MAY	JUN	JUL	TOTAL
Mth PROFIT	10179	941	4697	7598	1276	3817	7262	146	5271	8717	1800	8936	60641
Yr PROFIT	10179	11121	15817	23416	24692	28509	35771	35917	41188	49904	51705	60641	

REPAYMENTS

	AUG	SEP	OCT	NOV	DEC	JAN	FEB	MAR	APR	MAY	JUN	JUL	TOTAL
Repaymts-1st	0	0	0	0	0	0	0	0	0	0	0	0	0
" 2nd	0	0	0	0	0	0	0	0	0	0	0	0	0
" HP	1277	1296	1316	1335	1356	1376	1396	1417	1439	1460	1482	1504	16655

CASH POSITION (Inc. Depreciation but exc. VAT cash)

	AUG	SEP	OCT	NOV	DEC	JAN	FEB	MAR	APR	MAY	JUN	JUL	TOTAL
Cash - Month	9569	312	4048	6930	587	3108	6532	-605	4499	7923	985	8099	51985
Cash - Year	9569	9881	13928	20858	21445	24553	31085	30480	34979	42902	43887	51985	

- 1 -

109

1st AUGUST 1986 - 31st JULY 1987.

	AUG	SEP	OCT	NOV	DEC	JAN	FEB	MAR	APR	MAY	JUN	JUL	TOTAL
Wks in Month	4	5	4	4	5	4	4	5	4	4	5	4	
YEAR	2				INCOME (in £'s)								
Bar Sales	32538	36114	25596	24894	33660	23843	24193	31556	26297	26648	34361	29803	349503
Drink Cost	16920	18779	13310	12945	17503	12398	12580	16409	13674	13857	17868	15498	181742
Drink G.P.	15618	17335	12286	11949	16157	11444	11613	15147	12623	12791	16493	14306	167761
Food Sales	26622	29548	20942	20368	27540	19508	19794	25819	21516	21803	28114	24384	285957
Food Cost	11980	13297	9424	9166	12393	8778	8907	11618	9682	9811	12651	10973	128681
Food G.P.	14642	16251	11518	11202	15147	10729	10887	14200	11834	11991	15463	13411	157276
Machine take	1420	1576	1117	1086	1469	1040	1056	1377	1148	1163	1499	1301	15251
TOTAL SALES	60580	67238	47654	46349	62669	44390	45043	58752	48960	49613	63974	55488	650711
TOTAL G.P.	31680	35162	24921	24238	32773	23214	23555	30724	25604	25945	33455	29017	340289
					EXPENSES(in £'s)								
Bar Wages	4653	5164	3660	3560	4813	3409	3460	4513	3760	3811	4914	4262	49979
Food Wages	3727	4137	2932	2852	3856	2731	2771	3615	3012	3052	3936	3414	40034
Admin/Manage	1788	1788	1788	1788	1788	1788	1788	1788	1788	1788	1788	1788	21450
Print/Advert	235	235	235	235	235	235	235	235	235	235	235	235	2822
Entertainent	63	79	63	63	79	63	63	79	63	63	79	63	819
Clean/Garden	813	872	618	601	813	576	584	762	635	644	830	720	8467
Insurance	188	188	188	188	188	188	188	188	188	188	188	188	2258
Bank Charges	0	788	0	0	788	0	0	788	0	0	788	0	3150
Interest-1st	0	21090	0	0	21090	0	0	21090	0	0	21090	0	84360
" 2nd	0	1641	0	0	1641	0	0	1641	0	0	1641	0	6563
" HP	670	648	625	601	578	554	529	505	479	454	428	402	6472
Reprs/Renews	1411	1411	1411	1411	1411	1411	1411	1411	1411	1411	1411	1411	16934
Equip.Rent	70	70	70	70	70	70	70	70	70	70	70	70	840
Transport	131	131	131	131	131	131	131	131	131	131	131	131	1575
Heat & Light	0	0	1693	0	0	3387	0	0	3387	0	0	1693	10161
Telephone	236	236	236	236	236	236	236	236	236	236	236	236	2835
Rates/Water	659	659	659	659	659	659	659	659	659	659	659	659	7903
Depreciation	700	700	700	700	700	700	700	700	700	700	700	700	8400
Sundries	470	470	470	470	470	470	470	470	470	470	470	470	5645
TOTAL COSTS	15815	40306	15480	13565	39545	16608	13296	38879	17226	13912	39593	16442	280667
					PROFITS (in £'s)								
Mth PROFIT	15866	-5144	9441	10673	-6772	6606	10259	-8155	8378	12033	-6138	12575	59622
Yr PROFIT	15866	10722	20163	30836	24063	30669	40928	32773	41151	53184	47047	59622	
					REPAYMENTS								
Repaymts-1st	0	0	0	0	0	0	0	0	0	0	0	0	0
" 2nd	0	0	0	0	0	0	0	0	0	0	0	0	0
" HP	1507	1530	1553	1576	1600	1623	1648	1673	1698	1723	1749	1775	19653
				CASH POSITION (Inc. Depreciation but exc. VAT cash)									
Cash - Month	15059	-5974	8589	9797	-7672	5682	9312	-9127	7380	11010	-7187	11500	48368
Cash - Year	15059	9085	17674	27470	19799	25481	34792	25665	33045	44055	36868	48368	

1st August 1987 - 31st JULY 1988

	AUG	SEP	OCT	NOV	DEC	JAN	FEB	MAR	APR	MAY	JUN	JUL	TOTAL
Wks in Month	4	5	4	4	5	4	4	5	4	4	4	5	4	
YEAR	3												

INCOME (in £'s)

	AUG	SEP	OCT	NOV	DEC	JAN	FEB	MAR	APR	MAY	JUN	JUL	TOTAL
Bar Sales	38280	42488	30113	29288	39600	28050	28463	37125	30938	31350	40425	35063	411180
Drink Cost	19906	22094	15659	15230	20592	14586	14801	19305	16088	16302	21021	18233	213814
Drink G.P.	18374	20394	14454	14058	19008	13464	13662	17820	14850	15048	19404	16830	197366
Food Sales	31320	34763	24638	23963	32400	22950	23288	30375	25313	25650	33075	28688	336420
Food Cost	14094	15643	11087	10783	14580	10328	10479	13669	11391	11543	14884	12909	151389
Food G.P.	17226	19119	13551	13179	17820	12623	12808	16706	13922	14108	18191	15778	185031
Machine take	1670	1854	1314	1278	1728	1224	1242	1620	1350	1368	1764	1530	17942
TOTAL SALES	71270	79104	56064	54528	73728	52224	52992	69120	57600	58368	75264	65280	765542
TOTAL G.P.	37271	41367	29319	28515	38556	27311	27712	36146	30122	30524	39359	34138	400340

EXPENSES (in £'s)

	AUG	SEP	OCT	NOV	DEC	JAN	FEB	MAR	APR	MAY	JUN	JUL	TOTAL
Bar Wages	5474	6076	4306	4188	5663	4011	4070	5309	4424	4483	5781	5014	58799
Food Wages	4385	4867	3449	3355	4536	3213	3260	4253	3544	3591	4631	4016	47099
Admin/Manage	1877	1877	1877	1877	1877	1877	1877	1877	1877	1877	1877	1877	22523
Print/Advert	247	247	247	247	247	247	247	247	247	247	247	247	2964
Entertainmnt	66	83	66	66	83	66	66	83	66	66	83	66	860
Clean/Garden	853	916	649	631	853	605	613	800	667	676	871	756	8891
Insurance	198	198	198	198	198	198	198	198	198	198	198	198	2371
Bank Charges	0	827	0	0	827	0	0	827	0	0	827	0	3308
Interest-1st	0	21090	0	0	20765	0	0	20425	0	0	20068	0	82348
" 2nd	0	1641	0	0	1595	0	0	1549	0	0	1502	0	6286
" HP	399	372	345	318	290	261	233	204	174	144	113	82	2935
Reprs/Renews	1482	1482	1482	1482	1482	1482	1482	1482	1482	1482	1482	1482	17781
Equip.Rent	74	74	74	74	74	74	74	74	74	74	74	74	882
Transport	138	138	138	138	138	138	138	138	138	138	138	138	1654
Heat & Light	0	0	1778	0	0	3556	0	0	3556	0	0	1778	10669
Telephone	248	248	248	248	248	248	248	248	248	248	248	248	2977
Rates/Water	691	691	691	691	691	691	691	691	691	691	691	691	8298
Depreciation	735	735	735	735	735	735	735	735	735	735	735	735	8820
Sundries	494	494	494	494	494	494	494	494	494	494	494	494	5927
TOTAL COSTS	17360	42054	16777	14741	40795	17895	14426	39631	18614	15143	40059	17896	295389

PROFITS (in £'s)

	AUG	SEP	OCT	NOV	DEC	JAN	FEB	MAR	APR	MAY	JUN	JUL	TOTAL
Mth PROFIT	19911	-686	12542	13775	-2239	9415	13286	-3485	11508	15381	-700	16243	104951
Yr PROFIT	19911	19224	31766	45541	43302	52717	66004	62519	74027	89408	88708	104951	

REPAYMENTS

	AUG	SEP	OCT	NOV	DEC	JAN	FEB	MAR	APR	MAY	JUN	JUL	TOTAL
Repaymts-1st	0	6839	0	0	7164	0	0	7504	0	0	7861	0	29368
" 2nd	0	3652	0	0	3697	0	0	3744	0	0	3790	0	14883
" HP	1778	1805	1832	1860	1887	1916	1944	1974	2003	2033	2064	2095	23191

CASH POSITION (Inc. Depreciation but.exc. VAT cash)

	AUG	SEP	OCT	NOV	DEC	JAN	FEB	MAR	APR	MAY	JUN	JUL	TOTAL
Cash - Month	18867	-12247	11445	12650	-14252	8234	12077	-15971	10240	14083	-13679	14883	46329
Cash - Year	18867	6620	18065	30715	16463	24697	36774	20803	31043	45125	31446	46329	

- 1 -

Questions

1. How realistic do you think Porter's opening timetable is?
2. Do you think Porter has the substantive characteristics of a successful entrepreneur?
3. Is he right to be as confident as he appears about the licensing appeal?
4. Do his projections for the new business seem achievable and would they warrant the level of investment he is proposing?

Case 10
Tripos Motors

This case study has been prepared by *Colin Barrow* from material first published in *Venture Capital Report*

Rodney Gordon and his two colleagues were contemplating the likely response to their plans to produce two production component cars for exhibition at the National Classic Motor Show in May 1985. This would be a precursor to starting limited production on their Tripos R81 sports car. They needed £40,000 to produce the cars and could offer 20 per cent of the equity to a prospective investor.

History

In 1982 Laurence Abbott, who is an architect and sports car enthusiast and who had worked for Fiat's IDEA team in Italy for the previous two years designing an all-plastic car-of-the-future, decided that he would build himself an equivalent of the Lotus 7 kit car, but using the most up-to-date technology for running gear and suspension, and packaged in a superbly elegant body. His two partners in the architecture practice Tripos, who are also car enthusiasts (all three drive Porsches), quickly became involved too and helped to finance the work.

Having raced cars of all sorts himself for 30 years, Mr Abbott knew many experts to whom he could turn for specialist advice (as well as being a considerable expert himself, he has a collection of sports cars which he rebuilds and races, including two Aston Martins and two Jaguar E-types). For example, the chassis and suspension which uses very long radius arms down the outside of the car, was designed by Mr Abbott and Bob Egginton, whose company, Automotive Systems Development, is a specialist supplier to the motor racing industry with a reputation for producing the highest quality work, and which runs its own Formula Ford racing team.

The intention throughout was to produce a no-frills, high-performance sports car with adjustable suspension so that the car could be raced or used on the road, and with an elegant body. The body is moulded from self coloured GRP (no painting or finishing required) by Protoco, a specialist moulder in London. The moulds have been built to produce 100 to 200 body shells before they will need to be replaced.

Two years later, the Tripos team were so pleased with the elegance of their design and with the comments of friends and like-minded enthusiasts that they decided to exhibit the Tripos R81, as the car became known, at the National Classic Motor Show at the NEC to test public reaction and to see whether there might be sufficient demand to warrant limited production.

The results exceeded their expectations; great interest was shown by the public and motoring press alike, and the promoters received substantial coverage in the motoring press, of which the quote below is an example:

'The Tripos has beautifully smooth lines reminiscent of a 1960s racer: the mechanics, however, have benefited from much more up-to-date engineering.' (*Kit-Car*, July 1984.)

Despite saying that the car was not for sale, the promoters received many sales enquiries, and believe that they could have sold at least six to ten cars on the stand had they wished.

The prototype exhibited had originally been designed to take an Alfa Romeo engine and gearbox, but it was decided to redesign the chassis to take Ford components, which would give buyers a much greater range of engines to choose from. Since then work has proceeded slowly but steadily, with all three of the team concentrating mostly on architecture. The target is to produce a production prototype for exhibition at the National Classic Motor Show in May 1985, and to take orders and deposits at the show.

The Tripos R81 will be sold in component form only, since this avoids the need to obtain Type Approval, and the intention is to offer three kits as follows:

1. *Mini-kit*. Price £2,500. Includes chassis, body, list of parts required, and an assembly instruction manual.
2. *Standard kit*. Price £4,500. Includes chassis, body, hood and all parts except engine, gearbox, wheels and tyres. (So many different types of wheel are available that they are invariably sold as extras on kit cars.)
3. *Maxi-kit*. Price £6,000. An 'all-but-assembled' car needing only an engine, gearbox and wheels to be bolted in place and connected.

Architectural practices suffer an inherent problem of uneven cash flow, and during the last year the Tripos practice has had one steady job for the Bank of England where it is required to operate an office so that all drawings remain in the building, and has also undertaken design work on a number of other large schemes. If any of these are built, fees due to Tripos will be over £1 million, but meanwhile the cash position is tight, without being desperate. The promoters have enough resources to proceed with the development of the single production prototype for the National Classic Motor Show in May, but would prefer to raise £40,000 now, which would enable them to build two production cars, one of which could then be used as a demonstrator and one for loan to motoring correspondents. From the reaction to the prototype, the promoters believe that one of the two cars will be permanently used by motoring correspondents, who will then write reviews, so bolstering the sales campaign. £40,000 would also provide them with enough working capital to begin production and for marketing. Production will be by subcontractors, with assembly and packaging at Mr Abbott's house in Kent (two converted oast houses where there is a garage for seven cars and workshop space which would be sufficient for the production of up to 25 Tripos cars per year).

The market and competition

There are over 100 component or kit cars made in the UK, but the promoters believe that only about 10 are even remotely comparable to Tripos. Of these the nearest is the Caterham Lotus 7. Tripos will be sold at the same price as the Lotus 7, of which the promoters believe that about 200 to 250 are sold each year. The two are compared below:

	Caterham Lotus 7	Tripos R81
Engineering:	Essentially 1950s–1960s	1980s technology
Body shell:	Crude, bent metal panels	Elegant, through-coloured GRP
Performance:	Handles and drives superbly	Even better
Price:	Standard kit £4,500	Standard kit £4,500
Advantages:	25 years' reputation	Novelty value
	Nostalgic appeal	State-of-the-art engineering
	Thoroughly tried and tested	Extremely attractive body
		Free press coverage
Disadvantages:	Dated design	No track record
	Simplistic body	No 'marque' allegiance
	Long waiting list	

The men

Laurence Abbott is 43 and 'an inspired designer and a workaholic with tunnel vision'. (Rodney Gordon.) After a basic architectural education, he has worked with some of the most brilliant architects of his generation sometimes as a partner, but more often as a consultant since he works better on his own than in organisations.

Mr Abbott left the architectural school at Walthamstow Polytechnic in 1961, where he won the Chamberlain Award. He then worked with the Owen Luder Partnership until 1964, when he joined Team Four Architects and was responsible for the construction of a large house in Cornwall that won an RIBA award. From 1971 to 1976 he was a consultant to Piano and Rogers on the Pompidou Centre in Paris, where he lived for most of the time, overseeing the construction and doing much detailed design. From 1977 to 1983 he was a partner in Tripos Architects with the two other promoters, with specific responsibility for the design and construction of a factory in Essex for Neotronics. In 1981–82 he worked as part of the IDEA team in Italy, a multi-discipline team employed by Fiat to design a car-for-the-future, using new concepts and materials.

Mr Abbott now works as a consultant to Tripos, Rogers, Ove Arup and other architects, working from his house.

Mr Abbott has been interested in cars all his life and has raced a great variety, from Lotus 7s to Jaguars, as a club racer. He is the originator of the R81, owns 33 per cent of Tripos R & D Ltd, and will be responsible for production. He ceased to be a partner in Tripos Architects in order to concentrate on the R81.

Rodney Gordon is 51 and studied medicine at University College London 1950–52 before qualifying as an architect at the Architectural Association in 1957. From 1957 to 1961 he was employed as an architect by the LCC, where among other things he designed the Faraday memorial at Elephant and Castle.

From 1961 to 1968 he was a partner in the Owen Luder partnership, winning the RIBA bronze medal for London, and 1969–74 was the principal partner in Rodney Gordon, Abbott, Howard Architects. The practice built a headquarters building for Charington Lockett, a civic centre for Bishop's Stortford Local Authority and a 2 million sq ft industrial scheme in Birmingham. Since 1975 Mr Gordon has been a partner in Tripos Architects, which has built a number of large multi-million pound commercial developments for Samuel Properties, including a recently completed office complex at 66 St James's Street, London, which is occupied by Rothschild Investment Trust.

Mr Gordon will be managing director of Tripos Motors Ltd, the company which will be formed with the investor as the corporate vehicle for the project, and will have overall responsibility for the R81.

Ray Baum is 42 and is the administrative director of Tripos R & D Ltd. After qualifying as an architect at North London Polytechnic in 1959, he was employed as an architect by Derek Sharp Associates until 1962. From 1963 to 1965 he was job architect with Rodney Gordon, Abbott, Howard Architects, and in 1971 formed Co-ordinated Design Architects, which designed and supervised the construction of schemes for housing societies.

In 1972 Mr Baum set up the Solar Housing Society, and in 1976 amalgamated Co-ordinated Design Architects with Rodney Gordon to form Tripos. As a partner he has general responsibility for office management and procedures, and will fulfil this role for Tripos Motors.

At the moment, each of the three promoters owns a 33 per cent share of Tripos R & D Ltd. Tripos Motors Ltd will take over Tripos R & D Ltd.

Financial data

The promoters have prepared a 43-page business plan which contains detailed cash flow projections and which is available to potential investors.

Without an investment, the promoters will exhibit a single production R81 at the National Classic Motor Show in May 1985 and will decide on the next step after this. With an investment the programme will be as follows:

	£
January 1985	
2 chassis and suspension	
Jigs	400
2 chassis at £600	1,200
February 1985	
Finalise design of seating, windscreen pillars	
and interior cockpit layout	1,000
Commission windscreen (3 months):	
Tools	700
2 windscreens at £30	60
March 1985	
2 hoods at £350	700
2 body shells at £600	1,200
2 × all other components at £2,000	4,000

April 1985

Assemble and test 2 cars	2,000
Contribution to salaries and manufacturing costs (1)	2,000
Brochure, instruction manual, publicity	5,000
Total	18,260

Note

1. During the initial phase, Tripos Motors Ltd will pay £500 per month to be distributed by the three directors as they consider best as a contribution to their own time and expenses. Most of this will probably be paid to Mr Abbott, who will work two to three days per week on the Tripos R81, while undertaking consultancy contracts to pay his bills.

Thus, having spent about £20,000, Tripos Motors should be ready to exhibit two production cars at the National Classic Motor Show at the NEC in May 1985. At the show they will seek publicity for the car and also take orders. For a standard kit, a deposit of £300 will be required on placement of order, a further £3,200 on commencement of manufacture, and the final payment of £1,000 before delivery.

The promoters' detailed profit and loss projection for the first three years is summarised below.

Year		1		2		3
		£		£		£
Sales						
Mini-kits at £2,500	0	—	6	15,000	18	45,000
Standard kits at £4,500	5	22,500	40	180,000	84	378,000
Maxi-kits at £6,000	0	—	6	36,000	23	138,000
Spares		—		1,200		6,700
		22,500		232,200		567,700
Less cost of sales						
Mini-kits at £1,500		—		9,000		27,000
Standard kits at £3,000		15,000		120,000		252,000
Maxi-kits		—		24,000		92,000
Other		—		500		2,600
		15,000		153,500		373,600
Gross contribution		7,500		78,700		194,100
Less						
Fees to directors(1)		6,000		37,000		70,000
Other overheads		7,405		29,825		65,485
		13,405		66,825		135,485
Net profit		(5,905)		11,875		58,615

Note:

1. The directors will be prepared to link their salaries to the financial performance of the business.

The detailed cash flow projections show that only £23,000 of the £40,000 investment sought will be required in view of the positive cash flow resulting from deposits and prepayments. Nevertheless, the directors would prefer to raise £40,000 to allow for contingencies.

Financial structure

The promoters have designed an elegant, no-frills, high performance component car which they believe will offer better value, looks and performance than its nearest equivalent, the Caterham Lotus 7, of which about 200 to 250 per year are sold at the same price. Their optimism is bolstered by the enthusiastic response and reviews which the prototype received at the National Classic Motor Show in May 1984.

They now seek £40,000 in order to develop two production cars simultaneously, and to give them some working capital cushion. They have already been offered this by one of their architectural clients, but would prefer to keep architecture and the Tripos R81 completely separate. Their ideal investor would be an individual who shares their enthusiasm for the car. They would prefer to raise all £40,000 as equity when full Business Expansion Scheme relief would be available, but would also be prepared to consider a structure such as the one shown below:

Name	Contribution	%	Loan
Abbott	Project to date	27	
Gordon	Project to date	27	
Baum	Project to date	27	
Investor	£20,000	20	£20,000

The loan will be interest free, and repaid before the salaries to the existing directors rise above £500 per month each or £1,500 combined. The promoters would be quite happy with a passive investor, but would also welcome an investor who had some relevant skill to contribute and who could become a working director.

A freelance American motoring journalist at the motor show stand in May 1984 said that there could be sales of 500 per year in California alone.

Questions

1. How risky do you think the UK component car market is?
2. Do you believe that £40,000 is sufficient finance to get two cars made and up to the Motor Show?

3. Do the sales and profit projections seem realistic to you?
4. Given that the car is a success at the 1985 Motor Show, what options lie ahead of the directors? Which of these options should they choose and why?
5. What management expertise is needed to make sure that this venture is a success?

Case 11
Jensen Salmonids Ltd

This case study has been prepared by *Colin Barrow* from material originally published in *Venture Capital Report*

Jensen Salmonids Ltd was established in 1981, and the directors believe that they have developed a successful method of rearing salmon, achieving growth rates double those claimed by others. Several batches of salmon and trout grown in 1983–84 have been sold. By 1984 the company was poised to commence full-scale production and had begun to put out feelers in the venture capital market. They needed £200,000 to finance the project and were offering 35 per cent of their equity to investors in return.

Company history

Jensen Salmonids Ltd was started by Captain Knud Jensen and his son Jim in 1981. The initial research was carried out at the Central Electricity Generating Board's marine biological research centre at Fawley near Southampton, and showed that it was possible for salmonoids (the salmon or trout genus of fishes) to achieve good rates of growth in the English Channel.

In 1982 Captain Jensen obtained permission to set up a pilot plant in Southampton docks, and designed, built and crash-tested the cage equipment. The design is novel and has performed very well: no cages have been damaged or fish lost through storm damage. The pilot plant showed good results with trout, and the trial was successfully completed with all tests concluded. The fish were about to be sold when an out-of-control ferry which had lost the power of one engine hit the cages and damaged the fish. The ferry company bought the fish.

In 1982 the project moved to Portland, because the waters there were well-suited to aquaculture. The weather conditions in 1983 and 1984 were reputed to be the most severe experienced in living memory, but no fish were lost.

Unfortunately in July 1983 a major part of the trout stock, about 30,000 fish, was damaged and died from what experts believe to be deficient feed supplied by the manufacturers. The salmon stock reared in nearby cages and fed on feed from a different supplier was not affected. A claim was lodged with the suppliers, and the directors were confident of a successful conclusion to the claim with the award of substantial damages.

The salmon have been sold to fishmongers, restaurants and smokers, and all have intimated that they are very happy with the product and would like to buy increased quantities.

The site

The site is a series of rectangular cages, with buoyancy provided by the triangular box-section steel frame. Inside are hung 12 ft deep nets, with a further 30 in above the waterline, and a netting cover over the cage. The cages float in the sea, with the flat steel section at water level, so that waves wash over them, minimising water resistance in a storm. The flat steel section also provides a walking and working platform.

The cages are movable and interlinked, and the whole cage unit is tethered to two trawlers using a one-point mooring system. The trawlers are anchored in the harbour. The whole system moves with the wind, and the trawlers always point into the wind, breaking up heavy seas and protecting the cages. The trawlers can be used to tow the cages to other sites to avoid hazards such as pollution. A patent to cover the cage design has been applied for.

The initial development work was with trout and salmon, but after the successful growing of salmon, commercial work on trout was discontinued because there is great demand for salmon and higher prices can be obtained. As in Scandinavia, initial work was with both male and female fish, but male fish mature early and do not feed as well as females. Work in 1983 and 1984 therefore concentrated on female stock.

Captain Jensen has detailed results, and has worked closely with the Ministry of Agriculture, Fisheries and Food (MAFF). In about one year to 18 months after buying in the smolts at 25–40 grammes, the fish grow to an average weight of 6–7 lbs, which Captain Jensen believes he can increase to 7–8 lbs, and when sexless salmon can be introduced, in two or three years' time, further improvements will be made.

The results achieved by the company are double the growth rates of Norwegian or Scottish farms, with low feed consumption and high quality.

The market

UK consumption of fresh, smoked and frozen salmon products was estimated to be 25m lbs in 1984, and of this probably 15m lbs is smoked. A substantial amount is imported from Norway and Canada, but this is considered to be of lower quality and is sold at lower prices. Salmon imports in 1983 were in excess of 15m lbs, mainly frozen. Consumption in the UK has increased since 1980 by about 2m lbs per annum.

Jensen Salmonids can sell its fish fresh or frozen to fishmongers, direct or through Billingsgate – it has already sold salmon to Billingsgate, and in July, when there is competition from wild fish and the market is at its worst was obtaining £1.80 per lb. However, the wild catch is declining, and the market expanding.

One smoker has offered to buy all of Captain Jensen's fish. He currently buys 250,000 lbs per annum, and finds a price of £2 per lb attractive. When in full production, the farm will produce at least 300,000 lbs per year (50,000 fish at 6 lbs).

Marine Harvest, a subsidiary of Unilever, has several aquaculture units, and is believed to produce 1,000 tons per annum. A subsidiary of Norsk Hydro also produces a substantial quantity, and both companies could sell as much as they can produce, without affecting the market price.

The man

Knud Jensen who is Danish, is 53, and helped his father net fish while still at school. The Jensen family caught fish when they were plentiful, and then kept the fish alive in nets until the market prices had increased. After High School, Mr Jensen became an apprentice mate, until he went to nautical college where he obtained the highest ever mark in the Master's exams. He later studied engineering and naval architecture at Odense University.

After graduating he went back to shipping as marine superintendent of a line which operated a fleet of gas tankers. He became managing director of the company, and moved its headquarters from Denmark to Southampton because it had major contracts with Esso at Fawley, and much business based in London. The company was successful and expanded, but Mr Jensen left in 1980 after working for 13 years, because the owners wanted to exercise more control and move the headquarters back to Denmark.

In 1981 Knud Jensen started Jensen Salmonids with his son Jim.

Jim Jensen is 25. After High School he trained at a merchant navy officer training college in Svendborg and Esbjerg. He obtained his engineer's certificate and went to sea. He continued his studies, obtaining chief engineer and master certificates. During his time off he went to visit various fish rearing companies in Denmark and Norway, and also undertook some training in Norway. It was because he enjoyed the work and found it interesting that he decided to start a new career in the future modern fishing industry.

The company has one employee, who has worked for Jensen Salmonids for a year. He left school with A levels, and would have gone to aquacultural college but now believes that since aquaculture is in such an undeveloped state, it is more worthwhile to continue working at Jensen Salmonids. His job includes living on the trawlers 24 hours a day, to be on hand in case of difficulty.

One other full-time employee will be required when production is increased to commercial levels.

Profit and loss forecast

Year	1		2	3
Sales	—		360	720
Stock opening of sales	—		113	238
Gross profit	—		247	482
Overheads				
Depreciation	5		5	5
Rent and rates	11		10	10
Insurance(1)	11		21	22
Maintenance and transport	10		12	16
Salaries	10		12	16
Bank charges	7		5	4
Accountancy	5		3	3
Directors' fees	20		20	28
	79		88	104
Contingency	15		20	20
		94	108	124
Profit (Loss)		(94)	139	358

Note:
1. Comprehensive insurance through the Agricultural Insurance Service Ltd underwritten by Lloyds.

Financial data

Jensen Salmonids Ltd has appointed Coopers & Lybrand as accountants, and the latter have agreed to work closely with the directors to produce management accounts.

Forecast profit and loss accounts have been drawn up by the management for the first three years. The unaudited figures are shown on page 124.

The cash flow forecast is shown below. The quarterly balance figures have been rounded up/down to the nearest £000.

Cash flow forecast

	1	2	3	4	1986	1987	1988	1989
					£000			
Sales	—	—	—	—	360.0	720.0	720.0	720.0
Less cost of sales								
Materials (fish)	35.0	—	—	—	70.0	70.0	70.0	70.0
Materials (feed)	6.0	12.0	24.0	36.0	162.0	168.0	168.0	168.0
Production result	(41.0)	(12.0)	(24.0)	(36.0)	128.0	482.0	482.0	482.0
Fixed expenditure								
Rent, rates, phone etc	2.3	2.3	2.3	2.3	10.3	10.4	11.2	12.0
Insurance	0.2	0.2	0.2	0.2	1.1	1.8	2.8	2.8
Fish insurance	2.5	2.5	2.5	2.5	20.0	20.0	20.0	20.0
Maintenance, fuel	2.0	2.0	2.0	2.0	12.0	16.0	20.0	20.0
Salaries	2.0	2.0	2.0	2.0	12.0	16.0	20.0	20.0
Bank charges	1.8	4.6	4.5	4.4	16.6	15.1	13.8	12.2
Coopers & Lybrand	—	—	1.2	—	2.5	3.0	3.5	4.0
Directors' fees	5.0	5.0	5.0	5.0	20.0	27.5	30.0	30.0
Total fixed expenses	15.8	18.6	19.7	18.4	94.5	109.8	121.3	121.0
Balance	(57.0)	(31.0)	(44.0)	(54.0)	33.0	372.0	361.0	361.0
Cumulative (1)	(67.0)	(98.0)	(142.0)	(196.0)	(163.0)	209.0	570.0	931.0

1985 quarters

1. 1st quarter includes £10,000 of earlier expenses.

Notes:

1. Sales 35,000 fish weighing 6.5 lbs: 227,500 lbs. Price used lowest £1.65/lb but not less than £2/lb is expected. 227,500 lbs × £1.65 = £375,000, loss 4% say, = £360,000. Prices in excess of £2/lb are expected.
2. Fish bought in total cost £35,000 for 35,000 fish.
3. Feed. Conversion 1.6 lbs feed to 1lb fish.
   Price £500/tonne
   227.500 lbs fish use 364,000 lbs of feed or 165 tonnes costing £84,000.
4. All fixed expenses are based on known figures.
5. Further investment in nets and cages for first two years expected to be paid for by EEC grant for previous investments (grant not yet claimed).
6. Interest on cash not considered; it is assumed that business will be expanded.
7. Balance sheet not issued, as main part of capital expenditure already paid for.
8. No consideration of insurance claim.
9. Benefit from sexless fish not considered.
10. All at 1984 prices.

Financial structure

Captain Knud and Jim Jensen have developed sea cages and a method of successfully growing good quality salmon at twice the rate of other marine farms. This has been demonstrated by two years' successful production. The enterprise will be very profitable if the performance in full-scale production proves similar to the research and development results. Further expansion will be achieved by setting up more sites. In addition to these results, the company has a £400,000 insurance claim (re the bad feed), which the directors believe will be resolved in the company's favour. If the claim had already been met, funds would not be needed.

A number of investors are interested in investing in this project, which gives investors the opportunity to buy a share in a company with proven technology in a growth market. One investor has already committed his funds.

The directors of Jensen Salmonids are offering in total 35 per cent of the company for an investment of £200,000.

It is the directors' intention to launch the company on the OTC.*

Questions

1. How highly would you rate the Jensens' chances of getting £400,000 from the suppliers of the deficient feed?
2. Are their prospects of getting a patent on the cage design good? How important is that patent to the success of the venture?
3. Do you agree with Jensen's view of the market place expressed on page 123: 'both companies could sell as much as they can produce without affecting the market price'?
4. Does the fact that Coopers & Lybrand have been appointed accountants to the firm influence your view of the company's prospects?
5. What advantages do you see to the company seeking an OTC listing, and what do you believe are their prospects of so doing?
6. How do you rate their competitive advantage?
7. What part do you think that 'luck' has to play in the success or failure of a venture such as this?

---

*OTC is a form of stock exchange listing allowing the company shares to be traded.

Case 12
Phoenix Sportswear Ltd
Graham Beaver

Phoenix Sportswear Ltd is owned and managed by Stuart Williams who set up the business some 20 years ago after retiring from a career as a professional footballer. The shop is situated in Peterborough, an expanding town in Cambridgeshire, in what can be classified as prime secondary location, some 700 yards from the new Queensgate Centre which opened two years ago. Stuart, who is now 55 years old, wants to sell the business, due partly to his failing health and partly to the falling profitability of the establishment, which despite several attempts he has failed to arrest. His frustration is compounded by the fact that Olympus Sport in the new shopping mall appear to be doing very well, attracting many of his established customers, together with a new, young clientele.

Marketing and trading practices

Phoenix Sportswear kept predictable retail hours, opening every day at 9.30am and closing at 5.30pm, with the shop closing at lunch-time between 1 and 2pm. Lunch-time opening had been considered a possibility, but two part-time staff who he had employed since the business was established had to be considered and it was their wish to have a regular break to be able to go shopping and have something to eat.

The layout of the shop was neat and tidy, with sportswear acquired from most of the major suppliers. (A plan of the floor layout is given on page 128.) Stuart specialised in two main lines, football and cricket strip and equipment, with the window display reflecting this specialisation.

Once inside the shop, an impressive football display was arranged down most of the left-hand side with two full-sized football player dummies dressed in rival Liverpool and Everton strip. Behind them was a collage of press cuttings, football posters, programmes, and famous personalities from the sport. Within this

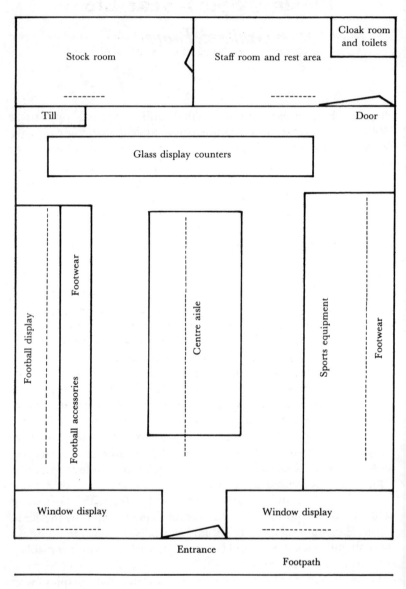

Fluorescent lighting – – – – – – – – – – – – –
Phoenix Sportswear: shop arrangement (approx area 1,000 sq ft – plan not to scale)

arrangement most of the football accessories, strip and footwear generally were displayed.

The centre aisle, which was free standing, contained primarily cricket and golf clothing and accoutrements, some tracksuits which invariably were on special offer, vests and tennis shirts.

The right-hand side of the shop was devoted primarily to other sports equipment, notably tennis rackets, golf clubs, some archery equipment, skiing accessories – and footwear generally – with the biggest ranges represented by Dunlop and Puma. The rear of the shop contained the heavy glass display cases which housed the bulk of the textiles, a small skiing collage and the till.

A door at the rear of the shop led through to a small staff room where he and his assistants could relax during the slack periods or lunch hour and make tea and coffee. Additionally, there was a stock room where Stuart kept replacement sizes for a range of sports equipment and footwear together with items that he would occasionally use as special offers to attract more custom. This mostly consisted of the more expensive football and cricket strip and golfwear which he had acquired at a very good price two years ago.

Stuart was keen to present a personal service to all his customers and both the assistants were instructed to be as helpful as possible in the selection of sportswear and equipment and to offer advice on colours, sizes and quality. He noted that sometimes there was frustration on the part of customers because many of the textile lines, eg tracksuits, tee-shirts, vests etc, were kept in the glass cases at the rear of the shop and therefore not readily available for examination. However, careful attention to customer needs usually overcame this problem area even if the service time took slightly longer sometimes. Furthermore, reduction in the incidence of pilferage was another benefit.

When a sale had been made by Stuart or his assistants this was entered into a ledger so that reordering of popular colours and sizes was made easier. Customers were invited to pay either by cash or cheque (providing a valid banker's card was produced) but no credit card facility was offered. This was a policy that concerned Stuart slightly but negotiations with Access some time ago were frustrated as they insisted on a 3 per cent payment on stock sold, and this was considered excessive. In order to contain the level of bad payment to a minimum, staff were instructed to enter the customer's address and home telephone number on the back of all cheques; after all, this was no more than sound business sense.

Buying and stocking policy

Stuart bought sportswear and clothing from most of the major suppliers, eg Adidas, Patrick, Nike, Dunlop etc, but never in any great quantities. He concentrated on lines which were compatible with the image and specialisation of the shop, notably football and cricket, and kept a full line of sizes and colours. Footwear, shoes, golf shoes etc, he mostly bought from Dunlop and Puma, considering the more recent lines, eg from Nike and HiTech to be of poorer quality. The Nike representative had approached him recently offering a very tempting arrangement if he would stock and promote the sales of their products, but as he discovered previously with representatives from Patrick and Adidas, their imposed credit limits were not sufficient and their insistence on payment he found intimidating.

Furthermore, his bank was not that sympathetic to an increase in his overdraft facility which remained fairly steady at around £12,000. If stock turnover could be enhanced to reduce this figure then perhaps some refinancing arrangements could be agreed so that more bulk buying of new stock might be effected. Apart from replacing sizes and colours in the more established lines, Stuart mostly bought the more lucrative offers from the various representatives when they called, eg discontinued lines or specially promoted lines in tennis rackets, tracksuits, skiing strip and squash equipment.

One of the many aspects of the trade that frustrated Stuart was that he could not exercise any real control over the level of margins that he required to make a good trading profit. Everybody it seemed required a discount, and if it was not forthcoming then a sale was lost. This was as applicable to new and established customers as it was to many of the football teams he supplied and the local authority business.

After several experiments buying from independent agents at prices lower than the established suppliers, eg Adidas, Nike etc, and despite assurances as to quality and delivery, he was usually left with even more stock that he could not sell in the short/medium term, and was forced ultimately to discount even these items. This reduced his margins even further and it annoyed him that he was selling goods at prices not compatible with his image of the shop.

At 55 Stuart had decided that he had had enough of the sportswear retail business. He seemed to be caught up in a vicious circle where turnover and profitability were gradually decreasing, his staff costs were rising as were his overheads generally and despite his best efforts he could not prevent the trend from continuing. He had made his mind up to sell the business and hoped that his two assistants would understand his dilemma, for to compound his frustration Stuart was a generous likeable man, who wanted to be a good employer.

Appendix 1

Summarised Profit and Loss Accounts 1980–84

Sales (£000)		*1980*		*1981*		*1982*		*1983*		*1984*
Footwear		65.7		70.2		74.7		78.3		76.5
Textiles		29.7		32.4		28.8		30.6		37.8
Equipment		10.6		11.4		11.5		12.1		12.7
Total turnover		106.0		114.0		115.0		121.0		127.0
Made up										
Credit sales		42.0		45.0		48.0		49.0		51.0
Cash sales		64.0		69.0		67.0		72.0		76.0
Gross profit margin		38.0		42.0		42.0		42.0		44.0
Overheads										
Staff wages and NI	6.0		7.0		7.0		8.0		8.0	
Director's salary and NI	8.5		8.5		8.5		8.5		9.5	
Rent and rates	8.5		8.6		8.9		9.1		9.2	
Heat and light	0.9		0.9		1.0		1.2		1.6	
Insurance	0.5		0.5		0.6		0.7		0.7	
Telephone/office expenses	0.7		0.7		0.8		0.9		1.1	
Printing and stationery	0.3		0.2		0.5		0.1		0.6	
Advertising and promotions	4.0		3.0		3.0		2.0		3.0	
Motor expenses	2.8		2.8		2.9		3.2		3.4	
Repairs and renewals	0.7		0.2		0.5		0.6		0.3	
Depreciation	2.0		2.0		2.0		2.0		2.0	
Legal and professional fees	0.3		0.3		0.4		0.6		0.7	
Bank charges and interest	0.2		0.3		0.3		0.4		0.5	
Bad debts	0.4		0.7		0.8		1.2		1.6	
Pension	0.5		0.5		0.5		0.5		0.5	
Miscellaneous	0.5		0.4		0.3		0.5		0.8	
Total overheads		36.8		36.6		38.0		39.5		43.5
Net profit margin		1.2		5.4		4.0		2.5		0.5

131

Appendix 2

Summarised Balance Sheets 1980–84

	1980	1981	1982	1983	1984
			£000		
Fixed assets					
Shop premises (leasehold) at cost	40	40	40	40	40
Motor vehicles at cost less depreciation	8	7	6	9	8
	48	47	46	49	48
Current assets					
Stock	44	47	47	44	45
Debts	17	18	18	19	20
Total assets	109	112	111	112	113
Less: current liabilities					
Trade creditors	18	20	20	23	25
Bank overdraft	12	12	13	11	12
	30	32	33	34	37
Net worth	79	80	78	78	76
Total liabilities	109	112	111	112	113

Appendix 3

Arthur Daley Holdings Ltd
Estate and Property Services Division
Business for Sale: Phoenix Sportswear Ltd, Peterborough

General

A retail shop trading in sportswear, clothing, footwear and sports accessories in a very good secondary location near to the much acclaimed Queensgate Centre and its many amenities. As a location for business Peterborough has much to offer. It is an historic cathedral city and also an expanding town, managed by the Peterborough Development Corporation. Expansion of the town started in 1970 and is already well over halfway almost to doubling the city's population by the late 1980s. The city's good location and vigorous development policy have made it the main employment and service centre of a region of 1,300 sq miles.

Background

Phoenix Sportswear Ltd, founded in 1964 by the present owner Mr Stuart Williams. Mr Williams wishes to retire from the business due to failing health.

Lease of 99 years with 79 to run, let on a fully repairing and in-suring basis with rent reviews every 10 years.

Current rental of £8 per sq ft. The basic operating costs are as follows:

Rent payable –	£8,000 per annum
	Payable quarterly in advance
Rates payable –	£1,200 per annum
	Payable in two six-monthly instalments
Heating, lighting, power –	Approx £1,600 per annum
No service charges are payable.	

Shop characteristics

The shop is of traditional brick and tile construction with a gross area of 1,000 sq ft, comprising the main shopping reception, a staff room/rest room, store room and toilets. It is single storey and in good tenantable repair, with a fine oak-panelled frontage.

Offers are invited in the region of £100,000 for this valuable retail business which will include approximately £15,000-worth of stock at present value.

Appendix 4

Sports clothing and footwear – market profile

During the 1970s a substantial increase occurred in the popularity of sport in the UK. By 1979 some 28 million people (or well over half the population) participated regularly in some form of sport-ing activity (see Table A).

Table A. Interest in sport in 1979/80

Population group	No of people	Percentage of population
Over 16 years	20.8	48.5
5–16	7.5	78.2
All	28.3	53.9

Source: Leisure Consultants' report, *The UK Sports Market*

Additionally (for England and Wales alone) around two-thirds of all days in that year spent on some form of leisure pursuit were devoted to sport (see Table B).

This proportion rises further if sports spectators are included and compares favourably with the 14 per cent of the leisure days spent on entertainment and culture (the next most important activity according to the Sports Council).

Table B. Relative popularity of sports compared to all leisure pursuits in England
and Wales 1979/80 (expressed in million days in the year)

Outdoor sports	1,110
Indoor sports	790
Total active sports	1,900
Spectator sports	150
Open air outings	350
Informal visits to buildings	170
Entertainment and culture	420
Total	2,990

Source: Sports Council

Accompanying the increasing importance of sport in the UK
has been an expanding market for sports equipment and accoutrement. The sports clothing and footwear sector of the leisure
market has grown rapidly in recent years. In 1982/83 the retail
value of this sector reached an estimated £245 million. This is
almost equally divided between clothing and footwear lines, and
is slightly smaller than the market for sports equipment. If the
closely related markets for swimwear and beachwear (estimated to
be a further £70 million) and hiking and walking clothes and
boots are included, the total size of the physical recreation
clothing and footwear industry is substantial.

In 1981–82 and 1982–83, due primarily to the recession, the
entire sports equipment market experienced stagnation, with little
or no growth, but some clothes and footwear sectors (particularly
training shoes and tracksuits) experienced a boom in trading
conditions.

Market size
An accurate assessment of the value of the sports clothing and
footwear market is extremely difficult for two main reasons:

First, there are few official statistics which relate directly to the
market, as *Business Monitor* publishes statistics only for sales by
UK manufacturers of sports footwear. These definitions – sports
clothing and footwear – are *not* used for trade statistics or market
parameters, each product line being grouped in far broader collections of apparel. Estimates of market sizes are thus based upon
information from trade sources.

Second, the size of the market depends a good deal upon definition. Estimates made by the trade vary widely for each product
group due to the difficulty of deciding exactly what constitutes
sports clothing and footwear.

There is a growing trend for sportswear to be used as fashionwear, with a strong fashion element in purchases, rather than for sport itself. Additionally, the market depends partly on what is considered a sport. For our purposes, the sports market covers soccer, athletics, tennis, cricket, angling, squash, badminton, table tennis, rugby, and a number of minor sports. Swimming is excluded (although swimming is a very large market in its own right) as are walking and hiking.

Trade opinion is that domestic production of sports apparel has, at best, stabilised in recent years, due to increasing costs and lack of price competitiveness (in common with most of the UK clothing industry). Imports have been increasing substantially in both the upper and lower sectors of the quality range. The bulk of imports are from the Far East, while western Europe and the USA supply many quality products (particularly running shoes). Many companies active in the UK market import from both the Far East and western Europe (eg Adidas). Exports are felt to have declined although some re-exporting from the UK is apparent.

Table C. The UK sports market, 1973–83 (consumer spending at current prices, £million)

Category of expenditure	1973	1979	1983
Sports equipment	145	412	445
Sports clothing	41	175	325
Sports footwear	27	119	
Total sports goods	213	706	770
Sports services	84	284	430
Total sports market	297	990	1200

Source: 1973–79 Leisure Consultants' report, *The UK Sports Market* 1983; Leisure Consultants' estimates

Spending on individual sports in 1981 is shown in Table D.

This decline is borne out by the only Department of Trade and Industry figures available: that of sports footwear (production) by UK manufacturers (Table E). In 1977, 8.26 million pairs of sports footwear were manufactured. By 1981 production had declined to 6.22 million and by 1982 (the latest figure available) the figure had fallen to 6.01 million. Peak output occurred in 1978 (at 10.05 million pairs). The value of production has declined substantially in real terms, in 1981 standing at some £29 million at manufacturer's selling price and in 1982 at £27.9 million.

Of the 1982 total, the bulk of sales in terms of value and volume were accounted for by shoes which had leather (as opposed to fabric or plastic) uppers, and were primarily soccer and rugby

Table D. Spending on individual sports in 1981 (consumer spending in £million)

Sports category	Sports goods	Sports services	Total
Athletics, indoor and outdoor	21	7	28
Badminton	19	7	26
Billiards and snooker	1	48	49
Boating, sailing, rowing etc	224	20	244
Bowls, outdoor and indoor	6	7	13
Boxing and wrestling	1	—	1
Cricket	23	3	26
Cycling	11	1	12
Darts	14	—	14
Fishing	34	10	44
Football, soccer	35	11	46
Football, rugby	6	2	8
Golf	73	54	127
Hockey (field)	3	1	4
Horse riding	14	31	45
Ice skating	1	3	4
Lawn tennis	36	9	45
Mountaineering	7	—	7
Self defence	1	—	1
Squash	19	27	46
Swimming	50	29	79
Table tennis	11	7	18
Walking and rambling	22	—	22
Winter sports	15	5	20
Other sports	61	2	63
Total	706	284	990

Source: Leisure Consultants' report

boots, golf shoes, training shoes and some racket games shoes. Unfortunately, in the absence of imports and exports statistics, production figures do not lead to direct parallels with the state of the market per se. Exports have declined and imports increased, while the market itself grew in 1977–79 and declined slightly in 1979–82. What is clear, however, is the dire state of sports shoe manufacture.

In 1979, according to Leisure Consultants (Tables C and D) the retail market for sports clothing was valued at some £17.5 million, and the sports footwear market at some £119 million. This total of £294 million had risen to around £325 million in 1981 and £351 million in 1982–83. Since 1973, therefore, a rise of approximately 430 per cent has taken place, which is substantially above the rate of retail price inflation. Growth in the market has accompanied increasing sports participation (cf the record applications received for competing in the London Marathon).

By way of comparison, Leisure Consultants estimate the

Table E. Sales of footwear by UK manufacturers 1978–81 (million pairs; £million at manufacturer's selling price)

	1977		1978		1979		1980		1981	
	Volume	*Value*	*Volume*	*Value*	*Volume*	*Value*	*Volume*	*Value*	*Volume*	*Value*
Footwear with uppers wholly or mainly of leather	5.35	21.00	5.51	23.51	4.55	23.26	3.76	20.97	3.84	21.33
Footwear with uppers wholly or mainly of woven or knitted material	1.42	1.75	3.18	4.49	1.47	2.39	0.74	1.58	1.15	2.34
Footwear with uppers mainly of other materials (eg poromeric, other plastic, or other synthetic material)	1.49	4.10	1.36	4.08	0.92	3.36	1.38	5.58	1.23	5.56
	8.26	26.85	10.05	32.08	6.94	29.31	5.88	28.13	6.22	29.13

Source: *Business Monitor*

market for sports equipment in 1979, 1981 and 1982 to have been £412 million, £445 million and £471 million respectively. The estimates for the clothing and footwear markets include swimwear and hiking/walking apparel.

In 1982–83 the value of the market as defined was estimated at between £220 and £230 million (see Table F) which compares with estimates for the total UK leisurewear market of over £3,000 million. Of the sports apparel market some £110 million relates to footwear, and slightly more – £115 to £120 million – to clothing.

The largest single sports apparel market is soccer. In 1982–83, approximately £33 million was spent on strip and boots and such items as tracksuits and training shoes for soccer players.

Athletics (including jogging) is the second largest individual sports market, valued at some £27 million. Third is tennis (£23 million), followed by cricket and angling (£21 million and £20 million respectively). The largest single clothing market is estimated to be that of cricket (£17 million).

Table F. The sports clothing and footwear markets by sport, 1982–83 (£million at retail selling price)

	Footwear market	Clothing market	Total
Soccer	20	13	33
Athletics and jogging	17	10	27
Tennis	10	13	23
Cricket	4	17	21
Angling	6	14	20
Golf	8	10	18
Squash	8	8	16
Badminton	4	8	12
Table tennis	9	—	9
Rugby	4	4	8
Others*	18	18	36
Total	108	115	223

*Chiefly riding, skiing, boxing, wrestling and judo

Source: Industry estimates.

When considering the market by product lines rather than by sports, between 20 and 25 per cent of the total is accounted for by training shoes – the largest single group. Tracksuits are second, with sales of over £35 million. Both these lines are sold to devotees of a very wide range of both indoor and outdoor sports, and to many who view such items as quasi-fashionable, or just plain comfortable!

The third most significant product line is so called 'white clothing' which comprises clothing for lawn tennis and other racket games, as well as athletics vests and shorts. For 1982–83 this sector was valued at between £25 and £30 million. Canvas shoes, commonly known as plimsolls, pumps or sneakers, also represent a significant market, worth some £15 million to £20 million.

Training and running shoes

In 1982–83 the sports market for training shoes was worth approximately £58 million, although total sales of these items to all consumers for use as casual wear were substantially greater.

Of the total market, some two-thirds by volume are of the bottom range 'black' variety (Table H), around one-fifth of the rapidly growing synthetic fibre material type, and 4–6 per cent of the white leather upper type. The remaining 8–10 per cent of the market is accounted for by running shoes for serious track runners, marathon runners and joggers. This sector has been growing rapidly with the well publicised London and other marathons each year, and the growth of serious jogging generally.

Table G. The sports clothing and footwear markets by product sector, 1982–83 (£million at retail selling price)

Training shoes	50
Canvas shoes	15–20
Boots (soccer/rugby etc)	12–15
Golfing shoes and clothing	18
Tracksuits	35–40
'White clothing'	25–30
Cricket clothing	17
Soccer, hockey, and rugby strip	15
Other*	30–32
Total	220–230

*Mainly angling clothing, riding boots and skiing clothing

Source: Industry estimates.

Table H. Running and training shoe sports market 1982–83

	% of Volume
Black shoes	66
Leather uppers (white)	4–6
Nylon	18–20
Serious runners' shoes	8–10

Source: Trade estimates

All the major footwear companies are represented in this growing, fast-moving and relatively lucrative market. In the 'black' shoe sector, Adidas is the leader with 16–21 per cent of the market by volume, followed by Nike, Patrick, Dunlop, Gola, Puma, Mitre and Le Coq Sportif, not necessarily in that order, each with some 4–12 per cent.

The above-mentioned companies are also active in the nylon and white leather segments of the business, with Adidas the overall leader.

The specialist running-shoe market, while small in volume terms, is appreciable in value terms, and is satisfied largely by imports from the USA, West Germany, and to a lesser extent Japan. Nike is the clear leader, with around one-third of sales, followed by New Balance and then Adidas (Table I).

Table I. Brand shares in the serious running shoe market (1982-83)

	% of Volume
Nike	34
New Balance	26
Adidas	12
Reebok	10
Inter	6
Pony	5
Kashu	5
Saucony	2
Total	100

Source: Trade estimates

Tracksuits

The tracksuit market, valued in 1982–83 at £35 to £40 million (substantially more if one includes those used for casual or fashion leisure wear) has received a great boost recently with the increase in jogging and marathon running.

It is estimated that between 0.8 and 1.4 million jogging suits are now sold annually, which could represent a third to a half of all sales of tracksuits to the sports sector. In addition to runners, purchasers include field games players and their clubs (which commonly buy several tracksuits for team substitutes).

Adidas and Atlas are estimated leaders in this market, each with about 20 per cent followed by Le Coq Sportif with around 10 per cent and a large number of other companies which have smaller shares.

A possible new product line in this sector could be tracksuit tops and bottoms sold separately, ie not co-ordinated. It is thought that this will receive the approval of many retailers and suppliers alike.

White clothing

In 1982–83 the sports market for 'white' clothing was worth approximately £25 million to £30 million and is one of the most image-conscious product ranges in the sports accoutrement market.

Quite apart from the growing demand for non-sport leisure-wear, actual playing wearers of 'white' shirts and shorts, skirts and dresses, are fashion conscious, and seek the latest trend (blue and white mixes being popular in 1982, for example). The fashion element is particularly strong in the women's clothing sector. However, the bulk of the market (particularly in the schools sector) remains functional (and white) although all the major suppliers cater for the fashion end of the market. Slazenger is the market leader in the 'white' sector of sports clothing sales, followed by Fred Perry and Dunlop (under Litesome label).

The fashion sector is estimated to be worth around 10 per cent of total sales, and is growing fast, with significant suppliers being the continental stylists such as Techini, Fila and Lacoste.

Table J. Brand shares in the white sports clothing market 1982–83

	% of Value
Slazenger	25
Fred Perry	20
Dunlop	20
Fashion companies (Technin, Lacoste etc)	8–10
Ascot	8–10
Others	15–18
Total	100

Source: Industry estimates

Football clothing and footwear

In 1982–83, the value of the market for soccer, rugby and hockey strip was some £15 million, and that of the boots market £12 to £15 million. Of these sports, soccer is by far the most important in terms of participation and sales.

Overall the market has declined in real terms in recent years with the effects of the recession and static participation numbers. A further effect of the recession has been the rapid decline in demand for individualised (more costly) team strip. There is a growing trend for teams to accept more standardised, mass-produced strip.

Table K. Brand shares of the soccer textile market 1982–83

	% of Value
Umbro	15
Bukta	15
Litesome	10
Star	10
Coffer	10
Others	40
Total	100

Source: Trade estimates

Table L. Brand shares of the rugby textile market 1982–83

	% of Value
Umbro	20
Bukta	20
Halbro	15
Europa	15
Others	30
Total	100

Source: Trade estimates

Table M. Brand shares of the soccer boot market 1982–83

	% of Value
Adidas	15–20
Patrick	15–20
Puma	8–10
Mitre	8–10
Gola	4–5
Dunlop	4–5
Others	35–40

Source: Trade estimates

Table N. Brand shares of the rugby boot market 1982–83

	% of Value
Adidas	20
Patrick	20
Winit	20
Mitre	15
Others	25
Total	100

Source: Trade estimates

Market leaders in both the soccer and rugby boot markets are Adidas and Patrick, holding approximately one-fifth each. Adidas has declined in importance in recent years, losing ground to several competitors. Patrick, on the other hand, has gained in

strength, partly due to the signing of Kevin Keegan for both promotion and endorsement. If the substantial schools market is
included, the share held by Adidas of the soccer boot market
increases to 25 per cent. A substantial portion of the bottom end
of the boot market is held by multiples' own brands.

Golf shoes and clothing

For 1982–83 the golf clothing and footwear market was valued at
approximately £18 million, of which clothing accounts for about
60 per cent. In the clothing sector, Slazenger is market leader,
with around 40–50 per cent of all sales. Muncingwear of the USA
and the British Lyle and Scott are notable, as is Pringle. Approximately 25 per cent of the market is in the hands of a number of
small suppliers.

Dunlop dominates the golf shoe market, with some 40–50 per
cent; Stylo is second (approximately 20 per cent) while an
estimated 35–40 per cent is accounted for by smaller suppliers.

Canvas shoes

The market for canvas shoes, pumps, plimsolls or sneakers is
worth between £15 and £20 million, and has remained relatively
healthy. This is primarily due to the fact that the product serves
a range of sports (and is accommodated within the wider leisurewear market). Dunlop is the clear market leader, with its very
successful Green Flash brand. This is the largest selling sports
shoe brand in the UK and holds an estimated 70 per cent of the
total market.

Cricket clothing

For 1982–83 the retail value of cricket clothing sales was
estimated at £17 million, and has declined in real terms in recent
years due to the falling popularity of the sport. Sweaters retail at
around £12–£20, on average, although joure (pure) wool
sweaters are more expensive, while cricket flannels cost around
£15–£25. Major suppliers to the cricket accoutrement market are
Duncan Fearnley, Grey Nicholls and Slazenger.

Sports clothing and footwear markets: anticipated future developments

There are two main aspects in the future of sport and the
associated markets for clothing and footwear in this country. The
first is the nature of sports facility provision, and the second the

nature of the recession with its impact upon both discretionary spending and on the long-term profitability and survival of suppliers and retailers to the market.

The extent of provision of sports facilities provides the ultimate brake on the development of sporting activity in the UK, which is still lamentably under-provisioned. A severe bottleneck exists for some sports, such as golf or athletics, with constraints imposed by the availability of suitable facilities. The waiting time experienced on public tennis courts in summer in London and most other major cities amply illustrates the nature of the problem.

The levels of investment required to build new gymnasia, sports centres, athletics tracks or golf facilities are extremely high, and are suffering at the present time. In the past, capital investment in sports and leisure facilities has been undertaken primarily by local authorities, schools and further education establishments. This is now subject to severe curtailment as spending cuts make their impact felt, and this creates uncertainty for the foreseeable future.

During the 1970s the Sports Council was instrumental in the promotion of the image of sport. Between 1973 and 1977 alone, provision for indoor dry sports increased by 300 per cent, and that for swimming pools by 70 per cent. However, a slowdown in the level of new construction has occurred since 1979. In its June 1982 report 'Sport in the community: the next ten years', the Sports Council outlined a three-pronged strategy for the future:

- First, to promote participation: by 1993 the Council hopes to have encouraged 1.8 million more people to play sport outdoors and 2.8 million indoors (despite falling numbers of children of school age).
- Second, to provide more facilities.
- Third, to encourage excellence in sport. Overall this strategy envisages an expenditure of some £215 million in 1983–88 of which £106 million would be invested in sports facilities. However, this appears to be over-optimistic in view of other legitimate claims on increasingly scarce resources.

While the demand for sport will depend ultimately on the provision of new facilities and on more intensive utilisation of existing capacity, sporting activity is almost certain to continue its growth. In 1979 a prediction was made that the growth in participants in sport between 1973 and 1991 would amount to some 21 per cent, of which badminton and squash would record some 59 per cent. Much of this growth has already occurred between 1973 and

1982, and further expansion is more likely to be steady but limited and very gradual.

The effects of all this upon the markets for sports clothing and footwear should be for a gradual increase in market size overall, despite the stagnation in real terms experienced in many lines since 1979. However, some product lines will grow while others will decline. The fastest moving sectors should remain items which are applicable to a range of sports, such as training shoes and tracksuits, products which are also in great demand in the amorphous leisurewear market. It is expected that new designs, colours and styles for these products will emerge quickly over the next two or three years. Soccer and rugby strip, on the other hand, could well decline, as may cricket clothing.

The overall leisurewear market, of which sports accoutrement is but a small sector, is expected to maintain an expansionary trend and it is anticipated that most suppliers of sports clothing and footwear will seek to continue their penetration into this lucrative market.

Consumers of sports clothing and footwear

There are considerable differences in consumer buying profiles and habits within this market, and in the levels of expenditure by individual sports players on their sporting activities.

A range of purchasing patterns exists and consumers vary from the casual amateur, who will make sports shirts and shoes last several years, to the dedicated professional who will continually buy replacement items. Furthermore, the apparel each purchases will differ greatly in quality and thus in price. Additionally, the economic climate generally influences the expenditure by individuals and clubs alike. When, as now, there is a recession, discretionary income falls and either purchases of sports accoutrement is deferred, or cheaper items are bought.

However, while clothing and footwear can be expensive, they are often only part of the story. A typical, enthusiastic squash player, for instance, can be expected to pay around 10–15 per cent of his total annual outlay on his sport on clothing or footwear, although sports such as marathon running can be garment intensive.

According to Leisure Consultants, in 1979 the popularity of sports varied from 5.6 million adult devotees (12.8 million total) for swimming to 100,000 enthusiasts for boxing. In that year alone some 28.3 million people in the UK participated regularly in some form of sport or recreational exercises. For the same year the Sports Council estimated that nearly 40 per cent of the national population participated regularly in outdoor sports. By any account, sport is extremely popular.

Differences exist in the consumer profiles of individual sports by region of the country, by age, sex and socio-economic group. According to the Sports Council, in 1982 the proportion of the population participating in sporting activity varied from 27 per cent in Wales to 41 per cent in the south and north of England for outdoor sport, and from 14 per cent in the south to 24 per cent in the West Midlands and East Anglia for indoor sport. Individual sports also show regional variations in popularity. Squash, for instance, is more popular in the south-east than in other areas of the UK. More is spent on sports clothing and footwear generally per head in the south-east than elsewhere.

One major feature of the 1970s was an increase in the number of women participating in sport, although there is still a trend for many of them gradually to give up their interest after marriage.

Expenditure on squash for a typical player 1982–83

	£
Membership	50–60
Playing fees	100–200
Clothing/Footwear	30
Racket	15–30
Balls	3–5
Total	200–300

Source: Squash Rackets Association

Running costs per year of a serious marathon runner 1982–83

	£
Shoes (2 pairs)	63.90
Tracksuit	18.00
Shorts (2 pairs)	11.00
Vests/tee-shirt	12.00
Socks (6 pairs)	12.00
Winter underwear	13.00
Gloves	2.00
Waterproof top	6.00
Woolly hat	2.00
Casio watch	19.95
Books	11.50
Magazines	15.00
Shoe inserts	11.99
Physiotherapy	21.00
Ointments/Plasters	10.00
Marathon entries	12.00
Total	214.34

Source: *Financial Times*, 6.7.82

Questions

For personal reasons an acquaintance of yours, Peter Simpson, has decided to take voluntary redundancy from his present employment and has set up as a retailer of sportswear and equipment, a trade in which he has always been interested. The sale of his house has raised £25,000 net of expenses and this, together with his savings over the years, gives him some £45,000. He also owns a one-year-old Volvo estate car.

After a long search of premises in the east of Britain, and discussions with many estate agents, Peter learns that Phoenix Sportswear Ltd is for sale and that the owner, Stuart Williams, is willing to consider a reasonable offer, providing that a quick sale can be realised.

After an initial meeting with Stuart Williams it is obvious that the shop, which enjoys a fairly good location, is not doing nearly so well as it could.

You have been asked by Peter Simpson, who has a good technical knowledge of the products he wants to sell but no real knowledge of establishing and managing a small business, for advice and guidance on how to run this shop successfully.

Details of the location, trading, buying and staffing practices of the business are given in the case history, together with a plan showing the current layout of the shop. A market profile of the sports clothing and footwear industries is provided in Appendix 4. In assisting Peter Simpson, prepare a report outlining your recommendations for improving profitability of the business, which should contain the following:

1. *Business objectives*
   What objectives do you recommend for the short, medium and long term? Attempt to construct realistic, consistent and measurable objectives.
2. *Marketing and trading policy*
   Analyse the current policy being pursued by Stuart Williams. What improvements and changes would you recommend? Advise Peter how he should assess customer needs, promote his products and respond to competitive pressures.
3. *Buying/stocking policy*
   Who should Peter buy from? What product items and lines should he stock and what should he expect from his suppliers? What changes would you recommend that he undertakes in order to introduce more precision and organisation in buying?

147

4. *Premises and staffing*

   What changes would you recommend Peter to undertake to improve the appearance and image of the shop? How many staff should he employ and what skills should they have? Would you advise Peter to employ the existing staff at Phoenix Sportswear Ltd – if so on what terms?

5. *Financial policy*

   Advise Peter how best to raise the necessary money to buy the business, maintain accounts, deal with cash flow and outstanding debtors, set selling prices, maintain control over margins etc.

6. *General comments*

   What other steps should Peter take to improve the performance of this business?

Case 13

Medsoft A

Colin Barrow

Medsoft is a new and very small high-tech venture situated in a town half way along the much publicised Silicon Valley, off the M4 motorway. They are in the business of selling dedicated microcomputer systems to hospital consultants. Their products allow consultants and clinicians to diagnose symptoms and monitor treatment results in a way that would not be possible without immediate access to a very powerful computer and a series of tailor-made programs.

The business concept grew in 1980 out of a chance meeting at a computer exhibition between Richard Kensall, then a successful department store owner and slightly disillusioned computer dealer, and an up-and-coming young doctor with a love of computers. The doctor's problem was that he had too large a volume of patient data to classify and analyse.

Although he knew that a computer could solve that problem, he could not access the hospital mainframe at convenient times. Kensall lent him a Sirius microcomputer from his stock and the doctor developed a program to handle his data.

Once the system was up and running, a stream of enquiries came in from other consultants in the hospital and eventually Kensall began to realise that he had stumbled across a significant market opportunity.

The amount of patient-related activity 'processed' by the National Health Service was enormous. The NHS cater for 35 million patient attendances and 5 million in-patients per annum. Most of this activity is channelled through 3,000 hospitals for which 16,000 consultants and a further 30,000 hospital doctors are responsible. The consultant/patient workload is spread across some 20 disciplines, the most active being general surgery, radiology, obstetrics, anaesthesia, and general medicine. A consultant and his department may be responsible for up to 5,000 in-patients and 20,000 out-patients each year. For each patient a record must be generated containing all details concerning the patient, his or her clinical history and indications, clinical test results, diagnoses, operations, complications and follow-up care. In 1980 almost all patient records were generated and maintained manually.

This meant that the records were prone to a high error rate; they were wasteful of administrative and skilled staff time; review and amendment of records was tedious; necessary 'housekeeping' functions (drug, instrument and time usage) were cumbersome to calculate manually; analysis across patient records to determine historical performance and outcome of the clinical team and to carry out clinical research investigations was virtually impossible.

Kensall believed that if he was to exploit this opportunity successfully he would need to set up a new business outside his department store. Although he was the majority stockholder his board were rather old-fashioned and did not understand this 'new-fangled' field of computers. They felt they should stick to what they knew best: buying for £1, selling for £2 and living well off a 10 per cent margin.

So, under the disguise of extending the store's computer department, Kensall, using the store's substantial and under-used overdraft facilities (about £¼ million) began to create Medsoft. He brought in Ivor Freedman, the former marketing director of a well-respected medical company and an old family friend, to help him get the business going. Freedman was attracted by the offer of 25 per cent of the share capital and, although his salary was modest, he had every hope of becoming very wealthy indeed when the company became successful.

Throughout the remaining months of 1980 and the early months of 1981, Freedman built up a small team of contract technical staff to develop a range of programs to run on the Sirius I microcomputer, then UK market leader. His logic was that without a product range they would not have a broad enough base upon which to build a substantial business supporting the sales and marketing organisation that would be needed. He did not want a one-product company, but recognised that the pace of competition in the software field was hotting up. Unless he could rapidly penetrate national (and international) markets, they could be knocked out before they were established.

Medsoft products had no direct competitors. At present, patient treatment data were either ignored, processed inconveniently on mainframes, or being done slowly and painfully on 'Sinclairs' with each consultant doing his own thing: the 're-inventing the wheel' syndrome. Freedman believed the medical equipment market was big enough to let in a new entrant without much upheaval, but only if they could maintain an element of surprise (a note on this market is included on page 157).

By the middle of 1981 four programs were at varying stages of completion and prototypes had been 'approved' by influential consultants who were all well-respected in their fields. Freedman felt that the time was now ripe to put a sales force in position. Product development had cost more and taken longer than planned so the selling operation would, by necessity rather than choice, be a 'budget operation'. In addition, money had only been going one way to date – out. Kensall's fellow shareholders were beginning to become alarmed at the size of the overdraft – and its constant upward movement. Sales were urgently required. The fragmented nature of hospital buying meant that decision-making power resided in over a dozen regional health authorities up and down the country. This called for a national sales effort from the start if any volume of orders was to be achieved and would-be competitors kept at bay.

Freedman decided to launch in America at the same time, as this market was six times the size of the UK's and more responsive to accepting high-tech products. As he was operating virtually as a one-man band he employed a freelance recruitment consultant to advertise for, and to short-list, his sales force.

He decided to go for 'commission only' people, offering the opportunity to earn in excess of £20,000 per annum. As a further inducement for them to make as many calls as possible he decided to offer a 'bounty' of £20 per demonstration: that is, every time a salesman managed to persuade a consultant to see and try out the computer.

Freedman was in the USA when the short-list of salesmen was prepared and Kensall decided to carry out the interviews himself. He had wide experience of selecting sales staff for the store and felt quite at ease with the task.

At the end of the day five sales people were selected, based in Aberdeen, Manchester, Birmingham, London and Cardiff. They were invited to attend a two-day product knowledge course later that month (May 1981) when Freedman and the programmers would explain the product and markets to them.

Freedman returned from the USA in early May having just appointed a young, enthusiastic company like his own to act as North American agent. Their territory stretched from Canada to Mexico. Freedman was much impressed by their willingness to take a stock order of £20,000-worth of programs as soon as they were ready. The only slight complication was that, while in the

UK Sirius was the market leader in the microcomputer market, in the USA it was a non-runner. The existing Medsoft programs would have to be rewritten for the IBM PC.

By the end of May the UK sales force had had their two-day induction programme and were now operational in the field.

At present the company could only afford to provide three computers for the five sales people. The Aberdeen and Cardiff salesmen had one each as they were out on a limb and the rest shared the remaining one.

One evening early in June 1981 Freedman sat at his desk trying to work out the likely profit projections for the forthcoming 12 months. To date they had spent over £100,000 just to get the products to this stage of development. Development costs for the three programs were running at £10,000 per month and looked like continuing to do so for a long time yet. Not only had they to bring the existing products up to scratch, they had to convert them for use on the IBM PC and extend the range of new products to keep the competition at bay.

Although the sales force was a commission only expense, they still cost £3,000 per annum each in expenses and 'bounty' payments. Freedman felt that, with over 3,000 consultants per salesman, it would be very poor if they could not sell one per month per salesman. Each sale would generate £10,000 revenue. Against that they would have to pay the computer manufacturers £3,000 for each machine and £500 per annum for a maintenance contract. The salesman himself would earn 15 per cent commission. The American operation could double those sales easily but the margins would not be so good. Every unit sold there would contribute around £2,500 to the UK overheads. He was uncertain whether they would break even before they broke the bank, but the Korner Report seemed to suggest that the current was turning in their favour (see Appendix 2).

Appendix 1

Management and organisation

Ivor Freedman – Managing director (42). BSc (upper second) in biochemistry from London University. Worked for Unilever (1965–68) as a product manager before joining Wainwright Medical as group product manager, hospital division. Remained until 1979 rising to marketing director. Pipped at the post for the divisional managing director's job so decided to accept redundancy and a part-time lecturing job at a business school.

Richard Kensall – Chairman (36). MA Oxford, PPE. Inherited the business from his father who was the second generation to run the family department store. Started in the packing department, took over on his father's death in 1977. Has never worked anywhere else. In 1977 he introduced a computer department into his store.

Contract technical staff
Andrew Brown – Physics graduate from St Andrews. Worked for Thorn-EMI in medical electronics and computing until 1976. Moved to Digital Equipment, writing both assembly, computer and interface programs. Became a freelance consultant in 1979.

Andrew Brown supervises two young graduates, Sally Jones (26) and Tony Johnstone (27) who both have extensive computer programming experience, but little business or medical knowledge.

Appendix 2

The Korner Report

The first report to the Secretary of State Steering Group on Health Services Information (Chairman: Mrs E Korner) was published in 1981. Its aim was essentially to recommend the characteristics (standards) and the minimum level of data to be kept within various areas of hospital and community health care activity in order to provide the local, district and DHSS management with the relevant, timely and 'integratable' information required to make the best decisions concerning the use of scarce resources. The standardisation of data (data 'sets'), and their subsequent collation, monitoring and reporting, is most efficiently managed with the aid of computers, and it is with this in mind that the Report was written.

   At the beginning of the Report reference is made (i) 'to the crucial role of clinicians in the management of resources and, *a fortiori*, to the need for information to enable them to fulfil it'.

   The introduction goes on to say that the aim of the recommendations is not to cut or contain the cost of information services within the NHS, but to provide a higher quality of information to assist management. The Report recognises that historically the

NHS has received poor value for money in its investment in information services. It states that implementation of its recommendations should give rise to benefits to patient services through better management services, even though inevitable initial and subsequent running costs must be incurred to achieve these benefits.

While the Report covers many areas of activity, a common theme runs throughout:

1. To know what resources/facilities are available (eg clinics, theatres, capital equipment, people).

2. To measure the activity processed by these resources (eg number of patient attendances; GP referrals; diagnostic tests) and who initiated the workload (by clinician; firm; GP; department).

3. To measure the rate at which work is carried out (eg length of waiting lists; time elapsed between the admission decision and admission date; rate of bed occupancy) and what work was *not* carried out (eg patients on waiting list at end of period; appointments made but not kept).

4. To use various parameters (eg specialty; admission type; type of patient) to establish correlations with performance measurements (eg non-attendance; the use of special (eg diagnostic) resources).

The use of microcomputer-based Patient Record and Analysis (PRA) systems

(a) Improving productivity
The development by Medsoft Ltd of its PRA systems was based on several aims:

(i) To provide the minimum data set concerning both people (eg patient, GP, consultant) and other resources (drugs, instruments, time) involved in the admissions, consultant episode and discharge processes.

(ii) To provide the clinical content required by the discipline for the comprehensive recording of clinical data.

(iii) To provide data review and analysis facilities to access the information required to aid better clinical and resource management decisions.

In providing the above within the structure of the Medsoft PRA programs, the clinician/department is able to generate the following type of information accurately and almost instantaneously.

Number of patients/attendances in any given period by:
- Sex/age
- Point of referral
- Type of procedure/procedural workload
- Resource utilisation

Level of patient demand (met and unmet) by:
- Number/type of patient(s)/admissions
- Number of patient referrals by source
- Time between patient referral, date on waiting list, date of admission
- Number on waiting list, or for whom appointment made, but not seen in period

Resources and time used by:
- Type/number of patients
- Workload initiator
- Type of procedure

Workload analysis by consultant/firm by:
- Resources/time
- Diagnosis, operations/procedures, complications
- Type and number of patients/attendances
- Number of non-attendances and cause

Medsoft systems therefore provide information to facilitate better management decisions in the following ways:

Operational management

(a) Patient management

1. What is the level of patient demand (by type of patient; point of referral)? Is this increasing/decreasing and why? How is the workload spread (by consultant; type of procedure)? Can the workload be more effectively rescheduled? Do the trends justify greater manpower or other resources?

2. What is the level of unmet demand and why (by patient type; consultant; type of procedure; source of referral; cancellations/DNAs)? Can unmet demand be reduced (by preemption; better scheduling; spread of workload; follow up)? Can more resources be justified?

3. What is the resource level and where (by instrument; diagnostic service; procedure; time measurement)? Who/what are the main users of a resource? Can a reduction in resource

utilisation be achieved? Can a greater resource allocation be justified?

(b) Paper administration

1. What secretarial/clerical time is spent on what tasks?

2. To what extent will this workload be reduced by the report/letter generating and record retrieval facilities of the automated PRA system?

3. For which additional tasks can the free time be used, and what would this have represented as additional secretarial/clerical costs?

4. To what extent is there an opportunity to share freed secretarial/clerical time with other users, and thus reduce overall running costs?

5. To what extent is the current administration system enhanced if no/little clerical support is available?

(c) Clinical management

1. To what extent might the data input discipline of an automated PRA system reduce record and associated errors?

2. What is the breakdown of patients (by type/history) by indications, diagnoses, operations/procedures, complications etc?

3. What are the causes of the results of the above analyses, what trends exist, and what clinical/surgical responses are appropriate?

4. Do the analyses suggest the need for re-allocating clinical or surgical resources?

5. To what extent do the analyses identify opportunities for further research, or material for papers or publications?

From the above it is clear that Medsoft Patient Record and Analysis systems can provide much valuable information as an aid to better management decisions concerning both resource utilisation and clinical/surgical performance.

The key to the effective use of this powerful information base is the structuring of a well considered and planned identification of the relevant management questions to be asked prior to adoption of the system.

Given the above, purchase of a Medsoft system for approximately £10,000 can be justified in terms of increased operational productivity (greater patient throughput; better use of administrative time; control over resource utilisation) and increased clinical awareness and thus enhanced patient care.

Below are two models that a department could use as the basis for specifically quantifying the productivity benefits of purchasing a Medsoft system, irrespective of clinical considerations.

Examples: Productivity pay-back on MICROMED PRA system

Department: 3 hospital doctors (various grades), 1 nurse, and 1 secretary dealing with 2,000 day-care patients per annum.

(a) *Running Costs pa*

	£
5 staff; salaries	65,000
Direct resource utilisation (materials and services)	20,000
Overheads (space and utilities)	15,000
Total Costs	100,000

(b) Cost of MICROMED system (hardware and software): £10,000.

Model 1

Patient booking and workload rescheduling, and improved paper administration allows *increased patient throughput of four patients per week*

> = 200 patients per annum = 10% increase in productivity
> = £10,000
> = *12 month pay-back*

Model 2

	£
• 30% increase in secretarial/clerical efficiency at £5,000 pa (ie greater work throughput)	1,800
• 12½% reduction in resource utilisation (eg fewer diagnostic tests)	4,375
• 5% increase in patient throughput (+ 2 patients per week)	5,000
	11,175

> = Total of 11% overall improvement in productivity
> = *12 month pay-back* (less than)

Appendix 3

The UK medical equipment market 1981

1. Industry structure*

The medical equipment industry is extremely diverse. Its products range, in cost and complexity, from disposable syringes to

*Reprinted by kind permission of Key Note Publications Ltd, 28-42 Banner Street, London EC1Y 8QE.

whole body scanners, and includes such varied equipment as cardiac monitors, replacement hip joints and incubators for premature babies. The high-technology end of the market includes computerised X-ray scanning systems as well as conventional X-ray apparatus, ultrasound equipment and sophisticated radiotherapy machines. At the other end of the market there are products such as disposable syringes, sutures and catheters which are used in hospitals in vast numbers every day.

By far the largest sector of the medical equipment industry in terms of numbers of manufacturers and total sales is the surgical instrument and appliance sector, which includes manufacturers of surgical instruments, sterilising equipment and operating theatre furniture, as well as manufacturers of disposable equipment.

A large sector of the medical equipment industry is electronics based. There are many different applications of electronics to medicine; for instance, electromedical equipment used to measure, monitor and record clinical functions such as heart rate and respiration. Equipment such as diathermy equipment is used for therapeutic purposes and there is a wide range of electronic instruments in use, for example, in pathology laboratories for analysing samples of blood, tissue and so on taken from patients. Nucleonic equipment such as gamma cameras are used to measure the uptake of radioactive isotopes by different parts of the body, to assist the diagnosis and treatment of various diseases.

Other sectors of the industry include medical engineering manufacturing equipment such as replacement heart valves, pacemakers and dialysis machines, as well as resuscitation, ventilation and anaesthetic equipment. There are also a number of firms manufacturing dental and optical equipment and orthopaedic appliances which are usually considered part of the medical equipment industry.

With such a wide range of products it is not easy to characterise the medical equipment industry. In the surgical instrument and appliance sector there are a large number of firms which tend to specialise in one particular type of product. For instance, Travenol produces transfusion kits and similar equipment, Eschmann manufactures surgical instruments, and OEC Europe Ltd (formerly Zimmer Orthopaedic) manufactures orthopaedic appliances. Many firms are part of larger companies some of which are foreign, usually American owned. Travenol and Abbott Laboratories are both American owned while Thomas Tilling is the parent company for five surgical equipment companies including Vessa and Dent & Hellyer. The number of firms in this sector has shown a steady decline over the past few years and employment has dropped as smaller firms have found it difficult to compete in the current economic climate. The number of UK manufacturers covered by the *Business Monitor* for the surgical instrument and appliance sector and the number of employees are shown in Table A.

Table A. UK manufacturers of surgical instruments and appliances

	1977	1978	1979	1980
Number of enterprises	171	152	136	94*
Employment in the industry (June Census figures in 000s)	28.3	26.9	26.9	26.1

* Coverage reduced by raising employment levels below which firms are not required to make a return.

Source: *Business Monitor PQ 353*

The electromedical equipment sector includes firms such as LKB Instruments and Technicon, who supply the medical market, and also sell equipment to other scientific and industrial users. Other manufacturers of medical equipment such as GEC, Vickers and, until recently, Thorn-EMI, are large firms with many interests other than the medical field. Foreign manufacturers have an important share of the market in some sectors. GEC Medical is the only major British owned manufacturer of X-ray equipment, other suppliers to the UK market being firms such as Siemens and Philips.

Some of the largest UK manufacturers of medical equipment in terms of sales, are shown in Table B. It should be borne in mind, however, that some companies may not be listed because they also have significant sales to other markets, or because they are subsidiaries of larger companies for which separate accounts are not available.

\ The diversity of the industry is reflected in the number of trade associations representing the different sectors. The UK Medical Equipment Industries Group seeks to represent the industry as a whole, but there are numerous specialist trade associations. Manufacturers of electromedical equipment may, for example, belong to the Electro-Medical Trade Association, or to the Medical Instruments Group of the Scientific Instrument Manufacturers Association. The trade associations representing other sectors include the British Surgical Trades Association, the Association of X-ray Equipment Manufacturers, the British Anaesthetic and Respiratory Equipment Manufacturers Association, and the Association of British Steriliser Manufacturers.

159

Table B. UK medical equipment manufacturers

		Sales £million	Products
Travenol Laboratories	11/80	40.5	Disposable medical equipment
Abbott Laboratories	11/79	24.0	Disposable medical equipment
GEC Medical Equipment Ltd	3/81	14.6	X-ray equipment
AD International Ltd	11/79	13.0	Dental equipment
Downs Surgical	3/80	14.4	Surgical instruments etc
Eschmann Bros & Walsh Ltd	6/80	10.8	Surgical instruments
OEC Europe Ltd	10/80	11.8	Orthopaedic appliances
Portex Ltd	8/80	8.8	Surgical plastics
SS White Ltd	12/80	8.1	Dental equipment
Vessa Ltd	12/80	8.0	Orthopaedic appliances
CR Baird International	11/79	5.8	Surgical goods
Howmedica (UK) Ltd	11/80	4.9	Orthopaedic implants
Medelec Ltd	12/80	4.1	Electrophysiological equipment
Davol International Ltd	12/79	3.6	Surgical goods
Dent & Hellyer	12/80	3.3	Sterile control equipment
Sonicaid Ltd	12/80	3.0	Ultrasonic equipment

Source: *ICC Financial Survey and Directory: Medical Equipment Manufacturers and Distributors*, 9th edition.

The major customer in the UK for medical equipment is the National Health Service. Sales to other customers such as private hospitals and clinics, universities and the armed services are small in comparison. Although the purchasing authorities in the NHS are individual regional and area health authorities, their funds are allocated by the government, and thus the Department of Health and Social Security (DHSS) has a considerable influence on the medical equipment market. The DHSS determines technical specifications and safety standards for medical equipment and negotiates central contracts for some equipment, notably X-ray equipment. It also has a considerable influence on purchases by health authorities of major capital equipment, for instance CT scanners and radiotherapy equipment.

The medical equipment market is, however, an international market, and exports are extremely important to UK manufacturers. British medical expertise in the building and equipping of hospitals is highly regarded overseas, and British firms have played a leading role in developing new medical technology. The British Health-Care Export Council exists to promote the sale and use of British expertise and medical equipment overseas, and it is the government's policy to encourage exports of medical equipment.

2. Market size and trends
The size of the UK market for medical equipment is determined principally by expenditure on the NHS which in 1978 was £7,800

million. Since the inception of the NHS in 1948, average annual expenditure per person has risen from just under £9 per person to £143 in 1978. Even after adjustment for inflation this represents an increase of 267 per cent or an annual average growth rate of 4.4 per cent (*Office of Health Economics Compendium of Health Statistics*, 3rd edition, 1979). In terms of the national output of goods and services, NHS expenditure rose from 3.7 per cent of GNP in 1957 to 5.5 per cent in 1978, and now stands at 6.0 per cent of GNP. However, this proportion remains lower than that of most other developed countries where typically about 7 per cent of GNP is devoted to health care.

The increase in NHS expenditure has been partly due to demographic changes and partly to an expansion of services, but pay and price rises account for the greatest increase. Since the introduction by the government of cash limits in 1977, the rate of increase in expenditure has slowed, and the present government's expenditure plans envisage an average growth rate in health care provision of between 1 per cent and 2 per cent a year.

It is not a straightforward matter to assess the proportion of NHS funds spent on medical equipment. Revenue expenditure on items such as disposables for the hospital service probably account for a substantial proportion of NHS expenditure on medical equipment but there is also considerable capital investment on larger items of equipment such as X-ray and pathology equipment. In addition there is expenditure on medical equipment for the community health services and family practitioner services, although this is very small by comparison. Almost all family practitioners' diagnostic equipment is bought by the doctors themselves, although syringes etc are supplied by the NHS. The distribution of revenue expenditure on hospital services is shown in Table C.

The private health care sector is growing rapidly. There are about 140 private hospitals in the UK with a total of around 5,500 beds, with a further 1,000 beds being added at present and plans for a further 1,000 beds. By way of comparison the average daily number of occupied general hospital beds in the NHS is over 200,000 with a further 100,000 or so psychiatric beds. It is difficult to assess what the private sector spends on medical equipment. For the most part private hospitals provide short-term, non-emergency medical and surgical care. Longer-term geriatric and psychiatric care is not available, nor are facilities for capital intensive treatments such as radiotherapy. While therefore the proportion of revenue expenditure by the private sector on

Table C. NHS revenue expenditure – hospital services in England and Wales (£million)

Patient care services	1974–75	1975–76	1976–77	1977–78	1978–79
Total	1196.5	1575.9	1817.6	2019.0	2292.8
Medical staff	176.9	244.1	279.1	298.4	336.8
Dental staff	3.7	5.7	6.6	7.4	8.6
Nursing staff	695.0	900.0	1026.1	1115.5	1256.5
Medical and surgical supplies*	152.6	200.7	244.9	301.0	353.1
Diagnostic departments	115.7	154.9	178.5	203.0	230.9
Other services	52.6	70.5	82.4	93.7	106.9
Administration and general services					
Total	874.4	1115.1	1247.1	1420.9	1572.0
Total revenue expenditure	2070.9	2691.0	3064.7	3439.9	3864.8
Medical supplies as % of total revenue expenditure	7.37	7.46	8.00	8.75	9.14

*Including pharmaceuticals

Source: NHS Summarised Accounts

medical equipment such as disposable equipment and electro-medical instruments is likely to be higher than that in the NHS, the scope for sales of very expensive high-technology equipment to the private sector is very limited.

Sales by UK medical equipment manufacturers are shown in Table D. In 1980, total sales were £475 million and sales by the surgical instrument and appliance sector accounted for £410 million or 86 per cent of this total. This clearly demonstrates that the bulk of expenditure on medical equipment is not on high-technology equipment but on items such as surgical instruments

Table D: +Sales by UK medical equipment manufacturers (£million)

	1977	1978	1979	1980	1st half 1981
Surgical instruments and appliances					
Sales	262.9	315.4	360.5	410.6	124.5
Of which export sales	110.8	126.0	148.8	164.1	..
Export sales as % of sales	42.1	39.9	41.3	40.0	..
Electromedical apparatus					
Sales	34.6	37.5	46.7	43.8	22.7
Of which export sales	17.2	16.2	24.4	24.2	13.5
Export sales as % of sales	49.7	43.2	52.2	55.3	59.5
Medical X-ray apparatus					
Sales	72.8	67.1	23.0*	20.6	10.2
Of which export sales	50.9	55.2	..	14.6	3.7
Export sales as % of sales	69.9	82.3	..	70.9	36.3

*Change in classification
+ UK and export sales
.. Not available

Source: *Business Monitor*

and disposables, which are relatively simple and inexpensive but which are used in very large numbers.

The export market is extremely important to UK medical equipment manufacturers. Many firms export a high percentage of their total sales, with Medelec, for instance, exporting 84 per cent of their sales last year. Although the figures, especially those for X-ray equipment, must be treated with some caution because of the difficulties of classifying medical equipment, it is clear that the surgical instrument sector has maintained its export sales at about 40 per cent of total sales while the proportion of export sales of electromedical apparatus has grown. The bulk of sales by UK medical X-ray equipment manufacturers are export sales though changes in classification make it difficult to assess any trends.

The main destinations for UK export sales are other EEC countries and the USA, particularly for electromedical and X-ray apparatus. Exports of medical equipment to the Middle East and Japan have also become significant in recent years. The EEC and the USA are the main source of the substantial imports of medical equipment to this country. Table E gives an indication of the levels of imports and exports but the figures should be treated with some caution. The classifications differ from those in Table D so that direct comparison between the tables is not advisable.

Table E. UK medical equipment and exports (£million)

	1977	1978	1979	1980
Surgical instruments and appliances				
Imports	47.4	58.0	69.9	78.1
Of which from EEC	23.0	30.7	39.4	43.5
Exports	85.5	96.8	113.9	132.8
Of which to EEC	27.1	32.2	42.2	47.2
Electromedical apparatus				
Imports	9.2	15.3	17.1	17.3
Of which from EEC	4.0	7.0	8.4	8.4
Of which from USA	3.2	5.7	6.1	5.0
Exports	14.0	23.5	25.2	20.3
Of which to EEC	5.0	8.9	10.8	7.8
Of which to USA	2.1	3.5	3.3	3.7
Medical X-ray apparatus				
Imports	23.6	27.1	31.5	32.0
Of which from EEC	15.2	19.2	23.2	21.8
Of which from USA	4.2	3.5	3.6	5.7
Exports	89.0	39.5	34.3	29.7
Of which to EEC	6.8	10.6	11.3	10.4
Of which to USA	50.8	5.8	6.5	5.2

Source: Overseas Trade Statistics

It is clear that the UK is a net exporter of all types of medical equipment with the exception of X-ray equipment. However, the substantial level of imports of medical equipment reflects the fact that the medical equipment market is an international market with many firms, both UK and overseas owned, operating through overseas subsidiaries. Nevertheless, for the majority of UK manufacturers the most important market is the NHS, but manufacturers of high-technology equipment must also look worldwide for their market.

3. Recent developments

Although the present government came to power committed to cutting public expenditure, expenditure on the NHS has in fact continued to increase. The increase has, however, been taken up largely by pay rises and the need to expand services to meet the needs of the growing numbers of elderly people. Health authorities have been under pressure from the government to make savings wherever possible and medical equipment manufacturers have found it difficult to maintain their level of sales to the NHS. At the same time the strength of sterling has hampered export sales. However, with encouragement from the government, the private health care sector has been growing rapidly, and sales of medical equipment to private hospitals and clinics have become more significant.

The government has also been responsible for two important changes affecting the NHS. First, a further reorganisation of the service is underway. On 1 April 1982 the present two-tier system of area and district health authorities will be replaced by a single tier of district authorities who will be (with the existing regional health authorities) the purchasing authorities. Second, the government has recently set up a Supplies Council (on which the medical equipment industry has a representative) to advise on purchasing policy for the NHS with the aim of getting better value for money. The Council is at present considering the possibility of recommending to health authorities a list of 'best buys' for a number of commodities, including medical equipment.

In the industry itself, the withdrawal of Thorn-EMI from the medical electronics market in 1980 caused a major upset. EMI had pioneered the development of computerised X-ray tomography (CT scanning), that is, the use of computers to construct an image across a 'slice' of a body from a series of conventional X-ray exposures. However, sales of whole body CT scanners did not live up to expectations. The UK market was effectively limited by expenditure on the NHS, and at a time when health authorities were hard pressed to meet all the demands on their funds they were unwilling to find the large capital sums required to purchase whole body scanners or to commit themselves to the very considerable staffing and maintenance costs of such equipment.

There was a similar story in the export market, particularly the US market where measures were taken to try to control health costs. In addition, there was intensive competition from Japanese and American companies who had developed their own range of CT scanners. Faced with mounting losses from its scanner business EMI merged with Thorn in 1979. At the end of 1980, Thorn-EMI withdrew completely from the medical electronics field. Their scanner development interests were sold to General Electric of America, who had already developed their own range of CT scanners, and Philips took over their existing UK scanning business.

There have been a number of other mergers in the medical electronics business, reflecting the high cost of research and development and the need for a worldwide market to recover these costs. In 1980 Vickers, which already had substantial interests in the medical engineering sector, acquired Medelec, a company specialising in the design and manufacture of diagnostic equipment for neurological disorders. With the support of Vickers' overseas subsidiaries, particularly in the USA, the company was thus in a strong export position. More recently Philips, with their interests in X-ray and other imaging systems, have formed a new joint company with the electronics firm Honeywell to develop in the medical electronics field, with the benefit of their existing worldwide distribution network. Again in the X-ray equipment sector, GEC Medical have acquired Picker, the USA based X-ray equipment manufacturer, which should assist their exports to the American market.

The development of microelectronics has had a significant effect on the medical equipment industry. The use of microelectronics has enabled the manufacture of electromedical equipment which is more reliable, simpler to operate and which can perform more complex functions than was previously possible. For example, the latest X-ray generators are microprocessor controlled, and microelectronics has been responsible for the rapid development of real-time ultrasound scanners, now available, which are relatively inexpensive and simple to operate, making it feasible, for instance, to undertake routine ante-natal scanning.

4. Future prospects

The government's current plans for health spending are for an increase in gross expenditure on hospital and community health services of 1.25 per cent in 1981–82 and 1.75 per cent in 1982–83 over the planned expenditure level for 1980–81 (*The Government's Expenditure Plans 1981–82 to 1983–84*, Cmnd 8175). However, the rising costs associated with demographic changes, notably the increasing numbers of elderly people, are expected to account for about 0.7 per cent of the increase which leaves only a small margin for improvements in medical techniques and desirable service developments. In the longer term, volume growth in health care provision is expected to average between 1 per cent and 2 per cent a year.

Medical equipment manufacturers are therefore likely to find difficulty in increasing their sales to the NHS, and the main scope for expansion in the home market is likely to be in the private sector. However, UK manufacturers are relatively well placed to expand in the export market, but there may well be further rationalisation in the medical electronics field particularly, which will enable manufacturers to meet the costs of research and development.

The main lines of development are likely to be the wider application of existing technologies, in particular microelectronics and materials technology. There is enormous scope, for example, for the integration of dedicated microcomputers with existing equipment so that clinical measurements can be analysed instantaneously, or stored for future recall, presented in different formats, or linked with other patient data for more effective diagnosis or treatment. The development of scanning and imaging systems is likely to feature strongly. The trend towards the use of ultrasound scanning, particularly real-time scanning in preference to X-ray imaging, is likely to continue and the new technique of nuclear magnetic resonance (NMR) imaging which is now being developed for clinical use may also become an established diagnostic tool. GEC Medical are expecting to make their first sales of NMR equipment in the current year, and a number of other firms are also developing NMR scanners.

In the current worldwide recession, however, customers will be looking critically at the price of new equipment, not only in terms of capital and running costs but also in terms of patient throughput, staff expertise and time. For this reason, manufacturers will have to concentrate on developing equipment which can solve medical problems more efficiently than existing equipment, for instance enabling a greater number of patients to be treated, or requiring less highly trained staff to operate. Technical innovation by itself will not be enough. Moreover, the largest market for medical equipment will undoubtedly continue to be for the relatively simple items of equipment which are in everyday use in hospitals and clinics throughout the world.

The impending reorganisation of the NHS is not likely to have much effect on the medical equipment industry, though in the longer term any changes in the basis of funding the NHS, such as those being discussed by the present government, might enable increased expenditure on medical equipment. In the immediate future, the government's priority for the NHS is more efficient use of existing resources, and any recommendations by the Supplies Council on 'best buys' for medical equipment would have a significant effect on the industry. Manufacturers whose products were not recommended would find it hard to sell to the NHS and would probably also find it hard to sell anywhere else. However, it remains to be seen which recommendations, if any, the Supplies Council will make.

Key Note reports publish over 150 titles and these are updated every 12–18 months. This extract has been taken from the 2nd edition report on 'Medical Equipment', a title which has been revised twice to date (May 1985).

Questions

1. How realistic, generally, do you believe Medsoft's strategy to be?
2. Do you think the UK sales force will perform successfully? If not, why – and what would you have done instead?
3. What key issues have Kensall and Freedman failed to address properly?
4. If they do achieve their planned sales will the business be profitable? When will it break even?
5. What would your strategy be to develop Medsoft into a profitable business?
6. Do you think the way that Kensall used his store's overdraft was a sensible one to fund this new venture?

Part 2: The Dawn of Reality
(One to three years)

Medsoft B

Colin Barrow

By January 1982 it had become clear that all was not well at Medsoft. The company's overdraft had grown to over £350,00 and the problem was made worse by the problems of Kensall's department store. Christmas sales had been satisfactory but they needed cash to finance a planned increase in sales. Their joint bankers lumped the store and Medsoft together as they were both effectively under Kensall's control. One or other of these businesses was going to be starved of cash – and soon!

The root of the problem was the extremely poor showing of the sales operation both at home and overseas. The Americans had budgeted for sales within eight weeks of receiving products. This did not materialise and as a consequence they had run out of cash just as their serious enquiries were beginning to build up. They asked Medsoft for financial assistance just before Christmas, were turned down and had effectively ceased trading.

In the UK, two of the five sales people carried out virtually no activity on Medsoft's behalf over the period. As commission only sales people they quickly realised that to pay the rent they would need to concentrate on faster selling products from other principals. In any case, only one of the four Medsoft packages was fully operational and that had only a very limited appeal in the market place.

To date only the Manchester and Birmingham sales people had sold anything at all. Sue Proudfoot in Manchester was 42 and had spent the last five years selling computers. She knew nothing about the hospital market but was a quick learner and an excellent saleswoman. She also had a working husband who could support them until she got her territory producing.

Adrian Crawford in Birmingham was 57 and had worked for one firm all his life. He took early retirement two years ago. He knew nothing about computers – he didn't even like them. Still, he didn't know too much about the other products he sold either, just enough to present a credible performance at a demonstration.

Freedman decided to restructure his sales organisation. He

decided to replace the non-performing sales people immediately and to change the whole force over to a mixture of basic salary and commission. The basic salary would be around £5,000 and the commission would be 10 per cent of sales – still giving good earnings potential.

As he still believed that exporting was the key to survival Freedman decided to recruit a field sales manager to look after the sales force on a day-to-day basis. At the same time he commissioned a management consultant to tell him why sales were so slow in coming through. Every doctor he spoke to thought the product excellent and wanted one (see the Consultants' Report, Appendix 1).

While Freedman was restructuring the sales organisation, Kensall was deliberating how to share the risk of this troublesome new venture. From being a mere sideline he now had a third of a million cash consumed by Medsoft and his main business was being stifled by lack of funds. He decided that the business needed a substantial injection of new capital from other shareholders to give Medsoft a more secure base from which to develop.

Freedman's plans for the USA were extremely ambitious despite his earlier setback. He prepared a four-year plan to set up a new sales operation in the USA to be run initially by him. He expected it would take around nine months of his time to get this plan off the ground and be able to return to the UK. Freedman's USA plan, as yet not discussed with Kensall, is shown in Appendix 2.

Appendix 1

Funding and decisions

1. Introduction
Selling computer capital equipment to hospital consultants poses some distinctive selling problems. In the first place the 'buyer' is rarely the 'payer'. This money has to be found from one source or another usually outside of their direct control.

Second, the customer consultant has to have the support of his peer group, and then that peer group has in turn to win an internal competition for approval, before a sale can begin to be achieved.

Third, microcomputers are a relatively new type of purchase in this market and the ground rules are still being worked out and procedures vary greatly from location to location.

Finally, the large number of people that have to be influenced to create a sale, and the nature of DHSS funding, make the time it takes to get an order unusually long, and the procedure itself confusing.

This report sets out to throw some light on these issues, their implication for Medsoft's sales force, and to give some guidelines for action.

The information was gleaned from meetings and discussions with the following people:

Ivor Freedman ⎫
Andrew Brown ⎪
Sue Proudfoot ⎬ Medsoft
Adrian Crawford ⎭

John Smith – Cardiac consultant and chairman of Hospital Group Committee, Fiveways District General.
Jean Black – Computer officer, Northward Health Authority.
William McTaggart – Assistant treasurer, Westbridge District.
Dr Mole – Southern General Hospital.

2. Summary

'Dedicated' micros in the health service is an important and rapidly growing market.

The decision-making process is lengthy and is resource expensive to influence. The funding process tends to concentrate purchases into three months of the year.

These factors all have important implications for the way Medsoft will sell, and of course on the performance of the business as a whole, in the next financial year.

3.

3.1 Computers in the hospitals

Computers in hospitals are a relatively new innovation, and micros even more so. At first the power lay with the 'mainframe' staff, who supported and ran a centralised hospital service and signally failed to satisfy medical users. Now the need for dedicated systems is well recognised, and a computer committee structure has begun to take over the decision/approval role.

It is not uncommon for a district hospital to have half a dozen different dedicated systems in various areas. One district has just approved £12,000 for a system to improve patient food ordering and cut down waste. Another has a patient record system for an 'open' diabetic clinic, as without such a system to recall records rapidly only a more rigid appointment system could be made to work.

There is pressure from government, from medical professional bodies, and from within the hospital itself, for consultants to use micros to help with research into treatment results and into patient handling and monitoring.

Medsoft's products seem to be well received in a market place that is hungry for products.

3.2   The decision-making process

The main source of funds is the DHSS via the regional health authority. There are some variations in the process described, but the general principles seem universal.

a) *Purchase decision*
   Consultant decides to purchase a Medsoft product.
b) *Project proposal*
   He should complete a 'project' proposal to communicate his need, plan and goals.
c) *Divisional committee/Computer committee*
   This proposal is submitted to:
   (i) His divisional committee, who are his peer group. They decide which projects should have their support.
   (ii) At the same time the proposal goes to the computer committee, who are interested in the 'computer credibility' of the proposal. They meet every couple of months, but the chairman of this committee usually has the authority to approve a project outside the formal meeting cycle. They are also interested in such factors as compatibility with other systems, networking possibilities and links with mainframe if they have one.
d) *Medical Executive*
   Once the project has been given approval by the last two committees, it is passed to the medical executive. This committee is made up of the chairman of all the medical departments, who set a professional priority on the projects. They have a preference for patient-orientated proposals. The priorities that are used fall into three categories, and are ranked within each. Category A are projects calling for the replacement of existing equipment; B are projects to extend or enhance existing equipment; and C are projects calling for new equipment. This final

category is the one that houses most microcomputer projects. These decisions are usually made between July and September, in time to pass to the district management team to incorporate into its strategic plan.

e) *District management team*

Once through the medical executive *all* capital requests for medical and scientific projects go to the district management team, which is a multi-disciplinary team consisting of medical nursing administrative and financial staff. They do not sanction regional funds, they only agree to pass proposals forward, or not. These proposals are incorporated into the strategic plan (a two-year ahead look) and the annual budget which is submitted to the regional health authority by February each year.

f) *Regional scientific officer/capital equipment advisers*

Once through the district management team the proposals go forward to the regional health authority where the scientific officer is usually involved in vetting computer capital requests. They, as the district management team, are concerned that the revenue implications of capital requests are fully considered, ie what will it cost to run and maintain.

Once a project proposal has successfully passed through these stages it will be approved for purchase, but only if sufficient funds are made available by region (more about money later). If the regional health authority makes less available than the district asked for, then the district management team and medical executive have to choose which to approve. They use the ABC categories to guide them in their choice.

It is important to note that if for some reason or other a project is not approved or is not funded in the year of approval, it drops out of the system and has to be re-submitted.

3.3 The funding process

While the annual project proposals are flowing upwards, the preceding year's strategic plan is being used to help the DHSS formulate its overall funding needs. Obviously at government level priorities are being decided with education, defence and industry departments etc, all competing for a finite sum. Additional funds from the DHSS can only come from other departments' budgets, increased taxes or internal improved efficiency. The process goes something like this:

March. By the end of this month the regional health authorities are able to let the district know how much their overall funding will be. For example, Somerset district's capital budget for 1981–82 was £7 million.* The overall sum allocated includes an allowance for estimated inflation. But as major items such as wage negotiations are not usually settled this early in the year, the district cannot release all its funds at the start of the year.

April. The district releases some of these funds to approved projects. During this month and May individual consultants will be told if they have been successful.

September. The district will carry out its half-yearly review of expenditure against budget. Usually with the conservative approach taken in March this will mean that further funds can be released to approved projects. Once again, consultants will be advised if they have been successful.

February. The year end review will probably release yet more funds, as the final picture of the year's expenditure pattern becomes clear. (For example, a mild winter in Somerset last year saved £12,000 in fuel bills; this sum was then available for other items.) Districts can carry up to 10 per cent of capital budgets over to the following year (1 per cent of revenue budget) so in theory funds could be available for some projects throughout the year, dependent on district policy on budget carry over.

3.4   Other sources of funds
While regional health authority funds are the main source of funds for computer capital projects there are some others. In the main, approval for these funds should go through the same decision-making procedure as for regional money.

HOSPITAL TRUSTS
Every hospital has funds left by benefactors and the sums vary from a few thousand to millions of pounds. There are two types of trust. The general trust houses funds that can be spent on anything, and the dedicated trusts are only available to a specific area, ie surgery, Ward A etc. Sums of up to £1,000 can be awarded by the trust administrator, who is usually a hospital treasurer. Negotiations for these funds at this level are fairly informal.

Over that sum district management team approval is needed in the usual way, but the requests can be made at any time and do

---

* There is a small amount of leeway between revenue and capital budgets.

not have to fit in with the general buying cycle. Policy varies from hospital to hospital, but as a general rule trust funds are used as 'topping up' money. So if a consultant can get £5,000 from another source, the trust may make up the balance for a £10,000 purchase.

PHARMACEUTICAL COMPANIES' RESEARCH BUDGETS
These companies are often prepared to help fund consultants' research projects, and will often respond favourably to a request from them provided, of course, there is some link between the project and the pharmaceutical companies' products or services. These funds have the advantage of not requiring approval through the normal decision-making channels.

WINDFALLS
These arrive from time to time, the most recent case being some Department of Trade and Industry funds for computer projects in the health service. This money is passed through the normal health service channels and district decision-making process.

THE MANPOWER SERVICES COMMISSION (MSC)
This operates a scheme that allows some investment in hardware and a wages contribution to create a computer training opportunity for young people. It is a spin-off from the Information Technology (IT) Centre concept pioneered by the MSC, but like all their schemes it requires some energy to get off the ground. Nevertheless it is a potentially rewarding area and as we have achieved a sale via this route, the method should be documented for use elsewhere. These funds also have the advantage of lying out of cycle funds.

DISTRICT RESERVES
Each district can spend up to £25,000 without any reference to the regional health authority. The only advantage of taking this route is that it eliminates the regional approval procedures.

THE HONEYMOON SYSTEM
This is an 'informal' agreement that grants newly appointed consultants some priority on capital budgets. The rationale is that old consultants tend to let things run down and a swift revitalising injection is needed to restore the balance.

Up to £30,000 or so can be spent under this heading, but it is a highly unofficial process.

4. Implications for the sales force

The decision-making process for computer capital purchases, and the funding process, have important implications for the sales force and the way in which they will secure orders.

4.1 Recognising an order

In the normal course of events recognising an order is not too difficult. Selling a microcomputer system to a consultant, however, presents some unusual 'buying signals' problems. The important points to consider are:

a) *'Prospects not suspects'*
   You have to gather enough information on your consultants to grade them into a priority hit list. The top grade has to be consultants who are interested in the product, are respected by their peer group and either have access to their own funds, are on the relevant committees, or for some other reason are powerful influencers.

b) *Pre-demonstration preparation*
   Before arranging a demonstration make contact with the chairman of the computer committee and the medical executive to try to establish their criteria for a successful project application.

c) *Demonstrate to as wide a group as you can*
   When you arrange a demonstration get as many 'influencers' along as possible. Use this to help smooth the consultants' path through the decision-making channels.

d) *'The sale'*
   The first step on the road to a sale is when the consultant agrees to buy and completes a project proposal to submit to his divisional committee and computer committee. You should help him with this, and so word it that it shifts the project out of the 'C' category and into 'B'. Get the date of the committee meetings from him. Keep a diary record of all key meetings.

e) *Monitoring progress*
   Once the proposal is in the pipeline you should monitor its progress and try to influence events as much as possible. Naturally this will vary from consultant to consultant, and hospital to hospital. It may be possible to help the consultant in his argument with the various committees, or even appear at them yourself.

f) *Buying dates*
   Remember decisions on funding are generally communi-

cated to consultants in April, September and February. Follow up at these times.

g) *If unsuccessful*

First make sure the project does not sink, and is brought up again, if necessary with modifications, and keep it in the decision-making channel. Either at this stage or much earlier look for alternative sources of funds. Talk to the hospital treasurer about trusts; contact the local office of the MSC and find out about IT money; investigate the probabilities of linking up with a pharmaceutical research project.

4.2 Time scale

This selling process is a long one and you should recognise it as such at the outset.

In general it seems that two months is the minimum period between a consultant initiating a project proposal and the district management team approving it. A further two months are taken up on the path to and from the regional health authority. As it will probably take a month or so to get the consultant to buy, from a cold start a firm order will take five months to secure.

This all serves to make it vital that you sift out the less likely prospects early on, and have as many live projects in the pipeline as quickly as possible.

5. Some other observations

These are some general points raised during various meetings and discussions:

1. Why should I buy from your Sirius agent? We can get our hardware locally, which is better for maintenance.
2. When will your programs be available on the Apricot/IBM?
3. Will the system 'link' in with other hospital systems? (This seems a red herring as no one really seems to know what they would like to link to.)
4. Price generally did not seem an issue. I was not much convinced by the 'price break' theory that suggested projects over £10,000 were easiest to get approval for.
5. Can we just buy the software as we have a Sirius?
6. Maintenance contracts did not seem to pose a conceptual problem as the consultants were used to having them with other equipment. Justification must be built into the initial project proposal.

7. Teaching hospitals and professors are a law unto themselves. Approval for capital expenditure seems much easier in this area.

8. In general there is more financial flexibility than the apparently rigid process suggests. I believe there is a continuous flow of orders for capital equipment working its way through the system, with three strong peaks (as indicated previously).

Appendix 2

Freedman's US strategy 1981–85

The USA obeys the 80:20 rule in terms of population coverage, the small north-east area holding 25 per cent of the country's population on 50 per cent of the land. The five states around the Great Lakes hold another 19 per cent of the population which, together with California (10 per cent), Texas (6 per cent), and Florida (4 per cent) make up 60 per cent of the country's total population.

This proposal assumes a geographical roll-out of the business over four years. A phased development of the business allows a gradual development of management control systems and marketing support activities in the light of the actualities of the market place. It thus reduces the costs of the learning experience, as well as reducing the start-up cash flow requirements.

In year 1 it is proposed to take on five representatives to cover the north-east region, with coverage expansion as shown below:

Year	Region	% Population	No reps	Units/Rep
1	North-east	24	5	18
2	West/Great Lakes	28	5	38
3	Mid and south-east/south central	29	5	62
4	North central/Rockies	17	4	80
		98[*]	19	

[*]Excludes Alaska, Hawaii and Puerto Rico

From previous experience with health care suppliers in the UK a representative should be able to build £250,000 worth of business per annum over the first three years, equivalent to 70 units of Medsoft software.

A summary of the USA organisation and budgeted earnings is given below:

No of employees by function and salary earnings

Function	Year 1	Year 5	£
Managing director	1	1	50,000
Product managers	—	3	35,000
Technical managers	1	3	43,000
Sales manager	1	1	43,000
Field sales managers	—	4	35,000
Representatives	5	19	29,000
Secretaries	1	2	14,000
Total employees	9	33	

It is proposed that our office is located in New Jersey, 'other' first year costs of £80,000 including £30,000 for office overheads based upon actual costs incurred by Medsoft Inc before they closed.

Management would be provided from the UK three months prior to start-up to identify a suitable office site, complete recruitment, develop the marketing support required in the field and for mass exposure of the product line, and to set up the financial and management control systems.

UK management would remain in the USA for a further three to six months to consolidate the start-up phase and recruit key replacement managers (ie a managing director and sales manager).

Arthur D Little's estimate of the health care environment in the developed countries is set out below:

Health care environment (1981)

Country	Population (millions)	Health care expenditure Billions $	% of GNP	$ per Capita
USA	225	192	10.0	1,045
Japan	120	48	6.5	610
UK	57	21	5.2	370
Germany	62	66	7.1	1,065
France	55	46	6.8	840
Italy	58	22	5.8	380
Other Europe	135	44	5.0	325
Western Europe	367	199	6.1	540

Questions

1. What do you think of Freedman's proposals to reorganise the sales force?
2. Draw up a job description for the field sales manager. What key tasks should this new person address himself to over the next three months?

3. If Freedman's present sales strategy is followed, when will they break even? (Make any reasonable assumptions and be prepared to defend them in your presentation.)
4. What questions do you think will be asked of Kensall by prospective investors in Medsoft?
5. Assuming that you had the spare cash and were prepared to invest it in a risk venture, what strategy(ies) would you recommend Medsoft to pursue now, and why?
6. Do you think that 'big company men' can ever make the transition to successful small businessmen?

Case 15

For a Few Pence More

Colin Barrow

John Holnbrook had spent all his working life with one major electronics company. He had seen it grow from a modest family venture into a powerful national company with a major share of the markets in which it competed. For the 15 years preceding his retirement he had been the chief editor of their technical handbooks.

For some years before retirement, Holnbrook had been casting around for some activity to keep him busy and to make some money to top up his pension. In June 1984 he followed up a card unit business for sale in his home town of Plymouth, since at one time he had been particularly interested in viewcards and photography etc. The idea of greetings cards seemed to him and his wife an attractive kind of business. The retail margins were high in the printed products trade in general, and cards had the additional merit of being a consumable product.

It was clear the little shop was not paying; the summer was here and people were going on holiday, of course, and there seemed to be reduced trade due to other traders nearby starting to sell cards. However, the business was being offered complete with all equipment (including cash register and music centre) and stock (£700–£800 at cost, approximately double this retail). It had been built up from scratch when the arcade opened two years previously, by the vendor, who had clearly put in a lot of work and fought several battles with the local opposition. It had originally been intended as a business for his wife, but she had become deaf, and he was running the shop himself with a woman as casual staff during the week, and a Saturday girl. The rent was all inclusive, and £70 per week. The vending price was only £3,000, including stock.

Holnbrook thought that when he retired in October trade would pick up, and if the shop paid the rent and part-time staff, he would have a rent-free outlet for other publishing activities. These included the writing and production of a number of DIY type booklets.

He revealed his anxiety about the state of his venture in this statement made to a former colleague:

'I am now engaged in the production of some DIY booklets, but the business has not picked up as expected due to the general recession. In October it was paying only for the part-time staff, and now, nearing the end of November, it is about paying the rent, leaving me to pay the staff out of my pocket.

The cash register produced an illegible journal roll, and it turned out to be obsolete so that a new ribbon could not be obtained to replace the tatty one. So I replaced it with a new electronic one, and this is now giving me some legible figures, and some interesting statistics. For instance, the slight rise for the last week of the month and first week in the new month is detectable, indicating the monthly paid element among the customers. However, more importantly, the till roll shows the time and date of purchase and the number of cash sales. Whereas I thought I was looking for customers, and the fault I thought lay with insufficient attraction into the arcade, last week and the week before we had 240 cash customers, 90 of them on the Saturday. Since these are not coming in every week for cards, but more likely once per month, the indications are that we have about a thousand regular customers. The trouble is the amount each is spending, an average of only about 60p.

We carry small stationery lines, some catering and party lines, and I have also taken on World Wildlife Fund cards and trading lines, which have proved a useful attraction. The shop is small (23 × 8 ft), strip lighting, double 6-ft windows and a glass door between them; there are four 5-ft card racks and one 4-ft, two table stands, various card and wrap stands for putting outside in the passage, several rows of shelves etc. and it is pretty full.

So here is the problem. I have 240 customers a week, coming, on average, for a card and a sheet of wrap or a couple of cards. They know the shop as the place to get their cards, which are top quality, a copper or two lower priced than elsewhere, nice bright atmosphere where they can bring in their prams and dogs, which no one else around allows. They are glad to get the packet of envelopes, or cake decorations, as a convenience if they need them in an emergency, and the occasional pencil and scrapbook, and there it rests. What I need is a second main complementary line which they need and for which they will come to accept us as their main supplier.

The previous owner tried records, but this was discontinued because the shop became jammed with non-buying school children, complete with their packets of chips from the bar next door, spreading the grease over everything. I am thinking of trying my surplus private books, at reduced price. We cannot do anything that other shopkeepers in the arcade are doing. I have a battery bar, specialising in micro batteries, but there is a jeweller who also does clocks and watches etc, and an electrical shop. So I cannot stock batteries.

I have a photocopier, and could produce leaflets to pop in their paper bags, provided the cost showed a return (an A4 costs about 3p, A5 1½p).

I need to persuade my customers to part with two amounts of 60p instead of one. I cannot just settle into retirement on my small pension when I feel so fit, and when my wife has over two years to go in her job before she retires.'

Questions

1. How realistic were Holnbrook's business aims?
2. What other steps should he have taken before buying the shop?
3. Comment on the steps he has taken so far to improve the performance of his business.
4. Do you think his analysis of the current situation is soundly based?
5. What alternatives lie ahead of him now and which would you recommend, and why?

Case 16

Pretty Things

Everett M Jacobs

Sue Hamilton, a 23-year-old graduate new to business, owned and managed a small ladies underwear shop called Pretty Things, in Sheffield. She opened the shop with a bank loan of £1,000 and £2,000 of her own in March 1984, and at first stocked only basic lines of underwear (including bras, knickers, slips, suspender belts, stockings, pantie-girdles and corselettes). However, in buying for the Christmas season, she ordered additional lines that she thought would be particularly suitable as gifts (including dressing gowns, nighties, slip and knickers sets, thermal vests and cosy tops, and 'sexy' underwear such as basques, waspies, playsuits, and revealing knickers).

It was clear by the end of November that Christmas sales were not proceeding quite as she had expected. She had spent £945 on the sexy underwear, but much of it remained unsold. Other lines were moving at an acceptable rate, but with so much of her limited cash tied up in unsold (and she was starting to fear, unsaleable) garments, Sue was beginning to sense a cash flow crisis in February 1985, when she would have to pay for goods she had ordered for the spring.

On a Saturday in mid-December, Sue still had no plan of what to do until an item on the first page of the local newspaper, the *Morning Telegraph*, caught her eye:

> 'Labour leader Neil Kinnock cheerfully accepted two kisses from a pretty Mother Christmas in Swindon, Wiltshire, yesterday. But he beat a strategic retreat when 32-year-old Liz Evans opened her red robe to reveal saucy underwear with black suspender belt and stockings. Liz, who runs a kissogram business, had waited among a small crowd outside the civic offices.'

The incident gave Sue the idea that she would be able to sell a lot of her sexy underwear to kissogram girls. She knew that she stocked just the kind of underwear that the girls wore when delivering their surprise messages and greetings. However, she did not know if there were kissogram agencies in or near Sheffield. She did not find any kissogram advertisements in that edition of the *Morning Telegraph*, but she found three in one of the local free distribution newspapers. She reasoned that there might be one or two more, and began working out her plan of action.

The 'basic uniform' of the kissogram girls was a basque, a lacy, figure-shaping undergarment covering the torso from the bust to the top of the hips with suspenders attached. The boob-a-gram girls favoured a waspie, which was similar in style to a basque except that it left a good deal more of the bust exposed. Sue had bought three dozen basques and three dozen waspies, both in mixed colours and sizes, from a leading manufacturer. She paid £11.99 for each basque, and £7.99 for each waspie, and sold them at the recommended retail prices of £17.99 and £11.99, respectively (all prices including VAT). This gave her a mark-up of 33.3 per cent on retail price. Sue knew that some popular newspapers sold basques to their readers for £7.99, and that it was sometimes possible to find clearance lines in the markets for £8.99, but she was convinced that her basques were of far better quality, had a greater variety of colours, and in general represented better value for money than the cheaper ones. Still, she had sold only three basques and two waspies so far, and was now willing to give kissogram girls a discount of 10–15 per cent in order to clear some of her stock. She therefore placed an advertisement in the personal column of the local morning and evening newspapers for four successive days with the following wording:

KISSOGRAM GIRLS – for very
pretty basques and waspies
at low prices, ring Pretty
Things at Sheffield 26444

The circulation of the *Morning Telegraph* was 45,000 (readership 50,000), and that of the *Star*, 150,000 (readership 400,000). The combined advertising rate was £1.45 a line, although she could have advertised exclusively in either paper at £1.05 a line. An advertisement appearing on three successive days received a fourth insertion free of charge.

After placing the advertisement, Sue sat back and wondered whether this would be enough to recoup her investment in sexy underwear.

Questions

1. Do you think Sue has chosen a worthwhile market segment to concentrate on and a sensible method of communications?
2. What else could she do to improve her business position?

Case 17

West Cornwall Woodwork
Maureen and Graham Davey

West Cornwall Woodwork began trading on 28 January 1985, designing and making up-market occasional furniture. The business takes the form of a partnership, the partners being Graham and Maureen Davey. Prior to starting business Graham spent eight years as a naval officer in the Fleet Air Arm and Maureen was a graduate in psychology.

The initial idea

In the late 1970s Graham, having established the beginnings of a career in the Royal Navy, began to have second thoughts about how he would like to spend his life. The idea of having a small country workshop, making pine furniture (the current trend in furniture) appealed, but realising that he was committed to the Navy for several years yet, he began to develop a hobby that would fulfil his creative needs.

At this stage the business was a long way off and Graham's priority was to establish the technical skills of making furniture. With no time to do a full-time course, these skills would have to be self-taught.

Starting to sell

As Graham's skills improved and he collected more equipment, friends began to take an interest. This led to the first sales of items of furniture – an important step from making for fun to making to sell. Graham and Maureen, now committed to Graham leaving the Navy probably in 1984, decided that they ought to find out about the business side of making furniture.

Maureen scratched the tip of the iceberg by attending a one-day seminar in London in 1982, run by the London Enterprise Agency. This opened up a Pandora's box as far as the idea of running a small business was concerned. Undeterred, they resolved to find out more.

The practice (1982-83)

Graham was now firmly committed to leaving the Navy in 1984, and they chose to use the intermediate time to good effect, to prepare themselves for the start-up on their own.

Graham's naval salary, then around £14,000 per annum, financed the purchase of capital machinery that would eventually set them off as a full-time business. Buying the machinery at this point allowed Graham to acquaint himself with its use. In mid-1983 they began to keep informal accounts and records of the small amount of business they were doing.

In the autumn of 1983 Maureen began a Start Your Own Business evening class at the Cornwall College of Higher and Further Education; she also took a typing course. The SYOB course lasted for a year and Graham was able to attend it from the beginning of 1984. By this time he knew he would be leaving the Navy at the end of September.

The run-up (1984)

Having established a small workshop (350 sq ft) not far from their home in Cornwall, they began to look at ways of testing the market, to find out exactly what they could expect to sell.

The initial idea of pine furniture (back in 1979) had been abandoned due to excessive competition and too small a margin on the scale that they could contemplate. It seemed that light hardwoods such as ash and oak were in fashion and popular designs were simple and functional.

It was hard at first to know what to do: should they approach shops and ask what the buyers wanted, or should they make some pieces first, to show potential customers what sort of quality they could produce? They chose the latter course, making a small range of occasional furniture. They then tried the local quality furniture shops; however, the response was not very promising. On the whole, the buyers liked the work and the styles, but thought that the price was more than most of their customers could afford, thus making the turnover too small to allow them to buy any pieces. The inference was that there was a gap in the market for quality-made occasional furniture, but that the price was critical.

At the same time, they began to take the trade magazine *The Cabinet Maker and Retail Furnisher*. Over the weeks there seemed to be a consistent stream of editorials saying that there was a shortage of well designed well-made English occasional furniture. This was the mainstay of Graham and Maureen's market intelligence; all they had to do was reach that market, which seemed to be mainly in the London area at the price level they could work at, while allowing a shop a 100 per cent mark-up as well.

They did, however, see one local outlet, a quality craft gallery that had a summer exhibition of crafts, with a commission of only 15 per cent on items over £250. They saw this as a good opportunity to try their work on the buying public. The selling price was based on cost plus 100 per cent mark-up, even though the gallery took only 15 per cent. In this way they could see if anyone would buy at a realistic manufacturing cost.

To their surprise, they did sell some pieces – four occasional tables at prices ranging from £150 to £330.

When to commence trading

Graham took advantage of an opportunity to attend a four-week SYOB course at Plymouth Polytechnic, as a pre-release course before leaving the Navy. Earlier in the year both Graham and Maureen had attended a one-day business workshop in London run by Thames Polytechnic. It was through these courses that they learned of the Enterprise Allowance Scheme and discovered that they would both be eligible for £40 per week.

There was only one slight drawback: Graham would need to be unemployed for 13 weeks after leaving the Navy. However, having thought through the financial aspects of this situation, they decided to join the Scheme. This meant that between September 1984 and January 1985 they were unemployed and not able to trade in any way or take firm orders that would imply they intended to trade before getting on to the Scheme. Instead, the time was spent carrying out further market research by collecting a list of potential customers and producing suitable material to send or preferably take to them.

A letter of introduction was sent out to 33 possible retail outlets, drawn from various sources. There were nine responses, two of which were negative, the other seven asking for more information and expressing a wish to see the photographs that had been offered.

Due to the lack of suitable transport and perhaps to a lack of courage the photographs were sent by post rather than taken by hand. While these photographs were very well presented in a custom-made, corporate-style folder they did not carry the same impact, nor provide the vital feedback that was later found necessary. The covering letter did, however, say that a follow-up visit was planned in the new year.

Cash flows and initial plans were also drawn up during this period. As the potential market area was in London, they saw the need to travel there fairly regularly in the early stages to meet buyers face to face. Since their only vehicle was a well-worn old van, they chose to lease a new one, thus giving them reliable access to London and the ability to carry a limited amount of furniture. The new van proved to be a good option not only from a reliability point of view, but being a diesel it was economical. Being leased it was a total tax loss, and they could claim the VAT back as it was a van.

VAT registration was not a necessary choice, the first year's turnover estimated as being well under the registration minimum. However, they registered anyway because they had over £7,000 of VAT receipts saved up from the various machines purchased over the past three years. This would bring in around £1,000 on the first VAT return. Also it was felt that if they were to deal mainly with shops, it would make transactions more standard because retailers normally buy from VAT registered suppliers.

The start

Trading began from the same small workshop they had had for the last 18 months (rented at £10 per week), equipped with the necessary machinery, all of which was paid for. The only draw-back in the set-up was workshop space, which was insufficient. There was only room for making furniture with no storage space for raw materials or finished goods.

The cash flow did not leave much room to manoeuvre. As the market and prospective customers were still a little uncertain, the choice between staying where they were in a low-cost workshop or moving to a bigger one presented a difficult problem. On the one hand there was the money that would be saved by staying put, on the other the potential nightmare of moving a whole workshop in mid-stream later in the year, assuming business took off as planned. They decided to move then and take the chance.

The idea of a bigger workshop was not a new one. For the past three years various ideas had been looked at, ranging from old warehouse sites, derelict barns and other commercial sites:

sometimes for freehold purchase, sometimes for leasehold and sometimes for rental under very loose agreements. For one reason or another nothing had come of any of these, usually due to lack of planning permission or poor access.

There was one other solution that had always been in the background, the English Industrial Estates Beehive workshop units. On a straightforward monthly payment basis these had always seemed expensive, but having exhausted all the other options only one choice remained for the new workshop site. The reasons for this were:

(a) Taking over a structurally sound building (no repairs were required).
(b) No planning problems.
(c) Good access.
(d) Easy to find.
(e) The building was well insulated and dry (very important for furniture making).
(f) All the services were on site: three-phase electricity, gas, water and telephone, plus toilet facilities.
(g) Tenancy agreement allowing three months' notice.
(h) No capital outlay in the lease premium.

So the £60 per week rental now seemed better value. What they were buying was no hassle and the ability to get on with making furniture, not doing up old properties and servicing bank loans.

There was, of course, a one-month moving period, when no furniture making could be carried out, but at the end of this period (end of March 1985), they had a fully operational workshop. This included a main work area, housing all the machinery and timber storage; a closed spraying area; and a modest (4.2m × 3.6m) office cum display area. This display area allowed the products to be exhibited to good effect to casual customers and the commission work to be discussed in relative comfort, away from the workshop.

At the same time as Graham and Maureen were planning the move to the Beehive unit came the first of many trips to London as a follow-up to the letters and photographs sent in December 1984. The first difficulty they encountered was that people were not that easy to pin down to an appointment. Not having enough positive responses from the places that had received the photographs, the only thing to do was to try some of the places that had not replied to the initial letter. This worked with surprising success, proving that a telephone call can often reach the person you need to see better than a circular letter.

So in February 1985 a small number of likely London shops were visited and presented with photographs of examples of the work done to date, illustrating the quality and style that could be produced. The main point of the visit was to discover market needs. All the shops were receptive to the furniture's quality and style, and were keen to give design briefs of what they felt would sell.

After designing two prototypes, the Daveys now have furniture at three shops in London.

Marketing the products hinges very much on feedback from the buyers and their design briefs for new styles of furniture that will satisfy the ever changing tastes of their customers. This is why it is necessary to make overnight trips to London, driving 600 miles for a 10-minute meeting with the buyer. Telephone calls work once established but, in the beginning, face to face contact is essential.

Sometimes luck can take over from careful planning. This happened at Liberty's when an appointment with the modern furniture buyer put the Daveys in the right place at the right time to meet the senior antiques buyer. He was looking for a small business such as theirs to make copies of furniture designed by Liberty's at the beginning of the century. This was a style similar to one of the pieces in their collection of photographs.

Finance

Apart from the sales revenue, the business has two other sources of income: £80 per week Enterprise Allowance (EAS) and £23 per week Family Income Supplement (FIS), which includes all the benefits of free prescriptions, dental treatment, milk tokens etc. The EAS was straightforward but the FIS required more effort in the form of a profit and loss account for the first month's trading and several letters of clarification to the department concerned. In the end it was awarded, being worth £1,300 in the first year, tax free.

Overdraft facilities from the bank of £4,000 provide the working capital for the business; however, the bank required a second charge on the family house to secure this facility.

The majority of capital equipment had been purchased well before trading began (around £8,000), but there are further items that will be required in the not too distant future. These will only be considered in the light of good order books and customers paying promptly.

Currently, a favoured method of finance is the long-term lease, especially in view of tax law changes, the philosophy being that you do not need to own it to make money out of it!

Financial management

At the critical start-up phase of the business when cash flow is more a term than a reality, a weekly cash balance is useful. The actual monthly cash flow is compared with the budget and graphs are also produced to show how closing balance sales and expenses relate.

The Daveys plan to do quarterly profit and loss accounts although a constant check is kept on the profitability of each job to ensure the margins stay where they should be.

Costing is often a difficult area; items that are considered are:

(a) What the market will stand
(b) Retail margins (usually around 100 per cent)
(c) VAT
(d) Material cost related to potential sale value, is the gross
 | margin (preferably around 70–75 per cent) enough?
(e) Can it be made in a time to match the contribution?

In the early stages of business there must be a certain amount of flexibility in applying these rules, so as to explore new markets, but a careful watch must be maintained if overall profitability is to be achieved.

Questions

1. What business are the Daveys in? Who are their major customer segments? What competition are they up against? Now write a list of benefits that they should use as their selling platform.
2. They relied heavily on their trade magazine for market intelligence. For a design-based business was this satisfactory?
3. How compatible do you think a workshop in Penzance and a market in London is? What are the essential issues to consider in choosing where to locate this type of business?

4. Do you agree with Graham's view of fixed assets as encapsulated in the statement 'You do not need to own it to make money out of it'?
5. Do you think all the preparation work paid off, or were there still gaps in essential knowledge and skills?

Case 18

Siop Swyddfa Post
David Kirby

Siop Swyddfa Post is a 42m^2 (450 sq ft) general store cum sub-post office located in Llaregub, a tourist/commuter village in mid-Wales. Situated some two miles from Llandrindod Wells (a town of 3,500 inhabitants) which functions as an inland tourist resort, conference centre and the principal shopping centre of the area, the village is approximately 30 miles from Newtown (9,250 inhabitants) and 41 miles from Hereford (47,000). The store is located in the centre of the village which, in 1980, had approximately 200 permanent dwellings (average household size 2.73 persons per household) and some 80 holiday homes (average household size 2.82 persons) on a site about half a mile to the south of the village.

The proprietors, John and Mary Brown, are in their early 40s. They came to the village from England in 1977 when they bought the business. Unlike many people in their position, they had previous experience of retailing, selling and renting televisions. Like the majority of Britain's village shopkeepers, however, their objectives in buying the shop were to make money, to be independent and to live in the country.

In 1980 the shop had a turnover of between £50,000 and £100,000. It sold groceries, greengroceries, milk and dairy products, frozen products, books and stationery, newspapers, pharmaceuticals, sweets and tobacco and small hardware and electrical items, mainly by self-service. In addition, it provided credit facilities and a delivery service, and although John and Mary felt that the future of the business, with its 200 to 250 regular customers, was 'secure' they were concerned about the increasingly high costs involved in its operation.

In September 1981 they enrolled in a training and advisory programme, organised specifically for village shopkeepers by the Mid-Wales Development Agency. The programme consisted of four weekend modules covering such topics as stock management (the definition of profit, stock mix, stock levels, problems of over- and under- stocking, practical methods of stock control), financial management (financial controls, measurement of losses, cash flow forecasting etc), in-store management (shop appearance, layout, merchandising etc) and customer management (identifying the nature and size of the market, increasing market penetration, reducing shrinkage etc). Each workshop included an element of project work and John and Mary were set exercises which they had to implement in their own store. To assist them a counsellor visited their shop after each module both to assist with the implementation of the various exercises and to advise on the various problems facing their business.

After attending the course, John and Mary decided to broaden the range of goods carried by selling bread and cakes and adding an off-licence. The off-licence had an immediate effect on trade, increasing sales by approximately £250 per week. At the same time, in an attempt to reduce costs and eliminate bad debts, credit facilities were discontinued, though customers could still obtain credit by Access and Barclaycard. Further cost savings were made. By 'shopping around' (as advised on the course) bank charges were reduced by £500 per year, and accountants' fees were reduced from £345 to £225 per annum. This latter saving was made possible, at least in part, by the better accounting procedures and financial controls which John and Mary had introduced as a result of the course. In turn, these measures enabled the proprietors to keep a closer check on costs and, in particular, to control overcharges and short deliveries, thus reducing the problem of shrinkage and saving 'many hundreds of pounds'.

Like most small businesses, buying-in was a problem and to overcome it the proprietors began to visit a major cash and carry warehouse some 60 miles from the shop at least every two weeks, buying between £1,000 and £1,500 of stock on each occasion. As a result, the stock range was broadened and, by selling at or below Shaw's recommended prices, a gross profit in excess of 20 per cent was achieved. Previously similar purchases at a local cash and carry had produced gross profit of between 13 and 15 per cent, all goods being sold at or above the prices recommended by *Shaw's Price Guide*. At the same time, John and Mary now take full advantage of any promotions which local cash and carries may be offering.

To advertise the store and to promote the special offers, the business now prints its own leaflets and distributes them every three weeks to the 250 households in its immediate catchment area. As a result, the shop has 'attracted some special offer only purchasers but we also acquired regular customers that we had never seen before'. Certainly this was borne out by a market research survey conducted in 1982, 11 per cent of the sample claiming only to shop at the store for special offers. However, whereas in 1981 a similar survey had revealed that some 18 per cent of the sample said they shopped at the store regularly for everyday or weekly purchases, in 1982 the proportion had risen to 30 per cent, while the percentage using the store in 'emergencies' or for 'forgotten items' had fallen from 53 per cent in 1981 to 44 and 33 per cent, respectively, in 1982. Despite the efforts of the proprietors to promote the business, some 33 per cent of the 1982 sample said they never used the store (some 6 per cent less than in 1981) and it would seem that there still remains scope for further market penetration. The market research survey revealed the main reasons given for not purchasing all food requirements from Siop Swyddfa Post are that 'it is too costly' (83 per cent), 'it does not stock everything that is needed' (28 per cent), 'we do not like the people who run the shop' (22 per cent), 'it is not convenient' (11 per cent), 'it does not have enough variety' (6 per cent), and 'bulk-buy elsewhere' (22 per cent).

By 1982 John and Mary recognised that in addition to the problem of high running costs, the business was now faced with problems of supply and too few customers, but despite these difficulties they regarded the future of their business as 'difficult but secure' and, through careful management and sensible diversification, they have managed to reduce costs and achieve greater market penetration, thereby increasing the profitability of the store. There is considerable scope for improvement and further development, however.

Questions

1. Do you think the actions that they took as a result of attending the course in September 1981 were both sensible and sufficient?

2. Using the most recent figures from the *Annual Family Expenditure Survey*, estimate the approximate size of the *total market* for the products sold by John and Mary in the immediate catchment area of their shop.

3. What is the *approximate* share of this total market which John and Mary achieve?

4. What more could John and Mary do to increase their penetration of this potential market?

Case 19

B&B Decorators
Everett M Jacobs

Bob Kenton and Bill Lester were each in their mid-40s in 1978 when they decided to become partners in a painting and decorating business. They came from the same part of Leeds, and both had completed national service and an apprenticeship in painting and decorating before they became professional decorators. Since 1958 Bob had worked for a large firm specialising in contract work (eg offices, halls, churches etc). Bill started at a small family firm of interior decorators in 1957, but after a few years became increasingly dissatisfied over his wages and despondent over any chance of advancement within the company. He moved to a somewhat larger firm specialising in domestic work in 1961, and then to similar firms in 1966, 1968 and 1973. Each move brought improved wages, but not the greater managerial responsibilities or higher status in the company that Bill was aiming for. Bill finally decided that his best bet was to set up on his own, which he did in mid-1976.

Bob and Bill had been friends for a long time, having met at their local working men's club. They had often talked about 'being their own boss' but Bob was still slightly surprised when Bill actually started his own business.'I thought it was just talk,' he told Bill. 'I never believed you would do it. I'd like to start up on my own too, but I'd always be worried about the regular income. I know I haven't got much now, but I know what's coming in and I can pay the mortgage and the other bills.' Bill admitted that he thought of the security angle also, but was convinced that working for himself would earn him more than working for someone else, even if he did not have work every week. 'You see, you can be competitive and yet make your money because you don't have the overheads of the big companies. And believe me, there's a lot of work around if you look for it.' He added that he was not worried about his mortgage because his wife's part-time earnings covered it. Bob pressed him on what he would do if in the end he could not find work, and Bill said, 'Well, if it should happen, which it won't, I have a little put away for a rainy day. But don't forget, there's always unemployment benefit if you're out of work for more than 14 days. And then of course – it won't come to that – you can apply for supplementary benefit.'

Bill's initial investment in his business was limited, since he already had the tools of his trade. He used part of his savings to buy a second-hand mini van with roof-rack for £850, and had some leaflets advertising his services printed. He would drive around the 'better parts of town', pushing the leaflets through the letter-boxes of houses where new residents had just moved in or where building work was going on. There were a few enquiries from the leaflets, but no work materialised. His first few jobs came from neighbours and then gradually as a result of recommendations. Tradesmen with whom he had worked previously were especially helpful in the early days. For example, a business consultant renovating a large old house asked the plumber if he knew of a good decorator. Bill was recommended and got the job. The consultant and his wife were soon recommending Bill to their friends. The wife said to one, 'He's not cheap, but he's not expensive, and look at the beautiful work he does. You can leave him on his own without fear – I gave him his own key – and he cleans up any mess. The only thing is that it took him longer than he said, but it didn't cost us extra because he stuck to his quotation.'

Bill's business began to build up, and after about a year he had to start refusing some work. He was fully booked for the summer of 1977 and could not take about six outside jobs. He also had to turn down some inside jobs that autumn because they were too big for one man. It was then that he began to encourage Bob to form a partnership with him. Bob originally rejected the idea because he still feared loss of job security; he was not fully convinced that he could earn more by being self-employed, and he did not want to give up his present job before Christmas, which was always a slow period for decorators. Bill stressed that, considering the work he had to turn away, they could each earn after expenses ' a minimum' of £100 per week (which was more than Bob was then getting). He added that Bob's experience with contract work would be very useful in getting some well-paying big jobs so that they could earn much more than that. Bob's employer's attempt to hold down wages in the face of mounting inflation, and Bill's continued reports of the business he had to turn away, finally made Bob change his mind. The two men formed B&B Decorators in April 1978.

The basic agreement was to divide income and expenses equally, except for the van and a business telephone. Bill used his van for domestic as well as business use (which is why he never painted his name, business, or telephone number on it), and it was arranged that Bob would pay only 25 per cent of the road tax, insurance, petrol and maintenance. Likewise, the telephone was for Bill's domestic and business use and Bob paid 25 per cent of the rental, 50 per cent of the cost of an additional directory listing (under 'B&B Decorators') and 50 per cent of the estimated cost of business calls.

Because of their different areas of experience, they agreed that quotations for domestic work should be done by Bill, and for contract work by Bob. Their basic policy was to charge trade prices for materials (or let the customers provide their own) and, as far as possible, to maximise their hourly wage rate for the job. In 1978 they believed that about £3 per man-hour was 'reasonable' for domestic work, and £5 per man-hour, the 'proper tradesman's rate', was suitable for contract work. By 1985 these figures were £5 and £8.50 per man-hour respectively. However, they were aware of competitive pressures, and would usually be willing to cut their hourly rates if they were looking for work, so long as they received what they thought was an acceptable minimum income. Their notion of acceptable minimum weekly income depended on the season, ranging in 1978–79 from £50 per man in the November to February period, to around £70 for the rest of the year (in 1984–85, £100 and £125, respectively). The concept of profit per se was absent from their calculations.

Calculation of quotations for domestic work was relatively straightforward, depending on Bill's estimates of the time the job would take and the cost of materials. On contract work, Bob had two strategies. His first, and preferred one, was to work out what big firms would charge for the job and then undercut that figure somewhat, on the grounds that B&B had very low overheads. His second strategy, used only if B&B were very short of work, was to tell potential customers that they would charge less for comparable work than the lowest quotation already received. The problem with the second strategy was that some firms unknowingly (or, B&B sometimes suspected, knowingly) called in 'cowboy' firms for quotations, which B&B had to undercut if they wanted to work. The cowboy decorators were usually not professionally trained, and were able to charge low prices because they rushed the job, took short cuts, used poor quality materials, and then did not stand by their work. B&B stressed that their 'lower than the lowest quotation' was for 'comparable work', but they could seldom bring themselves to work like the cowboys, even if they felt obliged to charge cowboy prices. Bob explained that 'we need the work so we're forced to quote cheap, but we can't very well sacrifice our reputation, can we?'

In most years, B&B usually obtained 40–50 per cent of the domestic work they quoted for, amounting to 30–50 jobs, and 33–66 per cent of the contract work, amounting to two to four large jobs (of which one might be for 'lower than the lowest quotation'). Their average weekly income per man, after business expenses but before payment of personal taxes and NI contributions, is presented in Table A. They did not register for VAT because the partnership's annual revenue was below the minimum registration figure.

Table A. Average weekly income per man*, B&B Decorators

	£
1978 (9 months)	105
1979	125
1980	136
1981	150
1982	145
1983	152
1984	155
1985 (first 3 months)	125

*Including NI payments

Until 1982, Bob and Bill were reasonably happy with the progress of their business. Their main problem in those years was a shortage of work in December. They had to sign on for unemployment in December 1978 and 1980 and would have done so in 1981 had it not been for two medium-sized cut-price jobs that they obtained at short notice. In 1982 and 1983 the mounting unemployment in Leeds and the vicinity was bringing more cowboys into the decorating trade, and this began to have a noticeable effect on their business. Bob's wife lost her part-time job in February 1983, and this put him under extra financial pressure. Although she found work again in May, he told Bill that he wanted to get back on his feet before he thought about buying a newer vehicle for the business. The odd weeks without work threatened both men's holidays financially in 1983, but they still managed to take their usual two weeks (Bill at the start of June, and Bob at the end of August).

In February 1984 a new organisation opened in Leeds called Trusty Tradesmen. Its plan was to offer the public free information about reputable tradesmen specialising in building, repair and related trades and who would guarantee their work. It cost £75 to register with Trusty Tradesmen, and then £20 per month to cover group advertising, office expenses etc. Bill was eager to join as a way of fighting the cowboys, but Bob was worried about the new overheads and whether B&B would be the only decorators that Trusty Tradesmen would recommend. After assurances of 'fair play' from Trusty Tradesmen, B&B joined and in the first two months received leads on six jobs. They failed to obtain any of them, which was unusual for them. On the sixth, they arrived to give a quotation for decorating a youth centre just as a notorious cowboy was leaving. They later found out that their quotation of £3,000 was third lowest of the six firms sent to the youth centre by Trusty Tradesmen, and that the job went to the cowboy (also registered with Trusty Tradesmen) for £1,300. Bob was furious, but they could get no satisfaction from Trusty Tradesmen and therefore cancelled their registration.

A warm summer in 1984 meant that B&B had a lot of outdoor work, but they were usually in the position of having to reduce their quotation before getting the job. If Bill saw that a prospective customer was unhappy with a quotation he would usually say something like, 'I think you'll find our price is fair, but if you don't think so, what do *you* think is fair?' Then he would bargain with the customer, and managed to get about two out of three jobs they went for. Still, there were quite a few weeks in the autumn when they had little or nothing to do. Bob blamed it on the cowboys, but Bill thought the problem was also that many of their old customers were now feeling the financial pinch and were not decorating as often as in the past.

Both men were on the dole from December 1984 to mid-January 1985, when a few domestic jobs were obtained. By the end of March, they had enough indoor work to keep them busy for the next three or four weeks, but had booked only two outdoor jobs for the summer (instead of the four or five they usually had by then). Replacing their van was becoming a more urgent problem as it would probably not get through the September MOT and was costing a lot in running repairs. Bill had always been the more optimistic of the two, but when he picked up Bob one morning at the end of March he had to confess, 'I just don't know what we can do to improve things.'

Questions

1. Are 'cowboys' B&B's real competitive problem?
2. How should they set about making their business run successfully?

Case 20
Datachase Ltd

This case study has been prepared by *Colin Barrow* from material originally published in *Venture Capital Report*

By the autumn of 1984 it had become clear that Datachase's cautious entry into the short run continuous stationery market had paid off. In April of that year Kevin Smith had formed the company to sell products bought in from a new firm in Northumbria, but with sales on a rapid upward curve the time was right to buy in their own printing equipment. With a view to raising £20,000 risk capital Smith set down this history of events and a description of his business area.

Products

The product range includes all business forms and letter-heads split up between those printed by traditional printers on continuous stationery, and those which are only printed by the modern machines introduced over the past 12 months.

The printing can be thermographed, on blind embossed or plain paper, and it can be produced in any colour. Individual forms or sets of forms can be printed including NCR forms.

In addition, all forms and letter-heads, even on heavy paper, can be microperforated in metric sizes. This is particularly useful in the case of letter-heads for mail shots: a company can run the letters out on continuous stationery using machinery that is cheaper and more reliable than a sheet feeder, and requires less attention. Some wordprocessing bureaux estimate that using continuous stationery will reduce their prices by 20 per cent.

The market

The market for company stationery is rapidly changing as computers become commonplace. There has always been a demand for bespoke continuous stationery, but until recently it has only been used by companies with large computers, and was not cost-effective unless produced in long runs of 30,000 forms and upwards. With the introduction of the microcomputer a new demand has arisen for short runs of high-quality continuous stationery, such as letter-headings, invoices and other business forms, and this in turn has stimulated demand for new types of printing press that can be set up quickly for short runs.

Datachase researched the market in detail, both geographically and by customer sectors. This research involved interviewing many different types of potential customer, and discussing his business plan with the company in Northumbria which is supplying Datachase until Datachase can set up its own press. A market survey produced requests for quotations from 70 per cent of the companies visited.

The research concluded that the most effective marketing approach would be to sell to the existing print trade. Although the profit margin for Datachase is lower, there is sufficient mark-up to allow both Datachase and the print customer to take a reasonable profit without making the price to end-users uncompetitive. The trade was chosen because Datachase will be supplying products which are not available at economical prices elsewhere, and it is common practice in the print industry to buy in products more cheaply than they can be produced by the printer. Datachase's specialist market is for short runs of continuous stationery, and even if the printers themselves set up their existing machines to produce this stationery, the final costs to customers would be substantially more than buying from Datachase.

The trade is broken down into three groups:

1. *Printers.* These supply customers both with material that they print themselves and with products bought in from outside.
2. *Print buyers.* These are the middlemen who order on behalf of end-users. Their main concern is price, provided that the printer can deliver goods of the required quantity and quality on time.
3. *Computer service agencies/Wordprocessing bureaux.* Their customers normally require relatively small amounts of bespoke stationery – otherwise they would be carrying out their data processing in-house. At the moment wordprocessing bureaux often use sheet feeders which tend to be expensive and unreliable.

Datachase will be selling its products nationwide through the print buyers, but will set up its own sales offices in two areas: the south-west (in Launceston, Cornwall) where the competition is limited and where they expect to be able to develop a strong local base; and in the Manchester area. The Manchester office will be run by Austen Lennon, a Datachase director. Production will be in the south-west when the presses have been bought and set up, but until Datachase has its own printing facility it will continue to buy in printed products from Northumbria.

The people

Kevin Smith, the managing director, is 35 and married with four children. He left school with O levels in 1965 to become an apprentice printer with James Galt & Co, a family company manufacturing and distributing educational stationery.

He has an HNC in printing technology with supplementary graphic design from a day-release course at Manchester Polytechnic and took a BFMP course in cost accountancy.

In 1972 he was made production and administration manager for the printing division of James Galt, responsible for purchasing, production control, management reports, production administration and union negotiations. The printing division had a wide range of presses and machinery.

It was apparent by 1974 that further promotion within this family business was unlikely, and he left to use his accounting skills at Hestair Hope, manufacturers of educational and commercial stationery, bookbinders and manufacturers of toys and jigsaws. He was cost accountant, responsible for 8,000 items, cost control systems, liaison with production and the development of computer costing and production control systems.

After attending an ICL Dataskil computer programming course in 1975 he implemented a variety of computer systems for accounting, production and stock control. In 1976 he was promoted to management accountant with responsibility for bought and sales ledger, budgets, financial statements and company secretarial duties.

In 1980 he left Hestair Hope to start a catering business with his wife. They had four contracts, including one with the Manchester Police Training School. The business was reasonably successful, making a profit of £10,000 in 1982–83, but Mr Smith was keen to start his own printing company. He perceived a gap in the market, and on the strength of this was accepted by the Manchester Business School to join their New Enterprise Programme. While on this course he met and talked with the printer in Northumbria, and became further convinced of the soundness of his ideas.

Austen Lennon, also a director, will be based in Manchester. He met Kevin Smith on the New Enterprise Programme course at the Manchester Business School. After O levels in 1965 he joined Bough, Cox & Dunn, high quality printers and book-binders and served an apprenticeship as a litho-press printer while attending the Belfast College of Art and Design. In 1968 he was promoted to assistant manager in the litho department.

After two years he was contacted by the Queen's University, Belfast, who had been looking for a manager with qualifications in lithography and photography to help set up a new department on the same basis as today's copy shops. He ran the department from 1969–74, with a staff of 18, but decided to leave in order to gain sales experience.

Mr Lennon then joined Century Newspapers in Belfast, where he was in charge of starting a news broadsheet, *Bangor Shopping News*, which was in print after four months and is still in circulation today. In 1975 he became sales manager of the Northern Publishing Office, a sheet printing company, and was responsible for sales and sales promotions throughout Northern Ireland.

In 1977 Mr Lennon left NPO to join his family's company, Lennon Holdings. In 1982 he left this family business, which is still trading, and after completing the New Enterprise Programme at the Manchester Business School, decided to start his own business.

Financial data

Datachase has prepared a series of financial projections – pessimistic, optimistic and most likely. All the figures shown in Table A are from the most likely projections.

Table A. Profit and Loss Accounts for Years 1 and 2

Year	1	2
	£	£
Sales (1)	99,655	286,000
Cost of sales (2)	41,648	111,540
Gross profit	58,007	174,460
Overheads (3)		
Establishment	2,521	2,868
Factory	15,823	21,097
Administration	13,635	15,196
Sales	2,341	2,466
Depreciation	5,223	6,964
	39,543	48,591
Net profit	18,464	125,869

Notes:
1. Sales level in Year 1 is based on target levels and may be exceeded because orders already exceed targets substantially. The Year 2 figures are based on those achieved by the printer in Northumbria and a similar business in Stroud.
2. Costs are related to those of the Northumbria and Stroud businesses.
3. There is no allowance for financing of capital, and Mr Smith allows himself only a subsistence salary.

The cash flow in Table B shows a summary of the working capital requirements.

Table B. Summarised cash flow showing the working capital requirement

Quarter	1	2	3	4
	£	£	£	£
Income from debtors (1)	3,000	13,715	29,055	39,260
Creditors (1)	2,662	6,639	11,332	15,312
VAT	(51)	(966)	(898)	(595)
Establishment				
Rent and repairs	370	619	540	540
Heat and light		126	75	251
Factory				
Wages		4,971	4,971	4,969
Power		154	154	154
Consumables and repairs		100	275	275
Administration				
Stationery	690	—	—	—
Post and telephone	399	199	199	208
Wages	1,803	3,312	3,314	3,315
Insurance	247	—	—	—
Audit		—	—	149
Selling costs	652	597	597	495
	6,823	15,851	20,559	25,073
Quarterly balance	(3,772)	(2,036)	8,496	14,187
Opening balance	—	(3,772)	(5,808)	2,688
Closing balance	(3,772)	(5,808)	2,688	16,875

Note:
1. Payments to creditors and from debtors are estimated at 30 days.

The cost of capital equipment is shown in Table C.

Table C. Cost of capital equipment

	£
2 Printing presses	36,600
1 Rotaprint two-colour press	35,000
1 Collator	6,640
1 Platemaker	2,500
Heating equipment	1,000
	81,740
Grant income	(12,261)
	69,479

The maximum outflow will be £69,479 for capital equipment plus £6,735 working capital in month 5, but they would like an element for contingencies until they establish a firm customer base. Such contingencies include late payment by debtors, the possibility of late delivery of the presses and initial problems in running them. It is estimated that a further £20,000 would be sufficient to meet such demands.

Financial structure

The directors have put together a financing package as shown below:

	£
Directors' equity	8,000
Grants	12,261
Loans	69,479
Investor	20,000
	109,740

The equity structure proposed is shown below:

Name	%	Contribution
K Smith	51	Project to date
A Lennon	16	Project to date
Production director*	8	(loyalty incentive)
Investor	25	20,000

*perhaps an investor

Questions

1. Do you think six months is a long enough proving period to warrant the capital expenditure proposed by Datachase?
2. Why should the Northumbrian supplier be so forthcoming with information that will ultimately cause him to lose a customer?
3. Do you agree with the rationale behind the proposal to run a national sales operation from the south-west and a Manchester office?
4. Does the project seem attractive to you as a potential investor?

The Shaftesbury Hotel

Colin Barrow,
from material provided by *Jill and Bob Crowther*

Jill and Bob Crowther are the proprietors of the Shaftesbury Private Hotel in Blackpool. They bought the hotel in 1983 from a couple who had run it as a 'sideline'. Their main business was a general store and the hotel's business seemed to come from the overflow from neighbouring establishments.

The Shaftesbury has 11 bedrooms and is located a five-minute tram ride from the centre of Blackpool. Nearby are other small hotels, a number of bed and breakfast places, and closer towards town a scattering of bigger hotels.

Jill was 28 when they bought the hotel. She had taken an HND in catering at Salford, followed by a spell as catering manager with Bowater Scotts, running a works canteen for 1,000 people. Bob, a few years older, trained as a confectioner and in 1982 was suddenly and unexpectedly made redundant. Within weeks the same fate hit Jill, and living in the north-east of England they had no illusions as to their job prospects. This was the impetus that forced them to think seriously about 'being their own boss' – but in what type of venture?

Two years later with some mistakes but rather more successes behind them, Jill was reflecting on past events:

'The main problem we faced was deciding what type of business to enter. Money was clearly an important factor, but we felt it was essential to get into something we both understood, especially as neither of us were business people. This led us naturally towards catering, but even that is a wide field. Eventually we decided on a hotel. This had the great virtue of being a bricks and mortar investment and so was easier to borrow against. It also provided us with a home.

Our problems didn't stop there. As we had no particular preference of location we contacted estate agents all over Great Britain. We ended up wasting an incredible amount of time chasing all over the place looking at quite unsuitable premises. We feel very strongly about the poetic licence taken by estate agents when describing property. Many a period hotel with "olde worlde charm" turned out to be a tumble down ruin full of junk.

Eventually we narrowed our search to Blackpool, partly because my mother had recently moved here, and partly because it's a really nice place to live. Finally we had two similar properties to choose from, the main difference being the decorative state and a difference in price of £5,000.

We were very uncertain and decided to ask our bank manager for advice. He checked the accounts of each business and said he would only consider finance on the Shaftesbury. He was convinced the other figures were "dodgy" – so our decision was made for us.

To finance the deal we were looking for £25,000 to match the money we could put in, and the next shock we had was the difference in both attitudes and interest rates of the major banks. Even on a relatively small loan such as ours the spread between the most expensive and the lowest interest rates was equal to a week's takings!

Finally we chose Barclays whose interest rate at the time was the most favourable; also they were the most helpful and free with advice. And they have continued to help us as required.

In Blackpool, as in other holiday resorts, the business is highly seasonal and the lending institutions wisely take that into account. We could repay our bank loan during the four peak working months only, instead of monthly payments. Discovering that certainly made a difference to our initial cash flow forecasts. In the end we decided to make four large payments and eight smaller ones so as to keep the interest to a minimum.'

Jill went on to talk about their experiences with setting up their accounting and bookkeeping systems and with tax planning:

'We were advised to register the business in my husband's name only and for me to draw a small wage. We were told this would be beneficial for tax purposes at the year end, although it was never made clear to us why that would be so. The same accountant advised us what books to use and which ledgers to keep. However, due to our total ignorance of accounting we made dozens of mistakes in our first 12 months, and these proved ultimately to be very expensive when it came to putting our first 12 months' trading figures together.

Our figures were in such a mess it took several months to get them in a satisfactory shape to submit to the Inland Revenue. To compound the problem Bob (my husband) had not paid any Class 2 self-employment contributions for the whole 12 months. So that on top of a £450 accountant's bill was a fairly unpleasant surprise to complete our first year with!

The upshot of all that is we've now got a new accountant who is extremely patient and very helpful. And because we now understand what is going on, our accounting bill last year (1984) was only £250, and the figures took days rather than weeks to prepare.'

The property itself was not without its problems, as Jill explained:

'Completion date was 4 March 1983, which left us with three months to get the hotel into shape for the season. There was a lot to be done but fortunately Bob is an excellent handyman so we managed to do much of the carpentry and plumbing work ourselves. Also from a maintenance position it is absolutely vital that everything is in working order when guests are here. We can't afford to wait a couple of days for a plumber or electrician to show up.

I realise that with any property unforeseen problems occur, but the money we paid out on surveyors' fees seems to have been completely wasted. They failed to discover two major faults which have since proved extremely costly.'

Eventually the Shaftesbury opened for business and guests started to arrive. Jill and Bob concentrated their energies on establishing a sound working routine. Jill ran the kitchen, Bob the bar and hotel rooms, and they both did the buying once a week, fighting off the hundreds of sales representatives who seem to flood in with 'bargain offers' when any new business opens its doors.

'The summer progressed and business was fair, although we started to feel apprehensive about the lack of bookings for the Illumination period.

Money we spent on various advertisements in different newspapers and journals met with very poor results. As a consequence we have felt wary of using them again. However, early in July we were approached by a local hotelier with a proposal that involved sharing a coach party for a peak Illumination weekend. He had been offered a booking for 40 clients but could only accept it as a total package. With all of our 11 rooms he could just accommodate the party. The weekend in question was free so I gratefully accepted. The fateful day

215

arrived, as did the coach, but with only 21 people on board, who were all accommodated in the other hotel. This left us completely empty for a whole weekend at the height of the season!

We were told it was due to last minute cancellations on the coach party, but as we had no contract with the other hotel there was absolutely nothing we could do but grin and bear it!

This, unfortunately, was not our only problem with the law of contract. We had been informed that when a booking had been confirmed and a deposit paid, if the customer didn't show up you could invoice them for two-thirds of the total, and if necessary the small claims court would help. However, our laws are not binding in southern Ireland or in Scotland. On three occasions we were left with empty rooms during peak weeks with no chance of payment. Now we demand a larger deposit from customers outside England.'

By the end of the first year's trading Jill and Bob had learnt a number of valuable lessons and were in good shape for the second season, which was relatively trouble free. During the closed season their profits and some savings were ploughed back into improvements. A new sun lounge frontage and refurbishments to the hall improved the appearance dramatically. They feel that this investment led to a higher number of chance customers during their second season. It also made it easier for them to increase their tariffs without any adverse effects.

They managed to secure a contract to put up the key staff of a major retailer who was opening a new store in the area. This brought in substantial regular business throughout the summer and even into the winter when business is traditionally slack. However, this was not without its problems. For example, 'long stay' guests have very different requirements from holiday-makers and in a small hotel that can be hard to handle. Jill is optimistic about the future.

'The accounts for our second season show that our gross profit is 68 per cent, an increase of 5 per cent on last year. On 1 April 1985 we registered the business as a partnership on professional advice. The percentage split of the profits will be such as to make my share small enough to be exempt from Class 2 National Insurance stamps. As to the future, bookings for the season are fair and our turnover should go up again. But we are anxious not to exceed the VAT threshold. In an extremely competitive business such as ours another 15 per cent on prices could put people off. Looking further ahead still, within five years we could be looking for something larger and be starting up all over again.'

Questions

1. Do you think their bank manager was the best person to advise them which hotel to buy?

2. What steps could they have taken to improve the quality of professional advice they received in the first year, particularly the accounting and surveying advice?

3. Segment the market for the Shaftesbury Hotel. Describe the particular needs of each of the segments. Prepare a marketing and promotional plan to increase the number of customers of each of the market segments you feel that the Crowthers should want to attract.

4. Do you believe they have been soundly advised as to the legal form that the business should take?

Case 22
Cotswold Leasing & Finance Ltd

This case study has been prepared by *Colin Barrow* from material originally published in *Venture Capital Report*

In the spring of 1985 Christopher Cartwright was reviewing the progress of his three-year-old business. The company had started life as a financial brokerage but in 1984 it began to act as a lending principal, providing funds to clients themselves. This appeared to be a profitable change in direction but to grow it would need more cash – and access to reasonably priced loan capital. Although profits to date had been modest at least they had been profits! And the future looked rosy with Cartwright's projections showing profits of £200,000 in 1987 and £400,000 in 1988.

Company history

Christopher Cartwright started Cotswold Leasing & Finance Ltd (CLF) in March 1982 as a finance brokerage specialising in arranging finance for low-value items of capital equipment for businesses. A finance broker receives requests from companies wanting to arrange leasing or HP finance. He contacts other finance companies until he finds one willing to finance the sale on reasonable terms, then he agrees the sale. He is paid by the financier, and in turn pays for the equipment.

For example, the customer of a catering equipment supplier wants to lease a microwave oven which is sold by the dealer for £3,000. The 36 monthly lease payments will be £116.70 + VAT. The catering equipment supplier will contact CLF with details of the customer and the equipment to be sold. CLF will contact several lessors (ie Forward Trust, Tricity Finance etc) and find one that will finance the lease. CLF telephones the catering supplier, and the sale is made. The invoice is passed to CLF who forward it to the lessor. CLF is paid by the lessor (£3,000 + profit £240), and pays the supplier (3,000). The end-user pays the lessor directly by standing order – 36 monthly payments of £116.70 + VAT.

In the first nine months to 21 December 1982 sales were £207,000 and in the year to 31 December 1983 had increased to

£672,000. In 1984 the directors decided to change the corporate structure of the company, and set up the holding company Commercial and General Finance Group Ltd. CLF thus became the regional subsidiary, and other subsidiaries were formed in Plymouth, Exeter and Bristol. At 31 December 1984 CLF was the only operating company in the group, although the Plymouth subsidiary was due to start operating on 1 February 1985.

The company's objectives were also changed: its dependence on brokerage was to be reduced, and it took on the role of lending principal, albeit in a limited capacity, which increased its profitability. This was funded by block discounting whereby a block discounting company offers a company such as CLF a line of credit – say £50,000 – in blocks of £10,000. CLF then makes sales to a total of £10,000, and 'calls off' one block, although the block discounter will give credit only up to a maximum of 60 per cent of the sale value, leaving CLF to finance the remaining 40 per cent.

Despite the improvement in profitability, however, the directors were very aware of the lack of capital to fund future development.

The service and marketing

The group has so far had restricted financial resources, and has therefore limited its market to arranging finance in the £500–£5,000 (retail value) bracket, with an average sale of £3,000 although sales of up to £30,000 are handled by the finance brokerage side.

The company has two main methods of selling its services: either through new equipment dealers, or direct to users who have used CLF before or who have been recommended.

Dealers use CLF to finance their sales for several reasons:

1. CLF's policy is to provide a reliable service, financing the same type of goods consistently: some other finance companies move in and out of various market sectors, so that dealers are never sure whether they are likely to finance a transaction.
2. Flexibility. The company offers a wide range of financing arrangements and terms, including leasing, HP and loans.
3. CLF is known to be a reliable and flexible payer.
4. Simple documentation enables even the most inexperienced salesman to complete a transaction.

CLF chose the low-cost capital equipment market sector because this type of business is not sensitive to the changes in capital allowances and consequently there are fewer finance companies fighting for this type of business. They are therefore able to charge higher rates, and on each transaction only a small sum is at risk. The company specialises in financing catering and low-technology equipment because these show a lower percentage of debtor default, and the equipment is not usually superseded for reasons of fashion or new technology.

CLF's sales manager approves dealers, who are instructed how to operate the necessary procedures and to conclude finance arrangements with acceptable customers.

CLF has 61 approved dealers, and a further 89 in various stages of negotiation, and most dealers use CLF exclusively. In some instances dealers expect to receive an introductory commission, but this facility is limited to four dealers and restricted to 1 per cent of sales volume. At the moment the increase in newly appointed dealers is being restricted because the company is unable to accommodate any large increase in sales, as they do not want to stimulate demand they cannot meet. Nevertheless, the company receives numerous enquiries every month and is currently concentrating on developing a number of national schemes.

The management

Christopher Cartwright, the managing director, is 30 and married with two children. He left Worsley Wardley Grammar School in Manchester in 1972 with A levels in economics and history to start work as an accounts assistant with Cussons & Sons.

In 1974 he joined British Telecom as a contracts engineer; in 1975 Fairey Engineering as a contracts administrator; in 1977 Ferranti Computer Systems in a similar capacity, negotiating multi-million pound contracts for the sale of bespoke computers to police forces, fire brigades, the Home Office etc. In 1979 in pursuit of better remuneration, he moved to the finance subsidiary of Williams & Glyn's, as a sales representative, and in 1981 he became branch manager of Manson Leasing in Cheltenham. Later in the same year he joined the ex-managing director of Manson Leasing in his own company, Grafton Mercantile Leasing Ltd, finance brokers as director and general manager. He left in 1982 to start Cotswold Leasing and Finance.

Cartwright's wife is a director of the company. She worked for Tricentrol (UK) Ltd for eight years as the manager of their

Cheltenham office, and for two years with Western Staff Agency as branch manager of their Cheltenham office.

Michael Vaughan Scantlebury, group sales manager based in Plymouth is 39 and married with two children. From 1963 to 1975 he was in the RAF after which, in 1977, he joined Highland Leasing as area manager for Devon and Cornwall. He was promoted to district manager for the same area, and later to regional sales manager for Scotland. He joined CLF in 1984, and will run the Plymouth subsidiary.

There is a sales manager in Cheltenham, and sales and accounts administrators.

Financial data

The profit and loss accounts for CLF for the years to 31 December 1982 and 1983, the draft outline for 1984 and the forecast for 1985 and 1986 are shown in Table A.

Table A. Profit and Loss Accounts

Year to 31 December	1982 £	1983 £	1984 £	1985 £	1986 £
Sales					
Brokerage commission	14,383	49,092	34,000	151,400	202,000
Own finance	—	—	27,000	108,890	264,245
Total	14,383	49,092	61,000	260,290	466,245
Block discount costs	—	—	14,000	46,110	117,980
	14,383	49,092	47,000	214,180	348,265
Administration	13,224	42,904	42,000	139,770	203,390
Interest	991	1,423	1,000	16,340	16,313
	14,215	44,327	43,000	156,110	219,703
Net profit	168	4,765	4,000	58,070	128,562

Notes:

1. Administration costs.

	Actual 1983 £	Forecast 1985 £
Salaries	14,498	49,500
Rent, rates, insurance	2,570	14,270
Light and heat	412	—
Telephone and post	4,206	8,600
Printing and advertising	4,291	9,000
Travel	6,148	12,200
Credit reference fees	5,584	10,500
Depreciation	1,923	3,400
Other	3,272	32,300
	42,904	139,770

Other in 1985 includes provisions for bad debts of £13,000, commissions to distributors of £7,000 and legal fees of £3,700.

The increase in administration costs in 1985 occurs because the group operate two offices, and there are additional staff: another salesman and three more administrators. There is also provision for bad debts for the first time; in previous years the company's principal business has been brokerage, with no need to provide for bad debts.

The directors have produced a detailed cash flow statement which is not reproduced here.

The draft balance sheet of CLF at 31 December 1984 is shown in Table B.

Table B. Draft Balance Sheet at 31 December 1984

	£	£
Fixed assets		11,000
Current assets		
Debtors	84,000	
Current liabilities		
Creditors	78,000	
		6,000
		17,000
Financed by		
Share capital		8,500
Reserves		8,500
		17,000

Questions

1. Do you think their four reasons why dealers should use them amount to a 'unique' proposition?
2. Is their strategy of market concentration soundly based, particularly their assessment of the catering and low-tech markets?
3. How realisitic do you think Cartwright's projections for sales and profits are? (Bear in mind that 51 dealers were needed to finance sales in 1984.)
4. How much additional finance should Cartwright look for if he is to achieve profits of £400,000 in 1988, and what form should that finance take?

Case 23
The Supreme Garden Furniture Company
Roger McMullan

The 1970s saw a tremendous upsurge in the home improvement market with the growth of many specialist DIY and gardening outlets selling directly to the public.

This growth coincided with an increase in available leisure time as a result both of a steady reduction in the average working week and a dramatic national increase in unemployment.

Gordon Smith had been made redundant in 1981, having been employed as a design engineer for the Lancashire-based subsidiary of a large national firm.

For a number of years his hobby had been making reproduction garden furniture. During recent years, prior to being made redundant, he seemed to spend more and more of his spare time making various designs of garden seats, benches and tables for friends and, as his reputation spread, for friends of friends.

Following the loss of his job, many of his friends encouraged him to turn his hobby into a business, but being by nature a conservative person and not wishing to be rushed into something which he might regret, he actively pursued his efforts to find another job.

However, as the months passed and he became increasingly disheartened by his failure to find a job which didn't mean having to uproot his family and move to the south of England, his thoughts turned increasingly to his hobby and he found himself evaluating the implications of establishing his own business.

With professional advice from his accountant he drew up a business plan incorporating cash and profit forecasts, an assessment of the market, his likely competitors, the plant and machinery required and the start-up capital which he would need.

With his redundancy money and by using a little, but not all, of his own capital, he knew that he could finance his working capital requirements as projected in his cash flow forecast for the first year without borrowing from his bank.

He realised that the garage in which he had always worked would be insufficient from which to run a business and he managed to acquire an 800 sq ft workshop on the ground floor of an old textile mill.

Gordon began producing a range of one-, two-, three- and four-seat garden benches in an authentic Victorian design, together with matching tables. Each item in the range was manufactured to a very high standard using top quality materials. The Victorian-style end sections of each bench were cast in aluminium by a local supplier using Gordon's own die which he had produced himself. He then had these sections treated in Telcothene powder coating which kept them rust-free and increased their durability.

The base of each seat was made from panels of kiln-dried African Iroko hardwood which he imported from Ghana through a Liverpool timber merchant. Gordon cut these to the required lengths in his own workshop where he assembled the completed benches.

The quality of the completed product meant that he was able to charge a premium price. Despite being often 30 per cent higher in price than his competitors – who were mainly small operators like himself – his product was highly regarded.

Shortly after the end of his first year of trading Gordon arranged to meet his accountant to review his progress. His turnover in the first year – despite initial teething problems with some of his wood sanding equipment and a lengthy rainy spell in late May and early July which hit sales – had been satisfactory at just over £38,000.

He was fairly pleased with himself, particularly as he had made a modest profit which he intended ploughing back into the business and he had indeed been able to finance the business entirely from his own start-up capital – a rare achievement, his accountant assured him, in an age when most business functioned with an overdraft facility, at least. His accountant impressed upon Gordon the need to plan ahead for the next 12 months and they agreed to meet again in a week's time to do so.

During the ensuing week Gordon gave a lot of thought to the future and, buoyed up by the success of his first year, he decided that the planning meeting should be devoted to exploring how he could best expand his business. However, as they looked in turn at each function of the business, Gordon's accountant very quickly began to highlight many of the deficiencies in the business which hadn't been apparent to him and which, particularly if he chose to follow his desire to expand, might ruin everything he had achieved.

Sales and distribution

From the outset Gordon had spent one day a week out on the road selling – initially in Lancashire, Yorkshire and Cheshire – and had found business easy to come by. In time, however, he found that the size of orders he was receiving from his main customers – garden centres – was small and he decided to spend three days in the London area taking samples of his product range from one garden centre to another in a hired van.

This proved to be a tremendous success and he found that the really huge garden centres in the south-east would sometimes order £2,000-worth of seats at a time, whereas in his home area a £500 order was exceptional.

This was all very well but he had only been able to repeat this three-day sales trip on one further occasion and he felt increasingly that the real volume market for his products was in the south-east, and he was in the north-west. The business could not sustain a sales representative on the payroll yet somehow he must find a solution to his problem.

Gordon had decided from the beginning that distribution of orders to his customers could only be handled by a firm of carriers. He had felt it was important that a bulky, awkwardly shaped product should be handled by a reputable firm with a good distribution network and so he had used a nationally known firm of carriers. The local depot manager was particularly helpful – Gordon often required collections at short notice and they had always accommodated him – even though there seemed to be big variations in the rates which he was charged.

His accountant quite rightly pointed out that there had been a dramatic increase in distribution costs in the latter part of the summer as business in the south-east had increased.

Marketing

Gordon was an engineer and the first to admit that he thought marketing was one way of making a straightforward job – selling – seem more complicated. The first year, he felt, was proof that the quality of his product would always guarantee sales.

He had dabbled at marketing to begin with – somebody had told him about a free direct mail scheme which the Post Office offer to first-time users. He arranged for a friend, who was a good amateur photographer, to take some shots of his range of seats and he had had a leaflet printed incorporating them.

In all, he sent out 500 leaflets to garden centres around the country. As far as he knew, 10 potential customers responded by phone and six subsequently placed firm orders. He wasn't sure about the exact number of respondents because during the week after the mailing he had been forced to spend the best part of three days away from the workshop.

Recently, he had been approached by the buyer from a large supermarket chain. This company had diversified into garden centres attached to their stores and wanted Gordon to produce the same range of seats for them under their own label.

To Gordon the offer had many attractions. Although on average his own seats sold at £110 and the own label range would be at a lower price – £75 – there was still a good margin in it for him and of course there were definite savings on distribution which would be made to a central depot once a month from just before Easter to August of the following season.

Gordon had spent a lot of time and effort getting the name of his own product range – Supreme Garden Furniture – known in the trade, but how could he afford to turn down the possibility of doubling his turnover in the second year, particularly when all of that business came from one customer?

As if he hadn't enough to think about, Gordon's accountant reminded him that his two main competitors had both taken stands at the previous year's Garden and Leisure Exhibition at the National Exhibition Centre, Birmingham. In view of Gordon's entry into the market and his obvious success, wouldn't they be likely to use this year's exhibition in three month's time to recapture some of the business which they had lost?

It also occurred to him that he must find some way of getting his Supreme range more widely known in the trade. His selling trips were usually successful but they were very time-consuming and he wondered if he couldn't try a different approach.

Finance

This was one area, in Gordon's view, where he had few worries. With the help of his accountant he had developed a system of financial control which, with his wife spending two hours a week regularly writing up his books, gave him an accurate picture of his current financial position.

It came as a surprise, therefore, when his accountant cast doubts on his ability to remain self-financing in the next 12 months. 'Don't forget,' he said 'that your selling season is short

– from just before Easter through to the end of the summer. In your first year, you spent the months during autumn and winter setting up your workshop, organising suppliers and establishing initial contact with your customers. We are now in September; have you thought what will happen to your cash flow in the next six months leading up to Easter?'

Gordon realised that his bank balance was likely to be totally drained in the next few months as he built up stocks for the season ahead. How could he overcome this imbalance in his cash flow? More to the point, how would the potential own label business affect his cash flow?

Staff

By nature a cautious person, Gordon had an in-built resistance to employing staff. Outwardly he explained to his friends that the business could not afford any employees. While this was in part correct, he knew inwardly that he couldn't trust others to work to the same exacting standards which he had set himself.

Often, when he was returning from a selling trip or finishing an order late at night in the workshop, he thought how invaluable it would be to have a conscientious craftsman to look after the production side of the business. However, it could take at least six months for such a person to bring a return in the way of increased business and he didn't see how he could sustain the additional overhead for so long.

Production/premises

One problem which Gordon had already recognised was that he was rapidly outgrowing his workshop. When he took deliveries from the timber merchant the quantities involved tended to swamp the workshop and leave him precious little room for production and storage of his finished product.

The owner of the mill complex had mentioned a week or two previously that he had another workshop of about 600 sq ft on another part of the site which was available on a three-year lease at nearly half the weekly rental of his workshop. Gordon thought that this was too good an opportunity to miss and that he could use the additional space for the storage of both timber and finished products. At least that would be one of his problems out of the way.

The way ahead

Gordon left the meeting with his accountant feeling rather dispirited and extremely confused. He wondered if he really needed to feel this way – after all, accountants are well known, he thought, for being prophets of doom. On the other hand, there seemed to be many home truths in the problems which they had discussed – unfortunately, they hadn't really come up with any solutions.

His accountant had concluded the meeting by suggesting that Gordon should give further consideration to all these issues and put his thoughts together in a written plan.

Questions

1. How well do you think Gordon has done in his first year?
2. Has he covered all the important areas in the analysis of his business, prior to embarking on the next 12 months?
3. How should he go about expanding his business? Prepare a list of key tasks he should carry out, and suggest some goals and objectives for him to aim for.

Case 24
Illustrated Tee Marker Boards Ltd

This case study has been prepared by *Colin Barrow* from material originally published in *Venture Capital Report*

Brian Hughes and Alan Lyddon had been burning the midnight oil to put together their plans for the next three years. Since starting in 1981 they had reached the end of 1984 with modest sales, but a firm conviction that at last their policies were beginning to pay off. However, the cost of arriving at that formula for success had been great and if the company was to move forward a fresh capital injection was required.

The product

Illustrated Tee Marker Boards Ltd (ITMB Ltd) offers illustrated tee marker boards to golf clubs, free of charge, in return for a contract to display the boards for 10 years. A marker board is situated at or near a tee in a prominent position, with a coloured illustration of the hole to be played, and an advertisement panel below.

Tees are normally marked by a tee box, displaying in figures the hole number, par and handicap, and the distance to the hole. The illustrated tee marker board provides much more information for the golfer, with its detailed plan, grid and numerical information. The board measures 20 x 24 in, and is made of unbreakable polycarbonate (as used for police riot shields), supported on a plastic-dipped steel frame. It stands approximately 3 ft high when installed.

Company history

ITMB Ltd was formed in 1981 by Brian Hughes, who designed the first boards and organised their installation in the Newport area. In a bid to expand, he then joined forces with John Farrow, a financier who invested £22,000, after which a further £75,000 was obtained through a government guaranteed loan. The company recruited a sales director and two salesmen through a well-known recruitment agency, bought cars, and geared up for a national marketing campaign. Unfortunately, there were problems with the marketing strategy, particularly selling advertising, and the staff did not perform as well as expected; although the sales director and one salesman were made redundant in early 1984, the company had by then spent much of the £75,000.

The directors reviewed the position and decided to give exclusive agencies for the idea in regions, making agents responsible for signing up golf clubs and for selling advertising. ITMB Ltd charges the agent £1,400 per club for the first year's rental of the boards, after which there is an annual charge of £1,000 per club. In return, ITMB Ltd provides the boards and sales leads. The advertising income per club is approximately £3,500 per annum, so the agent obtains c.£2,500 per club; the agent for East Anglia had regularly been making sales of £3,000 every three weeks, and his sales were rising. In four months he had completely sold six courses.

There are currently seven agencies in the UK and Ireland, one in Spain, and a licensing agreement with an Austrian company.

The market

There are in excess of 2,000 golf clubs in the UK, including 750 major 18-hole clubs with over 500 members. They were all mailshotted, and this resulted in 250 replies, with three to four enquiries still being received each week two years after the mailing. Hughes believes that, using exclusive agencies, the maximum number of clubs likely to take a contract is c.600.

The clubs are visited by the salesman or agent, and Alan Lyddon, the sales director, says that there is little difficulty in persuading club secretaries to sign a 10 year contract. The salesmen must then sell 18 advertisements, one for each board. (On some courses there may be two additional boards, each showing the whole course.)

The salesmen start with golf club members who run businesses, because they are easier to persuade initially, and have a high rate of annual renewal (currently 85 per cent). They then canvass other local businesses. The cost to advertisers is £150–£350 per board, per annum.

Lyddon will recruit at least two new agents every year up to a maximum of 15 and expects every agent to sign up eight courses per annum. By the end of 1985, 65 more courses will have boards installed (30 have already been installed), and by December 1986, he forecasts that he will have 169 golf courses installed, and over 500 by 1989.

The people

Brian John Howard Hughes, the originator of ITMB Ltd, is 33 and single. He was educated at Gowerton Grammar School and Newport College of Art and Design in 1970, where he studied graphics design, graduating in 1974. He gained his master's degree in 1975. Returning to Newport College of Art, he became a designer-in-residence, which included some undergraduate teaching. In 1977 he started the Brian Hughes Design Consultancy, while continuing to teach at Newport College of Art and Bristol Polytechnic. The design service now employs five and is used by medium and large companies requiring design input for their promotional and public relations activities. The work includes interior print and exhibition design. Clients include Ferranti, Hitachi, Sector Design Consultants, and Faber & Faber. He spends about one day a week on ITMB, in which he has invested £8,000, and has charged nothing for his time to date.

Alan Lyddon, the sales director, is 28 and married with one child. He left school with O levels in 1973, and joined the South Western Electricity Board as a trainee manager. In 1975 he moved to Caribonum, where he sold stationery supplies, and in 1976 to British Tissues, as a territory manager.

Lyddon then joined Slazenger, selling their golfing products, becoming top salesman in 1978–79 and 1980. He was promoted to control 25 major accounts, and was responsible for employing, training and motivating van salesmen and area managers. He joined Trendan Sports Ltd, a subsidiary of Martini, in January 1983 as area manager and in nine months doubled sales in his area, but Martini pulled out of Trendan Sports, and he was made redundant.

In March 1984 he joined ITMB Ltd, investing £10,000 in the company. Since joining, he has reorganised the sales, and initiated the change to exclusive agents. Turnover increased by 150 per cent in 1984 over 1983, and should increase a further 150 per cent in 1985.

A keen sportsman, Lyddon has represented Gloucestershire in football, cricket, table tennis and golf. He now concentrates on golf, has represented the county for 10 years, and has been elected as the next captain of the Gloucestershire Golf Union.

The company's accountant has prepared a series of financial projections including best, middle and worst cases. The profit and loss account (middle) forecast is shown in Table A.

Table A. Profit and Loss Account

Year	Actual 1983	Actual 1984	Forecast 1985	1986	1987
Number of agencies		5	9	10	12
Courses contracted and installed	6	30	102	182	278
	£	£	£	£	£
Sales (1)					
Agency sales	—	6,000	101,200	184,700	279,700
Advertising revenue (2)	16,922	50,541	32,000	35,000	35,000
	16,922	56,541	133,200	219,700	314,700
Less					
Direct costs (3)	49,909	67,655	55,462	86,439	110,483
Gross profit/loss	(32,987)	(11,114)	77,738	133,261	204,217
Less overheads	13,132	16,502	20,800	24,900	26,900
Interest	3,920	9,374	8,165	6,545	4,925
	17,052	25,876	28,965	31,445	31,825
Net profit/loss	(50,039)	(36,990)	48,773	101,816	172,392

Notes:
1. Sales are based on agents' estimated remittances to ITMB less 30 per cent.
2. Advertising revenue is from courses where the advertising is sold by ITMB. Advertising revenue in 1985 falls because some of the courses signed to ITMB are now operated by agents.
3. Direct costs include salesmen and expenses. In 1983 and 1984 there was a sales director, two salesmen and expenses; in 1985 there was only Mr Lyddon, who receives £8,000 plus commission. Other direct costs are mainly the depreciation of the boards. The material costs of a finished board are approximately £1,000: these are capitalised and depreciated over 10 years.

The accountant has calculated that an injection of £40,000 combined with the existing bank overdraft facility of £30,000 will enable the company to install ITMBs at 90 courses in the next 12 months.

The draft balance sheet as at 31 December 1984 is shown in Table B.

Table B. Draft Balance Sheet at 31 December 1984

	£	£
Fixed assets		46,198
Goodwill		12,000
Current assets		
Debtors	22,160	
Stock	1,050	
	23,210	

Current liabilities

Overdraft	32,466	
Creditors	17,849	
Loan and HP payments	13,766	
	64,081	
Net current liabilities		(40,871)
		17,327
Loan and HP repayments due after 1 year		52,117
		(34,790)

Represented by

Share capital	100
Directors' loans (1)	59,900
Profit and loss reserves	(94,790)
	(34,790)

Note:

1. The directors will capitalise their loans when the investor injects £40,000.

Questions

1. How much money should ITMB be looking for and in what form should that money ideally be (ie, equity, loans, overdraft)?
2. Do you believe in the formulae for success that ITMB has developed?
3. How attractive a proposition do you think being an agent for ITMB would be?
4. What strategy would you recommend they adopt from the position they found themselves in in January 1985.

Case 25
Zora Company Ltd

This case study has been prepared by *Colin Barrow* from material originally published in *Venture Capital Report* and from subsequent discussion with *Mr Gnjatovic*

Ljubomir Gnjatovic was explaining his latest business venture to Tim Rice, the managing director of a venture capital fund. The plan was to make and market a machine to produce high quality bricks from common earth. The market for this lay in the Third World where the transition from mud huts to houses was being impeded by the high cost of conventional building materials. This is a transcript of Rice's interview notes.

The product

The brickmaking machine produced by Zora Company Ltd works as follows:

1. Common earth which contains some clay, such as is freely available almost everywhere on the earth's surface, is passed through a sieve.
2. Water is then added to the earth to achieve the right consistency. If a specially water-resistant brick is required, then two chemicals, known by their trade names Consolid 44 and Consevex, may be added to water.
3. The Zora scoop, which holds precisely enough raw material for one brick, is then filled, and the earth poured into the brick chamber.
4. The heavy, steel top-plate of the chamber is then closed, and the hydraulic piston compresses the earth with a force of 35 tons. The motion of the piston is controlled by a simple lever. The piston is then lowered a little to take the pressure off the top-plate, the top released and the piston raised again to push out the finished brick. The top of the rectangular piston has a raised section to produce a frog in the brick.
5. The chamber on the present machine yields a brick of 11 × 5.5 × 4in. Future machines will have several interchangeable chambers to produce bricks of varying sizes and shapes.

6. The brick in this form is already extremely strong and cannot be broken, and is left to cure in the open. The bricks are ready for use after about eight days, and continue to cure and gain full strength for a further three weeks.

The cycle time of the present machine is 40 seconds, although a new machine is planned with a cycle time of only 12 seconds. One man should be able to produce 150 bricks per hour with this machine.

The following primary advantages are claimed for the system:

Ease of use. The machine is extremely robust and simple, and may be manually operated or powered by an electric or petrol motor, depending on local conditions. The power supplies are interchangeable.

Quality. The quality of the bricks produced by this method is only very slightly less than a conventional baked brick and is a great deal higher than that of the mud bricks widely used throughout much of the world, which are produced with little or no pressure. The major weakness of mud bricks produced without pressure is that they absorb water by capillary action and so erode relatively quickly. Nevertheless, a single-storey building will last for up to 25 years in a reasonably dry climate. The combined effect of the high pressure and the chemical additives is to produce a brick which is much stronger, and which will also resist water. Mr Gnjatovic believes that his bricks will last at least 25 years, and probably for 50 years or more.

Zora bricks could not be broken even immediately after manufacture, and the cured bricks seemed to be roughly equivalent to baked bricks in feel and hardness. They are currently having some proper strength tests conducted at the Building Research Centre in Watford. If even stronger bricks are required, 5–10 per cent of cement may be added to the earth mix.

Price. The machine to produce these bricks will be priced at £2,000 for the manual version, £2,500 for the electric version and £2,600 for the petrol version. This compares with a price of perhaps £200 for a single unpressurised mud brick machine, and several million pounds for a factory with a brick kiln. Since the earth is free and the only cost will be labour, chemicals and power, the cost of a brick produced by this system will be about 1p compared with perhaps 20p for a baked brick which must then be transported to the site. The following table expresses the above more succinctly:

Brick	Low-technology unpressurised mud bricks	Intermediate-technology pressurised mud bricks with chemical additive (Zora)	High-technology brick factory with kiln
Capital cost	£200	£2,000	£1m +
Cost of brick	< 1p	< 1p	20p + transport
Life of brick	25 yrs max.	25–100 yrs	100–300 yrs
Present usage	Very widespread in Third World	Only 6 machines in existence	Widely used in industrialised countries
Energy requirement	Natural curing	Natural curing	High temperature kiln

Brief history and reactions to prototype

In 1981 Mr Gnjatovic was in an aeroplane with a personal friend, Mr Koko, who was responsible for building the new capital of Nigeria, Abuja, a project for which Mr Gnjatovic was to supply aluminium windows. During the course of their journey Mr Koko said, 'You are an engineer: why don't you design a simple machine to make good bricks of earth which will operate in the wilds under its own power?' To begin with Mr Gnjatovic thought that his friend was joking, but later made many journeys to the interior of the country and soon came to realise that about 90 per cent of houses were in fact made of mud, and that mud is widely used as a building material throughout much of the world.

Back in England, he began experimenting and quickly realised the great increase in quality that could be obtained by compressing the earth, and later discovered that by adding the water-repelling chemicals, a brick which compares very favourably with baked bricks could be produced for a small fraction of the cost.

The first prototype machine went to Nigeria in late 1981, but by this time the Nigerian economy was beginning to experience problems, with the result that severe difficulties were put in the way of imports and no orders for the brick machine could be paid for. However, word of the machine had by this time reached Mr Muna, the president of the National Assembly of the Cameroons, who then came with his entourage to visit Mr Gnjatovic and was delighted with what he saw. Seven machines were ordered immediately and were shipped in 1982. When these proved highly successful in the field, a contract for a further 100 was issued, with a value of £305,000. The following paragraph quotes from a letter received by Mr Gnjatovic from the government of the Cameroons, acknowledging the receipt of the first machines: 'As I had thought, the importance of this machine can hardly be overestimated.... Government officials and leaders, as well as the governors of the different provinces have been thrilled by the machine'.

An agreement was made under which the company established by Mr Muna and the government of the Cameroons took the marketing rights for the Cameroons, Chad, Gabon, Zaire, Equatorial Guinea and the Central African Republic, and the initial order was increased to 300 machines with a value of over £900,000. Before the first order for 100 could be fulfilled, however, there were political troubles in the Cameroons, and several assassination attempts on leading political figures. The government changed and the contract lapsed.

To resurrect the project, Mr Gnjatovic approached the British Overseas Trade Board, who distributed a leaflet describing the machine in November 1983, and this resulted in over 200 enquiries from 50 countries including, surprisingly, many from Europe where the bricks would be used for agricultural buildings. From these enquiries they have now received five orders for trial machines as follows:

Uganda	2
Cameroons	1
Pakistan	1
Benin	1

When these machines prove their worth in the field, Mr Gnjatovic is confident that larger orders will result.

He has had discussions with a company who supply Iran with building materials, who have indicated a requirement for Iran for 500 machines per year. But the best indicator of the potential for the machines remains the order for 300 from the old company in the Cameroons, who based their order on having used seven machines in the field.

While any predictions about market potential must clearly be highly speculative at this stage, however, annual demand for his machines could be as follows:

Country	Annual demand
Cameroons	100
Rest of Africa	1,000
Europe	100
Iran	500
Middle East	1,000
India and Pakistan	500
China	1,000
South America	1,000
Other	1,000
Total	6,200

Marketing

The greatest problem will be marketing the machine simultaneously in so many countries. However, Mr Gnjatovic is making an arrangement with the Swiss company who supply the two water-repelling chemicals. This company has depots and agents in 23 countries and is happy to help market the machine in order to sell more of its chemicals.

In order to market the machine, Mr Gnjatovic proposes to attend building trade shows in as many countries as possible and to use these shows both to sell some machines directly to users and also to find agents to cover each country. The agents will be expected to attend building exhibitions in their countries and to demonstrate the machine regularly in the field, and Mr Gnjatovic will make a contribution to their expenses.

The man

Ljubomir Gnjatovic is 43 and was born in Yugoslavia, where he received a degree in machine engineering from Belgrade University. On graduating he became an engineer for a company manufacturing Massey Ferguson combines under licence, and frequently found it necessary to talk to English engineers. He decided to go to England, in order to improve his English, and finally arrived in 1962 staying with his uncle and aunt while studying English at a GLC college. When he finished the English course in 1964, Mr Gnjatovic decided to remain in England.

His first job in England was with Afib Engineering, who made costume jewellery, and for whom he worked for six months as a designer/engineer. He then began manufacturing costume jewellery himself in the basement of his uncle's house, trading as Zora Jewellery Ltd, and using a few simple machines which he acquired from scrap merchants.

During the next few years this company expanded steadily, both by increasing its range of products and also by using fewer subcontractors. The following table gives some relevant figures.

Year	Employees	Homeworkers	Sales
1964	3	15	£100,000
1970	14	30	£300,000
1975	20	50	£500,000

In 1970 the company, now called Zora International Ltd, moved into its present premises, an 8,000 sq ft factory on an 18-year lease in Hounslow.

Before 1975 the costume jewellery industry was highly structured and rigid divisions were maintained between manufacturers, wholesalers and retailers, and wholesalers would never order less than 10 gross of a particular design from a manufacturer. With the influx of Ugandan Asians, however, the industry changed dramatically and small manufacturers began to sell small quantities of jewellery direct to retailers, or even direct to the customer. The effect on Zora was that the average order fell dramatically, and Mr Gnjatovic remembers receiving one order from a wholesaler for just six units of one design.

At this level, the business becomes uneconomical in the UK, and to keep his machines busy Mr Gnjatovic began developing links with Nigeria, selling costume jewellery in even larger volumes, and also becoming a subcontractor to aluminium window and double glazing manufacturers in the UK.

Then in 1978 the Nigerian government imposed an import duty of 100 per cent on costume jewellery, so killing that side of Mr Gnjatovic's business at a stroke. However, having developed contacts in Nigeria, he was able to become a general trader to Nigeria, buying and selling a great variety of products.

Among these were the aluminium windows he was still manufacturing in London. His first large order for these to Nigeria was for £350,000 in 1980. This was completed and paid for in 1981, and was followed by an order for £1.4 million with further orders for £2 million and £3 million promised. After the first part of the first order had been shipped, in April 1982, the Nigerian government announced that an import licence was required. It was not until April 1983 and after 11 visits to Nigeria that Mr Gnjatovic finally obtained this licence. Even then he was unable to ship his goods, since by this time currency transfers were blocked in Nigeria. By October 1983 Mr Gnjatovic realised that the position was hopeless and that he could no longer keep Zora International afloat. The company finally went into liquidation in January 1984, owed over £200,000 from Nigeria. If the order for £1.4 million had been supplied as agreed and the £200,000 paid, there would have been £750,000 in cash in the company by January 1984.

In order to salvage what he could, Mr Gnjatovic formed Zora Company Ltd in October 1983, and the company repurchased various machines from the liquidator, including the rights to the brick machine.

Financial data

Table A gives the approximate economics of a sale of the petrol-powered brick machine.

Table A. Sale of petrol-powered brick machine

	1 Unit £	50 Units £	500 Units £
Cost, including materials, payment to subcontractors, assembly labour	1,200	950	800
Contribution to overheads and profit	1,400	1,650	1,800
Price (1)	2,600	2,600	2,600

Note:
1. Mr Gnjatovic's policy had been to price a single unit at over £4,250 and to give discounts for larger quantities, but he now believes that a better policy will be to lower the cost of a single unit, and to maintain this price regardless of quantity.

At the moment, Zora Company Ltd is continuing to manufacture double glazing as a subcontractor and also to supply and fit double glazing. Sales currently run at about £30,000 per month as follows:

	Monthly sales £
Supply and install double glazing	12,000
Subcontract manufacture	18,000
	30,000

At this level of business the company makes a net profit before tax of about £3,000 per month. The overheads to the company are as shown in Table B.

Table B. Overheads of Zora Co Ltd

	£
Rent	13,500
Rates	9,000
Water and gas	7,000
Gnjatovic's salary	15,000
General manager	10,000
Secretary	5,000
Telephone	6,000
Electricity	4,000
Advertising	5,000
Travel	2,000
Miscellaneous	2,000
Total	78,500

The balance sheet of Zora Company Ltd is approximately as shown in Table C.

Table C. Balance Sheet

	£	£	£
Fixed assets			
18-year lease on factory		12,000	
Machinery		30,000	
(Less HP on machine)		(10,000)	
			32,000
Current assets			
Stock	15,000		
Cash	4,000		
Debtors	12,000		
		31,000	
Current liabilities			
Creditors	(17,000)		
		(17,000)	
Net current assets			14,000
			46,000
Financed by			
Share capital			100
Loans from Mr and Mrs Gnjatovic			23,500
Profit and loss reserves			22,400
			46,000

Therefore, Zora Company Ltd has an accumulated profit of £22,400 after just six months of trading, and one strategy would be simply to move slowly forward, obtaining orders for brick machines as and when possible. However, this could be a mistake having seen the very good reaction to the machine in the field, and having twice nearly obtained larger orders. Gnjatovic believes the right thing to do is to risk some capital to promote the machine vigorously in as many countries as possible, as quickly as possible. To allow sales to pick up gradually by word of mouth and limited promotion is to run the risk of another manufacturer moving in, once the potential is realised. Mr Gnjatovic has applied for a patent on various aspects of the machine, but believes that in practice useful patent protection will be difficult to achieve.

Mr Gnjatovic therefore seeks to raise risk capital to be spent as quickly as possible on advertising and promoting the brick machine. He proposes two possibilities, and prefers the larger of the two.

	Preferred		Possible	
	£		£	
Activity:				
Tooling	2,500		2,500	
Salesmen for one year	25,000	(two men)	12,500	(one man)
Stock of finished machines	20,000	(20 machines)	10,000	(10 machines)
Visits to trade fairs	150,000	(30 fairs)	20,000	(four fairs)
Advertising in first year	50,000		5,000	
Miscellaneous	52,500		—	
	300,000		50,000	

Note:
A machine ordered on day 1 will arrive from the subcontractor on day 30 and be ready for shipment on day 35, against a letter of credit so that the proceeds from sales will go into the company's bank account on day 35. The subcontractor will not be paid until day 60 so that apart from the finished goods stock, no working capital should be required.

If the average contribution to overheads and profit is taken as £1,500 per machine, Table D gives the approximate financial outcome that might be expected at various levels of sales.

Table D. Approximate financial results at various sales levels

Sales of machines	50	500	1,000	2,000	5,000
	£	£	£	£	£
Contribution	75,000	750,000	1.0m	3.0m	7.5m
Overheads (1)	36,000	36,000	0.075m	0.1m	0.2m
Marketing	40,000	100,000	0.25m	0.5m	1.0m
	76,000	(136,000)	(0.325m)	(0.6m)	(1.2m)
Net profit before tax	(1,000)	614,000	1.175m	2.4m	6.3m

Note:
1. To begin with, Mr Gnjatovic suggests that the new company shares the premises of his existing business and contributes £36,000 or just under half to its overheads.

Mr Gnjatovic believes that sales of 2–5,000 per year could easily be achieved quite quickly if £300,000 is spent now on a marketing campaign. If the alternative of spending perhaps £50,000 on a marketing campaign is adopted, sales of 500–1,000 machines should be possible when the profits could then finance more marketing expenditure.

Financial structure

Mr Gnjatovic suggests the following structure for an investment of £300,000 in a new company, to which all rights to the brickmaking machine and its derivatives will be assigned. He would like all the investment to be in equity.

Name	Contribution	%
Mr and Mrs Gnjatovic	Idea and patents	60
Investor	£300,000	40

Mr Gnjatovic will welcome an investor who has access to markets abroad or experience of working abroad and who will be able to help achieve sales. A corporate partner would probably be ideal.

If no corporate partner can be found, Mr Gnjatovic suggests the following structure as one which might suit an individual willing to invest £50,000 and if possible to work at least part time in the company to help achieve sales.

Name	Contribution	Shares
Mr and Mrs Gnjatovic	Idea and patents	40
Investor	£50,000	30
Unissued		30

The £50,000 would be invested as equity and tax relief would be available under the Business Expansion Scheme, so that the net cost to an investor would be only £12,500 for a top rate taxpayer who spreads the investment into two tax years.

It is suggested that the unissued shares be issued to Mr Gnjatovic on the basis of his performance in achieving sales, as follows:

Machines sold by 1 June 1985	Shares issued to Mr Gnjatovic
25	5
50	10
100	15
200	30

Thus if Mr Gnjatovic is able to sell 200 machines by 1 June 1985, when the net profits should exceed £200,000 he will own 70 per cent of the company and the investor 30 per cent but if he sells less than 25 the investor will end up owning 43 per cent of the company.

Questions

1. After his experiences in Nigeria do you think Mr Gnjatovic is perhaps being unnecessarily adventurous with his new project?
2. What are the key issues that have yet to be addressed to ensure the new venture succeeds?
3. Do you think Mr Gnjatovic's previous business experiences make him more, or less, suitable for this new venture?
4. Given that you had access to the funds, which of the two proposals put forward would you choose and why?
5. How effective do you think Mr Gnjatovic's marketing plans are and what else could he do to secure orders?

Case 26
Wheatley and Company Ltd A
Nora O'Donnell,
under the supervision of *Dr JA Murray*

By the end of 1981 Mark and Helen Staveley knew that the business which they had started with such enthusiasm some 13 months previously was falling dangerously short of its objectives and would, if the trend was allowed to continue, be unable to survive for a further year. Set up to manufacture wholefood products for the growing Irish health food market, the company had experienced considerable difficulty in getting started and in organising sales and distribution of the product. At the end of November the Staveleys decided to curtail production severely for a few months while they assessed the lessons learned during the short productive life of the company. From an evaluation of their mistakes and the strengths and weaknesses of their company, they hoped to put together a plan which would ensure the survival of Wheatley and Company.

Background to launching the company

During the late 1970s the Staveleys felt attracted to the idea of setting up a manufacturing enterprise. They were no strangers to entrepreneurship, having launched a service organisation during the 1960s. That organisation had grown and prospered. The Staveleys wanted a new challenge: they wished to contribute to national development by manufacturing a high added-value product which would involve them in a market related to their own resources and aptitudes.

Mark's expertise was in the area of consumer goods marketing. Both Mark and Helen were vegetarians and interested in health foods. As health foods were not widely available for sale at the time, Helen had become expert in the preparation and cooking of nutritious wholefoods. The Staveleys felt that health food products fitted in well with their skills and began to research the market. They were not seeking a mass market, rather they wished to identify special niches where a small company could compete.

The Staveleys carried out some desk research on world health food market trends in the knowledge that the product chosen should have export potential, the market in Ireland being relatively small.

The health food industry

The Staveleys' research showed that worldwide the health food industry was of very recent origin, and had grown rapidly in the early 1970s. The recession in 1974/75 had slowed down growth somewhat. In comparison with the overall demand for food which was static during the 1970s, the health food market had grown at an average rate of 15 per cent per annum.

'Health food' is a generic term used to describe a very complex industry. The term covers not only wholefood products but also natural vitamins, food supplements, homeopathic remedies and even natural cosmetics. Mark Staveley said that the market consisted of several segments:

- diabetic/medical market;
- 'crank'-type market which looked for exotic herbs and roots;
- commodity market specialising in bran flour, nuts, beans and lentils;
- branded wholefood market usually consisting of biscuits, snacks or confectionery with comparatively few products available worldwide.

Underlying the growth in demand for health food products were two consumer trends. Consumers were turning away from processed foods and refined flour and sugar for foods with a high fibre content, mainly for health reasons. In addition, there was increasing concern about the unnecessary use of chemical additives in food to improve its appearance and to lengthen shelf life. As a result, more and more consumers were reading labels on foods, shopping around and adopting a discriminatory attitude to a whole range of different foods. Health foods were retailed through specialist and delicatessen shops and commanded large margins. The market in Ireland was completely underdeveloped. An English distributor supplied most of the demand for commodity-type products through a few specialist shops located in the main cities. There were very few branded products available.

The product idea

The original idea was to develop a range of products which would respond to the consumer trends identified. The Staveleys envisaged the production of breads, pâtés, biscuits, snacks, pizzas and all sorts of products based on the idea of pure and healthy ingredients. Helen Staveley had developed several recipes for all such products. The concept of 'home-cooked' quality would be used to create an image for the new products. In fact, the choice of product was endless and the main problem was to decide where to begin.

'The original choice does tend to push one in a particular way. One of the principal characteristics of lateral thinking, unfortunately, is that it begins and ends in the bath,' said Mark. After long discussion, the Staveleys decided to begin with biscuits. The Irish love biscuits, consuming IR£20[1] worth per head per annum. Realising that any change in diet is met with caution and suspicion in most Irish families, the Staveleys felt that biscuits would be the 'thin end of the wedge'. Housewives would try out a new biscuit more readily than any other food. Once introduced to the concept of health foods in this way, the housewife might be encouraged to replace other processed foods with 'natural' foods. Wholefood biscuits presented an opportunity to build up brand awareness and loyalty.

Seeking support

The Industrial Development Authority (IDA)[2] was approached for support. The bread and biscuit sectors, in the view of the IDA, had plant overcapacity and so the Authority had a policy not to grant aid to any new firms in that sector.

Disappointed, Mark Staveley turned to his local County Development Officer[3] whose reaction Mark described as 'lukewarm'. Yet this official arranged a meeting for Mark and Helen with IDA representatives and helped to put together a business plan which covered a description of the product and

---

[1] At the time: IR£1 = £ Stg 0.8002
IR£1 = $1.6158.
[2] The IDA has national responsibility for the furtherance of industrial development in Ireland.
[3] The County Development Officer is an employee of the local authority and has the task of fostering economic development in his county. He does this by ensuring maximum use of existing public services and by stimulating worthwhile new ideas for development.

market and an analysis of the 'fit' between the two; the basic competitive environments; sales forecasts; production forecasts and costs. (See Appendix 1 for some extracts from the plan.)

Prior to meeting with the IDA officials, Mark and Helen made up samples of two of the six varieties of biscuits proposed, had some labels printed and registered a business name. Through contacts in the food industry, Mark succeeded in placing the samples in a supermarket and in a few specialist shops. Consumer reaction was favourable. This exercise was, in the Staveleys' opinion, crucial in persuading the IDA to support the project.

The project proposal was put to the IDA in December 1979, and in February 1980 was approved for grant aid of 45 per cent of capital expenditure only. The remainder of the 'seed capital' and all the working capital came from the personal resources of the Staveleys and amounted to a total commitment of IR£50,000. This was the investment in a new limited liability company, Wheatley and Company – a name chosen for its wholefood and family business connotations.

The launch

Mark Staveley pointed out that when one goes into a business where one has no working experience, two potentially disastrous factors are likely to arise. First, everything takes more time. One has to learn all the details of the business and of the related suppliers. For example, cardboard boxes for biscuits – who makes such an item? How firm is firm cardboard and what do all these technical terms the supplier is using mean? Second, the inexperienced entrepreneur tends to rely on experts much more. This can lead to costly mistakes.

By Easter 1980 the Staveleys had entered into formal contracts for machinery (on the advice of experts) and buildings and had set July 1980 as the target date for start-up. The date was subsequently changed several times, as the machinery was not ready.

Then Helen Staveley became ill. Finally, in late October 1980 Wheatley and Company opened for business. A master baker and three young people reported for work. The young, unskilled operatives were used at the packaging stage which is the most labour-intensive part of the production process. The organisation structure was very simple. Mark was responsible for marketing, planning and administration. Helen's function was in the area of product control. However, because of her illness, she found that she could not contribute as much to the business as planned. The Staveleys felt that they were lucky to have the support of a very hard working, non-executive financial director.

Production

The production of biscuits uses well-known technology and is almost automatic. The ingredients are combined in a mixing bowl, then the dough is shaped into biscuits, weighed and baked. The baked biscuits are brought to the packaging area where they are packed into individual containers, weighed, labelled, put into an 'outer' of 24 or 18 packets (depending on size) and stored.

However, the particular ingredients used in the Wheatley range are different from the ingredients used in conventional biscuits. Nuts, dried fruit, seeds and wholewheat flour are used. The mixture is stiffer and accordingly it is more difficult to combine the ingredients. The Staveleys discovered that the equipment which they had been advised to buy was only suitable for a more conventional biscuit. It took another six weeks before the supplier was in a position to replace the equipment with machinery more appropriate to the required use.

Setting up the production line took considerable time, and then scheduling production became a problem. The Staveleys produced three varieties of biscuit at start-up. In the absence of market information they were unsure of how much of each variety to produce. They decided to build up stocks of 50 cases of each variety.

Packaging

The biscuits had a rectangular shape with 12 to 15 in a packet of either 150g or 200g weight depending on variety. The container was made of 'see-through' plastic and the inscription emphasised that only pure ingredients were used. A pastoral scene was printed on the lid of the container. The biscuits and packaging presented a 'handcrafted' appearance. Most other biscuits are packed in roll-type packages. The Wheatley products attracted attention because of their unusual shape. Shelf life was six months.

Selling and distribution

Mark Staveley positioned the biscuits in the wholefood market segment. The outlets chosen were specialist health food shops and gourmet and delicatessen shops. The sales volume through these shops was very small, and repeat business was slow. It became obvious to the Staveleys that the multiples would have to be approached. Most food products are retailed through supermarkets. The Staveleys were anxious to place their product in the specialist delicatessen shops within the supermarkets.

During the first half of 1981 Mark Staveley worked hard to get his products 'listed' at the head office of the seven supermarket groups. The buyers' requirements were that he prove that his products would give the multiples their expected return on shelf space, that certain levels of demand could be met and that 'listing' money be agreed. The system of listing is costly in time and money for the small manufacturer. Once listed, the manufacturer must approach each branch manager to obtain orders. While being listed will not guarantee orders, without being listed the branch manager will not even meet a manufacturer. The branch manager will order only if his customers demand the product, or if the new product has some complementarity with existing products on the shelves. In all but two supermarket groups who operate a central depot system, the manufacturer is responsible for delivery of the ordered amount to each individual branch at an agreed time. In selling to the multiples, the manufacturer must be aware of stock levels of his product at each branch so as to convince the branch manager of the need to reorder. Price is the major consideration of the multiples' management. Mark Staveley reckoned that he was very successful if he got 10 per cent over cost price from the multiples. As he could not afford expensive media advertising to 'pull' his product through the channel, he relied heavily on 'below the line' promotion – this involved contributions towards point of sale material, or 15 cases delivered for each 12 ordered.

The fact of being 'listed' carried no commitments from the buyer to the manufacturer. A product could be 'delisted' almost on a whim of the head office. Most food manufacturers would agree that the multiples have no loyalty to suppliers. According to one industry expert, dealing with the multiples is a question of the rapport between sales representative and buyer and of the experience of dealing.

By mid-1981 the Wheatley product was listed by one supermarket chain all of whose branches are in the Dublin region. At the time, Mark was serving around 100 small specialist shops in the greater Dublin area, and about 10 supermarket branches. Retail prices ranged between 43p and 53p per packet. Originally,

Mark did the physical distribution and merchandising himself. This meant making sure that the shelves were kept fully stocked and was very time-consuming. A van salesman was employed for a short time, but his services were dispensed with because of cost.

In August Mark appointed a national distributor to distribute the products to his existing customers and to 'break bulk' and sell in smaller amounts to the distributor's own network of small independent grocers. The distributor was a former colleague with whom Mark had worked very successfully in the past. He was selling a range of products for the specialist food market, and the Wheatley range broadened his existing range. Both men felt that there would be mutual gain from the promotional effects of a broad, well-balanced range at the retail level. They discussed projected sales. Mark produced his original forecasts (Appendix 1) and the distributor felt that he would have no trouble reaching the sales targets already set. In fact he gave Mark the idea that production (set at around 2,000 cases per month) would probably lag behind sales. The distributor indicated that he would work on a 22 per cent margin over the gross selling price of £8 per case. Product would be collected from the Wheatley premises. Staveley would issue invoices every 60 days.

By October it was clear that the agreement had broken down completely. Supermarket managers were on the telephone complaining of short delivery, late delivery and no delivery at all. A visit to the distributor's depot revealed 600 cases of unsold biscuits on the premises. By now 'delisted' with the peak selling period approaching, and stocks of over 1,000 cases of biscuits on hand, the Staveleys decided to slow production to a 'tick-over' level. Working capital was coming under severe pressure as creditors gave 30 days' credit on supplies. Many of the ingredients were imported so orders had to be placed well ahead of production. Most of the production staff had to be made redundant and Mark tried to sell as much stock as possible to small outlets. Sales achieved in the period January 1981 to November 1981 were 40 per cent of total planned production. These sales were made up of 15 per cent to the supermarket chain and 85 per cent to small specialist and delicatessen shops.

Mark and Helen felt anxious and depressed. They had confidence that the concept was still worth pursuing. Their considerable investment of money, effort and thought should not be thrown away. They were determined to go on. Commenting on the situation, Mark felt that they may have underestimated their weaknesses which he saw as a lack of knowledge of the market place. He felt that he and Helen had made many judgements without being sufficiently well-informed and experienced about the realities of the situation. On the positive side, the company was strong financially with no debt in its financial structure, and Helen and Mark were prepared to invest more of their personal capital to make sure that the project would be successful.

Appendix 1

Wheatley and Company business plan

Sales forecasts: £200,000 ex-factory prices
Production forecasts: 16,000 tons
Projected sales price: £8 per case of 24 packets

Projected profit and loss, 1980–81	
Sales	*100%*
Raw material	44
Labour	14
Factory overheads	15
Selling expenses	21
Marketing expenses	8
Administration expenses	6
Profit (loss)	(8)

Questions

1. Do you think the logic that led the Staveleys to adopt biscuits as the thin end of their marketing wedge was soundly based?
2. Is it ever wise to commit significant resources to a business area of which you have no working experience?
3. How could they have avoided the disastrous distribution problems that brought the business to a standstill in November 1981?

Case 27

Wheatley and Company Ltd B

Nora O'Donnell,

under the supervision of *Dr JA Murray*

Two years after Wheatley and Company Ltd had seen its early dreams in real danger of crumbling, Mark and Helen Staveley, its founders, owners and managers, were facing yet another stage in the firm's development. By November 1981 more than half of its employees had been made redundant and the company was re-building its sales operation from scratch. Reopening in early 1982 with a redefined business orientation and the accumulated experience of one year's disastrous trading behind it, the company went from strength to strength, developing not only the Irish market but also expanding into the UK. In the two years of renewed activity the company had experienced leap-frogging situations with growth occurring in uneven amounts.

By December 1983 the company was in the happy situation where sales raced ahead of production. Productive capacity was beginning to come under strain. The owners were preoccupied with what they considered the principal weakness of the company – its mainstream production efficiency. The need to increase productive capacity had to be faced together with the consequences of such a move. New personnel and new finance would be required which would change the company's structure fundamentally. The Staveleys, nevertheless, were of the opinion that the momentum for growth in the company was of prime importance.

Background considerations

In 1981 the company began producing wholefood products for the Irish market. Sales for the first year were 40 per cent of total planned production. Mark Staveley reckoned that sales had not materialised for several reasons. He felt that the demand for wholefood products in Ireland was small and undeveloped and suffered from a spartan image of intrepid consumers braving the world of rope sandals and sacks of bran. Mark said that he had underestimated the amount of time and effort needed to push a new product into this undeveloped wholefood market segment. His product was in a new category and such products are slow builders. As the financial resources of the company were limited Wheatley could not afford the promotional expenditure which the major manufacturing companies commanded. The structure of food retailing in Ireland – dominated by the multiples interested in large volume and quick turnover products – meant that the Wheatley products were seen as speciality items with little appeal for the ordinary housewife. Supermarket managers placed wholefood items in out-of-the-way corners of the supermarket. During the previous year Mark had discovered that the profile of the typical buyer of his product was aged between 25 and 40 ABC1 and female. He was convinced that he needed to broaden his customer base. To achieve this, Mark felt that he must reposition the Wheatley product within the mainstream biscuit market, so that the products would be perceived by customers as a non-speciality but high quality biscuit. He felt that his biscuits should be sold in competition with the ordinary biscuits available to customers. For this to happen, Wheatley products must be displayed beside other competing brands in the shops. Ordinary housewives were concerned about the nutritional value of foods and of the danger to health of too much refined flour and sugar in the daily diet. They should be given a choice of product quality at the point of sale. Already several distributors of imported speciality biscuits were adopting this strategy and were selling the products to multiples and not to speciality shops.

The biscuit market in Ireland

The market environment in which Wheatley and Company chose to compete is mature with an almost static demand pattern. It is estimated that the Irish consume approximately IR£20[1] worth of biscuits per capita per annum. The market increased slightly in value terms in 1982 to be worth between IR£60 million and IR£62 million. (See Appendix 1 for a breakdown of the branded biscuit market in 1982.)

The biscuit market segment is hard to define precisely as there is overlap between the cake and bread segment on the one hand and the confectionery segment – with snack bars – on the other. A recent example of the latter was the repositioning by Rowntree

[1]At the time: IR£1 = £Stg 0.7965
        IR£1 = $1.1929.

Mackintosh of their Kit-Kat product with the slogan 'it's a biscuit – it's a bar'.

The biscuit market can be broken down into the following three broad groups:

1. Unsweetened biscuits   – savoury, rusks, oatcakes, crispbreads and dry wafers.
2. Sweetened biscuits   – divided into two subcategories: Fancy Sweet – cream sandwich, mallows, fruit-filled, cookies and iced. Plain Sweet – shortcake, ginger, wheaten/digestive.
3. Chocolate biscuits   – half-coated chocolate biscuits and countlines which are individually wrapped chocolate biscuits such as club milk, telex etc.

Since 1979 there has been increased penetration of own label and some generics into the market place, and the major manufacturers introduced branded economy ranges in response to the greater emphasis on price. These value-for-money ranges were mostly in the sweetened biscuit group. The 1981–82 Wheatley range could be positioned in this group.

The market place in 1982 was extremely difficult for all biscuit manufacturers. Competition for market share was intense, not only between manufacturers, but also among retailers and wholesalers. The recession, the 6 per cent drop in consumer spending power in 1982, as well as higher labour costs, higher ingredient costs, higher energy costs, lower productivity levels because of shorter runs and a penal VAT (see Table A) increased the industry's difficulties.

Table A. VAT rate on biscuits 1980–83

Year	Rate %
1980	10
1981	15
1982	18
1983	23

Growth of the company

Early in 1982 Wheatley and Company recommenced trading. The primary objective was to build up a direct sales force and to get Wheatley products on to the shops' shelves. Mark was convinced that his product had shelf appeal. He felt that if he could get the product on the shelf, the customer would be attracted to it, buy it, and because flavour and texture were interesting would re-buy. Repeat business is the key to success in the biscuit market. Working with one van salesman, Mark began to rebuild contacts in the Dublin region concentrating on the multiples and larger wholesalers.

Multiples

There are seven supermarket chains (multiples – with more than ten branches) in Ireland. To introduce a new product to a super-market chain, the first step is to be 'listed' at head office as a supplier. Then the manufacturer deals directly with the branch manager to get orders. The branch manager has considerable autonomy and provides a product mix which he considers demanded by his particular customer group. Supermarket managers require a good return on shelf space, promotional efforts financed by the manufacturer and very low prices. Most multiples concentrate on the east coast where industry experts claim that 70 per cent of food sales are channelled through them. Only two chains have branches located throughout the country. One supermarket group operates only in the south-east and south of the country. The supermarket groups monitor each other's prices constantly, and if a product is sold cheaper by one super-market the rest 'delist' the manufacturer without warning.

Wholesalers/groups

Wholesalers serve two segments of the retail trade. On the one hand they have their own network of retailers and they also operate 112 cash and carry depots located throughout Ireland. The wholesaler serves a particularly useful function for the small grocer in the cities and in rural areas. Manufacturers usually command better margins when selling to wholesalers. There are seven major wholesale groups in Ireland, and over 50 per cent of the Republic's IR£1,000 million dry grocery trade is channelled through them. Some symbol wholesalers[1] offer a selling and marketing package to retailers – advice on shop layout, merchandising, and product mix. An essential link in the symbol wholesaler/retailer chain is the weekly Plof (price list and order

---

[1]Symbol wholesalers are those whose network of independent retailers promote their business under a common symbol such as Mace, VG and Spar.

form). This carries details of 5,000 plus lines offered by the wholesaler, including up to 1,000 items on special offer or bonus. The 'special offer' is supported by point of sale material produced by the wholesaler which is distributed free to any retailer who takes up the 'special offer'. The manufacturer is encouraged to support the special offers by 'below the line' promotion.

Independents

There are five very large independent retailers. Usually these retailers have less than 10 branches and are not affiliated to any group.

By 1983, Mark had built up sales through these outlets as follows:

	1982 %	1983 %
Multiples	45	55
Wholesalers	15	20
Retail	20	15
Speciality/Delicatessen	20	10

His sales force had increased to two van salesmen and one accounts manager. Apart from Kerry and Connemara where sales of the Wheatley products were taken care of by agents, the entire country was covered by direct sales under Mark Staveley's supervision. The selling involved extremely hard work. While the move to more sales with the multiples had meant increased volume for Wheatley and Company and lower prices to the customer, Mark found that specialist shops still stocked his product. In only two cases had a delicatessen owner refused to stock the Wheatley products saying that he could not compete with the prices being charged in the supermarket. Distribution was the responsibility of Wheatley staff in Leinster. Elsewhere, Coras Iompair Eireann (CIE – the National Transport Authority) was used for deliveries.

Product development

Early in 1982 Wheatley introduced two new half-coated biscuits to compete in the chocolate sector and made plans to increase the range of semi-sweet biscuits (ginger and wheaten biscuits). Packet sizes were kept at 150g and 200g. In 1983 three new, individually wrapped snack bars were introduced. These bars were given a new brand name and point of sale packaging was designed for them. The new Wheatley bars were made from pure ingredients and were popular items for inclusion in lunch boxes. Staveley found that the two chocolate-coated biscuits accounted for about 50 per cent of sales, while one or two other lines accounted for only 1 or 2 per cent. Retail prices ranged from 50p to 69p depending on weight of package and location of purchase.

There were 12 or 15 biscuits in each container depending on weight. Staveley was aware that the market place was becoming more price-conscious and that customers were looking for value-for-money products. He was contemplating selling the biscuits in larger sizes (250g, 500g). It appeared that prices were firmer in the larger packet sizes. During the 1983 Christmas season he experimented with boxes of assorted biscuits, packaged to reflect the healthy and quality image he was promoting.

Advertising

Advertising through trade journals, newspaper and magazine articles emphasised the twin themes of natural ingredients and Irish manufacture. The good-tasting qualities of the products were also highlighted. Staveley relied mostly on promotional methods to increase sales.

Profitability

Staveley said that profitability in the industry was very low. The average profit over the two years of renewed operations was 3 to 4 per cent of sales.

Competition within the biscuit industry

The estimated market share of the main competitors in the branded biscuit market is shown in Table B.

Table B. Market share of major competitors in the Irish market 1982

Company	Market share
Irish Biscuits	63% of which Jacobs 50% Bolands (Economy Range) 13%
United Biscuits	16% of which McVities 11% Pennywise (Economy Range) 5%
Burtons and Adams	7% (positioned in the value-for-money range)
Cadburys	6% (competes in the chocolate group)
Others	8% (about 6 brands involved – including Wheatley and Co.)

Source: Company records

Irish Biscuits, the market leader, offers a total of 50 different varieties of biscuit and competes strongly in all product groups. The brands are aggressively supported by media advertising. The advertising budget for 1983 was estimated to be near IR£0.75 million. New products are introduced constantly. In 1983 a wholefood-type biscuit was introduced. The biscuit is made with rolled nuts and sultanas to give a crunchy, healthy taste. The biscuit is sold in a roll pack, weighs 200g with 24 biscuits to the roll. Retail price was 30p.

United Biscuits – an English biscuit and food giant – entered the Irish market in the late 1960s and through aggressive promotion and advertising saw its market share rise from 5 per cent in 1976 to 16 per cent in 1982–83. United Biscuits compete in all the product groups and has several wholefood-type products.

Burtons and Adams Biscuits – English made – compete in the value-for-money, lower priced sector and rely on trade promotion rather than media advertising.

Cadburys have four half-coated and five fully coated products in the chocolate sector. It does not advertise to any great extent, relying on its excellent distribution network for sales.

Others include imported speciality biscuits such as the Bahlsen biscuits from Germany, Dutch butter cookies, two wholefood biscuit manufacturers – Farmhouse from Northumbria, and the Wheatley range. Also included is the Hill Range, Tennant & Ruttle and Rowntree Mackintosh who compete mainly in the countline range.

Distribution

Table C. Breakdown of main distribution outlets of two major manufacturers

	Irish Biscuits %	United Biscuits %
Multiples	35	48
Wholesale (includes cash and carry)	49	38
Retail (direct)	16	14

Export markets

During 1982 Mark Staveley began to research export markets. He explained that while Coras Trachtala (Irish Export Board) encouraged manufacturers to build a firm base in Ireland prior to exporting, he had found the structure of the distribution channels in Ireland were such that if he waited to build up the Irish market he would starve. He also felt that success abroad would ensure success at home. Besides, next door in Britain was a huge market place – £stg 840 million at retail prices in 1982. The wholefood end of the market was increasing at a rate of 10 per cent per annum, was well-organised with specialist shops of a very high calibre, and an escalating trend in the mainstream grocery trade to take products from the specialists' domain as they became profitable, high volume lines. Consumers were more aware of wholefoods and the market was maturing rapidly. Industry estimates suggested that by 1985, 1,400 'health' shops would be in existence with a turnover in excess of £179 million.

The strategy for entry to the UK market was to choose a wholesaler who supplied the wholefood and delicatessen sector. A longer-term objective was to expand into the multiples. Coras Trachtala was helpful providing promotional support and research back-up. It was with the agency's help that an importer and distributor was identified who seemed to have access to the chosen outlets. This distributor carried many other specialist lines for these outlets. However, he was of comparable size with Wheatley and Company and the latter's products made up a significant part of his sales. Staveley did not want to be a small supplier to a large distributor because in that kind of situation the Wheatley products might not be promoted properly.

Table D. Index of sales in domestic and export markets

	1981	1982	1983	1984*
Total sales	100	300	600	1,200–1,400
Export sales	—	10%	35%	50%

*Projected figures
Source: Company records

Most sales were made in three centres – London, Manchester and Glasgow. Staveley commented on the marked differences in taste in Ireland and the UK. While the half-coated chocolate biscuits sold extremely well in the UK so did Ginger Nobs which were unpopular in the Irish market. Staveley said that he had a policy of having a product range which was small enough to be efficient and large enough to be well balanced. He was constantly looking for more products which were unique as he believed that while the customer liked old favourites, variety was also sought.

Evaluation

Replying to questions about the strengths and weaknesses of his operation in late 1983, Mark Staveley pointed out that the company was much more experienced now, had an excellent reputation within the trade and a well-balanced range of products. The weaknesses he saw were a lack of capital and price constraints on his products. Price competition was intense with competitors seeking market share rather than profitability. Mark and Helen had financed the renaissance of their business and the major part of the expansion overseas as well as working capital out of their own personal funds. In 1983 working capital had increased by 20 per cent. Now they felt that they should 'dig in and build on what we have with a minimum of risk-taking'. The overseas operation was going very well, but the importer/distributor had very little strength with the multiples and further expansion would require the setting up of another distribution channel in the UK. Commenting on the threats he saw in the environment, Mark saw the improvement in the quality of competing products as posing a major threat. It was clear that all the major biscuit manufacturers were responding to the trend towards more natural and healthier ingredients in biscuits. Other threats were the increasing cost of raw materials and the effect domestic inflation had on overseas sales. He hoped that there would be a recovery in consumer spending soon.

Within his company, Mark saw production efficiency as a major area for improvement. During the past two years production crises had been commonplace. With one production line and eight varieties of product, scheduling was a major headache. He was considering commissioning a study of the production area by consultants. He knew that to sustain the growth which he forecast for sales of product he needed to recruit more middle-management. The organisation structure was similar to that at launch. But capital to finance growth was a problem, and profitability both in Ireland and in the UK was not sufficient to attract capital at competitive rates.

Appendix 1

Breakdown of sales of branded biscuits by product group 1982

	Total branded market	Growth in value 1982	Growth in volume 1982	Branded economy ranges % of the market
Unsweetened biscuits	%	%	%	
(included are savoury, rusks, oatcakes, crispbreads, dry wafers)	10	+ 3	− 1 ½	—
Sweetened biscuits (total)	60		+ 1	22
– of which Fancy Sweet (included are cream sandwich, mallows, fruit-filled, cookies, wafers and iced)	38			11
–Plain Sweet (included are semi-sweet shortcake, ginger, wheaten/digestive)	22	5		11
Chocolate biscuits (included are half-coated, and countlines)	30	+ 1	− 5	—

Source: Checkout, February 1983

Appendix 2

Biscuit industry in the UK

The number of manufacturers of biscuits has been declining steadily in the UK. In 1962 there were 115 firms; in 1972 50 firms; in 1982 27 firms. The decline is due in part to mergers and rationalisations within the industry. There are few independent firms. During the 1970s some new, small firms entered the market place, specialising in the 'home-made quality' type of biscuits and trading in the north of England and Scotland.

Table A. Market share in the UK biscuit market 1982

Company	%
United Biscuits	33
Nabisco brands	19
Rowntree Mackintosh	7
Burtons and Adams	7
Foxes	2
Cadbury	2
Other brands	4
Own label	26

Source: Industry experts

Staveley identified Foxes as the major competitor in the whole-food market segment. Foxes has seen its market share increase by 100 per cent in five years. Originally a regional brand in the north of England the company has increased its distribution network and in 1982–3 produced 50 varieties mostly in the homemade sector. Other competitors in the wholefood sector are Farmhouse, Turniss, Kippax, Shaws and Yorkshire.

In the total UK market there are over 1,000 lines of biscuits available (an average store may stock about 160), tremendous competition for shelf space, and continuous introduction of new brands and elimination of old brands. However, the population in England is static and UK consumers are generally eating as much as they need for nutritional and energy requirements [and as a result] there is unlikely to be any significant overall growth in demand for the industry's products.

There are some regional differences in demand patterns for biscuits as shown in Table B.

Table B. Weekly per capita in-home consumption of biscuits by region

(Weight in ounces)

	Total	Chocolate	Unsweetened	Sweetened
North England	6.73	1.74	0.15	4.84
Scotland	6.49	1.69	0.19	4.62
South-west	5.52	1.04	0.24	4.24
Wales	5.42	1.21	0.32	3.89
National average	5.40	1.12	0.23	4.05

Source: National Food Survey

Distribution

According to Nielson Surveys there were 56,590 grocery outlets in England in 1981. Although independent grocers (less than 10 outlets) own 83 per cent of all shops, only about 23 per cent of all food produce goes through them (this figure includes consideration of the major symbol wholesalers eg Mace). The six major country-wide multiple groups had 44 per cent of total sales with regional multiples holding about 20 per cent. Co-operatives and department stores make up the remainder. The multiples now direct 40–60 per cent of all product through centralised depots or through a nominated distributor, although Asda, the largest multiple in England, takes all deliveries direct from suppliers to stores.

Table C. Distribution channels for biscuits, 1982

	Share by value %	
Multiple grocers	46	
Co-ops	13	
Independent grocers	21	(includes groups/wholesalers including wholefood wholesalers)
Caterers	18	

Source: Monopolies and Mergers Commission

The biscuit industry has taken particular pains to deal directly with caterers in the UK by developing special pack sizes and pricing policies for them.

Source: Review of the Food and Drink Manufacturing Industry, 1983.

Advertising and promotion
The house name is featured most in advertising, with the exception of countline products, when manufacturers are at some pains to build up a 'personality'. Television and radio are used extensively, with point of sale materials also important. Promotion focuses on bonuses to trade customers – 15 cases for each 12 ordered. Competitions are also used.

Packaging
Staveley discovered that packaging was of tremendous importance in the UK. In Ireland his products were packaged differently to the major brands – in plastic, see-through, rectangular containers. Several biscuit ranges including some of the Foxes range and United Biscuits wholefood range were packaged in a similar way in the UK. Legislation in the UK insisted on greater attention to labels giving details of ingredients and specific inclusion of a 'sell by' date on each packet. The growing use of electronic point of sale equipment by traders put pressure on the manufacturers to add bar codes to packages.

Prices and margins
Recommended retail prices were issued by manufacturers but were not always followed. Margins varied between 17–25 per cent but promotional deals could reduce this to 9–12 per cent. In wholefood shops margins up to 30 per cent were normal. Biscuit manufacturing has never been regarded as particularly profitable. Efficiencies at production level give some manufacturers a competitive edge.

Trends in the UK market force

With the introduction of electronic bar coding and computerised inventory systems, smaller stocks are being held. Manufacturers foresee the introduction of more own label and economy range biscuits to respond to the consumers' emphasis on price and value for money. Manufacturers are moving away from assorted packs of biscuits (because of the high labour content at the packaging stage) and producing more countline products. Through improvements in distribution, imports have increased from 1–2 per cent during the 1970s to 4.5 per cent of total supplies in 1982. This trend is expected to continue. Exports of biscuits have been steady at around 11 per cent of output for several years. Recent emphasis on exporting policy at government level and the static market in the UK will, experts believe, lead to greater efforts to sell abroad by all biscuit manufacturers.

Questions

1. Do you share Mark Staveley's conviction that he *had* to broaden his customer base?
2. What dangers were associated with the repositioning strategy adopted for Wheatley products?
3. What do you think were the weaknesses and strengths of the plan to enter the UK market?

Case 28

Trendlight Ltd

Nora O'Donnell,

under the supervision of *Dr JA Murray*

In June 1980 Paul Sexton, chairman and managing director of Trendlight Ltd, felt reasonably optimistic about the future of his two-year-old enterprise. Set up in September 1977 to manufacture in Ireland and market in the UK a series of modern decorative light fittings under the brand name Trendlight, the enterprise had experienced fluctuating fortunes during its short life. Now, with new products, a new dynamic sales manager, and a recent injection of cash, Paul felt confident that his troubles were behind him and that it was almost as if he were starting afresh.

On 3 April 1978 Paul Sexton and four employees met in a disused warehouse which had been leased for a two-year period as a factory for the production of modern lightingware. Recalling this momentous occasion, Paul Sexton wryly remarked that the next few days were spent tidying up the warehouse and offices and purchasing items such as chairs, desks and heaters. That modest beginning was the result of some years of information gathering, decision-making and planning on his part.

Background to launch

Paul Sexton was about 40 years old. He graduated in 1958 from University College, Galway with a degree in civil engineering. He worked with two semi-state companies as an engineer for three years. In 1961 he embarked on a career with a public company whose main activity is the manufacture and export of unique hand-crafted product. For nine years, the company expanded rapidly.

> 'The whole thing was new to me and I had to learn it. I was frightened out of my life most of the time. I did various jobs there, and I was one of the earlier ones and titles didn't mean much but it was an engineer's dream .... I was in charge of all expenditure on building .... Equipment – we made our own

because people didn't make it for that industry . . . . Huge
expansion – we were building a factory every year . . . . I had
total responsibility for hiring architects and engineers and buying the land. This was the fascinating thing about it as against
semi-state bodies where you know responsibility is divided,
here you had the whole lot . . . and it was fascinating . . . Great
place . . . I loved it.'

During the early 1970s, growth at Paul's place of employment
began to slow down. The company's strategy became one of
growth by acquisition. Paul was put in charge of diversification
in addition to his day-to-day duties of purchasing manager and
chief engineer. Working independently, Paul investigated
hundreds of projects for diversification potential over the next
few years. In his search, he became familiar with the Industrial
Development Authority, a state organisation set up to promote
industrialisation in Ireland. He also worked closely with the
company's accountants in evaluating projects, and he gained
experience in presenting projects to the board of directors.

The recession of 1974–75 changed Paul's brief. With money
scarce, diversification was less attractive and the focus turned to
finding means of absorbing the spare capacity in companies
within the group. It was while he was looking for work for a subsidiary engineering company that he saw an advertisement in the
Financial Times for mechanical engineering subcontract work.
Alan Webster, the advertiser, required a company to manufacture lightingware to his specifications. Webster travelled from
England to Ireland at Sexton's invitation. Following discussion,
both men agreed that the project was not suitable as the subsidiary company was too big, and had all male employees.

Speaking of his feelings then, Paul said: 'At that stage, my
mind was pretty well on the line that I would find a suitable
product/project for myself, and that I would go with it.' Several
months later, Paul decided that Webster's problems might give
him the opportunity he sought to set up his own business.

Alan Webster

Alan Webster was 28 years old. He was a designer of light fittings
and furniture. He began his career as a designer with Terence
Conran, founder of Habitat. Habitat was a large retail chain,
head office in London, which specialised in well-designed,
modern and reasonably priced furnishings and fittings for the
homes of 'people with taste and little money.' Webster pioneered

and specialised in decorative, directional light fittings, that is, when the light is directed at the object or area to be illuminated. The reflector of these fittings was more of the same material as the base and was spun out of steel or aluminium. In 1969 Webster set up a factory to produce lights and plastic furniture to his designs.

He achieved some reputation as a designer in England and America. A piece of his furniture is exhibited in the Museum of Modern Art in New York. Sales were divided 50/50 between furniture and lighting products. His light fittings were on sale in specialist shops in San Francisco and New York, in Germany and in Habitat and several English chain stores. Webster did quite well until 1975. Then, because of the oil crisis, plastic furniture became uncompetitive and the business began to run into financial trouble. A major creditor sent in a receiver, who wound up the business. Webster reacquired the lighting end of the business from the receiver.

Paul explained his choice of Webster as a partner as follows:

'First, while it was apparent that Alan was not a great manager, anyone who can start from scratch and build up his own business to a turnover of £½ million caught my eye first. Second, he was a designer, which I felt was relevant. Third, he still had the market over in the UK and all that had happened to him was that he had failed in financial management.'

Developing his ideas on company formation, Paul said:

'Alan had what I thought were the ingredients I needed. I reckoned that I could get help from the Industrial Development Authority; that I could manage and produce myself. All I wanted was design and sales . . . and he appeared to have both, because he went bust with £100,000-worth of orders on his books. . . . I had always figured myself that the thing to do was not to start something new but pick up where the last guy usually failed . . . . I don't know of any industry that hadn't started like that . . . . You learn from mistakes and, of course, there is an initial market development that is very expensive as people change their habits and start thinking of something new, and you'd be better not having to pay for that. So, I thought I was getting something by teaming up with someone who had developed a market.'

The two men put the project proposal together during the winter of 1975/76.

The proposal

The project proposed was put to the Industrial Development Authority (IDA) for financial support by the Irish government early in 1976. It was proposed to set up a company to manufacture lightingware for floor, table, wall and ceiling mounting in Ireland. The MSTQ series, which had been sold successfully by Webster's old company, was to be the initial main product range. This series was extensive: each product had seven different models and each model was produced in three colours. These products were targeted at multiple department stores, up-market chain stores and some independent retail outlets. The MSTQ series was priced very competitively at approximately £5 ex-factory. Webster undertook to design a new series – the Cylinder series – and as a temporary measure, to organise the production of the new range under subcontract in England. This series had seven models and was designed specifically for specialist lighting shops and department stores such as Harrods. The Cylinder series was priced at approximately £15 ex-factory. The retail selling price of these items would be double the 'ex-factory' price.

The marketing of the product range would be the responsibility of Alan Webster, and a subsidiary, Trendlight (Marketing), was incorporated in England. The US market would be supplied with components which would be produced/sub-assembled by a local firm, with the marketing of the finished product being carried out by the distributor, Basic Concept Ltd (see Appendix 1).

The long-term strategy of the company was to manufacture the entire product range in Ireland and to continue to market in the UK, Germany, and the USA. This involved two stages of development. In the first stage of the project, employment was expected to reach 65. About one-third of this employment would be for skilled males. At the end of Stage 1, the company would move to a permanent factory in an industrial estate. In this second stage, employment was projected to rise to 125.

In late 1976, the IDA commissioned an international marketing consultancy group to carry out a survey to confirm the feasibility of the long-term strategy from a marketing point of view, the validity of the suggested sales volumes, the validity of the price levels suggested, and the acceptability of the product range.

The consultants' report was presented to the IDA in early 1977. The most significant feature of the decorative lighting market was identified as the large number of independent manufacturers selling on design, price and delivery. Potential markets for the modern lighting segment were worth £20 million[1] in the UK and around £1,000 million in the USA. The market was estimated to be growing at about 20 per cent per annum for the decorative sector. Main competitors of Trendlight in the UK were Anglepoise Ltd, turnover near £1 million; Pope Lighting Ltd and Lampways Ltd, both with a turnover of approximately £3–4 million in 1976. Vulcan Ltd, a small new company set up by Webster's former sales manager and a subcontractor, was signalled as posing a particular threat as it was marketing almost identical products as Trendlight's MSTQ series. German and Italian producers, particularly a very large Italian manufacturing company called Guzzini whose turnover was around £1 million in Italy, were seen as increasing their penetration of the English market. The product sold by Guzzini was extremely stylish and was sold through distributors in England. About 20 small companies with turnovers of about £300,000 to £400,000 were also very active in the market place.

Big store groups such as British Home Stores (BHS), Woolworths and department stores were the major outlets for domestic lighting. These stores purchased directly from the manufacturer or they imported their goods. BHS and Woolworths accounted for almost 40 per cent of retail lighting sales. Distributors of lightingware were typically small. Seventeen distributors accounted for 10 per cent of total sales in the retail lighting market.

The response to the design and quality of the Trendlight product – at this time the MSTQ series only, as the Cylinder series was still at the design stage – was favourable. The report concluded that if the new series maintained the standard of design and quality already achieved by the MSTQ series, the 'numbers would be easily achieved', and 'the products are good and the market is there for them'. Some oblique references were made to buyers who might be reluctant to do business with Webster because of bad delivery previously.

In July 1977 the IDA agreed to provide the following grants:

1. 45 per cent of the approved expenditure for Stage 1 estimated to total £200,000 on new machinery and equipment, subject to a maximum of £90,000 by way of grant;
2. 40 per cent of the approved expenditure for Stage 2 estimated to total £700,000 on land, site development,

---

[1] IR£1 = £1stg in 1977.

buildings and building services and new machinery and equipment, subject to a maximum of £280,000 by way of grant.

Subsequently, the IDA also agreed to take equity of £58,500 in the new company,[1] on the understanding that a nominee of the Authority would be appointed as a director of the new company. The Authority also made available a rent subsidy, a loan guarantee for a long-term loan, and an interest subsidy, as well as training grants (See Appendix 2).

In September 1977 the promoters set up a company, Trendlight (Ireland) Ltd, with a total capitalisation of £100. This was later changed to £130,000 when the equity agreement with the IDA was signed (see Appendix 1).

During the autumn and winter of 1977 both partners continued their separate activities. Sexton negotiated to buy a site on the industrial estate and to lease temporary premises nearby. He also took steps to recruit key production staff. He became increasingly concerned about his partner who seemed to be changing under the pressure of the uncertainty generated by the two years' delay in getting the project off the ground, and also because of difficulties he experienced in raising his share of the equity. Most of his cash had been invested in tools for the new lighting series and he had taken part in a trade lighting show. The partners agreed that it was important to keep a high profile in the market place in order to minimise any erosion of demand for their product until they could supply customers again. In March 1978 the equity agreement with the IDA was signed. Sexton resigned his position and moved with his family to rented accommodation in Dublin.

April to June 1978

Describing the first few months, Paul recalled:

'The biggest problem was finance, and the IDA wouldn't come up with their equity until I had come up with a loan. It was a chicken and egg situation. The IDA said, of course, our equity depends on you getting a loan. All the money we had was the

---

[1]The IDA Act, 1977 which resulted in the launch of the Enterprise Development programme gave the IDA new powers to supplement its financial support towards the fixed asset requirements of a project with aid towards the working capital needs where the project was being promoted by a first time entrepreneur.

money I had put in – £22,000. All Webster's equity was in kind rather than cash. And here I was going to the Industrial Credit Company Ltd (ICC)[1] and going through the whole thing and coming back again and going over to the bank. They were the only two I approached. But the bank refused me initially and you can imagine how I felt then. I can tell you I nearly went out of my mind. Well, here I was with people to pay and money running out. That's what delayed us getting started. I had to order a painting plant and big presses, and, of course, I had no money and I couldn't order them until the whole finance was sorted out. That was a very bad time. There were three or four months of total and complete waste. After I started, I did nothing. And, of course, the seeds of disaster were set then. I never went over to England to see what Alan was doing. He was organising the subcontract work for the Cylinder series and the sales and hiring people. I was stuck here every day going to banks and writing our forecasts. That was a very bad start.'

In June the bank agreed to lend £110,000 to the enterprise, the loan being guaranteed by the IDA. Instrumental in this was the IDA's nominee director. Appointed in June, he went with Sexton to the banks, and together they persuaded the bank to finance the venture.

July to December 1978 (first half; Year 1)

With the financial situation sorted out, Paul and his team got down to organising production. The original plan was that during the first few months most of the work would be subcontracted, and that assembly only would take place at the Dublin location. The personnel manager, with the help of Manpower, recruited 30 women, and with the help of AnCO[2] proceeded to train them to assemble the components.

The production engineer discovered that subcontractors willing to do the type of work required were either non-existent or too expensive. By July it was clear that complete manufacture would

[1]The ICC is a public company with a Stock Exchange listing. The Minister for Finance holds most of the issued share capital. ICC operates as a national development bank offering a wide range of financial facilities to Irish manufacturing, distributive and service enterprises.
[2]AnCO, the Industrial Training Authority, established in 1967 with the primary objective of raising to the highest international standards the skills of the Irish workforce at all levels in industrial and commercial activities.

take place at Dublin. This included metal-spinning, pressing, painting, finishing and testing. Two skilled metal-spinners were recruited in England. While the recruitment of these men was easy, retaining their services proved to be difficult. Until some two years later when Paul had trained two Irish men in the craft, these key positions were sometimes vacant. Other problems also arose. Sourcing of materials, particularly small components, special fasteners and screws proved difficult. Neither Paul nor his purchasing engineer had direct experience of the lighting industry. Alan, contacted by phone, proved to be unhelpful. He himself had always left that kind of problem to his production man. Second, Webster had no technical drawings of the MSTQ series. Paul and his production engineer had to work out tolerances by trial and error. Third, Alan insisted on components being assembled in a particular way for appearances' sake. It took several days to work out a system for doing this, and then the women had to be trained in the technique. Fourth, the emphasis on design and quality resulted in large numbers of light fittings being rejected.

> 'Knowing I was an engineer and not a designer, or customer oriented, I over-sympathised with what I saw as my weakness. I realised that we were in the design business, a very delicate business, because if the design failed, we failed, and because of that I gave Alan a great deal of leeway.'

> Paul Sexton

Production began in September. Sales targets of approximately £35,000 per month for the first six months were set by the two men. Webster projected sales every four weeks, and production levels were geared to these forecasts: 'I can't sell from the end of a production line. I must have stocks' he said.

Communication between England and Ireland depended on the telephone and telex and on the monthly board meetings in Dublin attended by the three directors and the senior staff. Webster undertook several trips to the continent and to the USA. Paul, concentrating on getting the production process functioning properly, had not found time to travel to England. After manufacture the products were despatched to England where they were warehoused. Delivery to the customer was the responsibility of the sales office in London. Invoicing was also carried out in London. In November Alan forecast sales worth £75,000 for December 1978. Trusting in his partner's forecasts, though shaken somewhat by the amount projected, Paul and his production team worked hard to produce the required number of lamps. In December Alan announced that the *Observer Colour Magazine* had agreed to make a special offer of two types of table lamps in the MSTQ series to its readers in January 1979.

January to June 1979 (second half; Year 1)

Early in January Paul made a trip to England. Examination of the accounts showed that in the period up to December sales of £30,000 had been made. Expenses were extremely high in London. Sales of the Cylinder series were minimal. Most sales were in the low margin MSTQ series. Some £25,000 was outstanding in payment to the subcontractors for the Cylinder series. Webster had been asked at a board meeting in December to cancel the subcontract and now Paul learned that he had failed to do so.

Feeling extremely let down, Sexton went next to France, Germany and Switzerland. Webster was forecasting very good sales in these countries. He had visited his contacts there during the previous autumn and had shown them the Cylinder series of lights. Distributors had been appointed in Germany, Belgium and Holland. Paul followed in Webster's footsteps. Everywhere he met with disappointing news. In France the older series of Trendlight lights – made in Ireland – were regarded as old-fashioned, while the new Cylinder series was ugly, too dear, and 'wouldn't sell'. In Germany no interest was shown in the products. While in Germany, Paul contacted a large firm who manufactured and distributed commercial lights – lights used in hospitals and office blocks. He proposed that the German company should license him to produce their lights in Ireland. He argued that he could produce very cheaply due to lower labour costs. While interested, the German company was non-committal.

In Switzerland Sexton concluded negotiations, initiated by Webster, with R & R Baltensweiller to manufacture under licence lamps designed by the latter. The agreement included the payment of a royalty of 6 per cent on sales. Webster proposed broadening the range with these highly specialised products. Returning to England, Sexton found that good news awaited him. The January *Observer* offer had 'a good response'. Due to this success the *Observer* agreed to a further mail order offer on 1 March (see Appendix 3). This second offer was quite successful, though the timing was unfavourable. Sexton commented that sales of lamps were somewhat seasonal – most sales being made in late autumn.

At a lighting show held in Earls Court, London in February, Paul discovered that the Trendlight stand – though lavishly and eye-catchingly designed – was being ignored by the major buyers. There and then he decided that another sales organisation was needed to sell the products in the volume needed to cover overheads. He decided to approach Lampways Ltd, a competitor, but with a large distribution network throughout the UK. Webster was helpful in making initial contact with the directors of Lampways as he agreed that there was an enormous gap between his forecasts and actual performance. He revealed that 70 per cent of his sales previously had been to Habitat and that after the liquidation of his company, Habitat had engaged another designer to produce lightingware for sale in that chain. Webster now agreed to continue to operate the design studio on a much reduced basis. A second designer was retained for a few months, but was then let go. Marketing was taken completely out of Webster's hands, the salesman was let go, and Sexton commenced negotiations with Lampways, negotiations which continued until June when an agreement was signed with the following terms:

1. Lampways would receive a 20 per cent commission on invoiced sales.
2. Lampways would supply a director to the Trendlight (Ireland) board.
3. Lampways would have the option of acquiring 26 per cent of Trendlight's shares at/or within three years, being those shares which are owned by the marketing and selling function, namely Alan Webster.

The negotiations had proved to be long drawn out because Lampways was worried about Vulcan Ltd activities. Finally, Trendlight agreed to change the product range somewhat and Lampways agreed to sell. Meanwhile, the initial loans had been well spent, and the bank was approached for a further extension of credit to allow Trendlight to stock up for a mail order offer planned by the *Observer* for the autumn of 1979. The *Observer* committed itself to investing £50,000 in advertising for this third mail order offer and projected sales worth £350,000. The bank extended a further £80,000. Subsequently, the IDA also agreed to increase their loan guarantee.

July to December 1979 (first half; Year 2)

In July Lampways began to sell for Trendlight in the UK market. The mail order commenced in September and continued until December. Results were very disappointing (see Appendix 3). Though Sexton had manufactured lamps worth £200,000, instead of 350,000, as a precautionary measure, he was still left with a large number unsold. Analysing the reasons for the failure, Sexton felt that the market had been saturated by the previous offers. He also felt that perhaps the *Observer* did not understand the product as the usual mail offer product was a tie, or a scarf or a shirt. Besides, because of a strike in the *Sunday Times* the *Observer's* circulation had been boosted only to fall off in the autumn when the strike was resolved. The *Observer* tried unsuccessfully to buy advertising space in the *Sunday Times*, for the Trendlight products. Advertisements were placed in women's magazines and the response was very poor. The recession was beginning to bite in England, and this was a further cause, Sexton felt, for the failure to achieve substantial sales.

Meanwhile, the relationship between Lampways and Trendlight was proving to be unsatisfactory. Sales were disappointing, and in December Lampways was taken over by a large commercial company in the UK. The new management was not interested in continuing the association between the two companies and terminated it. Sexton felt that he was lucky in recruiting the services of John Wright, former sales manager of Lampways Ltd. John Wright was a well-known and well-connected salesman. He did not, however, wish to continue to work for Lampways under the new management.

By December 1979 all lending institutions were unwilling to extend further credit. Sexton approached Foir Teoranta,[1] who lent £45,000 (Appendix 4).

January to June 1980 (second half; Year 2)

On 2 January Alan Webster resigned from the board of Trendlight (Ireland) surrendering all his shares, and was replaced by John Wright. Under Wright's direction, 'slowly and expensively' Trendlight products broke into the department stores in

---

[1]Foir Teoranta provides assistance for industrial concerns which may be in danger of having to close down or suspend activities because of inability to raise necessary capital from commercial sources. Such concerns, however, must be basically sound and capable, if necessary with reorganisation, of becoming profitable.

England, and better sales were achieved. Wright insisted that a new product be manufactured to widen the range.

Sales were mostly in small amounts and often lamps were returned. Trendlight had about 150 accounts in England by June 1980 but over 70 per cent of the turnover was represented by less than 30 accounts. Control of the sales function in England caused headaches. While a new young accountant had been recruited to monitor sales, he was based in Ireland. Invoices were sometimes late in being issued and large credits were given. Co-ordination of the sales and production functions was difficult because of a lack of consistent communication.

Analysing trends in the light fittings industry in mid-1980, Sexton realised he was dependent upon the property markets. Property markets in England during the previous two years had been stagnant. There were signs in mid-1980 that this inactivity would continue for a further period, but it was seen as likely by all the commentators that a revival would take place in 1981–82. The increasing demand should cause prices to improve with a resultant growth in profits and increased stock turnover.

Sexton decided to look for ways to diversify. He reckoned that the decorative lighting market was too competitive and too difficult to service in the long term. He decided to intensify his attempts to penetrate the Irish market.

Kilkenny Design Workshop[1] was commissioned to design table, floor and pendant lamps. A Scottish firm was commissioned to design recessed commercial lights known as downlighters in the trade. Trendlight began to target the commercial sector of the lighting market in Ireland, estimated to be worth £4 million per annum. Through the Product Identification Unit of the IDA, Sexton was put in touch with an American producer of energy-efficient lights. Negotiations were begun to manufacture under licence the range of large area lighting fixtures for sale in Ireland. Royalties of 7½ per cent on sales were sought by the Americans. These fittings were specified by architects for large factories, supermarkets and power stations. There was no other manufacturer of such fixtures in Ireland. Sales in Ireland were Sexton's responsibility.

At the same time, Sexton began actively to look around for another partner. Several large public companies were approached

---

[1]The Kilkenny Design Workshop was established in 1965 by the Irish government to advance good design. One of its functions is to stimulate product design innovation and to provide practical design assistance to industry.

and two in particular showed interest in taking equity in Trendlight (Ireland). At the end of June negotiations were still continuing.

Appendix 1

Summary of initial project proposal

Sales targets	Units sold 000s	Sales value £000s
Year 1	80	400
Year 2	160	800
Year 3	200	1,000
Unit value (ex-factory) = £5		

Markets	%
UK	30
EEC	30
(predominantly Germany)	
USA	40

Profit and Loss Account indices	
Sales	100%
Costs	
Raw material	44.0
Direct labour	10.5
Administration costs	10.5
Distribution costs	7.5
Selling costs	10.0
Factory overheads	8.5
Net profit	9.0

Share capital

	Total	12% redeemable cumulative preference shares	A. ordinary shares	B. ordinary shares	C. ordinary shares
Authorised £1 each	130,000	58,410	200	40,533	30,857
Issued and fully paid up	130,000	58,410	200	40,533	30,857

The redeemable preference shares had priority to the payment of dividend before any classes listed above and ranked prior to other classes in the event of liquidation. The A. ordinary shares conferred on the holders the right of management and control of the company, the B. and C. ordinary shares were non-voting. The shares were held as follows:

	%
IDA	45
Webster	38
Sexton	17

The cumulative preference shares were held in total by the IDA. These shares could be redeemed during the period 1 July 1979 to 31 December 1985, by ordinary resolution and at the written request of Sexton only. In a separate agreement Sexton agreed to transfer seven shares to Webster to make the eventual shareholding:

	%
Webster	55
Sexton	45

Proposed organisation structure

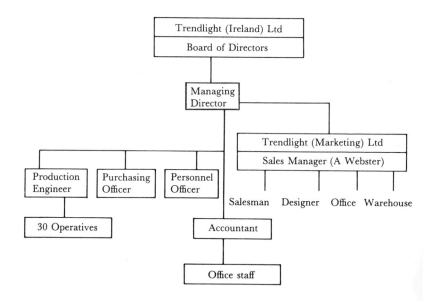

Appendix 2

The IDA agreed to make available to the new company:

(a) a rent subsidy of £7,020 per annum for a period of two years or 45 per cent of the actual rental costs of Stage 1 buildings whichever was the lesser;

   (b) a loan guarantee on the long-term loan of £110,000 which could be procured by the company for Stage 1 of the undertaking;

   (c) a five-year interest subsidy of £30,780 towards the interest payable on a long-term loan of £110,000 subject to the rate of interest actually paid by the new company not falling below 4 per cent per annum;

   (d) training grants of approximately £50,000 over three years.

Appendix 3

Sales by month from January 1979–June 1980 (Sales in £000)

		UK	Mail order	Ireland	USA	Europe	Subcontract	Total
Jan 1979		8	11	1	—	—	—	20
Feb		8	15	1	—	—	—	34
March		3	6	3	25	—	—	37
April		2	5	5	—	2	—	14
May		7	1	5	10	—	—	23
June		2	8	2	—	—	—	12
July		2	—	1	6	—	—	9
Aug		1	—	1	9	—	—	11
Sept		3	3	4	—	1	—	11
Oct		5	25	5	8	—	—	43
Nov		6	25	4	—	1	—	36
Dec		9	23	3	4	—	—	39
Budgeted								
Jan 1980	10	6	10	2	—	—	1	19
Feb	10	3	4	2	—	—	2	11
March	30	24	—	1	—	—	3	28
April	25	18	—	4	8	—	4	38
May	20	6	—	4	—	—	5	15
June	20	21	3	1	—	—	2	27

Notes:
1. Credits and trade discounts amounted to £55,000 for 1977–79.
2. Budgeted sales from January 1980 from J Wright.
3. Projected sales for general accounts July-December 1980:

    July 1980   £20,000
    Aug 1980   £30,000
    Sep 1980   £30,000
    Oct 1980   £35,000
    Nov 1980   £35,000
    Dec 1980   £20,000

4. Plans were under way for special subcontract work for an Irish company in summer 1980 estimated at £30,000.

Appendix 4

Consolidated Profit and Loss Account for the 30 weeks ended 27 June 1980

	1980 IR£	1979(1) IR£
Sales	299,736	175,456
Cost of sales	(297,006)	(137,696)
Gross profit	2,730	37,760
Selling and adminstration expenses	(163,700)	(139,165)
Bank interest and charges	(47,057)	(11,389)
Start-up expenses (2)	—	(99,259)
Net profit (loss)	(208,027)	(212,053)

Balance Sheet, 27 June 1980

	1980 IR£	1979 IR£
Current assets		
Cash on hand	38	138
Debtors and prepayments	86,088	37,975
Stocks (3)	240,925	200,886
Intercompany account	—	94,623
Total current assets	327,051	333,622
Current liabilities		
Bank overdraft (4)	237,607	98,822
Creditors and accruals	146,025	107,942
Total current liabilities	383,632	206,764
Net current assets (liabilities)	(56,581)	126,858
Fixed assets, net (5)	63,223	89,722
Investment in subsidiary	—	500
Term loans (6)	(210,000)	(210,000)
	(248,358)	(7,080)
Financed by		
Share capital	130,000	130,000
Accumulated deficit	(378,358)	(122,920)
	(248,358)	(7,080)

Notes:
1. The prior year figures reflect the results of the Group for the period 1 September 1977 to 13 July 1979.
2. Start-up expenses represent expenses incurred by the company prior to the attainment of normal production levels.

3. a) stocks comprise the following:

	1980 Group IR£	1979 Group IR£
Raw materials	99,848	89,289
Finished goods	141,077	111,597
	240,925	200,886

b) Stocks are stated at the lower of the first-in, first-out cost and net realisable value. Cost includes an appropriate allocation of production overheads.

4. Bank borrowings comprise:

	1980 Group IR£	1979 Group IR£
Bank overdraft	268,338	102,336
Term loan No. 1	50,000	50,000
No. 2	110,000	110,000
No. 3	50,000	50,000
	210,000	210,000

The borrowings are secured by:
a) a fixed and floating charge over the company's assets
b) a guarantee from the IDA for IR£204,000.

5. Fixed assets, net:

			1980	
a) *Group*	Cost IR£	Government grants IR£	Accumulated depreciation IR£	Net book value IR£
Leasehold improvements	3,275	—	3,235	40
Plant and machinery	123,742	50,728	11,263	61,751
Office equipment	5,944	—	1,618	4,326
Motor vehicles	5,207	—	607	4,600
	138,168	50,728	16,723	70,717

	Cost IR£	Government grants IR£	Accumulated depreciation IR£	Net book value IR£
b) *Group*				
Land deposit	20,500	—	—	20,500
Leasehold improvements	3,275	—	1,596	1,679
Plant and machinery	113,206	44,832	4,500	63,874
Office equipment	8,673	—	795	7,878
Motor vehicles	4,683	—	1,034	3,649
	150,377	44,832	7,925	97,580

6. Long term loan. The company obtained an IR£45,000 loan from Foir Teoranta during the period to 27 June 1980. The loan was secured by a second floating charge

over the assets of the company. The first charge over company assets is held by the Bank of Ireland as security for the term loans issued, as noted in Note 4 above. The repayment terms of this loan are as follows:

a) A moratorium on interest and capital repayment until 31 March 1982.
b) Gross interest is payable from 1 April 1982 to 30 September 1982.
c) Repayment of the loan and capitalised interest to commence on 31 September 1982.

Questions

1. Do you think that Paul Sexton and Alan Webster had the potential to be ideal business partners?
2. What problems were likely to result from splitting the business into a manufacturing unit based in Ireland and a sub-contracting and marketing function in England?
3. Why do you think Alan Webster's first business failed?
4. How realistic do you think Trendlight's initial projects set out in Appendix 1 were?
5. What options lay ahead of Sexton in January 1979 and which would you recommend him to take?

Case 29

Highland Ltd
Richard Thorpe

Highland Ltd originally started as an independent outdoor pursuits centre at Shiel Bridge. In order to compete with other outdoor pursuit centres which enjoyed the benefits of local authority subsidies and grants, its director, Frank Rose, began to manufacture outdoor protective garments. Although untrained, he had a flair for make-up and design, but because of his lack of business expertise and his preoccupation with teaching at the school, he did not devote as much time to the manufacturing business as he should. In order to repay a loan raised to start this business and to buy premises, he was forced to sell the centre at Shiel Bridge and move to rented accommodation in Inverness.

Frank Rose required additional funds and Andrew Robertson and his wife were willing to put money into the business in return for a place on the board. Andrew and his wife soon took over the running of the business – he as managing director, she dealing with the accounts. Frank Rose increasingly turned his attention to the outdoor centre, now run from some small cottages that had once been instructors' accommodation and were still owned by the company. From the time of the move to Inverness he contributed no new designs and his contact with the manufacturing side of the business was minimal.

The manufacturing company moved to its first new location in April 1977 and took with it machines and raw material stock (see Appendix 1). The main customer, Weir's of Glasgow, fed the company enough work to make this small business viable. Overheads for the one-room flat in Inverness in which the firm now operated were small and staff relationships were informal. A skilled and competent machinist, Judith Harling, had been employed as the first worker at the new location, as it was not possible to take any of the machinists from Shiel Bridge. From then employment increased steadily until about November 1977 (see Appendix 2).

The directors were trying hard with their limited resources to get the business on to a proper footing. Although there had been no attempts to attract new custom, it was assumed that there would be a ready market when production capacity could be made available. Approaches to retailers were, therefore, discouraged as Andrew Robertson held the view that it was no use going to the market until he had the capacity to satisfy the demand when it came. He was convinced demand would come when the company went to the market.

Boom in an oil-related industry

Out at Loch Kishorn on the beautiful Applecross peninsula, Western Oil Ltd were building the biggest concrete oil platform that the world had ever seen. Stoner Garments Ltd, agents for waterproof and protective clothing, were anxious to supply jackets to this very lucrative market of some 2,000 manual workers. As a local supplier, Highland Ltd could produce jackets almost to demand and provide quick delivery. Highland Ltd, together with Stoner Garments, designed a jacket that was acceptable to Western Oil in terms of both quality and price, and a first order in waxed cotton cloth was soon received for 500 jackets.

Highland Ltd set about production, paying a commission fee to Stoner but invoicing and delivering direct to the construction site. Subsequent orders came direct from Western and Stoner was conveniently ignored and a local myth became established that Mr and Mrs Robertson had cornered the market for waterproofs at Kishorn. The real story was slightly different, the new relationship being closely connected with their office girl attending a local dance where she met a Stoner employee who asked her where she worked and what she did. From November 1977 additional staff were rapidly recruited and trained by Highland Ltd, and the company expanded to occupy all the tenement floors in the Inverness building. Business was booming with orders of 100 to 150 garments per week at an invoice value of £1,600 plus. Although Weir's continued to give Highland work, Kishorn Jackets, as they became known, absorbed the whole of the extra labour recruited until September 1978, 14 people then being employed (see Appendix 3). The effect on the finances of the business can be seen in Appendix 4. Many of these employees had been attracted to work at the factory by the opportunity to earn high piecework wages. Without exception all were trained and skilled machinists, and many had come from the local trouser factory which was going through a bad period.

The business was racing ahead of itself, tenancy had been

secured on a new 'advance' factory of 6,000 sq ft by the end of 1978, and occupation was planned for 1 January 1979.

While accepting the need for greater efficiency, Highland was a company in which the philosophy and raison d'être mattered a great deal. There was a realisation that although the stated objective of the company was to maximise profits there were secondary objectives that it wished to pursue. These were embodied in the company's philosophy and although never written down, key elements were easily identified.

There were underlying differences in the way different people saw the company philosophy even between the directors, some stressing one facet more than another, depending on their own interest and motivation. The following list is, therefore, not in any order of priority:

- Concern for people.
- Informal style relationships.
- People should enjoy working for Highland.
- The quality of life at work should be of a high standard.
- Management should respect their staff and show evidence of this in the systems they introduce.
- The company supports the aims of the Mountain School to provide a certain kind of developmental experience for young people which is not available elsewhere.

The continual reaffirmation of this philosophy served to attract people to the company who shared those views, but contradictions often arose.

At the end of 1978 the company employed 14 machinists (see Appendix 3), all of whom were fully trained and worked under the direct control of one supervisor, Judith Harling. When necessary, Judith was assisted by one of the younger, full-time machinists who was paid an enhanced day rate to offset any loss of piecework earnings such duties might involve. Neither Judith nor this girl, Mari Graham, had been supervisors before and it was no secret that Judith had been promoted to supervisor because she had been with the company the longest. She had a difficult temperament and it was a rare week that one or other of the girls would not burst into the manager's office threatening to resign. However, Judith was admired for machining skills, but was not an effective supervisor, often assuming too much and demonstrating new work methods too quickly. However, she could spot the best ways of tackling a problem and make a professional job. Mari, on the other hand, was sympathetic to learners and was often used for training new machinists, the manager making some excuse or other to have Mari do this rather than Judith.

The cutting department was under the direct control of David Gosnold, the cutter/designer. David joined the company soon after it moved to Inverness and was fiercely loyal to the Robertsons. David came to the company to find self-expression in an environment in which he felt able to progress. His designs were simple but functional. However, he was not a pattern cutter and often work he had done which went to the machinists was of a poor standard and caused them difficulty. When work was rejected, the machinists blamed the cutter, while he blamed the quality of machining caused by girls rushing on piecework. Arguments often ensued as a result of this conflict.

Before the move to the new factory, the office had been the nerve centre of the business. Five people shared a tiny room. When, early in 1977, the company moved, a whole section of the factory was partitioned off for offices, and not only were individuals now located in their own rooms, they were physically separated from the rest of the factory. At Shiel, access to the office had been much easier, adding to the informality of the working arrangements.

Soon after the move, Andrew Robertson became ill. He had played a major role in the factory's move to the new premises and the management of related problems. His absence at this time resulted in considerable anxiety and uncertainty within the factory. A management void was created that badly needed to be filled. Mrs Robertson, in contrast to her husband, was remote and unapproachable. She gave the impression of being hungry for power, enjoyed being called 'the director' or 'the chief accountant'. Presumptuous and boastful, she was tolerated to a point. She could not delegate and often did jobs herself for which she was entirely unsuited. The organisation chart she drew and distributed is shown in Appendix 5.

Marketing policy

Between April 1977 and January 1978, following the oil connection, the company had experienced a dramatic increase in output and profits. Whereas initially the output had gone almost exclusively to Weir's it now went to Western Oil (see Appendix 6).

Having moved to new premises, the company felt that these would provide the ideal environment for a 'take-off'. It was also considered that the 1979 market for sportswear may have been missed due to an eight-month delay in occupying the new factory, but there was still confidence that the modest programme of product development and design would yield results when retailers saw the new garments. Prior to becoming ill, Andrew Robertson had assured the workforce that some preliminary marketing had been done, therefore retail outlets could be offered the existing product range. A sample box of Highland products was sent to every reputable retailer selling mountaineering clothing and equipment. 'Take-off' was then awaited. The company's emphasis on quality cannot be overstated. The managing director felt that Highland's strength lay in the quality of its products. As shown in Appendix 7, he wanted high-volume industrial breadwinners, plus a range of high-quality specialist sportswear.

Production policy

Garment manufacturing has three basic processes: cutting, making or machining, and packing.

Cutting cloth is usually done by band knife or vibrating blade and once a pattern is laid out, as shown below, several thicknesses of material can be cut through at once, in this case as many as 30 at a time. Although the laying out takes longer for 30-thick cutting, the cutting operation takes only slightly longer for 30 than it does for one.

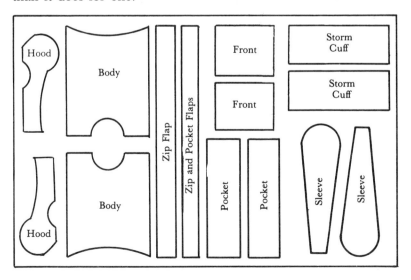

Once cut, the garments are split into bundles and passed to machinists where the pieces are sewn together. Usually one girl sews sleeves, another cuffs, another overlocks etc. At Highland Ltd, girls made through, that is, obtained, all the items for one complete garment and made up one complete jacket. This was thought to give the girls a certain amount of job satisfaction. It was recognised that speed would be sacrificed, but it was thought that the quality of Highland's garments merited this method of manufacture. The policy, however, had the following implications:

1. Machinery had to be similar, so that girls could do all operations on their own machines. Some jobs proved difficult to do on one machine but all jobs *could* be done this way.
2. Girls often used to make up the garments sectionally in any case. Recognising that it took only fractionally longer to machine five cuffs than one, once they had laid them out, they would make up all five jackets sectionally themselves, or place themselves informally in groups and make up a number of jackets together.
3. The quality could be tightly controlled and checked back to individuals as each girl marked her name on the items she machined.

Finished garments were moved through to the packing area where they were finally inspected, despatched to customers or stored against future orders. The final inspection invariably revealed a large percentage of garments below the required quality, although confusion existed, often manifesting itself in anger as to what exactly quality levels were when garments were taken back to machinists for reworking. Unpicking is time-consuming and fiddly work and in the end often results in a second quality garment as material is damaged in the process of rework (see factory layout, Appendix 9).

Stock

Those garments made for the Western Oil Company and Weir's were almost always made directly against a customer's order. All machinists in the company were trained to undertake work on all the different designs and because of the inequitable payments system this meant each type of garment had to be shared out as fairly as possible between the various machinists. In an attempt to combat the small cutting and making orders from individual retailers, larger batches were devised to obtain some economies of scale. Those garments not despatched immediately were put into store.

Costing and wage payment

Over the years an accurate record of material usage had been kept, but present labour content and what was possible were more difficult to judge. One of the supervisor's main functions was to estimate the time it would take to complete a garment. This information was passed to Mrs Robertson who would calculate a piecework rate. For a number of reasons, these rates did not always reflect job content and the following problems could be identified:

1. Rates drifted due to girls using or developing different make-up methods after the rates had been set. This would be natural as they became more familiar with the work and simply became more efficient. No method was ever written down or agreed.
2. Wage differentials developed between girls caused by different machinists applying different methods to similar jobs.
3. Slack and tight rates because of rate drift resulted in vast contrasts in earnings and problems in the equitable distribution of work as shown below.

Earnings differences between skilled workers – 40-hour earnings.

Employee	Week A £	Week B £	Week C £	Week D £	Average on 4 weeks £
Annette Thornton	69.60	86.73	77.49	87.83	80.41
Roe Scott	57.15	46.54	48.67	63.00	53.83
Valerie Sanderson	54.07	51.58	45.00	62.22	53.22
Fanny Mitchell	38.40	56.91	46.87	65.47	51.91
Heather Wright	73.17	87.69	78.75	92.20	82.95

4. Differentials caused by operatives on day rate. Operators were sometimes required to move to a day rate because of shortage of work, specialised work, or repairs. As the basic rate was low compared with their previous earnings girls were unwilling to do this. A further complication was the existence of two basic rates. One was the basic rate of 82p per hour, the other an enhanced day rate of 96p per hour paid to some women when, and only when, they were making a certain kind of high-quality complicated jacket. The part-time sample machinist was always paid at this rate. Some girls were earning only the basic rate of 82p per hour but not because they were insufficiently skilled to do piecework and 'specials'. Disputes would

arise about the methods of payment if, for instance, one girl was not paid the enhanced day rate when she thought she ought to be. The complicated jacket, in her opinion, was an equally difficult and skilled job as making jackets that didn't warrant the higher rate of pay. They just didn't take as long. The problem could be exacerbated if women thought others were getting the higher rate for some jackets when they were not. The higher price had been introduced at the time of pressure for orders and was meant to reflect a number of things–the skill of the operative, the need for quality on intricate work and expensive material, so as to (a) not let the machinist suffer in any way; (b) reduce the chance of rejects.

As the standard of machining increased the two-rate anomaly remained. There was great reluctance to see this rate spread to other garments. Indirect workers, such as packers and checkers and supervisors, were also paid on a day rate basis. They often felt that when the factory was in full swing they too would have to work hard, yet any increase in effort was not reflected in their wages. The following wage levels were paid to indirect workers:

	£
Dayworker	44.00
Packer/checker	56.00
Supervisor	68.40
Cutter	96.00

More recently the wages in general had been the cause of some bad feeling. It was considered by some in the workforce that they were being badly paid compared with other workers in the locality. One machinist had seen an advertisement about wages councils and minimum pay and had brought this to the attention of management.

Garments were never inspected until the final operation and although this was a thorough check, it was generally recognised as being too late. Girls would rush on piecework to obtain maximum earnings and this often caused rejects. Rejects at this late stage would result in unpicking jackets in the girls' own time or completely recutting the jacket. Often there were spectacular arguments as to where the fault lay – in cutting or machining.

It would not be unusual for girls to be on piecework for some of the week and then be moved on to day work. This could be due to a number of factors but often it related to work on new styles. In addition there was a process whereby the supervisor would issue work fairly between operatives to attempt to balance earnings.

This was not always possible. Sometimes management would push a rush order and (particularly true of Kishorn work) this would be given to the fastest and most skilled machinist. In their own interests girls would want to maximise their individual earnings and stay on piecework. Average hourly earnings for some piecework over a period of two months can be seen in Appendix 8.

Jealousies among the workforce were rife. There were allegations that the supervisor had favourites and the distribution of good and bad work was becoming a problem that was difficult to solve.

Pricing

Pricing and tenders for all work on the basis of a fixed percentage (55 per cent) on direct labour and materials.

Appendix 1

Accounts for year to 30 September 1977

(as presented by the company accountant)

Balance sheet

30 September 1976

£	£		£	£
32,389		Fixed assets		10,065
		Current assets		
	8,117	Stock and work-in-progress	13,679	
	6,274	Debtors	6,262	
	5	Cash in hand	66	
	14,396		20,007	
		Less current liabilities		
	£3,200	Short-term loans	£4,200	
	3,000	HP creditors	2,501	
	736	Capital creditors	350	
	11,095	Trade creditors	2,542	
33,138	15,107	Bank	3,152	12,745
(18,742)				7,265
13,647				17,327
5,000		Loan from government		—
8,647		Net surplus at 30 September 1977		17,327

represented by

			Authorised	Issued		
		Share capital				
		Ordinary shares of £1 each	£17,000	£13,200		
		A. ordinary shares of £1 each	8,000	6,500		
	16,500		£25,000	£19,700	19,700	
	1,070	Loan from directors			4,569	
		Surplus on sale of property		£6,899		
	—	Less/building grants repaid		3,942	2,957	
	17,570				27,226	
	8,923	Losses carried forward			9,899	
8,647					17,327	

Trading Profit and Loss Account

15 months to 30 September 1976

£	£		£	£
38,168		Sales		37,377
8,310		Course fees		6,159
46,478				43,536
	23,893	Materials	11,116	
	13,615	Wages and NI	14,984	
40,931	3,423	Provisions	4,901	31,001
5,547		Gross profit		12,535
—		Interest received		485
160		Profit on sale of vehicle etc		570
5,707				13,590
	2,982	Salaries	3,614	
	1,418	Repairs and removals	431	
	392	Carriage	271	
	3,266	Car and travelling expenses	2,211	
	766	Power, heat and light	719	
	576	Rates and insurance	700	
	316	Telephone	603	
		£ 966 Interest–loan	£ 690	
		2,155 bank	2,175	
	3,557	436 HP	660	3,525
	690	Stationery and advertising	398	
	812	Miscellaneous	874	
16,860	2,085	Depreciation	1,220	14,566
11,153		Deficit for year		976

Appendix 2

Recruitments until November 1977

Name	Date of employment	Age	Category	Status	PT/FT
Judith Harling	07.04.77	40	Supervisor	Married	F/T
Betty McFarlane	30.06.77	28	Machinist	Married	P/T
Margaret Murry	30.06.77	27	Machinist	Married	P/T
Christine Howson	01.06.77	24	Accounts office	Married	P/T
David Gosnold	01.08.77	23	Cutter	Married	F/T
Mari Graham	11.08.77	19	Machinist	Single	F/T
Fanny Mitchell	08.09.77	28	Machinist	Married	F/T
Christine Reid	08.09.77	45	Checker	Married	F/T
Linda Taylor	06.10.77	38	Machinist	Married	P/T

Appendix 3

Recruitments after November 1977

Name	Date of Employment	Age	Category	Status	PT/FT
Valerie Sanderson	15.12.77	21	Machinist	Single	F/T
Fiona Hinde	15.12.77	18	Packer/Checker	Single	F/T
Kate Morton	15.12.77	18	Cutter assistant	Single	F/T
Roe Scott	22.03.78	20	Machinist	Single	F/T
Moira Watts	22.03.78	21	Store person	Single	F/T
Anne McIntyre	20.04.78	42	Machinist	Married	P/T
Heather Wright	03.05.78	24	Machinist	Married	F/T
Annette Thornton	03.05.78	20	Machinist	Married	F/T
Heather Livesey	28.05.78	37	Machinist	Married	P/T
Jo Moyes	19.07.78	27	Machinist	Married	F/T
Cathy Plank	16.08.78	23	Machinist	Married	F/T
Sue Jardine	01.10.78	17	Machinist	Single	P/T
Cathy Sclater	08.11.78	37	Machinist	Married	P/T
Alex Walker	01.09.78	55	Driver/Mechanic	Married	F/T

Appendix 4

Balance Sheet as at 31 December 1978

	£	£	£
Fixed assets			19,350
Current assets			
Stock and work-in-progress		35,505	
Debtors		15,481	
		50,986	
Current liabilities			
Short-term loans	4,200		
HP creditors	6,462		
Capital creditors	1,504		
Trade creditors and accruals	8,300		
Bank overdraft	12,567		
		33,033	
			17,953
Total net assets			37,303
Represented by			
Share capital			

	Authorised	Issued	
Ordinary shares of £1 each	17,000	13,200	
A. ordinary shares of £1 each	8,000	6,500	
	25,000	19,700	19,700
Capital reserve			2,957
Directors' loan			4,569
Retained profits			10,077
			37,303

Trading and Profit and Loss Account

15 months to 31 December 1978

	£	£
Sales		
Industrial	155,058	
Recreational	41,723	
		196,781
Cost of sales (materials and direct labour)		
Industrial	100,159	
Recreational	25,172	
		125,331
Gross profit (36.31% on turnover)		71,450
Fixed costs		
Wages and salaries		
Directors	10,000	
Manager	5,250	
Clerk/Typist	2,250	
Forewoman	2,525	
Quality control clerk and assistant	3,824	
Cutter and assistant (semi-variable cost)	853	
Cleaner	320	
	25,022	
Rent, rates and insurance	3,624	
Heat and light	895	
Telephone and postage	2,430	
Petty cash	2,660	
Transport	1,942	
Maintenance	913	
Stationery	345	
Accountancy	1,650	
Interest charges	4,538	
NI	1,420	
		45,439
		26,011
Depreciation		6,035
Net profit for period		19,976
Losses brought forward		9,899
Profit carried forward		10,077

Note: There will be no liability to corporation tax in view of capital allowances on fixed assets acquired during the period and capital allowances and losses brought forward.

Appendix 5

Organisation Chart

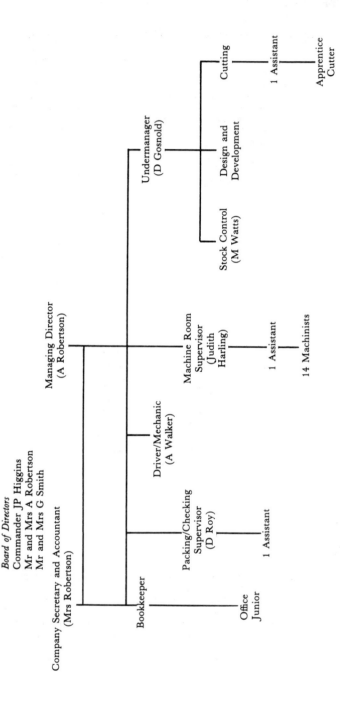

Board of Directors
Commander JP Higgins
Mr and Mrs A Robertson
Mr and Mrs G Smith

Managing Director
(A Robertson)

Company Secretary and Accountant
(Mrs Robertson)

Undermanager
(D Gosnold)

Cutting

1 Assistant

Apprentice Cutter

Design and Development

Stock Control
(M Watts)

Machine Room Supervisor
(Judith Harling)

1 Assistant

14 Machinists

Driver/Mechanic
(A Walker)

Packing/Checking Supervisor
(D Roy)

1 Assistant

Bookkeeper

Office Junior

Appendix 6

Breakdown of sales: 15 months to 31 December 1978

	Industrial £	Recreational £
Weir's retail business		30,879
Weir's wholesale business		5,944
Trail Gear (Export)		1,335
Centre Sports		1,089
Western Oil	151,047	
Outdoor Centre		424
Tartan Inc (Export)		745
PQ Construction	3,542	
Regional Council		239
Taylors		540
Mountain School		528
Sundry Sales	469	
	155,058	41,723

Sales to Western Oil per month

	£
October 1977	5,212
November	6,090
December	6,920
January 1978	7,778
February	9,114
March	10,237
April	10,851
May	11,798
June	14,043
July	13,525
August	13,332
September	12,283
October	10,310
November	10,129
December	9,425
	151,047

Appendix 7

Product range

Hightop Jacket	–	Foul weather outdoor garment in heavyweight neoprene designed for mountain use.
Summit Jacket	–	Foul weather outdoor garment in oiled cotton design for mountain use.
Fisherman Jacket	–	Outdoor lined jacket in waxed cotton designed for fishermen.
Shirts	–	Wool and wool/acrylic shirts in various tartans designed for mountaineers.
Kishorn Jacket	–	A well-designed jacket with over-trousers produced in heavyweight neoprene for industrial use.

Appendix 8

Table of average hourly earnings of pieceworkers (including trainees)

	Average over 8-week period prior to that (7 January 1979 to 4 March 1979)
Betty MacFarland	183.19
Margaret Murry	166.56
Linda Taylor	129.00
Annette Thornton	162.00
Heather Wright	153.00
Cathy Plank	135.00
Fanny Mitchell	135.00
Jo Moyes	135.00
Sue Jardine	160.00
Valerie Sanderson	108.00
Anne McIntyre	132.22
Moira Horburgh	129.84
Roe Scott	133.35

Appendix 9

Factory layout

Factory toilets / Office toilet

Mechanics' workshop

General office   Manager's office   Director's office

Canteen

Cutting table

Small inventory store—zips, thread, etc

Superintendent's office

Cloth stock

Finished goods store

Machinist area

Total area 6,000 sq ft.

Questions

1. Is Robertson's view that 'it is no use going to the market until he had capacity to satisfy demand' a realistic approach to marketing in an expanding business?
2. How effectively are Highland servicing the various market segments for their products?
3. To what extent do you see the directors' behaviour and decisions as being consistent with their business philosophy?
4. What problems is the payment system causing and what should be done to improve the situation?
5. How important are 'design' and 'quality' to the business?
6. Do you think the move to the advance factory will have an effect on company communications? What could be done to minimise adverse effects, if any?

Part 3: Growing Concerns
(Three years and over)

Windancer
John Thompson

In spring 1982 Tim Langley, inventor of Windancer and the air-wheel which makes it a unique land yacht, was concerned about his company, Tim Langley Airwheels. He had invested £20,000 of his own savings in the business and so far had been unable to raise *any* external finance. His product is innovatory and consequently high risk. In the trading year ended 30 September 1981 the company made its first profit: £350 before tax. Since the company was formed in 1978, accumulated losses have amounted to some £12,000.

The company is very small, yet its potential market is huge. The product has an international market potential, but the company cannot afford the necessary investment to attack it. Cash flow problems are forcing it to tread very cautiously.

1981 was a good sales year (70 yachts were sold), but 1982 had started only sluggishly. Langley was unsure about what he should do. He could not really afford to increase his advertising and marketing – but how else could he stimulate sales and revenue? Certain options were available to him (see page 313) but each of them had a question mark hanging over it. There must obviously be others he had not yet identified.

The following summary has been prepared by a detached outsider and shown to a number of people who are looking for businesses they can invest in.

The product

The airwheel
The airwheel is a light, chunky bouncy wheel whose tyre is treadless. It exhibits a number of useful properties which make it ideal for movement across both soft and rough ground:

(a) Low pressure, approximately 5 psi. This is equivalent to an average man standing on one foot. Consequently it is less likely to sink than 'normal' tyres when the ground is particularly soft.

(b) There is no real wall or tread stiffness – the airwheel has a tough thick, flexible outer skin covering an inner tube. This allows 'give' when the wheel has to cross uneven, unmade ground. The fact that it rides over obstacles (of a reasonable size) rather than having to mount them improves the speed and reduces the propellant force requirements.

(c) The low pressure minimises the likelihood of cutting or piercing.

(d) The width is around half the diameter providing a virtually square footprint under a full load. It can, lightly loaded, traverse ground inaccessible to pedestrians.

(e) It has so far been produced as large as 32×16 in (diameter × width) and could be manufactured as large as 120×60 in.

(f) The wheel provides an automatic cushion effect, eliminating the need for shock absorbers.

(g) The wheel flattens on ground capable of supporting the (low) inflation pressure, spreading the load and eliminating sink, a prime cause of high drag with 'normal' tyres.

(h) Wheels of sufficient size, lightly loaded, can be expected to run on the surface of water at speeds in excess of 15 mph. The buoyancy of such wheels on lightly constructed vehicles, reasonably lightly loaded, would ensure safe flotation when partially immersed.

Additional notes

(a) The airwheel enjoys patent protection.

(b) The wheel was originally conceived with the idea of boat-launching in mind. This has not proved a commercially viable proposition *so far at least*. A number of reasons are involved: many launching sites are concreted because of known difficulties; launching trailers should ideally double as car trailers; airwheels have no tread etc.

(c) The wheel itself attaches to frames with specially developed quick release retainers. An added advantage.

(d) The commercial development has centred on the Windancer, a superior land/sand yacht.

Windancer

Windancer is best explained by the company's marketing literature (see Appendix 1). It is unquestionably a leisure product, felt in some quarters to have a direct appeal to keen windsurfers who can pursue their sport on land. It has a proven wider appeal, but it is a not inexpensive purchase which initially attracted almost exclusively A/B consumers.

Windancer is suitable for all family members, with possibly the 30–50 age group being the prime target. Used carefully in light winds it behaves in a docile manner. With a special, larger mast and sail it is capable of very high speeds – this has been proved by an Isle of Wight yachting enthusiast. It will sail in winds of 12–15 mph upwards and, given a reasonable blow and an experienced pilot, 30 mph can be achieved without any modification.

It is not a traditional windsurfer, for two reasons primarily. First the wheels; second the 'pilot' sits down as opposed to standing up as is more typical for windsurfers.

Manufacturing Windancer

Windancer is manufactured 'from square one' by Tim Langley. Only the carrying bags for the collapsible model are bought in ready made. Other materials bought are in basic form.

The workshop in Yorkshire is capable of producing the bases, frames, hubs, tyres and sails which involves mould-making, brazing, welding, plating, construction and assembly, spray acrylic finishing and the manufacture of the quick release retainers, bearings, sliding connections and hubs etc.

Capacity – with the current staff of two – is estimated at around 200 per year, which could be stretched. This had to be something of an estimate (which could be low) because the level has never been required. The premises are capable of accommodating several more workers and generating a far higher output.

Manufacturing costs

Materials £72 ⎫ £128 – averaged for both models. These are
Direct labour £56 ⎬ 1982 figures – in the past material costs
⎭ have been higher.

Manufacturing overheads are low.

The premises are wholly owned, and premises and equipment are valued at £15,000. However, only a small proportion of this, covering cars and equipment, is actually included in the company's balance sheet. The level of working capital in the business is very low and it must be assumed that additional working capital can only be generated by sales, not loans.

Distribution and pricing aspects

Given some guarantee of volume Tim Langley could sell Windancer ex-works for prices in the region of £156 and £196 (inclusive of VAT) for the fixed frame and collapsible models respectively. A 60 per cent distributor margin could then place the product on the market between £300 and £375. However, what should the price be?

A competitor, *landsailer* (believed to be of inferior quality by Langley), is priced at £298 for a board plus £120 for the sailing rig. These are recommended retail prices, inclusive of VAT. This model, incidentally, allows sailors both to stand up and sit down; Windancer is exclusively seated, but product development could easily involve a stand-up version.

Windsurfers come in many varieties and many qualities. A survey of 80 alternative boards (inclusive of sails) in 1981 showed a range of prices from £160 (kit form) to over £700. The mean was £415. Special clothing, of course, is an essential extra.

The VAT inclusive recommended retail prices of Windancer in 1981–82 were £430 (fixed frame) and £550 (fully collapsible) – but they have been available discounted from some independent distributors (see Appendix 2).

Market size and potential, incidentally, is difficult to quantify. However, the windsurfer market has grown to 14,000 units in the UK in five years. It is much greater on the continent, especially in France.

The organisation

Company history

The company began in 1978 when Tim Langley decided:

a) to refine and develop properly an idea (for the airwheel) he had had for some time; and

b) to purchase an old vicarage in Yorkshire and convert it into two flats and a workshop.

This took 18 months and the company began trading in 1979. Product refinement continued throughout 1979 and 1980.

Windancer sales

1979	(part)	10
1980		30
1981		70
1982	(part)	25

including spares total revenue less than £50,000; these figures ignore all sales of individual wheels

Most sales have been to individual private buyers, generated by advertising (see below). Some have been via distributors who also responded to the advertising.

Personnel

The company 'employs' Langley, his youngest son (early 20s) full time and his wife (part-time secretary)

Langley was a fighter pilot (Spitfires), and is a graduate engineer – though initially he was employed as a millworker and lorry driver. After the war he worked in the aircraft industry as a designer and later in manufacturing management. Prior to forming his own small company he was a management consultant. His work experience was almost exclusively in large and international organisations.

Selling and advertising

Selling has essentially been direct from the company's base. Magazine display advertising has been used to generate enquiries which have been followed up personally by Langley. Definitive figures for enquiries/advertisements and enquiry conversions are not available. However, 'attributable sales' to advertisements are given below, aggregated for a number of years. Overall *Exchange & Mart* has proved by far the most successful in terms of aggregate enquiries and sales, but it has shown diminishing returns.

Analysis of advertising 1979–81

Magazine	Advertising cost (inc artwork) as % of sales
Exchange & Mart	9.0
Scottish Field	8.0
Country Gentleman	15.0
Chandler & Boatbuilder	6.0
Scouting	
Adventure Sports	
Sussex Life	no directly attributable sales
Devon Life	
Norfolk Fair	

During 1980–81–82 approximately £1,000 per year has been allocated to advertising.

Exhibitions etc

A further £1,000 per year has been allocated to showing Windancer at the Boat Show and certain agricultural shows, and demonstrating it in country parks, stately homes etc. Much *interest* has been generated, but it has not proved a successful *selling* opportunity. A question must concern whether a more professional salesman than Langley would have produced greater returns from the opportunities.

Financial summary

Profit and Loss Account
for the year ended 30 September 1981

	£	£
Sales		23,000
Less		
Direct wages	4,200	
Purchases	9,000	
		13,200
		9,800
Less		
Director's additional remuneration	3,000	
Motor and travelling	2,000	
General administration/manufacturing overheads	1,800	
Advertising	1,000	
Marketing expenses	1,000	
Depreciation	250	
Auditors' remuneration	400	
		9,450
Profit before tax		350
Less		
Tax		2
Transferred to reserves		348

Balance Sheet as at 30 September 1981

	£	£
Fixed assets		
(after depreciation)		1,250
Current assets		
Stock	500	
Debtors and prepayments	3,100	
Cash at bank	5,400	
	9,000	
Current liabilities		
Creditors	2,050	
Directors' loan account	20,000	
Bank overdraft	—	
Tax	2	
	22,052	
Net current liabilities		13,052
Net deficiency		(11,802)
Represented by		
Authorised, issued and fully paid share capital		100
Profit and loss account deficiency		(11,902)
		(11,802)

Specific developments

Sole distributor

In 1981 a Humberside trader approached Langley and asked for sole UK distributorship. This trader had *not* previously been involved in this type of product. A trial was agreed, aiming for 120 yachts/year at an arranged call-off. Generous margins were agreed relative to the recommended retail price, and payment was to be on collection.

Some 30 items were sold during 1981 in the Grimsby area alone (good winds and flat terrain). However, Langley terminated the trial because the distributor was discounting against the recommended retail price not altogether consistently and Windancer prices began to vary substantially. Langley was unhappy about this.

Assessment

- Professional selling sold Windancers more effectively than the company itself was able to.
- Manufacturers lose some control with this type of arrangement, a fact of life Langley found hard to accept. Unfortunately, of course, any complaints/rectifications are likely to come to the manufacturer.
- Possibly the wrong 'partner' was selected; possibly insufficient attention to detail could be levelled at Langley.

The Australian market

- Proposal made to Langley from Australian importer early 1982.
- Jointly financed company, especially to promote Windancer. Langley purchases 25 per cent of equity.
- Agreement on transfer price. Langley to receive 5 per cent of the sales revenue in return for his equity stake.
- Arrangement would only cover Sydney which is something of a hilly area.

Assessment

- Nothing has come of this yet, ie Langley has not formally responded.
- Australia is 'leisure-mad' and spending reflects this. Market potential may well exist; possibly Sydney is not the most suitable area?

The Middle East
- Langley approached by an exporter based in Cheshire.
- Discussions led to the following suggestion:

Special company formed to produce purely for Middle East exports. Langley Airwheels are suppliers and continue to hold patents. Langley holds 50 per cent equity of new company.

Target production: 40 a week, 2,000 a year
Price ex-works: £210 – collapsible model

Probably 20 employees required – but capacity of workshop may limit this to about 10, balance by subcontracting.
In anticipation the exporting company bought seven Windancers, for cash, early in 1982. Two immediately in trial in Dubai.

Initial reports
- Insufficient wind! Winds are thermal, in the main, and inadequate, especially well away from the Gulf Coast. Best sales potential inland.
- This proposal may therefore be moribund. But sales potential – *not* even 1,000 a year though – does exist. Larger sail required.

UK department stores
- Contact made with the man who has the franchise for 'Ocean Leisure' in Lillywhites (London). 'Ocean Leisure' is 1,000 ft of sales space turning over £250,000 per year. Contact could expand retail distribution throughout UK if it proves worthwhile.
- Two Windancers taken for display/trial and priced at £300 and £375 (VAT inclusive) (spring 1982).

Initial reports
- They are not moving 'quickly'.
- General fear: the leisure market, at least the segment Windancer falls into, may be 'dead' in 1982.

Appendix 1

Selected quotes from company literature

Designed for you. Whether you want fast sailing in strong winds or tricky terrain or whether you want just quietly to glide across miles of smooth sand – WINDANCER – provides both.

WINDANCER is enjoyed by the whole family – even four generations. The very young, in lighter winds, riding with Dad. Others in similar conditions cruising quietly along taking the air. The sportsmen and women of the family taking it into winds and terrain which will challenge reaction and all possible requirements for thrills and excitement.

We dare say that WINDANCER is the most versatile, most easily used, most readily transported, and most easily stored wind-powered vehicle in the world.

The most versatile because of its range of reaction in winds up to gale force and down to 10 or 12 mph. Also because, riding on our patented AIRWHEEL, it can sail where no other wheels can go. Even its small size and comparatively small sail results from the low drag where the wheels are painting brushmarks over ground where pedestrians are making deep footmarks.

The most easily used because 90 per cent of the UK population can sail within a few miles of home. Recreation grounds, football pitches, any even, small area of short grass field will do. Also on 90 per cent of beaches around the coast. Wherever you are or wherever you go, WINDANCER sailing will be available not far away.

The most easily transported. The mast and boom dismantle into about 4-ft lengths. The wheels can be removed in seconds and the whole vehicle assembled and dismantled in about five minutes.

The most easily stored. It's bound to be if it dismantles and transports as easily as it does.

Fixed frame model. The frame of this model is 5 ft long by 4 ft wide and only 3½ ft high. It can easily be put on any car roof-rack by one person. The remainder of the machine, including mast and boom sections, can be neatly put in the boot of a car.

Fully collapsible model. Two bags contain a complete WINDANCER which takes five minutes to erect to its full size of 10 ft long, 4 ft wide and 14 ft high. Total weight is only 32 kilos and it is designed to be transportable in a car boot.

We are proud of it, it is ours and yours if you want it, and it is unique in the world. If you like it for the qualities we describe, do not waste time seeking alternatives, there are none. The AIR-WHEELS make it possible and these are covered by patents, so incidentally is the WINDANCER itself.

Appendix 2

Airwheel Windancer – price and order sheet

- Trade prices reduce as purchases accumulate.
- Mark-ups increase from a minimum 33 per cent to over 70 per cent. These result from the relationship between prices and accumulated purchases in any 12-month period.
- This gives easy, order by order control of prices and margins.
- We benefit jointly through steady expansion of sales, and a product life comparable with sailboards, with which Windancer shares many attributes.

The table enables you to identify your unit price against accumulating purchases.

	Unit prices for this order			
Total units purchased during past 12 months to date (include this order)	2–4	5–7	8–11	
				Prices for higher accumulations in
Fixed frame (recommended retail price £374)	£281	£267	£252	follow-up table
Fully collapsible (recommended retail price £480)	£360	£342	£323	Please request this when appropriate

All prices subject to VAT at current rate.

Trade prices start at two units purchased. *New customers* are advised that any first trial order for *one* Windancer will be charged at full recommended retail price but credit of £60 (fixed frame) or £70 (fully collapsible) will be offset against their next order.

Questions

1. Do you think Langley has selected the right product in which to incorporate his invention?
2. How sound do you think his approach to his chosen market has been?
3. What options lie ahead of Langley now? Which should he pursue and why?

Case 31
Weston Precision Turnings Ltd
Rick Brown

Weston Precision Turnings Ltd (WPT) is a small company manufacturing turned metal parts for the motor industry, located on a new industrial estate near Leamington Spa. The company was founded some 15 years ago by the present managing director, Bill Weston, who has an engineering background. WPT has 35 full-time employees, several of whom are skilled machine setters and fitters. A factory manager looks after the production side, while Bill Weston concentrates on sales, design and administration. At present WPT is operating below capacity; several machines are little used, and the factory could accommodate a further 15 employees provided sufficient work could be found.

All of WPT's sales are of custom-machined parts, and over the years the firm has supplied all the major British motor manufacturers as well as some of the large component manufacturers. Nevertheless, business was not easy to get, and competition from other turners was stiff. Recently Bill had been forced to take on some business for a French company, which had been offered to him by their buying agent, even though this was at a very slim margin. One of Bill Weston's problems was that his overheads were high partly because lack of business meant that several machines and part of the factory space had to stand idle.

The French buying agent reported back that his company was pleased with the first batch, and was prepared to grant a further contract for at least a year, involving 60,000 units initially. Bill saw this as a good opportunity, although he knew the price would have to be very keen. Four parts were involved, and the agent gave WPT sets of engineering drawings to work out an estimate. Armed with the initial factory-cost estimates, Bill sat down to work out the price. His normal profit mark-up was 10 per cent on total costs, although for large orders he normally added only 7½ per cent. One of the four parts accounted for 40,000 units or two-thirds of the total contract, so Bill decided to concentrate on this one first, and prepared the estimate shown in Figure 1.

Bill then telephoned the French agent with this information

	£
Direct material	1.60
Direct labour	0.90
Direct cost	2.50
Overhead (130 % of direct labour)	1.17
Total cost	3.67
Profit (7½ % of total cost)	0.28
Price	3.95

Figure 1. Part number 1057: summary costing (£)

but was told that the price was nowhere near acceptable. After some discussion, Bill offered to cut the profit margin by a further 2½ per cent explaining that he was now working on half his normal profit. This brought the price down to £3.85, but the buying agent explained that his company bought components all over Europe, and that Bill would need to get 'somewhere near £3' to win the contract.

Bill Weston was very disheartened by this, but decided to look again at the figures. The factory manager agreed after discussion that the material estimate could be trimmed by 4p, and that after retiming the job, the labour estimate could be reduced to 87p. WPT's accountant also looked at the overheads. The charging rate of 130 per cent had been calculated by the accountant based on Bill's forecast of overhead and output at the beginning of the year, representing overheads of £360,000 and direct labour of £282,000 as shown on WPT's profit and loss account, Figure 2. After looking at the overhead and direct labour figures in detail,

	£000
Sales	1150
Direct materials	446
Direct labour	282
Total direct costs	728
Overheads (see note)	366
Total costs	1094
Gross profit (sales – total costs)	56

Overhead recovery rate: 130% of direct labour

Figure 2. WPT: budgeted Profit and Loss Account.

Note (Figure 2)

Overheads	£
Rent	100,000
Rates	50,000
Administration	50,000
Selling and marketing	60,000
Heat, light and power	30,000
Insurance and legal	25,000
Directors' fees	25,000
Sundry	26,000
	366,000

	£
Direct material	1.56
Direct labour	0.87
Direct cost	2.43
Overhead (120% of direct labour)	1.04
Total cost	3.47
Profit (5% of total cost)	0.17
Price	3.64

Figure 3. Part number 1057: revised summary costing (£)

Bill and his accountant decided that some savings in the original overhead forecast could be made, although they felt the direct labour forecast was still accurate. Nevertheless, expected overhead savings allowed them to reduce the charging rate to 120 per cent. Using all this information, Bill prepared a new costing, shown in Figure 3.

Bill felt he had done quite well in getting the price down to £3.64, and prepared quotations for the other three parts on the same basis, then telephoned the French buying agent. The agent told him he had received an alternative quotation for less than £3.64, and that although he would like to give WPT the business, he could not do so at that price. Finally, Bill had no option but to offer the business at next to break-even, and offered part 1057 at £3.50, which left him with a profit of only 3p per unit, or less than 1 per cent. Bill explained to the buying agent that this meant cutting his normal margin by 90 per cent, and that it was impossible to go any lower. The French buyer repeated that he wanted WPT to have the business, and was sympathetic to Bill's problems. Finally, he said that provided Bill was prepared to offer the other three parts on the same basis ie a mark-up of 1 per cent on total costs, he would place contracts for these with WPT.

However, in order to give WPT a contract for part 1057, the maximum price he could offer was £3.25. He said Bill could have a few days to think it over, but must let him know within a week. Bill was left to ponder whether or not to accept the order on these terms.

Questions

What should Bill do?
1. Reject the contract.
2. Accept the work on the three minor parts but reject the contract for 1057.
3. Accept the contract for all four parts, and attempt to negotiate the buyer up to, say, £3.35 for 1057.
4. Take the £3.25 and hope to cut costs somewhere along the line.

AP Smith (Vending) Ltd

Michael Beaumont

Mr and Mrs AP Smith established this business in 1975 using £10,000 cash which Mr Smith had received from the sale of his former one-man business as a wool merchant when recession in the wool trade threatened the future of the business.

This vending business commenced with the purchase of a round of cigarette vending machines established in three small sites within five miles of their home. The sites were in pubs and clubs and were purchased from a friend who wished to reduce the workload of his own business owing to poor health. This business is a high turnover, low profit margin operation involving a lot of cash handling and good personal relationships with the site managers or stewards.

Initially there was insufficient income to support the couple and so Mrs Smith took up employment as a secretary/clerk to provide the main income for the couple while most of the income from the sites was ploughed back into the business. The cars were sold and replaced at first by a single light van for deliveries and collections. They moved house into an older bungalow which had the advantage of plenty of parking and loading space, quick access to the ring road and a very large basement for secure storage, packing and filling.

During the first two years teething problems were overcome by cutting out holidays so that Mrs Smith could carry on the business while Mr Smith went to courses in machine maintenance or to trade exhibitions. It was fortunate that Mrs Smith had experience in clerical work and Mr Smith in the running of a small business but there were problems in the new roles and working together as a team, particularly as leisure interests and social contacts had to be severely curtailed.

Expansion

This began with the acquisition of a large and busy new site on the other side of Leeds about nine miles away but placed conveniently close to the ring road (site no 5). The site at a popular working men's club required several machines and a turnover large enough to provide an income in itself. The club had become dissatisfied with the service of their first operator within six months. They demanded a high standard of service on a seven-day week basis up to 9pm if necessary on social evenings and including New Year's Day and Boxing Day. There was a useful sideline of cigars and tobacco sold from behind the bar. They expected a few free hand-outs for veterans and pensioners on special occasions. Ever since its acquisition this site has had the highest turnover and been the most demanding. It was the forerunner of other clubs making expansion possible.

The present

At the time of writing the business is well-established. Mr and Mrs Smith are both fully employed in the business, in fact they are both overstretched. Staff can be divided into two sections:

Basement staff. These are jokingly referred to as the troglodytes by Mr Smith. They include *Mrs Smith*: she works most of the time in the basement but also covers a small local site for a change of scenery. *Mrs Thwaite*: a reliable and hard-working single parent employed full time but unofficially so. She is in charge while Mrs Smith is out. *Mrs Dodds*: a part-time worker. *Mrs Breams*: also a part-time worker doing four hours a day.

Road staff. These service the sites, being allocated certain sites as their responsibility but not working Saturdays, Sundays or bank holidays. They include *Mr Smith*: he covers site no 5 and new sites initially plus any sensitive sites. *Mr Briar*: he is an old friend of the couple who was made redundant a couple of years earlier from his responsible position at the age of 47. He is provided with a van which he can use privately. *Mr McQueen*: he took early retirement at 60 and works a four-day week. He is also provided with a van which he can use privately. He is a very reliable worker and is paid less than Mr Briar. He is less trouble than Mr Briar who is a bit touchy about being given orders by Mr Smith. He is also no problem with his bookkeeping records, unlike Mr Briar who is sometimes a bit slack and has in fact had one or two rows with Mr Smith when reproached on this matter. The good thing about Mr McQueen is that you can 'just forget about him'. On the other hand, he is a bit slow and the Smiths are just hoping that he does not slow down any more. *Bill and Dolly*: they are a couple of vending machine operators who are working a few sites for the Smiths two days a week and providing their own cars for the job. They will not take on any extra work but are willing to stand in if there is an emergency. They have given the Smiths a few useful tips at times and are always very alert to any site problems. They could easily expand their own business but Dolly has an invalid Mum and her husband Bill is a keen Leeds United supporter.

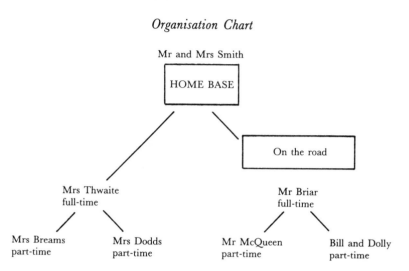

Organisation Chart

Problems of expansion

Two new sites have recently become available to the business. Both are large sites in the no 5 category but not quite so large or demanding. They require six days servicing a week but can manage over Sundays and bank holidays if well stocked. There is also the chance of acquiring, at a reasonable price, a chain of four small sites operated by a widow who wishes to sell up and move to the south coast. The basement could accommodate the extra stock but extra labour would be needed both in the basement and on the road.

Possible additions to staff have been considered. There is no problem at all in obtaining basement staff through local contacts of Mrs Smith. Alternatively, Mrs Breams could work full time but this would cost almost twice her present hourly rate because of additional costs such as tax, insurance etc.

Mr Smith has two contacts for road staff. One is young Fred Green, an efficient and fast worker who could easily be enticed from his present employer based a considerable distance away.

He would appreciate the opportunity and would not need to be handled quite so carefully as the present road staff. However, he could possibly become too ambitious later on. There is also Mr Meadows, another office worker made redundant and a former colleague of Mr Briar. Mr Smith is unwilling to employ complete strangers on the road staff because of the high risk involved in a job with large cash handling aspects. The Smiths have in fact, had two cash snatches already during operations at sites.

There are other less definite possibilities for expansion as some competitors in this business are frankly 'a bit slack' in the service they give to customers. However, any expansion beyond the additional sites already mentioned would require (a) additional new premises (b) proper paid office staff (c) additional security measures (d) more systematic and careful provision for tax, insurance etc.

Present problems

Security. There have been two thefts of cash from vans while machines were being serviced at sites. It is feared that local thieves may be watching and studying the movements of the staff servicing machines. There is also risk of vandalism to machines on site and these cannot be insured except at prohibitive rates. In addition there is the risk of house burglary and of a cash snatch while taking the change to the local bank as the cash has to be carried several yards down the street owing to parking restrictions (a matter Mr Smith has frequently complained about without result).

Management. There are occasional mini-crises when Mrs Thwaite has to be absent to deal with emergencies concerned with her young son who is maladjusted. There are also occasional rows concerning Mr Briar and disagreements between Mr and Mrs Smith on how best to deal with him.

Sites. Sometimes the demands for service are unreasonable but this tends to be from the bigger and more profitable sites. On a couple of the sites the manager or steward is known to be slightly dishonest and fiddling the claims for refunds but still leaving a good profit margin. A 'showdown' could quite easily cost the firm the site.

Vehicles. These are a big expense for the business and, as Mr Smith says, 'We are providing private transport for half our staff.' Yet from another point of view there is a great need for a spare car or van because there has been a crisis whenever a vehicle is off the road for any reason.

Takeover. An offer has been made by a large competitor which would give the Smiths a good return on their capital and effort while paying Mr Smith a quite reasonable salary for a five-day week up to retirement and with car provided. There is a veiled threat that he could be put out of business any time they wanted but there has been no evidence of any moves in that direction.

Questions

1. What suggestions can you make concerning improvements in security and in improving vehicle economy and efficiency?
2. Discuss the issue of whether Mr Briar should have been taken on in view of his attitude to 'being bossed about'.
3. Discuss the issue of whether it is best to appoint personal friends or whether it is better to select from advertisements or by some other method.
4. How do you think the problem of fiddling by site managers should be dealt with?
5. Consider the alternatives between appointing Fred Green or Mr Meadows. What criteria should you apply?
6. Discuss the pros and cons of accepting the 'takeover offer'.

Case 33

Noblelight Ltd

This case study has been prepared by *Colin Barrow* from material originally published in *Venture Capital Report*

In the spring of 1984 David Littlechild was putting the final touches to his plans for a new factory on the Cambridge Science Park. Flushed with the success of winning the 1983 *Daily Telegraph*/National Westminster Bank Enterprise Award, the company seemed set for growth.

Company history

Noblelight Ltd was started in December 1978 by David and John Littlechild. John Littlechild, the technical director, had previously set up a flashlight manufacturing unit for another company and David Littlechild, the managing director, owned and was running a precision engineering business, Shearline Ltd, which he had started in 1970.

The business has been profitable from the start. Until 1982 its principal products were continuous wave and pulsed lamps, but after this date the company began to make custom-designed power supplies, trigger transformers and lamp holders. Laser users are the main market for the lamps, although other uses (such as spectral analysis) are beginning to develop.

Noblelight was the first company in the world to give guarantees on its lamps. Initially they were guaranteed for 100 hours, but when the competition followed this by issuing a similar guarantee, Noblelight extended its to 300 hours. Noblelight exports about 60 per cent of its production, and is the largest manufacturer of continuous wave lamps for lasers in the UK and probably Europe. It is acknowledged to have a world technological lead in continuous wave lamps for use in lasers. Noblelight is currently halfway through a two-year project to improve the cathodes used in pulsed lamps and, when completed, the programme will have cost £250,000 (partly funded by a government grant).

The products

A flashlamp is a constant-volume envelope of transparent, impervious material (eg glass) with electrodes sealed at opposite ends, containing a purified noble gas at a pressure generally less than one bar. Flashlamps are used in solid state lasers or spectrophotometers.

When a current is passed through the electrodes, a discharge is caused, which can be pulsed or continuous wave (CW). The light emitted from this discharge has a wide spectral band similar to that of the sun. The laser user requires this type of light output, and the art of making the lamps is to produce a lamp with consistent output which will last a long time.

The manufacture of a lamp starts with the silicon or glass tube, which is cut to appropriate length and shaped if necessary. The anode and cathode are sealed into the ends of the envelope, and air is evacuated before the envelope is filled with a noble gas. The complete lamp is then ready for testing. The quality of a lamp, its performance, life and character of operation are determined by the construction methods, envelope material, electrodes, operating equipment, drive circuitry, the radiation properties of its arc discharge, gas composure and pressure, and the interaction of all these factors.

Noblelight's policy has always been to buy in only raw materials, and to manufacture everything in-house so that quality can be controlled at all stages of the process. They design and make every component including the electrodes. Every product is assembled and tested on jigs with equipment and tools designed by Noblelight's staff.

Each lamp is tested and burnt-in before despatch. Less than 1 per cent are returned for replacement under guarantee. Some lamps from each batch are subjected to complete testing.

A lamp will last 300–1,000 hours. Some users keep their lasers operating 24 hours a day to make maximum use of a very expensive asset. A lamp is sold to end-users for £30–£200.

The company also designs power supplies, trigger transformers and lamp holders for its customers.

The market

David Littlechild has recently commissioned some market research because it was not possible to find any published information on the market size or usage of lamps. It is believed that the market for lamps is hundreds of thousands and is expanding quickly, because the cost of lasers has dropped, reliability has increased, and so more lasers are sold.

Flashlamps are used in all solid state lasers, which are more widely used in the scientific industry than gas lasers. Solid state lasers are medium-powered and used for cutting, welding and trimming with applications in medicine, industry and scientific research. The largest market is the USA, followed by Japan and West Germany.

Noblelight's lamps are sold in the USA by ESI, thought to be the largest manufacturer of solid state lasers in the world. ESI also represent Noblelight in Japan and the majority of Europe.

Noblelight markets its products in the UK itself, and takes stands at exhibitions in the UK, Europe, Japan and the USA. Sixty per cent of sales are exported, and although overseas sales are handled by distributors, the customers receive the product in Noblelight packaging and therefore know the manufacturer. There are about 500 end-user customers.

Current competition comes from several small US manufacturers and ILC, an American company which specialises in laser lamps. ILC went public in 1983. There is also competition from some European companies, most of which are subsidiaries of major companies. David Littlechild believes that the real competition will continue to come from the USA.

The people

David Littlechild is 35. After leaving school he became an apprentice instrument maker and at the end of his training he moved to Cambridge University's engineering laboratories for a year. In 1970 he set up his own precision machining company, Shearline Ltd. The company expanded quickly and is shortly to move out of the premises that it now shares with Noblelight. Shearline has its own management and is running very profitably at full capacity. In 1978 David Littlechild set up Noblelight with his brother John.

John Littlechild is 39. He undertook a glass-blowing apprenticeship after leaving school and worked for several companies until 1975, when he set up a flashlamp section at TW Wingent. The new section was successful but lacked investment, so John Littlechild decided with David that it should be possible to go it alone, and left to start Noblelight. John Littlechild's expertise has developed through self-instruction and practice, and he is now one of the world's leading flashlamp technologists.

All the other managers are in their 30s. Noblelight employ:

Roger Hines, workshop supervisor, who has worked with flashlamps since 1975 and was previously with TW Wingent.

Rex Fulcher, who has recently joined Noblelight and was production manager of flashlamps at TW Wingent.

John Moore, the senior glass-blower and part of the development team, who used to work for the flashlamp section of English Electric Valves.

Noblelight also employ an electronics engineer and will be taking on a new marketing manager. There are three full-time and one part-time administrative staff, and 19 production staff.

Roy Haliwell, who used to work for PA Consultants and now has his own practice, is currently doing research for Noblelight into pulsed lamps. He is an expert on cathodes.

Financial data

The profit and loss account for the past three years and actual to 31 March 1984 are shown in Table A.

Table A. Profit and Loss Account

Years to 31 March	Audited 1982 £	Audited 1983 £	Final draft 1984 £
Sales	171,329	255,364	473,013
Direct costs	58,093	77,742	141,561
Gross profit	113,236	177,622	331,452
Research and development	—	19,500	45,915
Overheads	28,825	59,362	72,585
Depreciation	7,863	15,262	20,548
Directors' remuneration	30,599	48,391	55,062
	67,287	142,515	194,110
Net profit	45,949	35,107	137,342

Notes:
1. The audited accounts for 1983 show a net profit of £45,107 which includes the £10,000 prize from the *Daily Telegraph*/National Westminster Bank Enterprise Award for Small Business.
2. The drop in net profit in 1983 is because £20,000 was paid to top up the pension fund and £19,500 was spent on research and development.

The £500,000 sought will be used to pay for part of the new building (total cost £500,000), partly to fund the research and development programme (total cost £250,000 over two years less government grant of £87,000), and partly to fund working capital.

The balance sheet as at 31 March 1984 is shown in Table B.

Table B. Balance Sheet as at 31 March 1984

	£	£
Fixed assets		384,409
Current assets		
Stocks	62,907	
Debtors	141,230	
	204,137	
Current liabilities		
Creditors	112,251	
Bank	93,309	
	205,560	
		(1,423)
Total assets less current liabilities		382,986
Other liabilities		
Amounts falling due after more than one year		149,920
		233,066
Deferred taxation		58,376
		174,690
Capital and reserves		
Share capital		1,000
Profit and loss account		173,690
		174,690

Financial structure

The business is half-way through a research and development programme which is showing signs of success and which will establish Noblelight in another market, that of pulsed lamps. This will signal a major step in the company's growth.

The company could fund the purchase of the new factory on the Cambridge Science Park, and the research and development programme from bank borrowings and retained profits, but the directors feel that this could restrain growth in the immediate future, and therefore if a suitable investor can be found, they are prepared to offer shares in the company in return for a capital injection of £500,000. They suggest the following structure:

Name	%	Contribution
David Littlechild	65	Company to date
John Littlechild	25	Company to date
Investor	10	£500,000 convertible preference shares

331

The new shares will be convertible into ordinary stock within five years, at which time the investor will own 10 per cent of Noblelight.

The directors will have service contracts and are prepared to offer various guarantees to protect the investor's interests.

Questions

1. Do you think giving guarantees on the lamp's life is a sound competitive strategy?
2. How significant an event do you think winning the Enterprise Award was for the company?
3. Do you think the company is making the most effective use of its working capital?
4. What level of sales and profits would the company require to justify a further £500,000 of capital being employed in the venture?
5. Could they really fund the new factory and their development programme from bank borrowings?
6. What significance do you attach to the suggestion that convertible preference shares are used to fund the venture?

Case 34
Third Scale Technology Ltd

This case study has been prepared by *Colin Barrow* from material originally published in *Venture Capital Report*

Anthony Hopkinson is 49 and the major shareholder and managing director of Third Scale Technology Ltd (3ST), the company which he formed in 1978 as a vehicle for his paper recycling machines.

After Eton, he served for 12 years in the Scots Guards until 1965, when he joined Norman Marshall, the partworks publishing division of British Printing Corporation. Part of his job was to arrange for the production of binders with Easibind. After a year he was persuaded to join a small paperback publisher, but this job was not a success and so in 1967 he joined Easibind as wholesale and export manager.

In 1970 he joined his family company, Automatic Business Machines, of which his father was joint owner and managing director. The company imported and sold electronic business machines and had about 70 employees with sales of about £2 million. The expectation when he joined was that he would in time take over his father's role. However, although he remained with the company throughout the 1970s, he never really believed in the products or enjoyed the job. Finally, in 1979, the 50 per cent share of the business which was owned by his family was sold.

Having served with the army in many poorer countries, Mr Hopkinson had always been appalled at the contrast between the poverty of the Third World countries and the profligacy and waste in the affluent West. Having thought about this, he decided that the most positive thing he could do would be to devise a process to recycle some of this waste in such a way that it could be used in the Third World. He decided that the best prospects were offered by paper recycling since, coming from trees, this is a renewable resource and the recycled products could be used as substitutes for plastics, which are expensive and non-renewable, coming from oil.

His first experiments were conducted in the early 1970s when he designed a kit for small-scale home papermaking. This kit is now marketed by Recycled Paper Products Ltd. Finally, in 1978, he formed Third Scale Technology Ltd and in 1979, when the family shares in ABM were sold, this became his full-time occupation.

Large-scale automated paper-recycling machines have always existed, but these are expensive (£100,000 plus) and consume huge volumes of paper, both of which make them inappropriate for Third World countries. Mr Hopkinson's concept was to provide a cheap (£3,000) machine which could be operated on a small scale, to use the waste paper in a local area, probably transported by the local population, to produce useful items such as biodegradable plant pots and packaging materials, for use by the local community. After several years of experiment with different machines, he has been entirely successful in this aim. Some 50 of the first machines were sold in 27 countries in 1983, and in response to many requests the company developed a slightly larger machine – the Melpack – and also an egg-tray mould to go with it. So far 16 of these have been sold, all but two to developing countries.

The Melpack paper pulp moulder

The Melpack machine works as follows: waste paper is first placed in the 'pulper' where it is continuously agitated in water by an impeller. The lumpy pulp from this is then transferred in a bucket to the 'refiner' where it is cycled continuously through a shredding/scraping device which separates the individual fibres and produces a fine pulp. This in turn is transferred by bucket to the moulder. The moulds are made from a fine wire mesh to which a vacuum is applied, so that when the mould is lowered into the pulp, water is sucked through the mesh leaving a layer of fibres on the mould, whose thickness may be adjusted by time and vacuum pressure. The mould is then inverted and located on an inverse mould above it. The vacuum is then transferred to the inverse mould so that pulp adheres to this, and the mesh mould is then withdrawn. A tray is placed under the inverse mould, the vacuum is reversed, and the product is then deposited on the tray and removed for drying.

It is quite possible for one person to operate the machine, but the normal manning level is two – one to feed in the raw paper and prepare the pulp, and the other to operate the moulder. A typical moulding cycle will take 40 seconds, so that outputs of 60 trays per hour are easily attainable.

The quality of the final product may be varied considerably. The addition of wax causes the final product to become resistant to water, and it may be made to last for a season (eg a geranium pot). By adding compost, a plant pot is produced which is very easily degraded and which also feeds the young plant. Vegetable dyes may also be added to produce colours.

Financial data

In small quantities, waste paper is free in most parts of the world, but it may also be collected in bulk, when it commands a price of about £18 per tonne which compares to a price for wood-pulp of more than £100 per tonne.

The potential profit from operating the machine may be seen from the example of plant pot production in the UK. The Melpack machine, with two operators, will produce 60 sets per hour, of 15 plant pots each. Each set may be sold to garden centres for 30p who will retail them for 60–90p. The weekly operating economics might then be approximately as follows:

Sales	£	£
30 hours		
(1) × 60 sets/hr × 30p		540.00
Cost of sales		
Paper at £18/tonne	32.40	
Compost additive	50.00	
Labour two at £80	160.00	
Power	5.00	
Transport to garden centres	50.00	
		297.40
Gross profit/week		242.60

Note:
1. This assumes that two people spend 30 hours in the week producing and 10 hours distributing the sets to garden centres.

In general the quality of the final product is quite suitable for plant pots in the UK but not for egg-boxes, which require a better finish. This is not a problem in the Third World, however.

The profit and loss statement for 1984 was as follows, shown together with the projection for 1985, assuming that no product manufacture is undertaken:

		1984		1985
Sales		£		£
Machines (1)	12	35,892	12 at £3,200	38,400
Via agents (net)			12 at £2,240	26,880
				65,280
Gross contribution	(63%)	22,732	(60%)	36,480
Sales of signs (2)		4,267	£3,000/month	36,000
Gross contribution		1,707		14,400
Total gross contribution		24,439		50,880
Overheads				
Mr Hopkinson		—		7,500
Mr Payman		7,100		7,500
Power, rent, rates (3)		700		700
2 cars and running costs		6,700		6,700
Telephone		800		1,200
Other		7,500		7,500
		22,800		31,100
Net profit before tax		1,639		19,780

Notes:
1. The economics of the sale of a machine are approximately as follows:

	£	£
Sale price (inc one mould)		3,200
Cost of components (a)	750	
Vacuum motor	60	
Refiner motor	120	
Miscellaneous	150	
Cost of moulds	120	
	1,200	
Gross profit	2,000	(60%)

  (a) The basic assembly is manufactured by a subcontractor, and this is the price from him.
  (b) Each machine takes three man-days to assemble and pack, but Mr Hopkinson and the only other employee Mr Payman, the development engineer, between them have the capacity to assemble all the machines for 1985, so that this cost is included in overheads.
2. During a lull in machine sales in 1984, Mr Hopkinson began selling signs to local companies around Cambridge. This has been very successful with many companies coming back to request more signs, having been pleased with the first set. He is confident of achieving sales of £3,000 per month, without disrupting his work on paper pulp machines.
3. The company is run from rooms at the back of Mr Hopkinson's house, which is owned by his wife and used as a conference centre by local businesses.

The balance sheet of Third Scale Technology Ltd is approximately as follows:

	£	£
Fixed assets		1,500
Current assets	—	
Current liabilities		
Bank overdraft	20,000	
Creditors	10,000	
Net current liabilities		(30,000)
		(28,500)
Financed by		
Share capital		100
Profit and loss		(28,600)
		(28,500)

The overdraft at 31 March 1983 was about £23,000 so that some progress has been made during the last year.

Mr Hopkinson is guaranteeing the bank overdraft and the bank has been pleased with the progress in the last year and is happy to see the arrangement continue.

Mr Hopkinson believes that the company could continue quite well on its present upward course without any investment. Orders for the paper pulp machines presently stand at four, two for delivery in January and two for February, with a steady stream of enquiries coming as a result of word of mouth and in response to various BBC World Service programmes which have featured his machines.

However, now that the existing machine has demonstrated its potential and has been well received in the field. Mr Hopkinson believes that it would be sensible to market the machine in a more systematic fashion. He has also received many requests for a machine which is semi-automated, and which would stand between the present Melpack machine costing £3,000 and a fully automated plant costing £100,000 plus. He has in mind a machine with a capacity of about 250 trays per hour which would retail for about £12,000. This machine would have greater potential for sales in the UK and other developed countries. He has outline designs for such a machine and estimates that the development would cost £16,700 and take three months to complete.

Questions

1. How successful do you think the company's overseas sales activities have been?

2. Do you think a company such as this can succeed with the great majority of its sales spread across so many export markets?
3. Do you think there is a UK market for the Melpack machine and if so, what sort of people might buy it?
4. Given that Hopkinson would like to raise the whole of the capital needed to launch his new £12,000 machine, would you be prepared to invest £17,000 to buy a 25 per cent stake in his company?
5. In Hopkinson's position what would you do now?

Case 35

Russell Shears Ltd

This case study has been prepared by *Colin Barrow* from material originally published in *Venture Capital Report* with additional material provided by *Russell Shears*

The company

Russell Shears Ltd are a small company in Rotherham who manufacture and market scissors for the UK market. In 1983 they were poised to launch a new product which they hoped would restore the company's fortunes.

During the preceding years, in common with other UK scissor manufacturers, the company had suffered financially, at first from the effects of cheaper imports and then from the impact of plastic bow scissors. In response to this latter threat, they began importing Lindex plastic bow scissors made in Italy, and this product accounted for 60 per cent of their sales. Their sales in 1981 were about 150,000 compared to £250,000 in 1980 and the workforce, which had been 87, had been contracted to 23.

As a result of these difficulties, and also as a result of expenditure on developing their new product (the direct expenditure to date had been £50,000), the company was in a weak financial position and needed to find a new investor.

However, the picture was not quite as gloomy as might at first appear. First, by dint of a cost-cutting exercise (staff reductions being a part of that), the company's losses had been stemmed and a small profit had been made in the ten months to October 1982. Furthermore, sales prospects for existing products had improved significantly and with orders in hand it looked likely that 1983 sales could reach £500,000.

The market

The scissor market is very large and also subject to fashion. Approximately 22 million pairs of scissors are sold in the UK each year, and possibly 400 million pairs worldwide. Prices range from 35p to £10 for the major selling brands, with an average price of about £3.

The recent history of the scissor market in the UK illustrates

339

Balance sheet at 31 October 1982

Current assets	£	£
Cash in hand	75	
Deposit account	24	
Sundry debtors and prepayment	27,646	
Stock in trade	26,947	
		54,692
Current liabilities		
Sundry creditors	42,845	
Bank overdraft (1)	30,015	
Bank loan (1)	20,216	
HP accounts	790	
		93,866
Net current liabilities		(39,174)
Long-term liabilities		
Unsecured long-term loan		(12,876)
Net liabilities		(52,050)
Fixed assets (WDV)		35,409
Net deficiency		(16,641)
Financed by		
Share capital	1,000	
Directors' loan accounts	2,104	
		3,104
Less deficiency brought forward	21,043	
Plus profit Jan–Oct 1982	1,298	
		(19,745)
Net deficiency		(16,641)

Note: 1. Secured.

how rapidly the market can change, which creates both problems and opportunities for scissor manufacturers. On the one hand, their existing styles may suddenly cease to sell, while on the other a new design, and especially a cheaper design, may capture a large market share in a very few years.

In the early 1970s there were approximately 50 manufacturers in the UK selling all-metal scissors which were either cast iron (bad), cold forged (better), or hot forged (best). Few scissors were imported, and the manufacturers competed among themselves on more or less equal terms with similar labour and material costs. During the 1970s cheaper scissors began to be imported, mostly from the Far East, and the UK manufacturers steadily lost their market share.

In 1977 the development of the plastic bow (handle) scissor by

Fiskar's of Finland caused a revolution in scissor manufacture. After some initial market resistance, the public accepted plastic in scissors, and by 1980 this design accounted for no less than 60 per cent of the UK market, where it was marketed by Wilkinson Sword, and a similar amount elsewhere in the world. Of the remaining 40 per cent, 30 per cent was retained by the UK manufacturers, and 10 per cent was accounted for by Far Eastern and other imports of plastic bow scissors.

By 1982 Wilkinson Sword's share of the UK market had slumped to 20 per cent, the traditional UK manufacturers had 20 per cent, and the remaining 60 per cent had been taken by no fewer than 26 manufacturers of plastic bow scissors. This pattern has been followed in the USA and other countries. Initially the Fiskar design enjoyed dominance, but their market share has slipped as prices have been undercut by cheaper look-alikes.

Some idea of these latest problems besetting UK scissor manufacturers can be gained from the fact that there were 32 UK companies in the field at the beginning of 1982 and only 9 by the spring of 1983.

The new product – Shearline 2000

These Russell Shears scissors were developed over a period of six years and the company believes that their design is substantially more revolutionary than the Fiskar design was in 1977. Furthermore, since almost no labour is involved in the manufacture, the ability of Far Eastern manufacturers to undercut on price will be limited.

The economics of the sale of a pair of the new scissors are as follows, all manufacture being by subcontract except for the grinding, which will be undertaken by Russell Shears.

	£
Cost of blades	0.38
Pivot and clip	0.25
Plastic moulding	0.42
Packaging	0.03
Total cost including labour	1.08
Margin to Russell Shears	1.42
	2.50
Margin to retailer	1.84
	4.34
VAT	0.65
Final price to public	4.99

Although the concept of the product has been amply proved, the company was initially unable to achieve sufficient quality in production. In order to overcome these production problems Nick Quick, a production engineer, was approached and at the time of the case he believes that these problems are now solved.

The company have patents on the concept of Shearline 2000 in the UK, Finland, Canada and the USA. The scissors offer the following primary advantages:

1. Greatly reduced manufacturing costs

Conventional high-quality scissors are manufactured by hot forging steel. The cost of a pair of stainless steel blanks after forging, but before the many finishing processes, including heat treatment, straightening, grinding and fitting, is over £1 per pair, and the final cost of manufacture about £2 on average.

By contrast, the finished cost of the new scissors which will be of at least equal quality, is about £1.08. Not only is the material cost very much reduced, but the labour content is cut by over 75 per cent.

2. High quality

The new scissors are at least as stiff as conventional scissors, and are heat-treated to a Rockwell hardness of 56, which is significantly harder than ordinary scissors (Rockwell 50–52), giving a near permanent edge. The process of heat treatment is induction heating, so that only the edge is hardened. This means that not only does no distortion occur (so eliminating the straightening process), but the rest of the blade retains its resilience.

3. High visual appeal

The secret of the new process is to use an L-section of thin-gauge steel to give the stiffness required and so embed all but the cutting edge itself in an ABS plastic. This gives the designer the opportunity to introduce all the colour and variety of shapes that he wishes, and liberates him from the constraints of working with all-steel blades.

Scissors with plastic bows were first introduced into the market in the mid-1970s, and have since captured an amazing 80 per cent of the world market. The combined effect of extending the plastic down the blade, and the much lower price, could result in equally dramatic inroads being made by the new scissors. The public has already demonstrated its enthusiasm for plastic in scissors.

4. This is the first truly ambidextrous household scissor. If one appreciates that the number of left-handed people is increasing as each decade passes, due to the fact that schools now allow left-handed children to be left-handed, then a considerable proportion of the public are not being catered for. Apart from the inconvenience of needing scissors of each type in each household where there is a left-handed person, there is an obvious advantage for retailers who need stock one type instead of two.

5. **Differentiation**

The new scissors are a marketing man's dream. Not only are they immediately distinguishable from all other scissors on the market in appearance, but the design is such that the two blades may be separated very simply for cleaning. This will enable those marketing the scissors to differentiate them even further from competition. ('Do you still have old-fashioned, unhygienic . . .?' etc.)

The first design for the scissor shape was undertaken by Edwin James, who won a scholarship to the Royal College of Art on the strength of it, and which the Design Council have requested permission to exhibit. This had not yet been granted, however, for fear of stimulating competition, which might seek to infringe the patents. However, the company has taken out insurance to enable it to fight any company attempting to do this. The patent has been independently valued at £4 million.

The people

Brenda Powell is 53 and is joint managing director of Russell Shears, of which she owns 49 per cent. The company was founded by her father in 1946, five years after he had retired early, aged 45. At this time she had her own physiotherapy business, but she joined the company in 1956 to help her father, and became sole managing director when he died in 1960. She continued to run the company by herself until 1980 when her husband sold his own construction business to join her.

Mrs Powell knows many of the buyers for major stores very

well and expects to continue playing a key role in obtaining substantial orders.

Nick Quick is 39 and a lecturer in production engineering at Birmingham University. In 1962 he obtained a BSc in mechanical engineering at Salford University, while serving a five-year apprenticeship with Metropolitan Vickers (AEI), after which he obtained an MSc in production engineering from the Cranfield Institute of Technology.

After working in Chrysler central staff for seven years, he then returned to take an MBA at Cranfield in 1971, before starting his own furniture business in Sheffield, specialising in fitted kitchens and bedrooms, which he ran for 10 years, making a modest profit.

In February 1981 he sold the business to become a lecturer in production engineering at Birmingham University, where he has been able to bring some of the resources of the University to bear on the problems associated with the integral moulding of steel and plastic. He has also prepared the financial data for the company, and visits Russell Shears once a month to help with accounts etc in addition to regular meetings.

Mr Powell is 55 and ran his own small construction company from 1950 to 1980 when he sold out in order to help his wife in Russell Shears with the acute problems then facing the company, caused by the recession. While she visits the customers and secures sales, he handles the administration, which he enjoys.

The final member of the team will be responsible for marketing but does not wish to be named. He is 30 and has been marketing executive for Russell Shears since 1982 and sells their traditional scissors on commission. Having started his own marketing company in 1973, he also has the sales agencies for many other products, and is a very successful salesman, now selling over £2 million of goods per year and earning commission of 2.5 per cent. He would like to invest £10,000 in the business for an equity stake, and to have rights to sell in the UK for a commission of 2.5 per cent.

Future plans

The company needs an investment of £150,000 to bring their new product successfully to market. Russell Shears would prefer to find an industrial partner who shares their enthusiasm for the product, and who would be able to maximise the commercial potential of the new scissors both in the UK and abroad simultaneously. This new money will be used as follows:

	£
To pay for tooling and dies (1)	20,000
To pay Russell Shears for work to date	50,000
Working capital for launch (increase in stock etc)	50,000
Contingencies	30,000
	150,000

Note:
1. Over the last two years Russell Shears has worked closely with the Manpower Services Commission who have agreed to purchase an injection moulding machine (£20,000) and also the mould tooling (£12,500 a shuttle mould capable of producing 2.5 pairs per minute), provided the work is undertaken by Danum, a sheltered workshop employing handicapped people. Since the moulding operation and the packing are both highly repetitive, non-skilled tasks, Mr and Mrs Powell are very glad to agree to this. The first 50,000 units, however, will be produced by Alan Grinders Ltd, the company which will produce the mould in order to prove it in production.

The time-scale for the launch in the UK is as follows, as soon as the funds are available:

Lead time on manufacture of tools	12 weeks
Proving tools at production rates	12 weeks (maybe less)
	24 weeks

The manufacture will be entirely by subcontract, except for the grinding.

The price of £4.99 is deliberately chosen as the psychological gateway to large volume sales of scissors. The present prices charged for scissors of similar quality range from £6.95 (Kitchen Devil) to £9.95 (Wilkinson).

The profit and loss account for the UK market alone will therefore be as follows, at various levels of market penetration:

	5%	10%	50%
Unit sales	1m	2m	11m
Contribution to Russell Shears @ £1.42	£000	£000	£000
Overheads (1)	1,420	2,840	15,620
	53	55	75
Net profit before tax	1,367	2,785	15,545

345

Note:
1. The overheads of Russell Shears for the 10 months to October 1982 were as follows, before directors' remuneration:

	£
Office salaries	6,142
Rates	1,438
Insurance	1,825
Depreciation	4,226
Pension premiums	2,598
Advertising	1,609
Audit and accounting	1,551
Miscellaneous	4,400
	23,789 = 28,546 in 12 months

Mr and Mrs Powell would like to draw salaries of £10,000 each, and also to pay Mr Quick a retainer of £5,000 per annum both to secure his continuing contribution to production engineering needs, and to reward him for his efforts to date, which have been largely unrewarded. Total overheads will therefore be £53,000 in a full year. The existing administration should be able to handle the increased level of sales without difficulty. While it would be possible to increase these overheads substantially with a large advertising budget, Mrs Powell sees no good reason for doing this. Point of sale material, and promotion of the product by the mail order catalogues, should in themselves be sufficient to secure sales.

Questions

1. What real strengths do Russell Shears have to help them launch their new product successfully?
2. Who do you think is the most important member of the management team?
3. How unique do you think the new scissors' advantages really are? Will they be sufficient to protect the company from eastern competition?
4. Which of the three levels of market penetration, 5, 10 or 50 per cent, do you think most likely to be achieved by the company for its new product?

Case 36
The Dearne Valley Foundry
John L Thompson

A management buy-out opportunity

In September 1981 Peter Marshall, managing director of the
Dearne Valley Foundry, was considering his increasingly uncertain future. His firm was part of the Yorkshire Foundries
Group, which had recently experienced such severe cash flow
problems that a receiver had been appointed by the company's
bank. Peter Marshall knew that it was not Dearne Valley
Foundry that had brought about the downfall of the Group, but
one of the other subsidiaries. Dearne Valley had recently been
trading at a loss, but was, he felt, a viable organisation with
genuine long-term prospects.

Marshall knew of the increasing number of management buy-
outs taking place in the United Kingdom and thought this might
well be the solution. Was it worth the risk? How many of his
senior colleagues would support such a scheme? How should the
foundry be valued? Could enough money be raised? What potential sources of funding existed? Was a foundry a glamorous
enough investment to attract external capital of the magnitude
required? And would the receiver be aiming for a quick sale of
individual companies in the Group, or would he pursue all
possible avenues for selling the Group intact before he considered
splitting it up? Perhaps most important of all, was this the sort of
challenge he wanted?

The iron foundry industry

The Dearne Valley Foundry's major market is rolling mills but
it also supplies the glass industry and manufactures components
for cranes and fork-lift trucks, together with several other
products.

The foundry *industry*'s most important customer is the motor
industry, but the majority of the suppliers to this are located in
the Midlands. Aluminium castings were, however, eroding the

iron foundries' market share from the early 1970s onwards, and this was compounded by a fall in vehicle production in the late 1970s. The iron foundry industry was declining.

Other important markets are the steel industry (second largest segment), building, engineering, water and gas (pipes and tubes), shipbuilding, coal-mining and railways: all heavy industries, and all affected to some degree by the recession in the late 1970s and early 1980s.

The recent story of the iron foundry industry therefore has been a story of decline. Output, employment and the number of firms have been reduced steadily over a 20-year period.

Table A. UK iron castings production, 1963–81

000 tonnes

1963	3,700
1968	3,600
1973	3,450
1978	2,700
1980	1,820

While the recession has brought about closures and capacity reductions, it may in the end prove to be beneficial to the industry – or at least to the firms which survive it. Generally it is the least efficient foundries that have closed, and those remaining could emerge leaner, fitter and more profitable. In the future it seems likely that UK iron foundry output will continue to decline, but production will be concentrated in fewer, more modern units operating with minimum labour requirements. Nevertheless, they will still be mainly small to medium-sized companies rather than large firms.

Foundries have never been major exporters, selling typically less than 10 per cent overseas. But they have been forced to turn this way recently and useful markets have been developed.

One favourable trend has been input costs. The major raw materials used by iron foundries are pig iron and ferrous scrap, and the prices of both have fallen during the recession. The low level of activity throughout the steel and foundry industries should continue to hold them down.

Historically the Dearne Valley Foundry has been a profitable operation with a specific and identifiable market for its products, which was not expected to disappear in the foreseeable future. Dearne Valley has fortunately been protected against foreign competition to a large extent by its specialisation in heavy iron castings. It also has relatively few UK competitors.

Dearne Valley and the Yorkshire Foundries Group

The Dearne Valley Foundry was established at the end of the last century. By the early 1970s it had developed into a small public company with a turnover approaching £1 million from approximately £300,000 net assets. However, the normally profitable company lost £70,000 in 1973. The board was ageing and felt they should seek new blood to run the company.

A prominent local businessman with experience in the industry, Graham Benson, was invited to be chairman. He accepted, and brought with him Tim Watkins to be the new managing director. Watkins' background was in selling. Benson himself owned a small specialised foundry (Benson's (Foundry)), which was easily absorbed into Dearne Valley in exchange for a small personal shareholding. Benson Holdings (of which Graham Benson was also chairman) then quickly became a significant shareholder in Dearne Valley with a 30 per cent holding, the largest 'individual' holding.

New staff were needed and were appointed, beginning with an experienced metallurgist and a roll designer. Peter Marshall was appointed in 1974 as company accountant. His experience was entirely in large corporations but he was seeking the challenge of a smaller, less formal organisation. In 1976 he became general manager.

In 1978, with the last four trading years yielding almost £1 million of profit, two significant developments took place.

First, the company decided to diversify into the steel foundry business, and bought Northern Foundries Ltd from a major Sheffield steel company. Northern manufactured carbon and alloy steel castings and, in terms of turnover, were almost as big as Dearne Valley. The group also held a 90 per cent share of a Canadian selling subsidiary.

Second, the organisation was restructured with Yorkshire Foundries Group becoming the holding company (see Figure 1). Peter Marshall was now a director and general manager of both Dearne Valley Foundry Ltd and Benson's (Foundry) Ltd (which now operated as an independent subsidiary), but he was not a member of the Yorkshire Foundries Group board, which consisted of Benson, Watkins and two non-executive directors.

In reality Northern Foundries had been bought very cheaply, for it had been allowed to run down. Major customers had been lost and plant replacements and new investment had been neglected. Major changes were required. The team who had

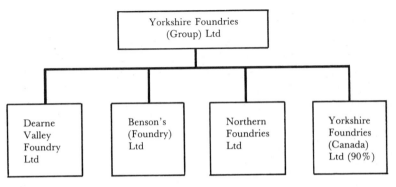

Figure 1. The group structure, 1978–81

succeeded at Dearne Valley were confident they could do the same with their new acquisition.

A major investment programme was immediately begun, using reserves earned by Dearne Valley supplemented by loan capital. The rate of new investment was dramatic. Fortunately investment took place throughout the group; Dearne Valley was not neglected, although the commitment was less than it had been during 1974–78.

But the recession deepened and imports of steel castings grew. Interest rates rose and it quickly became clear that the investment programme had been overambitious. Northern Foundries had laid down capacity equivalent to the whole UK market, which they had totally misread. Interest repayments became a real problem, and a major share issue to reduce the overall debt burden was considered impractical. Moreover the group traded at a loss in 1979–80 (see Appendices 1 and 2).

Dearne Valley fared rather better, but Marshall too had his problems. In 1980 the home market was 'drying up' and in October the workforce was reduced from 262 to 216. Orders were sought abroad. The company was literally buying work to prevent further redundancies. For the year ended 31 July 1981 a trading loss of £124,000 was recorded against the profits of £314,000 the previous year. The order book was low and the workforce by necessity was reduced again, this time to 176 (see Appendices 3 and 4).

The group as a whole was in trouble. The trading loss of £212,000 (year ended 31 July 1980) was predicted to treble to a £650,000 loss for 1980–81. Peter Marshall toured the financial institutions seeking support. It was a lost cause, and in September 1981 a receiver was appointed to the Yorkshire Foundries Group.

Peter Marshall's dilemma

Peter Marshall wasn't a fool. He could see the foundry industry was still in trouble. And yet he felt that Dearne Valley was basically sound and viable. His results over the years (see Appendices 5 and 6) bore out his firm conviction that it was not Dearne Valley that had caused Yorkshire Foundries to crash. On the contrary, his efforts had delayed the day of judgement.

He had talked to various institutions who had refused to support the ailing group, but who had spoken more kindly about an independent Dearne Valley. He had sounded out the group company secretary, Barry Phillips, a chartered accountant, who agreed with him and was genuinely interested in a possible buy-out. Other managers at Dearne Valley *might* be interested, but he was not yet sure. Marshall knew he could find £15,000 from savings and a loan against his house. Phillips was able to offer £10–12,000. But was this enough?

On the positive side Marshall had contacted a number of Dearne Valley's major customers. While unable to commit themselves specifically about future requirements most of them expressed a willingness to buy from the company in the future if Marshall masterminded a buy-out – as long as past quality, delivery and competitive pricing strategies were maintained.

Appendix 1

Yorkshire Foundries Group

ᵢ **Group Profit and Loss Account, year ended 31 July 1980**

	1980 £000	1979 £000
Turnover	8,138	8,175
Profit before interest and tax	54	552
Interest charges	266	72
Profit/(loss) before tax	(212)	480
Taxation	(113)	261
	(99)	219
Extraordinary items*	35	63
	(64)	282
Dividends paid	11	44
Profit/(loss) transferred to/from reserves	(75)	238

*1980: subsidence compensation; 1979: profit on sale of property.

Appendix 2

Yorkshire Foundries Group

Group Balance Sheet, 31 July 1980

	1980	1979
	£000	£000
Fixed assets	3,129	1,919
Current assets		
Investment	19	—
Stock and work-in-progress	961	978
Patterns	39	46
Debtors	2,424	2,212
Corporation tax recoverable	59	—
Cash and bank balances	5	7
	3,507	3,243
Current liabilities		
Bank overdraft	552	162
Creditors	2,048	2,297
Hire Purchase	190	54
Current taxation	54	144
Proposed dividend	—	33
	2,844	2,690
Net current assets	663	553
Net assets employed	3,792	2,472
Financed by		
Share capital	295	295
Reserves (1)	1,073	895
Share capital and reserves	1,368	1,190
Grants	300	95
Deferred tax	712	788
Bank loan	800	249
Hire purchase	612	150
Capital employed	3,792	2,472

Note: 1. The 'reserves' include asset revaluation at Northern Foundries.

Appendix 3

Dearne Valley Foundry Ltd

Profit and Loss Account Summary, year ended 31 July 1981

	1981 £000	1980 £000
Turnover	2,771	4,192
Trading profit/(loss)	(124)	314
Taxation	(91)	154
Extraordinary item	47	—
Profit/(loss) transferred to group accounts	(80)	160

Appendix 4

Dearne Valley Foundry Ltd

Balance Sheet extracts, 31 July 1981

	1981 £000	1980 £000
Fixed assets		
Land and buildings	291	316
Plant and machinery	273	298
Other equipment, inc vehicles	109	133
	673	747
Current assets		
Stock and work-in-progress	209	291
Patterns	25	34
Debtors	664	1,028
Cash and bank balance	1	280
	899	1,633
Current liabilities		
Overdraft	159	—
Creditors	590	808
Hire purchase	8	20
	757	828
Net current assets	142	805
Net assets employed	815	1,552

Notes:
1. The land and buildings have not been revalued since the mid/late 1970s. They are worth more than their book valuation, maybe by as much as 30 per cent when the property market becomes more buoyant.
2. Plant and machinery (and other equipment) have been depreciated from historic costs. At auction they might fetch one-third of book value overall.
3. Most stock is reasonably new, certainly most of it is usable. Very little is in need of being written off.

Appendix 5

Yorkshire Foundries Group/Dearne Valley Foundry

Results summary, 1974–81 (Years represent 12 months ended July of year in question)

	1981 £000	1980 £000	1979 £000	1978 £000	1977 £000	1976 £000	1975 £000	1974 £000
Yorkshire Foundries Group								
Sales		8,138	8,175	4,487	2,764	2,599	2,156	1,513
Trading profit/(loss)		(212)	480	352	242	264	270	175
Net assets employed		3,792	2,472	2,019	1,186	967	668	466
Profit ÷ Assets %		(0.6)	19.4	17.4	20.4	27.3	40.4	37.6
Dearne Valley Foundry								
Sales	2,771	4,192	3,750	2,985				
Trading profit/(loss)	(124)	314	365	262				
Net assets employed	815	1,552	1,815	1,810	From 1974–78 Dearne			
Profit ÷ Assets %	(15.2)	20.2	20.1	14.5	Valley constituted most of			
					the Group sales and profit			

Appendix 6

Dearne Valley Foundry

Selected items from management accounts

	Year ended July			
	1981	1980	1979	1978
Contribution % of sales	25.6	31.7	32.7	N/A
Fixed costs % of sales	30.1	23.4	22.1	N/A
Exports as % of sales	24.7	22.2	12.3	7.2
Tonnage output	6252	7865	8714	7240
Productivity				
Hours/tonne	39.2	44.1	41.8	48.5
Sales/employee £	13,300	16,200	14,650	11,760
Absenteeism, %	4.9	9.2	8.4	9.2

Questions

If Marshall were to consider a management buy-out then:

1. How should he value the foundry?
2. What potential sources of money are there to fund such a venture?
3. Is the market sufficiently glamorous to attract external capital of the magnitude needed?
4. Is this a worthwhile challenge for Marshall?
5. If he and his colleagues buy out the company, what style of management should the managing director of the resurrected venture adopt and why?

The sequel

Peter Marshall, managing director of Dearne Valley Foundry (1982) sipped his whisky and idly glanced at the Cambridgeshire countryside as his train sped relentlessly northwards. Had he gone too far this time, he pondered?

His company had been bought from the receiver just over six months ago. It was trading profitably, if at a somewhat low ebb, with a workforce of 150. In masterminding the buy-out he was convinced he had done the right thing. He had, however, just quoted a Swedish fabricator for sufficient castings to occupy his current plant capacity fully for the next two years. Maybe it was fortunate he did not expect to win the business. If he did, he would face the implications when they arose. Was it too soon to expand? Could he manage the necessary subcontracting so that loyal customers who had stayed with him would not lose out? Perhaps he should have another whisky.

The buy-out

Within a week of his appointment the Yorkshire Foundries Group receiver had closed Northern Foundries Ltd, and announced a date for the auction. He was running the rest of the Group as a going concern and seeking prospective purchasers.

Marshall acted quickly. He struck up an arrangement with the company secretary, Barry Phillips, and they were subsequently joined by six other functional managers from the old Dearne Valley Foundry. Between them they could muster £60,000, but with quite significantly different levels of contribution.

Marshall contacted and talked to a wide range of institutions and found key support from the Industrial and Commercial Finance Corporation (ICFC) and a leading union pension fund. The pension fund invested £45,000 in return for equity, ICFC likewise. Thus they each received 30 per cent of the shares, the management team retaining 40 per cent. This was backed by loans from ICFC and CIN (the NCB Pension Fund), totalling £350,000, supplemented by a clearing bank overdraft and government grants.

A number of major companies were seriously interested in acquiring the foundry, but only two actually bid against the managers. The buy-out succeeded and Dearne Valley Foundry (1982) Ltd was registered in January 1982.

Land and buildings were purchased at an independently assessed market price; plant and machinery for about a third of book value; new and recent stock at cost and old stock discounted. The name and outstanding contracts were also included in the deal. Debtors and creditors were excluded and the government took over responsibility for redundancy rights and pensions.

New plant and equipment were immediately ordered, in particular a sand reclamation plant. The aim was improved productivity and cost savings rather than capacity expansion. Prior to trading the balance sheet was approximately as follows:

Dearne Valley Foundry (1982)

	£000
Land and buildings (estimated value)	350
Plant and machinery and other equipment (at cost, but including new plant on order)	250
Stock/work-in-progress	200
Cash/bank balance	150
	950
Financed by	
Share capital	150
Loan (ICFC)	350
Grants	325
Overdraft	125
	950
Net assets employed	825

The organisation

The board of Dearne Valley Foundry (1982) was four members, including Marshall and Phillips. The ICFC and pension fund nominated the others. The other six equity-holding managers are members of a policy-making directorate, which Marshall seeks to manage by consensus. In reality Marshall exercises considerable executive authority. The institutional shareholders receive a fixed dividend on their 30 per cent holdings; the managers *may* receive dividends as a form of bonus. The reduced workforce have retained their earnings level. However, greater weight is attached to incentive schemes than was the case previously.

The markets

The period of destocking which dampened the home market appears to have ended, but things are still tight. European markets are depressed and North America is in the middle of a destocking programme. Prices are highly competitive. Being more independent and more able to take higher risk decisions,

Marshall is ensuring that Dearne Valley compete aggressively, He is also looking to diversify into higher quality iron castings.

The big enquiry

Dearne Valley supply ½ to 5 tonne castings to a Swedish navigational aids company who fabricate marker buoys and sinkers. This company is diversifying and wishes to tender for a contract to erect 16 iron lighthouses in the Seychelles. They will each be 40 metres high, constructed of cast iron tunnel segments, and they must be able to withstand a 100 mph wind velocity. Marshall has agreed to quote, fully appreciating the job would equate to two years' full capacity. He also appreciated the risk involved until the first lighthouse had been erected and tested on site.

He was convinced his colleagues would support his decision. He was less convinced he really had any strategic plan for the next three to five years. He had met and renegotiated successfully with all his major customers. Orders were building up, albeit slowly. But some diversification was paramount if the company was to fulfil its genuine potential within a still declining industry.

Having said that, Marshall was concerned about the pace of change. The company was not used to any major changes of direction, product or working practice. But if ever there was a suitable time it was now. Morale and commitment throughout the works were higher than Marshall felt they had ever been previously. He must not destroy the support he had; but at the same time he must produce results and justify the faith the workforce had in him.

Questions

1. Is 40 per cent of the business enough to give the owner directors effective control of the business?
2. What dangers are inherent in the consensus style of management that Marshall is seeking to adopt?
3. Was the decision to go for the Swedish contract a wise one at this stage in the new company's life?
4. Do you agree with Marshall's assessment that 'some diversification was paramount'?

Case 37
Cifer Systems Ltd A (1972–76)
John Howdle and Peter Chadwick

Beginnings

During the early part of 1972 two employees of Graphic Displays, a subsidiary of Kode Ltd, based in Calne, Wiltshire were thinking about starting their own business. Tony Akers, aged 32, an ex-RAF trained electronics engineer, and Geoff Craddock, aged 23, an electronics graduate were working as commissioning and design engineers respectively. Both were interested in starting an independent business offering an electronics contract design service. The two engineers were joined in this venture by Gerry Crisp, aged 40, a draughtsman during the earlier part of his career and currently sales manager of Graphic Displays. Changes in company organisation were under consideration at the time, which led Tony Akers to believe that 'they couldn't do much worse on their own'.

However, with no personal capital between them, they required initial financing, and after several visits to a local branch of Lloyds Bank, when they attempted to 'educate the manager in the world of electronics', they eventually persuaded him to grant them an overdraft facility of £5,000. No formal business plan was presented, though some financial figures were given and a number of potential contracts were cited. The overdraft facility was backed by a 'joint and several guarantee' of the directors and their spouses, based on the £30,000 collateral of their homes. At the time a fourth employee of Graphic Displays, Terry Cosgrove, aged 33, an experienced electronics engineer, decided not to join the venture, having recently moved house from Bedford (see Appendix 1 for brief biographies). The business idea was based on a perceived need to offer a contract design and small-batch production service within the computer industry and it was decided to form a limited company. This form of organisation was chosen as suppliers in the industry tended to prefer dealing with limited companies rather than partnerships.

In deciding what to call the company, three of their initial

359

suggestions were not acceptable to the Registrar of Business Names. Eventually though, after devising anagrams in a pub one evening, they managed to produce a name which fitted with their desire to have the company name linked with the computer/ systems area – 'Cifer Systems Ltd'. However, due to an industrial dispute within the Civil Service it took 17 weeks for the name to become officially registered. Until then, the overdraft facility could not be used, in spite of the fact that all three founders had left their previous employment and could not register for unemployment benefit. Cifer Systems started with an issued capital of 1,002 £1 shares held equally between the directors.

Premises

The new company was eventually registered on 2 August 1972 and moved into premises at 26 Lowbourne, Melksham, Wiltshire. The building had previously been used as a doctor's surgery, but was now very dilapidated with a severe damp problem. The 14 year repairing lease that the three directors had negotiated reflected the premises' structural condition. The first three years' rent was for a nominal 10p per annum, rising gradually until the eighth year, when market value would be charged.

At first most of the directors' time, including evenings and weekends, was taken up with building and decorating; as one of them put it '10 per cent of our time was spent on electronics and 90 per cent on building'. It took 18 months to complete the major repair work, partly because the cash flow dictated the rate of purchase of building materials. Moreover, the business could only support two of the directors full time, so Gerry Crisp carried on working for another computer firm as a sales consultant.

Cifer Systems started trading by gaining design contracts for clients such as the Ministry of Defence and the Electricity Research Council. These initial projects, though, were limited to those requiring mainly design expertise and minimal manufacturing capabilities. Early in 1973 Terry Cosgrove, who had been party to the original discussions to set up Cifer Systems, left Kode Ltd to join the company full time as a director. Further contracts were undertaken for a number of other organisations and the new company was gradually establishing itself, but salaries were set at 'survival rates' – enough to cover mortgages and housekeeping. The peppercorn rent during the start-up period was seen by Terry Cosgrove as 'a major contribution to our survival in the first two years'.

At the end of the first trading year (September 1973) the company reported a sales turnover of £23,639 and a net profit of £4,285 (see Appendix 2 for Balance Sheet and Profit and Loss Account).

Manufacturing a product

By the beginning of 1974 the number of client organisations had grown and Cifer Systems was now employing two other staff – a receptionist and a technician/wireman, Dave Harrold – though all three directors were still undertaking many of the production operations such as soldering and assembly. The work pattern was typical of many jobbing businesses – peaks and troughs – resulting in what Terry Cosgrove described as 'us having to work all hours as invariably the customer wanted completion yesterday'. However, the trading year 1973–74 proved to be a difficult one with the combined effects of the oil crisis and the three-day week. The financial results at September 1974 reflected this tighter operating environment in the United Kingdom, with sales turnover down to £17,120 and a reported loss of £1,419. Although directors' remuneration had fallen by nearly £1,000 over the previous financial year, overheads and wages had risen, and the bank felt that the company was close to overtrading.

The directors, therefore, decided to devise a product which they could manufacture on a limited scale in order to reduce the impact of the troughs in the contract design business. First thoughts included a computer-controlled digital clock, since they had needed to build one as part of the specification for one of their contracts, after finding that no one was supplying them. However, having spent several months looking at this and other ideas they decided to design a visual display unit (VDU), after talking to Stuart Gregory, a college friend of Geoff Craddock, who was then working in computer science research at Westfield College, University of London. The VDU market was in its early stages of development and the product appeared to be technically straightforward (though the directors have since seen the complications!) and capable of being manufactured in small quantities at the Lowbourne premises. Stuart Gregory was, therefore, commissioned to design a 'card' or printed circuit board for Cifer Systems. A prototype VDU was subsequently built and Gerry Crisp, who had joined the company full time, began to assess the product with some potential customers. The reaction was favourable and Cifer decided to launch their first VDU – designated Model 127 after the code used by Tony Akers on the specification drawing – in November 1974, at the COMPEC Exhibition in London.

A visual display unit is a device for inputting data to a computer system and for displaying information to the user via a cathode ray tube. The unit incorporates a keyboard similar to that found in a typewriter and a small screen similar to a portable television in size. Logic electronics interpret the binary code for sending information to and from the computer, and for generating a character set made up of dots. In their most basic form, colloquially known as a 'dumb' terminal, VDUs only provide for communication to and from the mainframe with no information-processing ability on the VDU. The 127 model was a 'dumb' terminal.

The Cifer Systems model was largely designed by Tony Akers with a glass fibre casing manufactured outside. Similarly, all the electronic components were externally sourced. These components were then made up into units using a large number of hand-soldered joints, and tested after visual inspection.

The market for VDUs and the product launch

The market for VDUs at that time was following the pattern established in the United States and some European countries, notably France and Germany. The development of VDUs allowed greater use to be made of mainframe computers in a variety of organisational applications, and they were replacing existing mechanically based input machines. The major computer manufacturers already made and sold their own VDUs as part of their hardware, but there was a growing market for display units sold direct to independent 'systems houses', dealers/distributors and other users. Systems houses (characterised along with the larger computer companies as original equipment manufacturers – OEMs) designed computer systems for small to medium-sized business users, and in general tended not to manufacture their own hardware but did provide software, training and support. They thus supplied a package, buying the hardware such as the central processing unit, VDUs and printers and designing the software themselves which formed a 'turnkey' operation for the user, ie the user just 'turned the key' and had an operating system ready to use without the need to employ their own software specialists.

Cifer Systems did not commission or undertake any basic market research to determine the size or structure of the market, but believed that VDUs were an 'enormous market' and intuitively felt that the terminal end of the overall computer market was showing very rapid growth (see Appendix 3 for synopsis of NEDO reports). Tony Akers recalls that during November 1974 he 'worked all hours to get five 127s up and running the night before the opening of COMPEC' and that the company came away with two firm orders and a number of enquiries which they could follow up. Indeed, Cifer's first VDU sale to Lincoln College of Education was still operating successfully eight years later and the company has subsequently repurchased it for sentimental and display purposes.

The average selling price for VDUs was £700 to £750 with top of the range models selling for £2,000 or more. The directors of Cifer Systems worked out the price of the 127 on a cost plus basis and then deliberately priced it higher than the average at £800 to £900 depending on discount. This was done to limit the rate of sale of their VDU, as the directors still felt that the contract design and small batch production work would provide them with a substantial proportion of their turnover.

Financing further growth

Sales of the 127 grew steadily and by September 1975 they had sold 48 units, the majority to systems houses with the balance to individual end-users, particularly universities and colleges. The systems houses were becoming an important group of customers as they bought in volume. During the financial year 1974-75 VDUs accounted for nearly 40 per cent of the £93,000 turnover, and VDU manufacture had been allowed to dominate their activities during 1975 at the expense of the design and development business, in order to generate a significant presence in this sector of the market. None the less, a contract for £12,000 was completed for Joseph Lucas Ltd during the summer of 1975 and a substantial £150,000 project for a government department was finished in December of that year.

The expansion of VDU manufacture meant that by early 1976 Cifer Systems was producing the 127 model at the rate of between 20 and 30 per four-week period and employing 15 other staff, seven of whom worked on direct production; others were employed in the test section and there were two part-time sales engineers. A buyer was recruited to be responsible for the purchasing and stock control functions, and Mike Sharp, an ex-colleague from Graphic Displays, joined Cifer as company secretary. The latter had already been working for Cifer Systems in a part-time capacity for one year, the provision of financial administration having been undertaken previously by Geoff Craddock. Mike Sharp's major contribution was to remove the pressures of day-to-day accounting procedures from the other directors and to implement formalised systems. Each director now became responsible for a particular section of the business: Tony Akers as production director; Terry Cosgrove as managing director; Geoff Craddock as technical director; and Gerry Crisp as sales director. At times, though, they each did the other's role and continued to work 50 or more hours per week and often at weekends.

Production of the 127 model was being constrained by the lack of space at Lowbourne (1,000 sq ft) and they needed a larger facility to build their new model, the 224. This had been developed for one of their major OEM customers who required a more versatile machine. The 224 had a larger keyboard, different interfaces, additional facilities and a more up-to-date cabinet, but was still technically similar to the 127. Annual sales of the new machine were forecast to be in the region of 150 units, and further sales could be expected to other customers. In addition, Cifer Systems was developing a model extension, the 244P, offering built-in text editing and data preparation. The new machines were, in the jargon of the industry, becoming 'smarter' or more intelligent since they provided for some data processing prior to input into the mainframe computer. As Terry Cosgrove put it: 'It is the intention of Cifer Systems Ltd to continue development of its microprocessor-based terminals, to cater for the newly developed data transmission methods and to allow us to emulate the more expensive American produced terminals.'

Further development activity was under way with a major British company of a new visual display controller for their range of medical electronics products. This unit would offer the company a potential market for 400 display units per annum, at a unit cost of £600 and provide Cifer with the opportunity to develop another product to meet the needs of a large number of users who required a general application display unit at a lower price.

However, the envisaged growth could only be accommodated by enlarging the company's manufacturing capacity, and this meant that Cifer Systems' immediate requirement was for premises of around 6,000 sq ft. By chance, a newly built, 9,000 sq ft single-storey factory had become available in Melksham at Avro Way on the nearby Bowerhill Industrial Estate, due to a change of plans by the original client. The industrial estate was owned by West Wiltshire District Council and a developer had built a factory which included a small amount of land for expansion. This was offered to Cifer on a 99-year lease for a total of £55,000.

The company's current overdraft facility would cover the necessary fitting out costs, but there was a longer-term borrowing requirement for the purchase of the property itself. Initial soundings were made with a number of insurance brokers and financial advisers who suggested some city contacts. Several merchant banks were approached, but were found to be only willing to lend a maximum of 50 per cent of the sum required, and also insisted on a substantial equity stake in the business. The directors of Cifer Systems felt reluctant to part with a sizeable block of shares; however, the interviews conducted with the various city lending agencies did help the board to improve and refine their proposal documents.

In June 1976 Cifer made contact with Technical Development Capital (TDC), a part of the ICFC (see Appendix 4 for details of ICFC and TDC). Terry Cosgrove rang the local Bristol Office of ICFC, and he and another director were invited to present their proposals the following Monday. The directors spent the weekend drafting and typing their proposal with one finger! Despite their reluctance to sacrifice equity, they had come to realise that this was the price of further growth.

Appendix 1

Key personnel – brief biographies

TA Cosgrove, Managing Director.
BSc (London) maths and physics.
  4 years design engineer, Davy & United Instruments Ltd.
  4 years development engineer, Solartron Electronics Group Ltd.
  3 years product engineer, Texas Instruments Ltd.
  2 years chief engineer, Graphic Displays, subsequently Kode International Ltd.

AJ Akers, Production Director.
13 years RAF. Sergeant and chief technician in wireless and radar technology.
2 years quality assurance engineer, Kode Ltd.
1 year commissioning engineer, Graphic Displays Ltd.

GD Craddock, Technical Director.
BSc (CNAA) engineering.
3 years student trainee, The Plessey Co Ltd.
2 years electronics engineer, The Plessey Co Ltd.
1 year design engineer, Graphic Displays Ltd.

G Crisp, Sales Director.
11 years design draughtsman with British Aircraft Corporation, Peto Scott Ltd, and Hope Bros Inc USA.
4 years sales representative with Elliot Bros Ltd and Pye-TMC Ltd.
7 years sales manager, Kode Ltd.
2 years sales consultant, Digico Ltd.

MA Sharp, Company Secretary.
7 years assistant company secretary, Methodist Newspaper Co Ltd.
2 years company secretary, Graphic Displays Ltd.
4 years sales associate, Hambro Life Assurance Ltd.

Appendix 2

Extracts from the Trading Profit and Loss Accounts 1972–77

	Year ended Sept 1973 £	Year ended Sept 1974 £	Year ended Sept 1975 £	9 months to June 1976 £
Sales	23,639	17,120	93,650	132,601
Operating expenses	7,374	3,503	53,314	75,081
Gross profit	16,265	13,617	40,336	57,520
Overhead expenses	3,768	4,809	12,720	13,822
Wages and NI	1,750	4,642	8,710	13,701
Directors' remuneration	6,462	5,585	14,610	14,306
Net profit (loss)	4,285	(1,419)	4,296	15,691

Extracts from the Balance Sheets 1972–77

	Year ended Sept 1973 £	Year ended Sept 1974 £	Year ended Sept 1975 £	9 months to June 1976 £
Fixed assets	1,797	2,754	5,247	9,444
Current assets				
Stock and work-in-progress	850	4,055	21,506	37,829
Debtors	5,082	2,263	22,050	27,167
Total assets	7,729	9,072	48,803	74,440
Current liabilities	6,128	10,496	45,931	55,877
Net assets	1,601	(1,424)	2,872	18,563
Share capital				
Authorised	2,000	2,000	2,000	2,000
Issued	1,002	1,336	1,336	1,336
Reserves				
Profit and Loss Account	599	(2,760)	1,536	17,227
	1,601	(1,424)	2,872	18,563

Appendix 3

1. The electronics industry: brief synopsis of the economic assessment of the electronics industry to 1972, published by NEDO Electronics EDC in 1970

The output of the UK computer industry, which constitutes part of the overall electronics sector had shown rapid growth, achieving total deliveries of £209.2 million in 1970. Export deliveries amounted to £90.7 million and had shown a faster rate of increase in 1968–70.

Nevertheless, imported products were taking an increasing share of the home market especially in peripheral equipment. Indeed, the latter was taking an increasing proportion of the total market – 1966 15 per cent; 1967 20 per cent; 1968 23 per cent – which reflected the greater emphasis on 'add-on' equipment, multi-access and interactive systems. The UK manufacturers' share of the peripheral market, though, had been virtually static during this period. The electronics EDC highlighted the peripheral segment as one on which the UK industry should concentrate and instanced the US experience where moderate-sized firms were able to concentrate on a narrow part of the segment and become market leaders.

The EDC did point out a number of difficulties which home

367

manufacturers were likely to encounter within the UK computer industry:

(a) Potential shortages in the supply of qualified and skilled manpower, especially of computer software personnel. (The UK electronics industry in general has a higher density of qualified manpower in research and development activities than any other industry other than chemicals and aircraft.)

(b) The funding of research and development to provide for the commercial exploitation of new developments. (The research and development effort for the UK electronics industry in general is approximately five times as important in relation to capital expenditure as the average for manufacturing industry.)

(c) The size of the UK market (relative to the US) did not give home manufacturers the opportunity of funding product development across the volume of sales that the US manufacturers typically had in their home market. This factor highlighted the importance of exports for UK manufacturers and the role of government purchasing in supporting home products. (UK government was the largest purchaser of computers with $c.14$ per cent share of the home market.)

(d) A significant fall in prices per unit of performance, as technological developments enhanced the capability of computers at no higher cost.

(e) As a whole the electronics industry has grown three times as fast as the national average, and key sectors within the industry have grown faster still. The allocation of resources out of current cash flow needed to provide the total capital investment to sustain future demand represents a far greater burden than is the case of other industries, whose growth rates are nearer to the national average.

2. The annual statistical survey of the electronics industry published by NEDO (October 1973)

a) Output and deliveries by UK manufacturers of electronic computers and related equipment 1967–72 (£000)

	1967		1968		1969		1970		1971		1972	
	Total	Export	Total	Export	Total	Export	Total	Export	Total	Export	Total	Export
Digital computers	62,492	21,441	77,179	25,803	86,596	36,370	123,437	55,519	101,776	46,857	109,374	48,214
Analogue computers	1,452	293	1,931	233	2,575	498	779	124	798	20	329	46
Data transmission equipment	2,849	838	3,235	1,132	7,918	2,973	18,092	9,010	12,543	6,052	25,380	18,638
Peripheral equipment	27,561	12,775	27,112	11,614	44,720	19,416	66,898	26,058	78,242	36,671	70,176	30,491
Total deliveries	94,354	35,347	109,475	38,782	141,809	59,257	209,206	90,711	193,359	89,600	205,259	97,389

Source: Department of Trade and Industry

b) Percentage factored (1) deliveries of electronic computers and related equipment in UK 1970–72

	1970 %	1971 %	1972 %
Digital computing systems (2)	41	43	41
Analogue and hybrid computers	71	39	64
Data transmission equipment	17	39	38
Peripheral equipment for computing systems	34	35	43

Source: Department of Trade and Industry

Notes:
1. Factored equipment sold by firms who do not make it, and in the present context is almost synonymous with imported.
2. Other than computers, inseparable from other capital equipment (eg radar and navigational aids).

Appendix 4

Background note on the Industrial and Commercial Finance Corporation Technical Development Capital (summarised from the 1974 ICFC Annual Review)

In the autumn of 1973 after 29 years of separate existence, Finnance Corporation for Industry (FCI) and the Industrial and Commercial Finance Corporation (ICFC) were merged under a new parent company, Finance for Industry (FFI).

The shareholders of FFI are the Bank of England and the English Clearing and Scottish banks. The primary function of the group is the provision of finance for the development of British industry. FCI makes finance available to the larger private and public companies in amounts ranging from £1 million upwards.

ICFC provides finance and related services to small- and medium-sized businesses in sums ranging from £5,000 to £500,000 or more. The finance scheme is tailored to the requirements of the situation and may include secured or unsecured loans, preference, preferred ordinary, or ordinary shares, property and development leasing and plant purchase. Interest rates are market rates, typically on the low rather than the high side of the current market, and expenses are modest. Rates are fixed for the period of the loan and repayment terms are normally spread over periods of up to 20 years to suit requirements. An important element in compiling a package is to avoid placing too severe a strain on projected cash generation. The Corporation's close relationship with the clearing banks makes the negotiation of security cover easier, particularly when the clearer already has a charge on the business's assets.

Since ICFC's formation in 1945, over £375 million has been provided to around 3,000 companies throughout the UK. During the financial year 1973–74 over £44 million was invested of which half was to existing customers. There are 19 branches of ICFC in the UK and pre-tax profits to year ended 31 March 1974 were over £6.5 million.

Only 4 per cent of the companies in which ICFC has invested had an ICFC representative on the board, indeed the following is an extract from the 1974 *Annual Review:*

> 'It is accepted that most private businesses value their independence and are eager to develop their own management style

and learn from their own experience. It is not ICFC policy to intervene in the day-to-day management of customer companies nor to obtain control of a customer's business. There are inevitable exceptions – for example, where there is an obvious gap in the management strength ICFC may take the right to appoint a nominee director to help fill this gap.'

ICFC has a number of operating subsidiaries such as ICFC-NUMAS a management consultancy for smaller businesses, and Technical Development Capital (TDC). The latter's objective is to help entrepreneurs create new, or expand existing, businesses based on worthwhile technological innovation. The closer any product, process or service is to commercial realisation, the greater the likelihood of favourable assessment. TDC looks at all cases but states in the FFI 1974 *Annual Review*:

'Appraisal is assisted if a meeting is preceded by a brief, written description of the project, its history, details of any patents granted or pending and background of the proposed management. In addition, TDC should receive estimates of the market potential, cost and pricing structures, and an indication of the total finance required and how it is to be used. If the case is being presented by a company, details of its trading record are required.'

During TDC's 12 years of operation, over 100 small businesses had been assisted, a minority shareholding combined with a medium- or long-term loan being a widely used arrangement.

Note: At the time of writing Finance for Industry Ltd has been renamed Investors in Industry Group plc, and Technical Development Capital has been renamed the New Ventures Division.

Questions

1. How important a decision is choosing a business name? What factors should you consider and why?
2. What market research could have been undertaken to confirm their subjective view that the VDU market was 'enormous' and that it was a desirable one for them to enter?
3. How compatible were Cifer's two business activities? What strategic implications do you see this change in direction having on the company and the directors?

4. Do you agree with the bank's assessment that Cifer were 'close to overtrading' in 1974?
5. How much money should they look for to finance their expansion plans? Where should they look and what form of financing is appropriate to their needs (eg loans, overdraft, equity, grants, HP, leasing, etc)?

Case 38
Cifer Systems Ltd B (1976–81)
John Howdle and Peter Chadwick

Financing expansion

Cifer Systems launched its first computer terminal product late in 1974. In 1975 terminal products accounted for about 40 per cent of the annual turnover of £93,000. The success of the company's 127 range convinced the directors of the scope for expansion in the terminal market. In spring 1976 Cifer Systems approached a number of financial institutions to raise the capital required to purchase the leasehold of a single-storey factory on the Bowerhill Industrial Estate near Melksham in Wiltshire. In June 1976 the directors submitted a proposal to Technical Development Capital (a part of ICFC).

TDC subjected the document to very thorough scrutiny and the initial meeting was followed by a second meeting with the area manager of TDC on site in Melksham. The outcome of these meetings was favourable and an agreement to assist was arrived at, in principle, within about two to three weeks of the first interview. In practice, the documents were not finalised until the end of September 1976. TDC imposed a number of conditions on their loan of £50,000:

1. Certain fees, which were owed to the directors, should remain within the business for the duration of the TDC loan.
2. A guarantee was sought from the bank to the effect that it would provide a growing overdraft facility as the business expanded.
3. TDC should have an option to purchase up to 20 per cent of the equity of Cifer Systems at a fixed price.

The offer of financial support was seen as a mixed blessing by the directors of Cifer Systems. On the positive side, the injection of capital would enable the company to transfer its production operations from a converted doctor's surgery into a new purpose-built factory unit on an industrial estate. Set against this was the burden of servicing a substantial loan, together with the implications of surrendering a proportion of their equity stake in the business. After considerable debate and some taking of sides the directors decided that acceptance of TDC funds would provide the means to expand the business. Although the directors were somewhat reluctant, in their view TDC were 'covered quite nicely by the building'.

Throughout the negotiations to acquire the new factory Cifer Systems continued to manufacture VDUs on their original site at Lowbourne in Melksham. Cifer had outgrown the capacity of these start-up premises (see Cifer Systems A) and urgently required more room in which to produce their latest machine, the 224 (a more advanced version of the 127). Lowbourne was clearly inadequate for a company of 20 people (including directors) with an annual turnover of £204,247 and net profits of £17,652.

The move to Avro Way

Raising the funds to purchase the new factory was a major step for the company, but much remained to be done before Cifer Systems could commence production at the Avro Way site. £45,000 of the loan was released on signature of the agreement with TDC; the remaining £5,000 was withheld subject to completion of the interior of the factory building. Delay in purchasing the new factory had a two-fold effect on Cifer Systems: it reduced the rate of expansion and increased the cost of fitting-out due to the high rate of inflation. In order to minimise costs, the directors of Cifer undertook much of the work themselves. The building was essentially a single-storey shell with only a rough concrete floor. Priorities included laying a proper floor, erecting ceilings and partitions and providing all necessary services, such as plumbing and wiring.

Tony Akers, now the engineering director, recalls working through November and December 1976: 'We were back in the building business,' installing the complete electrical system in the factory. Frequently the temperatures were sub-zero, but by January 1977 'the centre bay was operational'. The task of making the new factory habitable was one which involved almost everybody. On one weekend, late in 1976, the company held a painting party. 'Everyone turned up in old clothes, staff, families, the lot. We provided a pile of paint and brushes and everybody grabbed a wall . . . that's the sort of response you get from staff in a very small organisation'.

Once production was established in the centre bay, attention turned to preparing the offices in the first bay of the factory. The offices were occupied in May 1977. By mid-year production of terminal units was in excess of 50 units per four-week period (for details of the factory layout see Appendix 4). For a short period Cifer Systems retained their original premises at Lowbourne, but once the new factory was fully operational the lease was sold for £2,500.

The product range

By 1976 it was clear to the directors of Cifer Systems that the immediate future of the company lay in the production of high quality VDUs primarily for the original equipment manufacturers (OEM) market. Production of a standard product with a growing market seemed to offer a more secure source of revenue than the company's original 'design and prototype production service for electronic equipment'. Some residual contracts for specialised electronic work remained, but they were rapidly being completed and not being replaced. The company's involvement in the development of the visual display controller for medical electronics was abandoned. This project was deliberately stopped because it was seen to be diverting the company's efforts away from its major objectives. In retrospect, the decision to avoid too great a dependence on another company's products is thought by the directors to have been an important assertion of manufacturing independence.

In 1977 the company's 224 range of terminals was launched. This product was technically very similar to the 127, but embodied several additional features, including a bigger cabinet, a larger keyboard and different interfaces. The 224 was designed to meet the needs of the company's important OEM customers.

During 1977 it became clear that Cifer Systems needed to develop a new product which would eventually replace both the 127 and the 224. To this end a new VDU, designated the 026, was designed and put into production. The 026 was first sold late in 1977, but its lifespan was little over a year and by June 1979 no more 026s were being produced. Only 276 units in total were sold. This was because the 026 did not offer any great advantages over previous models and the technology employed in the product was becoming dated. Lacking any claims to being highly innovative, the 026 received a somewhat lukewarm response from Cifer's customers.

A similar fate afflicted Cifer's next attempt to introduce a new VDU product. The Cub was launched in July 1978 at a price of

£359 (one off to an end-user). The Cub was conceived as a low-priced VDU, aimed at a segment of the market which was cost-conscious but not looking for great technical sophistication. Cifer believed that they could produce an acceptable VDU, in the right price range, by building a unit based on the chassis of a stripped down, portable, domestic television. The advantage of this approach was that Cifer would be able to keep costs to a minimum by making use of the scale economies normally only available to a volume manufacturer of television sets. The Cub was reasonably successful: approximately 400 units were produced over a period of two years, but its sales performance was overshadowed by Cifer's new and current model range, the 2600, which was launched in March 1979. The 2600 range embodied the latest microprocessor technology and involved a radical reappraisal of Cifer's VDU products. (The development of the 2600 is described on page 378.)

With hindsight, it is plain to see that the Cub was a viable product aimed at a significant sector of the market. However, Cifer transferred its attentions to the 2600 because the potential rewards to the company were greater. The Cub involved just as much marketing effort as the higher priced 2600 range, but generated substantially less revenue. Further, the Cub was seen to be downgrading the company's image.

Market performance

The evolution of Cifer's product from the original 127 to the 2600 range was not without its difficulties. Events 'took a turn for the worse', in the months of June and July 1977, when the company experienced a two-month lull in orders. This problem was compounded when the company's two most significant OEM customers cut back their orders at almost the same time. This forced the company to go into a three-day week and provided a salutary shock to the management. The company's heavy dependence upon two major customers, accounting for approximately 50 per cent of output was clearly demonstrated. The downturn in sales was fortunately only a temporary phenomenon, caused by overstocking on the part of these OEM customers. The potential impact of such discontinuities in demand was not lost on the directors of Cifer Systems.

Despite this setback, production of VDUs built up steadily at the new factory, and a rate of 80 per four-week period was achieved by the end of 1977. Sales of the 224 and, to a lesser extent, the 026 sustained the company into 1978.

Throughout the formative years of Cifer Systems the founders of the company were in touch with another electronics specialist, Stuart Gregory. Indeed, it had been Stuart's expertise in VDUs which had first attracted Cifer towards this type of product. By mid-1978 Cifer was anxious to fill the gap in its product range which had opened due to the poor sales of the 026. Stuart Gregory joined the company as a director in July 1978. On 30 August 1978 4,000 ordinary shares were issued to Stuart Gregory as consideration for acquisition of the issued share capital of the Clockwork Data Company Ltd (a freelance design consultancy). Effectively Stuart Gregory became a director of Cifer Systems, with a significant shareholding in the company in exchange for the design and technical concept of the Cub. Stuart Gregory is seen by the other directors as an 'ideas man', 'a catalyst' with 'a feel for the needs of the market'.

Finance

There is no nominated finance director at Cifer Systems Ltd. Mike Sharp, the company secretary, undertakes the task of maintaining the company's accounting records. Responsibility for the company's financial performance has been accepted on a collective basis by all the directors. The Balance Sheets and Profit and Loss Accounts are given in Appendices 5 and 6.

It is evident from Appendix 6 that Cifer Systems has enjoyed a very rapid growth in sales turnover. Financing this expansion has involved a close and developing relationship with Technical Development Capital (TDC). The initial loan (discussed on page 373) has been supplemented by further loans to provide for the company's growing requirement for working capital. These negotiations were conducted by Geoff Craddock in his new capacity of managing director, having changed roles with Terry Cosgrove, who became technical director. By July 1977 the company had completed the first phase of the new factory at Avro Way. The second production area within the factory was due for completion by autumn. In anticipation of an increased need for working capital, the company sought a facility from TDC of £50,000 in July 1977. The forecast need was for £43,000, but Geoff Craddock requested an additional £7,000 to provide more leeway. As he explained in the application to TDC, 'some of the management time currently devoted to cash flow monitoring can be more effectively used. With the current turnover approaching £70,000 per period, errors of £10,000 in any given week have proven extremely difficult to avoid.'

This facility was agreed by TDC and has been followed by other similar financing arrangements. Cifer Systems enjoyed a significant growth in pre-tax profits during the financial years 1977 and 1978, and this enabled Geoff Craddock to negotiate the release of the directors' personal guarantees to the bank. However, the results deteriorated in 1979. This was the result of the costs of developing the 2600.

The development of the 2600

Stuart Gregory joined Cifer Systems at a time when the directors were going through a period of radical reappraisal. There had been considerable discussion about the future direction of the company and in particular about the design concept of the next Cifer VDU. It was clear that a new product was needed and if sales were to be maintained, the new model must be developed with great urgency. As Tony Akers put it, 'the company had reached a sink or swim situation'.

Decisions had to be made about a specification for the 2600 range. These were finalised and approved by the board on 15 December 1978, despite a divergence of views among the directors. The new product was to be a radical new design with a microprocessor at its heart. It was to incorporate the best of the new technology which had recently become available. The circuit designs had been thought out and finalised by the time of the company's annual Christmas party. Tony Akers, the engineering director, worked flat out with his staff on the mechanical aspects of the product. In spite of the progress made in developing the 2600, dissension about the overall direction of Cifer continued among the board members. This was finally resolved during April 1979 when two of the founding directors (G Crisp and G Craddock) left the board and sold their equity stake in the company to the other directors.

The 2600 was in production by April. The first 10 VDUs were built before the prototype top cover had arrived. When it came, it fitted perfectly. Stuart Gregory was responsible for getting the electronics right and in the event the overall design concept, which was based on flexibility, has proved to be right.

The pressures of launching a completely new product in under six months were formidable, but the ultimate success of the exercise proved a great boost to company morale. By the end of 1981 over 5,000 units of the new range had been sold. This figure easily exceeded the total production of all the earlier models combined.

Production

In the early days of the company production was largely organised and controlled by Tony Akers. This situation changed when John Woolnough was recruited to take over the production role, thus freeing Tony Akers to concentrate on his engineering responsibilities within the company. John Woolnough joined the company in 1976, when there were about 15 people employed on the production side of the business. He joined Cifer Systems from Smiths Industries, with a background of production management expertise in the electronics industry. His task was 'to create a production organisation based on a policy of growth'. By the end of 1981 the production department had grown to some 70 people (see Appendix 3).

Assembling a VDU

The task of the production department is to manufacture the products required by the sales department. While the company sells a range of VDUs, approximately 80 per cent of the components are common to all products. The main variables which must be accommodated are:

(a) Colour of tube (choice of three)
(b) Very simple or 'smart'
(c) Special facilities required (customising).

The production system at Cifer is based upon bringing together a range of sub-assemblies within the lead times necessary to produce the whole product. Sub-assemblies are manufactured, visually inspected, then tested. Once they have been satisfactorily tested, they come back into production as working items and are brought together into a working VDU with a keyboard. Up to this stage (about three weeks' labour in progress) production is not really customer conscious. The final week in production is devoted to creating a product which exactly marries up with the customer's specification. The customising process may involve adding specific programmed chips, additional keys on the keyboard or any other special features.

Estimated works costs (in %) were:

Materials	60
Direct labour	15
Production overhead	25
Total	100

Nature of the production process

The manufacture of VDUs at Cifer involves the employment of two groups of employees, a large group without any specific knowledge of electronics and a smaller group who are highly educated in a technical sense. The first group are concerned with assembling a variety of items on to the chassis of the VDU, the second group require the expertise to test or customise the finished product.

To date, production at Cifer Systems has been rather labour intensive. One of the most common manual operations is soldering. Each VDU will contain several printed circuit boards. Some of these may be very small, others will involve over 2,000 solder joints. Typically the printed circuit boards in one VDU will require over 5,000 solder joints. Operations such as soldering lend themselves to the introduction of more sophisticated production equipment.

In 1980 a wave soldering machine was purchased and this has generated substantial improvements in productivity. The machine is only used for about two days per week, yet it is capable of producing the same output as six or seven operators. However, the major impact of this process is to make significant improvements in the quality of the printed circuit boards produced (typically faults are easier to identify and there are fewer of them). As production volumes increase there will be further scope to make production more capital intensive. While the product itself is technically advanced, sophistication in production is largely a function of volume. New capital equipment offers substantial improvements in the reliability of the final product, which in turn leads to cost savings in test and after-sales service.

Cifer are currently (1981) occupying every available inch of space in their present factory. Indeed a number of additional Portakabins have been brought on to the site to provide additional accommodation (see Appendix 4).

Organisation structure

As the company has grown in size and complexity the four directors of Cifer have tended to become more closely associated with specific areas of responsibility. Tony Akers is now engineering director and concentrates upon research and development. He is concerned with designing new products for Cifer, employing the best in modern technology. This role is performed in close consultation with Stuart Gregory, the marketing director. Stuart Gregory runs the company's sales organisation and is vitally concerned with Cifer's performance in the market. VDUs enjoy a life cycle of about three to four years at present. The timing of new product launches and the inclusion of new technology is fundamental to maintaining market share. As the Cifer VDUs have become increasingly 'intelligent', the company has expanded its software capability. The systems analysts and programmers form an added dimension to Stuart Gregory's area of responsibility.

John Woolnough is Cifer's production director and has responsibility for responding to the volume and mix of products required by the sales team. He also has to react to the problems of how to produce new products which emerge from the engineering department. Part of the engineering department's task is to design products which are easy to produce, as well as being attractive to the user.

Terry Cosgrove is the managing director who endeavours to co-ordinate the overall activities of the company. Invariably, he is the person who negotiates with third parties over finance, buildings and other issues which are of long-term importance to the company. He has also retained responsibility for negotiating with two of the company's major customers. This is perhaps illustrative of an organisation structure where there is no chief executive as such. While Terry Cosgrove is nominally the managing director, in reality the directors organise and run the business as equals, since none has a dominant shareholding and three directors' votes are required to institute a major change in policy. During April 1979, Oliver Newland (previously of Touche Ross Accountants) became associated with Cifer in the capacity of financial consultant.

Marketing

Marketing at Cifer Systems is a complex mixture of technical awareness, cost-consciousness and trying to understand what the market wants. The task of understanding these different strands rests with Stuart Gregory, the company's marketing director. Keeping abreast of developments in the market requires constant vigilance and the ability to recognise important new directions as they emerge.

In Stuart Gregory's view, 'as a small company you've got to limit the number of things you're going to try to do'. Cifer Systems have opted to sell mainly to OEMs and to large end-users. For these customers the VDU is only one part of a total system. Cifer 'try to sell in quantities of 20–500'. As a company they are not really organised to service sales of single units. The company policy at this point in time, is to sell VDUs in substantial numbers to buyers who are fully versed in the technology of the product. To this end, Cifer Systems are deliberately negligent on promotional literature. 'If salesmen are provided with too many glossy leaflets these will get into the hands of the small end-user.' Cifer do not have the capability to service a multitude of small customers and can count their customers in hundreds rather than thousands and 'make money out of about 100 of them'.

Pricing strategy and competition

Cifer design their products to sell within a particular price range. This involves trying to establish what the customer wants and expects to purchase at a given price. Cifer's task is to build a product with the required facilities for the target price range. Most of Cifer's current range of VDUs sell within a price band of £600–£2,000. Over the last few years Cifer have tended to move their products further up-market. Cifer are aware that the VDU is very much at the front end of any computer system. The appearance of the product is important and Cifer deliberately steer clear of the cheaper end of the market, in order to maintain the company's quality image.

The market for VDUs in the UK may be broken down into several broad areas:

(a) Large mainframe systems (eg IBM and ICL). This sector of the market is normally closed to the small independent manufacturers of VDUs, as the computer majors produce their own terminal units.

(b) Systems houses (see Cifer Systems A). The systems houses and smaller computer manufacturers sell complete computer systems built up from hardware bought from a range of specialist producers.

(c) Large end-users. There are a range of end-users with sufficient expertise to build up systems to suit their own needs.

(d) Small end-users. Independent organisations buying VDUs in small numbers for particular applications.

A large number of companies offer to supply terminals to the end-user (see Appendix 1). A much smaller group of companies are actually engaged in the manufacture of VDUs. In 1981 there were about 15 suppliers (including importers) who were actively competing in the UK market. Cifer believed that they ranked among the top two or three companies (by volume) supplying that sector of the market which was not tied to the manufacturers of mainframe computers (ie (b)–(d) above). Newbury Laboratories were thought to be producing about 1,000 units more per annum than Cifer Systems. Cifer were selling at a premium of approximately £150 above the Newbury price. However, Newbury also manufacture printers and thus have a rather different product range to sell from Cifer. Another company, Lynwood, also compete in the VDU market, but sell at considerably higher prices than Cifer and mainly to end-users.

Between them these three companies account for a substantial share of the UK market, but rarely meeting in head-on competition. This can be explained by their different approaches to pricing and to the different types of customer. The market is also subject to the attentions of large and successful overseas manufacturers, notably DEC (the Digital Equipment Corporation).

For some of the reasons described above it is difficult to be definite about the size of the UK market for VDUs. Cifer estimate that the market available to them in 1981 was of the order of 30,000 machines. With production close to 8,000 machines, Stuart Gregory considered that Cifer's share was already becoming 'dangerously large'.

The sales organisation

Stuart Gregory is responsible for the company's sales force. The UK is split into three regions as shown on page 384.

Both the northern region and the south-east region were due to recruit a third salesman each, whilst the south-west regional office, based at the factory at Melksham, was planning to add a technical salesman. The company operates with an open invitation for good technical people to move into sales, subject to a three-month trial period.

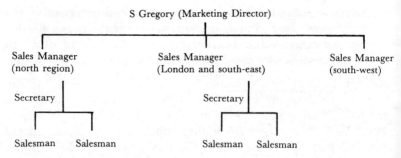

Cifer would not claim to have a very large or sophisticated sales organisation. For instance there is no national sales manager – the regional sales managers report directly to Stuart Gregory. The company does not have a system for computerised mailing, despite their ready access to the necessary hardware. The main problem for Cifer, towards the end of 1981, was trying to keep abreast of demand.

Another preoccupation at this time was the need to strengthen the company's capacity to provide both programming and technical support to its customers. A software department was set up, once again under the control of Stuart Gregory, to operate as a sort of contract software house for Cifer's major customers. The ability to assist customers with their programming problems is seen to be an important part of Cifer's marketing stance. Software support may prove to be a prerequisite to the sale of Cifer VDUs.

Technology and the market

Cifer Systems have grown rapidly by focusing on one major product within the wider market for computers, computer peripherals and software. Some of the earlier distinctions between products have begun to blur. Cifer's product is steadily being made more 'intelligent'. It is worth asking at what point does an 'intelligent' terminal become a desk-top computer? Cifer do not produce a dedicated wordprocessor, but a Cifer VDU can easily be adapted for word-processing. Given the growth and technical proximity of these related products, how should Cifer Systems devise a strategy for the future?

Stuart Gregory provides some insights into the way in which he thinks about the product and the market. Technology has an important part to play:

'I'm a natural buyer . . . really it is all about technical specula tion. We sit and look at a chip. I look at the things the chip makers produce and decide what computers are going to be built out of those chips . . . . The market is actually led in the end by engineers, who actually put the chips together and build in exciting things, that people then sell to customers under some pretext or other.'

Keeping ahead of the competition requires an open mind and the freedom to pursue original ideas. To this end, Stuart Gregory refuses to conform to the norm of the nine-to-five office day. He has a reputation within Cifer Systems for being difficult to contact and for both arriving late at work and leaving late. He does not confine this approach to himself, but is concerned for his research staff. He worries about 'the adverse influences on their radical ways of life'.

Pursuing new product ideas and improving on current products means being aware of what is happening in the market. This is achieved at Cifer by the directors having regular contact with the company's significant customers. Stuart Gregory says that he is constantly 'looking for the right ingredients for next year's cake'.

Employee relations

By the end of 1981 Cifer Systems were employing 107 people. Labour turnover in the company was very low. About 25 per cent of the staff were female. One of the advantages of a company which is experiencing substantial growth is that it continues to provide new opportunities for ambitious and well-qualified staff.

Retaining staff is one thing, but attracting able people to work for Cifer Systems is seen by several of the directors as one of the major constraints on the growth of the company. Mike Sharp is responsible for the legal aspects of recruiting new staff. He deals with the employees' contract of employment and other aspects of employment at Cifer Systems. There is no formal trade union organisation, although some members of the workforce are individually members of trades unions. However, a lot of attention is paid to good working relationships and the directors have tried to retain an informal atmosphere. All employees are paid monthly by cheque and in addition the company pays for BUPA and life insurance. A common eating area is provided for staff and a free vending machine is available to all.

John Woolnough has been instrumental in the introduction of a staff council with a brief to enhance communication between the workforce and the management of the company. It meets once a month and is seen as a way of improving commitment and dialogue as the business grows. The staff council is intended to represent all employees, but tends to reflect the views of the majority, who work in the production departments. Terry Cosgrove uses the staff council as a means to explain news of both company successes and failures. The company retains a tradition of the annual Christmas party.

New developments

By the end of the 1980–81 financial year Cifer Systems had achieved an annual turnover of £2.7 million. This represented a record growth of 75 per cent over the previous year and was based upon the success of the 2600 series. The 2600 had been subject to considerable development since its launch in 1979. The 2600 series now included general purpose ('dumb') terminals, 'smart' terminals and, at the top of the range, the 'very smart' user programmable 2684. Demand for the 2600 was such that once again Cifer Systems had run out of factory space. Indeed the factory was surrounded by Portakabins (see Appendix 4). Output had reached a level approaching 8,000 units per annum and Cifer were forecasting sales for 1981–82 at a level of about £5 million.

The company was poised to launch its latest and most advanced product to date, the 1880 range of desk-top computers. These computers offered considerably more memory than anything previously produced by Cifer Systems. The 1886, priced at £2,700, included storage on two floppy discs. At the top of the range the 1887 offers one floppy disc together with a Winchester disc drive. This model provides greatly enhanced random access memory (RAM) and 12Mbytes Winchester disc storage. The Winchester or 'hard disc' gives rapid access to memory, plus greater storage capacity. The higher specification of the 1880 range took Cifer out of the VDU market and into desk-top computers and a price range of £2,700–£5,400. A range of applications software allowed the company to offer what amounted to a small business system, up to a maximum price level of £12,000.

In order to accommodate this level of expansion Cifer Systems had laid plans to double production from their Avro Way, Bowerhill factory by constructing a £300,000 extension. The local press headlined the creation of a substantial number of new jobs as a result of a greatly expanded production area. The 1880 range was due to be announced at COMPEC early in 1982.

Suppliers of visual display terminals in the UK

Ampex (GB)		x
Business Computer Systems	0	
CTL	0	
CALCOMP Ltd		x
Comart Ltd	0	
Control Data Ltd	0	
Cossor Electronics	0	
Cotron Electronics	0	
Data General	0	
Data Logic	0	
Datapoint UK		x
Digico Ltd	0	
Digital Equipment Corporation		x
Ericsson Information Systems		x
Facit Addo		x
Ferranti Computer Systems Ltd	0	
Fortronic	0	
Hewlett Packard		x
IBM (UK)	0	
ICL	0	
Lynwood Scientific Developments Ltd	0	
Marconi Radar Systems	0	
Motorola	0	
NCR	0	
Newbury Laboratories	0	
Olympia Business Machines		x
Philips Business Systems	0	
Plessey Displays	0	
Prime Computers (UK)	0	
Quest Automation	0	
Siemens		x
Sperry Univac		x
Systime	0	
Televideo		x
Tektronix		x
Wang (UK) Ltd	0	
Westrex	0	
Zenith Data Systems		x

Key: 0 denotes those companies manufacturing (or direct providers of a service) in the UK.
x denotes those companies without own works in UK.

Evolution of the Cifer range

Product	1972	1973	1974	1975	1976	1977	1978	1979	1980	1981
127										
224										
026										
Cub										
2600										
1800										

Appendix 3

Production department – organisation chart (1981)

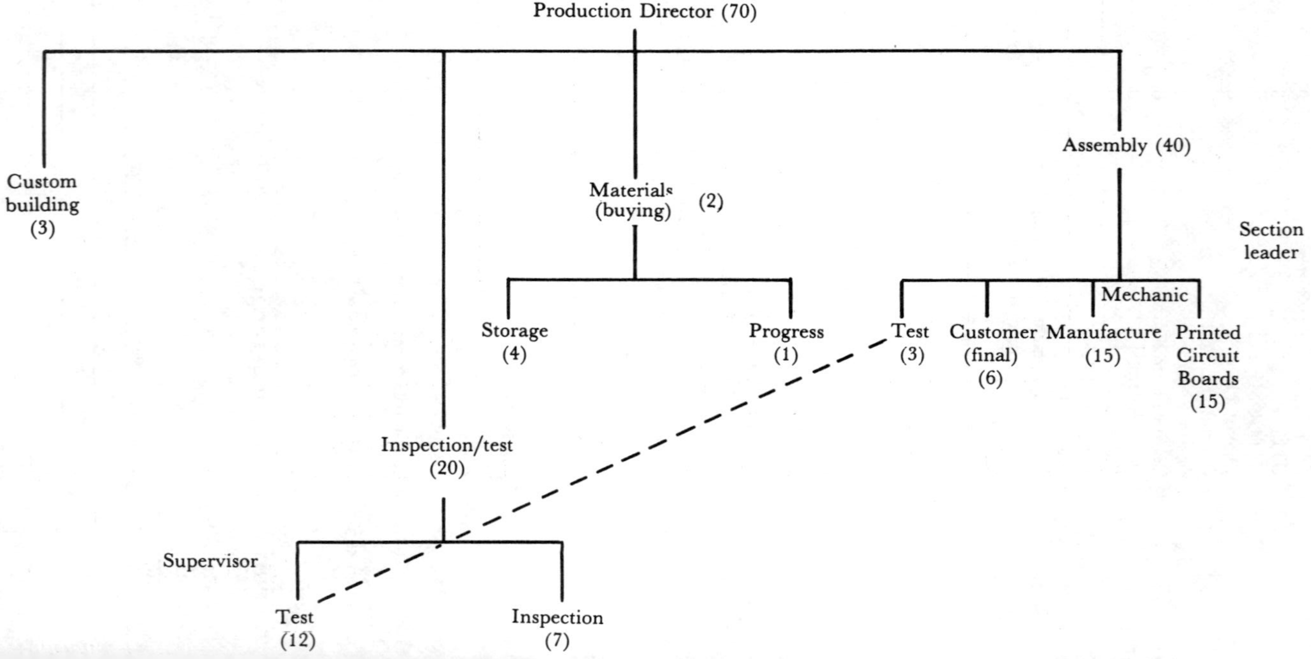

Production Director (70)

Custom building (3)

Assembly (40)

Section leader

Mechanic

Printed Circuit Boards (15)

Customer Manufacture (15)

Customer (final) (6)

Test (3)

Materials (buying) (2)

Progress (1)

Storage (4)

Inspection/test (20)

Inspection (7)

Test (12)

Supervisor

Appendix 4

Factory layout (1981)

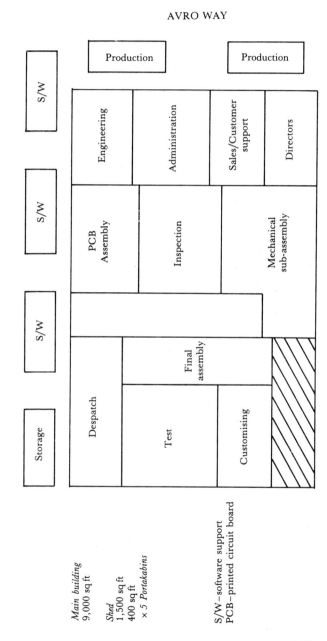

AVRO WAY

| Production | Production |

| S/W | Engineering | Administration | Sales/Customer support | Directors |

| S/W | PCB Assembly | Inspection | Mechanical sub-assembly |

| S/W | | | |

| Storage | Despatch | Final assembly / Test / Customising | |

Main building
9,000 sq ft

Shed
1,500 sq ft
400 sq ft
× 5 *Portakabins*

S/W – software support
PCB – printed circuit board

389

Appendix 5

Cifer Systems Balance Sheets (1975–81)

	1975 £	1976 £	1977 £	1978 £	1979 £	1980 £	1981 £
Fixed assets	5,247	68,053	97,589	141,698	179,493	186,765	241,287
Shares in subsidiary				32,735	200	200	200
Current assets							
Stock and work-in-progress	21,501	46,917	60,988	169,859	142,678	228,512	374,010
Debtors/prepayments	22,050	42,439	105,216	129,405	223,114	333,252	643,105
Building society			203	222	240	265	
Cash in hand and at bank	5	10	9	21	16	18	39,809
Current assets	43,556	89,366	166,416	299,507	366,048	562,047	1,056,924
Total assets	48,803	157,419	264,005	473,940	545,741	749,012	1,298,411
Current liabilities							
HP liability		3,916	3,576	2,935	12,405		
Creditors	28,046	52,290	98,572	119,329	179,842	347,103	785,932
Bank overdraft	17,398	29,400	23,478	52,406	105,536	128,063	
Portion of mortgage						15,600	20,000
Dividend payable				994	520	3,172	15,584
Advance corporation tax					223	1,359	6,763
VAT	183	1,217	3,526	3,707	18,398		
Current liabilities	45,627	86,823	129,152	179,371	316,924	495,297	828,279
Net assets	3,176	70,596	134,853	294,569	228,817	253,715	470,132
Represented by							
Share capital	1,336	16,000	16,000	25,000	25,000	25,000	25,000
Share premium				39,920	39,920	39,920	39,920
Reserves (profit and loss)	1,536	4,524	44,768	86,060	(42,545)	18,903	266,978
Mortgage loan TDC		45,000	45,000	70,000	125,000	93,775	120,000
Directors' loans	304				81,442	76,117	18,234
Plus other loans		5,072	29,085	73,589			

Cifer Systems Profit and Loss Accounts (1975–81)

	1975 £	1976 £	1977 £	1978 £	1979 £	1980 £	1981 £
Turnover	93,650	204,247	520,804	830,083	1,018,999	1,551,000	2,732,316
Net profit	4,296	17,652	40,244	42,286	(81,375)	60,533	309,915
Less							
Bank charges and interest	2,804	2,206	3,255	3,951	11,232	19,729	8,492
Loan interest	—	—	8,549	9,362	13,873	18,417	22,174
Directors' loan interest			875	2,581	579	6,048	882
Depreciation	761	2,719	4,206	11,550	27,050	43,688	58,336
Auditors' remuneration	100	150	300	280	450	1,150	1,500
Directors' salaries and fees	14,610	21,430	48,000	68,500	41,970	62,521	147,066
Profit/(loss) before taxation	4,296	17,652	40,244	42,286	(81,375)	60,533	309,915
Taxation	nil	nil	nil	nil	977	1,593	7,216
Profit/(loss) after taxation	4,296	17,652	40,244	42,286	(82,352)	58,940	302,699
Extraordinary items					59,213		
Prior year adjustment						(6,200)	38,000
Dividends payable				994	1,040	3,692	16,624
Directors' fees written back					(14,000)		
	4,296	17,652	40,244	41,292	(128,605)	61,448	248,075
Balance brought forward	(2,760)	1,536	4,524	44,768	86,060	(42,545)	18,903
	1,536	19,188	44,768	86,060	(42,545)	18,903	266,978
Less							
Amount utilised for capitalisation issue		14,664					
Reserves	1,536	4,524	44,768	86,060	(42,545)	18,903	266,978

Appendix 7

The Cub

Scope

This guide will cover the standard V24 interface ASCII code version of the CUB VDU. If the VDU is supplied or used without a keyboard as a read-only display, then all references to keyboard operation should be ignored.

1. Description of equipment

The CUB is a non-intelligent low cost display terminal suitable for a wide variety of applications.

The CUB consists of two items, a lightweight portable monitor unit housing the display and interface electronics, and a separate keyboard unit. The display format is 16 lines each of 64 characters. Display characters are drawn with a 7 × 11 dot matrix on a 9 × 12 character cell. This format allows the display to be used as an interactive terminal or as a secondary data display.

When the CUB is used as a terminal it is supplied with a 60 key keyboard. The keyboard can generate all 128 ASCII codes and includes caps-lock and repeat function keys. The keyboard is connected to the display unit with a short length of lightweight cable terminated in a 5 pin DIN type connector. The keyboard normally operates with the displays in full-duplex mode, but a switch option is available on the display to allow half-duplex (local echo) operation.

Operator controls for brightness and volume are provided on the front of the display unit. Preset controls, not normally required by the operator, are situated on the rear panel of the display unit.

2. User Controls

2.1 Front panel controls:

MAINS SWITCH: This is located at the top of the front panel and is a Push-On, Push-Off switch. Power On indication is provided by the red light on the base plate.

BRIGHTNESS: This control sets the Black level for the display. It should be set in conjunction with the contrast control.

VOLUME: With the volume at minimum the unit will not respond to BEL Code (CTL G).

2.2 Preset controls:

These controls are situated on the rear of the unit. They should not need frequent adjustment.

VERTICAL HOLD: This control should be set to the centre of the range that gives a stable picture.

CONTRAST: This control adjusts the intensity of the white portions of the display. The correct setting for this control can be achieved by using the following procedure.

Questions

1. Should the directors have undertaken so much of the fitting out work at Avro Way themselves?
2. What do you think of the way in which new products are developed at Cifer? How could they improve on their process of developing and launching new products?
3. Do you agree with Stuart Gregory's comment that Cifer's share of the market in 1981 was already becoming 'dangerously large'?
4. What problems do you see ahead of Cifer's management in implementing their 1982 growth plans, particularly with respect to doubling the factory size?

Case 39

Eaves & Washbourne Ltd F

Nigel Campbell, Paul Washbourne
and Stuart Craimer

Ron Washbourne was a co-founder of the company, together with his nephew Stan Eaves. Ron's son Paul joined the firm and at the time of this case was nominally production director. Don Ellwood, the managing director, had joined five years earlier after being introduced to Paul as a 'suitable candidate' by mutual friends. He was a metallurgist who had trained with British Steel. Prior to joining Eaves & Washbourne he had taken an MSc at the London Business School.

The company's principal activities are making and marketing machine tools and operating as a subcontractor.

On 22 April 1980 Eaves & Washbourne held a board meeting at the Allesley Hotel in Coventry to reach a decision over a major investment. The previous three years had been a period of steady growth with profits rising from £63,000 in 1977 to £313,000 in 1979 (see Appendix 1). In this time the company greatly developed its business with three main customers.

The earlier cases in this series appeared in *The Small Business Casebook* by Sue Birley (Macmillan, 1979). The cases in this book deal with the issues that faced the business between 1980 and 1982.

A video is available to accompany these cases; for details, contact Dr Nigel Campbell, Manchester Business School, Booth Street West, Manchester M15 6PB.

Crosfield Electronics

The first of these was Crosfield Electronics, makers of electronic graphics equipment for the printing industry. They had been important customers of Eaves & Washbourne's for ten years and had been bought by De la Rue, a large public company capable of supporting Crosfield's rapid expansion.

Crosfield bought all the components for its colour scanning machines from outside sources and Eaves & Washbourne had become the sole supplier of the main base casting, the machine slides, bearing housings and leadscrews. The precision of the finished machine depended on the extreme accuracy of these machined and ground parts. Such technical expertise demanded a close personal relationship between the management of both companies. The co-operation between Eaves & Washbourne and Crosfield was such that the mechanical parts of Crosfield's new machines were jointly designed to suit the capabilities of Eaves & Washbourne's machine shop. The closeness of the relationship was furthered by Crosfield's investment of £150,000 in a thread-grinding machine and measuring equipment. These were installed at Eaves & Washbourne in order to meet the increasing demand for high precision leadscrews and, by 1980, Crosfield were annually ordering around £900,000-worth of components from Eaves & Washbourne, around 40 per cent of turnover.

Parker-Majestic

Additionally, the purchase of the Parker-Majestic licence from Dr Blythe provided the company with slow, but consistent, progress in their manufacture and selling of the two main Parker products, small surface-grinding machines and boring spindles for automatic transfer lines. A sizeable and expensive sales and marketing effort would have been needed to accelerate the company's sales of grinding machines against their large and well-established British and European competitors. Rather than make such an investment, the company decided to rely on new business and repeat orders. These were mainly from subsidiaries of international American companies. By the late 1970s 30 to 40 machines per year, at a value of around £5,000, were being produced.

While shying away from the large investment needed in the surface-grinding machine market, Stan, Paul and Ron recognised the potentially larger space for expansion in their Parker boring spindles trade. The number of customers was limited to around eight builders of automated machinery – mainly for the car industry. This meant that customers could be serviced without additional sales personnel.

Eaves & Washbourne's position in the boring spindle market was helped by the general lack of faith in the only other serious British competitor who was unable to supply products of sufficiently high quality. Additionally, the Parker Spindle had a high reputation with car manufacturers and American car companies often specified Parker boring machines on any transfer machines they ordered. Due to this, Eaves & Washbourne were able to build up their spindle business in the 1970s until it was worth around £25,000 per annum. The decline of the British car industry, however, offered little hope of further growth.

In 1976, with trade slack, a chargehand suggested that Paul Washbourne contact Parker-Majestic to see if he could obtain any direct work from them. This was not really the object of the Parker licence, but luckily Parker were very busy because the car companies were re-equipping their plants to produce smaller and more economical car engines (American legislation, precipitated by a rise in oil prices, forced the car makers to improve average fuel consumption from 15 to 27 miles per gallon). There was, therefore, a large demand for transfer-line machinery and for new cylinder blocks, cylinder heads, con-rods, gearboxes etc and Parker were one of the main suppliers of boring spindles to the transfer-machine makers.

With Parker unable to cope with this massive influx of work, Paul's call came at an opportune time. Trade with Eaves & Washbourne also offered a number of advantages to Parker other than the alleviation of their capacity problem – the lower wages paid in Coventry meant that spindle manufacture, even after the payment of freight and import duty, worked out favourably for Parker. As Parker's customers, the transfer-line manufacturers, also sold a fair proportion of their machines to European car plants they could avoid import duty by using spindles made within the EEC.

Parker immediately placed orders for Eaves & Washbourne spindles and, by 1980, they were making £700,000-worth per year. Parker had become a major customer, taking about 25 per cent of Eaves & Washbourne's output, some of which was delivered to customers in the UK.

Charmilles

The third company was Charmilles, an old-established Swiss engineering company based in Geneva. They were a leading producer of spark-erosion machines. This was a method of removing metal by passing an electric spark between an electrode and the workpiece and, in the 1960s, it was the fastest growing and technologically most exciting field in metal removal. Through the use of new technology Charmilles had become internationally successful, though they were handicapped by the scarcity and high cost of skilled labour in Switzerland. Their production methods were progressively modern with the latest computer-numerically-controlled (CNC) machines and they had been the first company to replace the time-consuming manual scraping of machine slides by precision grinding.

Their success was such that Charmilles were anxious to develop sites outside Switzerland. Britain offered cheap skilled labour and so Charmilles set up a factory at Gloucester for assembling their machines. Their aim was to find British subcontractors to manufacture all the parts locally. Their demanding quality requirements, particularly for the machine slides, made this a difficult task. One of their service engineers knew of Eaves & Washbourne and this led to Paul and Terry visiting the Gloucester factory. Initially, they were frightened by the extreme accuracy demanded, though Charmilles offered full technical assistance. Paul and Terry realised that this was an opportunity to build up new expertise in a fast expanding market. Work from Charmilles increased, but importantly, it was supplemented by technical advice and many of Eaves & Washbourne's staff visited Geneva to learn the latest machining and grinding techniques at first hand.

Investments and success

Due to the big influx of orders from Crosfield, Parker and Charmilles, the company rapidly expanded with turnover rising from £762,000 in 1976 to £2,256,000 in 1979. In 1978, to meet the demands of such expansion, the company decided to embark upon a major investment plan. This was precipitated by the need to move with new technology, particularly that seen at Charmilles. Unless Eaves & Washbourne invested in the latest CNC machines they would be hopelessly uncompetitive.

Stan was particularly enthusiastic for investment as the government allowed 100 per cent capital allowance against corporation tax for investment in new plant. If the company made £200,000 profit and bought £200,000 worth of new machinery it paid no corporation tax. Alternatively, they would pay 52 per cent corporation tax on profits. These advantages were supplemented by the government's offer of a straight cash grant of 30 per cent on the cost of new plant to encourage the machine-tool industry's investment in new equipment.

Between 1978 and 1980 around £600,000 was invested, mainly on four CNC machines (at around £100,000 each) with the

EAVES & WASHBOURNE LTD F

balance being spent on the buildings, measuring equipment and the replacement of eight ageing conventional machines.

The people

These major changes were orchestrated by the management of Paul and Don. Ron Washbourne retired soon after Don's arrival, while Stan continued to run the assembly shop at the Cross Road premises about two miles away from the main site. Nominally Don was managing director and Paul production director, but basically they worked as a partnership with Don looking after financial and commercial affairs, the Parker-Majestic business and smaller customers, while Paul concentrated on the production side and the trade with Crosfield and Charmilles. Paul explained Don's role:

> 'When Don first arrived at the company his main expertise was on the financial side and, since at the time we didn't have a qualified accountant, Don was most interested in forward planning on the financial side and cash flow.'

Both Paul and Don were anxious to improve the calibre of all personnel and emphasis was laid upon apprentice and operator training, supervisors were sent on management courses, a computer programmer was recruited and two graduate trainees, one in engineering and one in economics, were brought into the company.

There was growing recognition of the company's success. In February 1980 the Department of Trade and Industry invited Paul and his wife Carla to a reception for small businessmen given by Margaret Thatcher at 10 Downing Street. Trade journals also covered Eaves & Washbourne's investment in the latest technology.

Their success also attracted a number of offers for the company. Crosfield were prepared to buy half the business at one point and Jim Salmon, formerly a technical director of Crosfield became a non-executive director of Eaves & Washbourne. A major bank was also interested in buying a sixth of the company for £160,000. This valuation was based on five times the average of the last three years' profits and did not take specific account of the onset backing. In view of this Paul Washbourne started to look at the possibility of demerging the operations so that the Cross Road site would be in a separate company (Deedmore Road was rented).

Even so, Don and Paul were aware of the insecurity of relying on three customers, even though each was a market leader in a different field and Eaves & Washbourne had established close relationships with them all. Don observed: 'We were very busy, very profitable, but we were very aware that we were dependent upon three legs – the legs were Parker-Majestic, Crosfield and Charmilles.' They aimed, therefore, to attract and develop two or three more accounts. The first step in this direction was made at the 1980 International Machine-Tool Exhibition at the National Exhibition Centre. Here, with the help of Crosfield's marketing department, they mounted an impressive stand. They attracted a major customer from the aerospace industry whose business was likely to be worth around £200,000 per annum, but the exhibition was generally disappointing.

The next move?

Shortly afterwards, however, Charmilles approached Eaves & Washbourne with the proposition of doubling their volume of orders from £30,000- to £60,000-worth per month. The excitement of the offer was tempered by the risk – it meant investing £100,000 in a new machining centre, £250,000 in a special grinding machine and £50,000 on a new building, a total investment of £400,000. Unlike the earlier investments, this demanded a large loan with interest rates running at 14 per cent. Stan, and to a lesser extent the others, felt that they could get additional work for the new grinding machine. They also estimated that the margin on this work and the new work from Charmilles would be comparable to the margins they were getting from other machines. However, this further concentrated Eaves & Washbourne's reliance on one of its three major customers.

To lessen this risk, Paul asked Charmilles if they would enter into a contract by which they would pay a financial penalty to Eaves & Washbourne to cover interest charges in the event of a downturn in demand. The Swiss management, while expressing their confidence for the future, were unwilling to give guarantees upon the levels of trade in five years' time. Charmilles had also discovered a London company who had successfully completed grinding trials and were prepared to make a substantial investment to deal with Charmilles' work.

At their board meeting, the Eaves & Washbourne board had to decide whether to proceed with their investment in the trade with Charmilles through a major and risky capital outlay.

Appendix 1

Financial results

Profit and Loss Account

	1976	*1977*	*1978*	*1979*
Turnover				
Home	732,289	877,380	1,256,614	1,762,102
Export	30,323	190,443	637,243	493,673
Total	762,612	1,067,781	1,893,848	2,255,775
Trading profit	31,290	63,555	272,894	312,990
After charging				
Directors' emoluments	35,866	39,362	61,206	94,952
Auditors' remuneration	1,200	1,450	1,700	2,250
Depreciation	31,123	34,102	47,332	78,159
Disposal of fixed assets	—	—	—	—
Hire of plant and machinery	1,612	2,785	3,294	9,818
Interest	25,333	27,649	18,575	24,484
After crediting				
Rents receivable	78,755	21,763	27,333	29,734
Profit on disposal of fixed assets	2,572	2,846	1,256	5,347
Interest receivable	33	29	425	1,284
Profit before taxation	31,290	63,555	272,894	312,990
Taxation	19,440	30,529	149,690	156,628
Profit after taxation	11,850	33,026	123,204	156,362
Balance sheet				
Fixed assets	270,770	335,390	449,080	817,940
Goodwill	14,974	14,974	15,692	15,374
Trade investment	3,000	3,000	3,000	3,000
Current assets				
Stock and work-in-progress	176,781	259,972	231,751	295,490
Debtors and prepayments	184,166	282,067	306,299	743,376
Taxation recoverable	6,320	6,072	—	—
Cash at building society	447	476	500	531
Cash at bank and in hand	353	116	20,782	4,109
	368,067	548,703	559,332	1,043,506
Less current liabilities				
Creditors	209,869	333,041	328,525	717,305
HP Creditors	43,792	48,020	43,951	37,259
Short term loan (secured)	53,681	123,561	3,250	—
	308,769	504,622	375,626	754,564
Net current assets	59,298	44,081	153,771	157,640
Total assets	348,042	397,445	621,543	993,954
Financed by				
Share capital	10,000	10,000	10,000	10,000
Reserves	157,119	190,145	313,349	469,711
Deferred taxation	101,050	131,605	251,760	435,248
Medium-term loan	34,080	25,176	13,332	53,330
Long-term loan	—	—	—	—
Mortgage	45,793	40,519	33,202	25,665
Minority interest	—	—	—	—

Questions

1. How well has the company performed over the past four years?
2. How big a risk could they afford to take?
3. Should they invest and take on the extra trade?
4. What other options are open to them to broaden their customer base?

Eaves & Washbourne Ltd G

Nigel Campbell, Paul Washbourne and Stuart Craimer

See case 39 for the background.

Buying the Waldrich

Central to the company's large new investment, once it was decided upon, was the purchase of a Waldrich grinding machine. The addition of this machine was keenly advocated by Terry Hutchinson to release the workload on other machines and enable fulfilment of existing orders. Charmilles' representative, Dick Kirkham, a personal friend of Paul's, also exerted a great amount of pressure on Eaves & Washbourne's management for this purchase. Waldrich were renowned as the best slideway grinders in the world and Charmilles used such a machine at their Geneva headquarters.

The purchase of the Waldrich was an interesting one. Don and Paul heard of a suitable machine being auctioned. It was eight years old and being sold off by one of the Stavely companies, no longer able to operate. A limit of £150,000 was set on Eaves & Washbourne's bidding. During the auction it became clear that Eaves & Washbourne were in competition with another company who had received the same promises of work from Charmilles, providing they had a Waldrich. They too had a limit of £150,000. When the price reached this figure, it was Don who raised his arm to add another £1,000. Eaves & Washbourne had taken the risk and had the machine.

Installing the Waldrich took a further two to three months with the construction of stronger foundations and new buildings. The pressures for speedy completion and operation were large. Terry Hutchinson explained:

> 'At the time we were doing work for Charmilles, it was a growing market and they always wanted more work than we could cope with – they were promising us even double what we could handle, but obviously to do that we needed more equipment.'

The Charmilles business was large and the possibility of expansion provided grounds for great optimism. To supplement the Waldrich, a CNC machine was in the process of being delivered to Coventry – this had cost a further £100,000 with £50,000 for a new building.

Crash

Before the Waldrich could be brought into operation, Dick Kirkham contacted Eaves & Washbourne. His news was simple – instead of doubling its orders, Charmilles would no longer be placing any orders at all with Eaves & Washbourne. Charmilles were ending their British operation and severely curtailing their work in Geneva in response to the world recession.

In the space of a few words, 13 per cent of Eaves & Washbourne's business disappeared and the investment anticipating another 13 per cent was rendered redundant. Yet, the Waldrich was ready for use and the CNC equipment was irrevocably on its way – the investment had been made and had to be carried through and justified somehow. Terry summed it up as 'a very stressful and depressing time'; Paul was more forthright and called it 'devastating'. Later he philosophically noted: 'More businesses go bust because they're expanding than because they're contracting.'

The international situation

Of course, Eaves & Washbourne's was not an isolated case of a company suffering a massive fall in demand. The machine-tool industry was in a state of collapse and, moreover, this was a totally unforeseen situation. As subcontractors, machine-tool makers were the first to be hit with larger corporations cutting subcontracting work before rationalising their own production. In the Coventry area, the machine-tool industry was decimated: Alfred Herberts, who had employed 10,000 people in the 1970s, closed; Wickmans reduced their workforce from 2,500 to 400; Matrix from 2,000 to 400; and Webster and Bennett, employing 700, closed completely.

The news from Eaves & Washbourne's other customers was equally bleak. After the boom in the American car industry, there was a period of startling recession, and massive corporations, such as Chrysler, were on the verge of bankruptcy. The industry had finished its re-tooling and Parkers were left with greatly diminished order books and so, in turn, were Eaves & Washbourne. Trade with Crosfield was also adversely affected. Over the years Crosfield had amassed a stockpile and so, in difficult times, they could simply reduce orders to cut costs for a while. They did so, and Eaves & Washbourne were forced to reduce their shopfloor workforce from 120 to 40 with the increasing likelihood of a three-day week. This was narrowly avoided when the company won an order on the Friday before the proposed start of three-day working.

The policy of recovery

In order to cope with such a collapse, all work at Eaves & Washbourne was rationalised to a bare minimum. The management had a plan which could cope with any volume of work between £100,000 and £35,000 a month. At the lowest level this involved using the talents of wives and relatives rather than paid staff. Don Ellwood's confidence in this plan was such that he never contemplated the company closing. Stan Eaves was similarly optimistic, though Paul Washbourne found it increasingly difficult to see why Eaves & Washbourne should survive when so many were failing.

While managing in the short term, the company also had to find itself more orders. Two technical sales representatives were appointed in 1981. They rigorously covered all of England, but failed to attract a single large customer in their first 12 months. The company also prepared a large number of publicity leaflets on their spindle production, the uses of the Waldrich and their crack detecting expertise, which were widely distributed.

The people

In these difficult times Paul Washbourne became steadily convinced that the company would not survive and, with so little confidence in the future, he felt it better that he leave the company's running to Don, Stan and John Phillips, who had joined as the company accountant in 1980. Stan moved to Deedmore Road to take a more active management role. The very survival of Eaves & Washbourne was questionable, but this was further complicated by competition for the managing directorship between Don, Stan and John Phillips and the desperate need to formulate successful and incisive policies for the future.

Appendix 1

Financial Results

	1980	1981	1982
Profit and Loss Account			
Turnover			
Home	1,984,615	1,577,504	1,841,333
Export	663,504	881,192	573,219
Total	2,648,119	2,458,696	2,414,552
Trading profit	193,189	61,717	(30,178)
after charging			
Directors' emoluments	97,969	84,738	73,612
Auditors' remuneration	2,650	3,650	4,250
Depreciation	138,542	186,159	158,618
Disposal of fixed assets			705
Hire of plant and machinery	3,198	3,568	—
Interest	80,100	96,009	84,118
After crediting			
Rents receivable	35,555	30,289	38,960
Profit on disposal of fixed assets	—	465	—
Interest receivable	45	746	874
Profit before taxation	193,189	61,717	(30,178)
Taxation	55,218	234,293	5,956
Profit after taxation	248,407	296,010	36,134
Balance Sheet			
Fixed assets	1,024,763	1,241,177	1,112,295
Goodwill	15,843	15,843	15,843
Trade investment	3,000	3,000	3,000
Current assets			
Stock and work-in-progress	388,300	328,591	245,797
Debtors and prepayments	747,232	502,592	492,885
Taxation recoverable	—	—	—
Cash at building society	576	628	682
Cash at bank and in hand	4,799	16,644	22,660
	1,140,907	848,455	762,024
Less current liabilities			
Creditors	472,141	377,013	289,635
HP Creditors	75,025	221,800	131,300
Short-term loan (secured)	42,395	55,536	61,487
	589,561	654,349	482,422
Net current assets	165,414	8,349	66,713
Total assets	1,209,020	1,268,369	1,197,851
Financed by			
Share capital	10,000	10,000	21,000
Reserves	717,987	1,013,857	966,307
Deferred taxation	348,837	141,800	140,150
Medium-term loan	86,664	66,600	46,656
Long-term loan	27,649	27,312	23,000
Mortgage	17,701	8,418	—
Minority interest	272	322	738

Questions

1. With hindsight, what could they have done to protect their position when they took on the Charmilles order?
2. Do you share Paul Washbourne's pessimism about the prospects of success for their policy of recovery?
3. What else could the company do to ensure survival?

Index